Cyril of Jerusalem, Mystagogue

North American Patristic Society
Patristic Monograph Series
Volume 17

Cyril of Jerusalem, Mystagogue

The Authorship of the Mystagogic Catecheses

ϟϾϾ

Alexis James Doval

The Catholic University of America Press
Washington, D.C.

Copyright © 2001

The Catholic University of America Press

All rights reserved

Printed in the United States of America

The paper used in this publication meets the minimum requirements of
American National Standards for Information Science—Permanence
of Paper for Printed Library materials, ANSI z39.48-1984.

∞

LIBRARY OF CONGRESS CATALOGING-IN-PUBLICATION DATA

Doval, Alexis James, 1953–

Cyril of Jerusalem, Mystagogue : the authorship of the
Mystagogic catecheses / Alexis James Doval.

p.   cm. — (Patristic monograph series ; vol. 17)

Includes bibliographical references and index.

ISBN 0-8132-1079-8 (alk. paper)

1. Cyril, Saint, Bishop of Jerusalem, ca. 315–386.   I. Title.

II. Patristic monograph series ; no. 17.

BR1720.C88D68 2001

270.2′092—dc21

2001028743

To my Mother and Father,
Patricia and John Doval,
with love and gratitude

Contents

Figures and Tables

Foreword

The Patristic Monograph Series began publication in 1975, with Michael Sage's volume on St. Cyprian. The publisher was the Philadelphia Patristic Foundation, Ltd., which, because two seminaries had merged, had its editorial offices in Cambridge, Mass. The initial plan was to produce softbound books by photo-offsetting typewritten pages and to sell them at a low price, so that the results of original research in patristics could be made widely available to scholars in the field. The undertaking was successful, and the Philadelphia Patristic Foundation published twelve volumes in the series. In 1988, the series was taken over by the North American Patristic Society, and Mercer University Press was engaged as publisher. The series moved to hardbound books, and new technology made it possible to have the equivalent of typeset books. Between 1988 and 1997, Mercer University Press published four volumes in the series.

In 1999, The Catholic University of America Press became the publisher of the series. The present volume, *Cyril of Jerusalem, Mystagogue: The Authorship of the Mystagogic Catecheses,* by Alexis James Doval, is the seventeenth volume in the series and the first to be published by The Catholic University of America Press.

It is a pleasure to present Alexis Doval's book to the North American Patristic Society and to the scholarly world. Books in English on Cyril have not been abundant, and Doval's book fills a real need. Moreover, interest in the history of the liturgy has grown in the past several decades, and the *Catecheses* of St. Cyril of Jerusalem are one of the most significant witnesses to the state of catechetical instruction, and to the rites of baptism, chrismation, and the Eucharist, to survive from the fourth century. But the statement just made already implies the conclusion reached by Doval: that Cyril is the author of the five mystagogical catecheses that conclude the series of twenty-four. In a careful study, Doval builds the case for his conclusion, step by step. But he does a good deal more: in the course of his argument, Doval treats history, theology, liturgy, and several other topics, so that his book is both an exacting study of the question of authorship and a wide-ranging treatment of Cyril of Jerusalem and his thought.

The North American Patristic Society is pleased to work with The Catholic University of America Press so that, together, they can foster the growth of the Patristic Monograph Series and see it flourish.

Joseph T. Lienhard, S.J.
Fordham University
Editor, Patristic Monograph Series

Preface and Acknowledgments

This book began as a small part of a larger intended doctoral thesis on the liturgical theology of Cyril of Jerusalem. As I started my research, I discovered that nearly every significant study dealing with the *Mystagogic Catecheses* included a treatment of the disputed authorship of the text and, hence, prepared to include my own. But as I surveyed the various studies, I was struck by how much they differed in their scope and conclusions. Each scholar emphasized different parts of the question, many were unaware of the findings of others, some studies that still carried weight were now outdated, and the final judgment on the authorship question continued to be split.

I realized, then, the possibilities of a major project that could serve two purposes. First, the question of authorship could be settled once and for all. Second, since this would require a more comprehensive examination of Cyril and his catechetical works than had yet been done, the dissertation could be a significant new resource in Cyrilline studies. For the study would need to include, on the one hand, historical material such as Cyril's personal life, his ecclesiastical career, and the political situation in which he lived, and on the other, theological topics in the areas of liturgy, sacraments, and dogmatics. Further, since I would be examining a time period of over thirty years in the latter part of the fourth century, which was a time of theological fecundity, the formulation and development of doctrine would also be an important component.

The project was immensely satisfying, and colleagues and teachers have urged me to make the results more available to the academic community by getting the dissertation published. I feel honored to be able to do so, and my hope is that this volume can be useful to anyone studying Cyril's life or thought. I do not claim to have exhausted every area or topic, but I hope to have provided many opportunities for further study in the field.

I would like to thank the following for permission to use copyrighted material. The drawing of the Church of the Holy Sepulchre on page 26 is by K. J. Conant and was taken from "The Original Buildings at the Holy Sepulchre in Jerusalem," *Speculum* 31 (January 1956), page 17, plate III. The table on pages 41–42 originally appeared in my article, "The Fourth Century Jerusalem Catechesis and the Development of the Creed," *Studia Patristica,* vol. XXX (Leuven: Peeters Press, 1997), pages 296–305. The plan of the west end of the Holy Sepulchre Church on page 87 is based on an original by C. Coüasnon © The British Academy 1974. It is reproduced by permission from *The Church of the Holy Sepulchre in Jerusalem* (London: Oxford University Press for the British Academy, 1974), plate VIII.

Many of my teachers, colleagues, and friends have helped me along the way, and I would like to thank them also. First of all I thank Edward J. Yarnold, S.J., who first introduced me to Cyril and the field of early liturgy in my undergraduate days at Oxford. He then supervised my doctoral studies in 1988 and has consistently given support and encouragement. I thank Gerard Ledger for his supervision of the stylometric portion of the study, as well as the Oxford University Computing Services, especially Stephen Miller and Susan Hockey, whose patient technical guidance was essential. I am also indebted to Sebastian Brock and Penelope Johnstone at the Oriental Institute, who provided invaluable assistance with Syriac and Arabic texts. I am grateful to my thesis examiners, Anthony Gelston and Kallistos Ware, who have persistently urged me to get this study published. I thank the North American Patristic Society for accepting the manuscript for their Patristic Monograph Series and especially the series' editor, Joseph T. Lienhard, S.J., for his help on readying the manuscript. I thank also the Faculty Development Office at Saint Mary's College for providing financial support. To many other friends and colleagues in Oxford I am grateful: the many librarians of the Bodleian Library, especially Mary Sheldon-Williams, for their bibliographical assistance; the De La Salle Brothers in Oxford for their hospitality and support; and the Franciscan community of Greyfriars Hall, especially Ben Cullen, OFM Cap., Charles Serignat, OFM Cap., Stephen Innes, OFM Cap., Thomas Wienandy, OFM Cap., and Gregory Shanahan, OFM. Finally, I thank Dr. Felicidad Oberholzer who read the manuscript many times over and offered countless suggestions for clarifying arguments and improving style.

Abbreviations

Works of Cyril

P   *Procatechesis*

C   *Catecheses 1–18*

M   *Mystagogic Catecheses*

Other Ancient Works

AC   *Apostolic Constitutions*

AT   Hippolytus, *Apostolic Tradition*

BH 1–5   Theodore of Mopsuestia, *Baptismal Homilies*[1]

DS   Ambrose, *De Sacramentis*

IE   Egeria, *Itinerarium Egeriae*

HE   *Historia Ecclesiastica*

LXX   Septuagint

Mingana   A. Mingana, trans., *Commentary of Theodore of Mopsuestia on the Lord's Prayer and on the Sacraments of Baptism and the Eucharist.*

PK 1–4   John Chrysostom, *Baptismal Homilies*, Papadopoulos—Kerameus Series

Stav. 1–8   John Chrysostom, *Baptismal Homilies*, Stavronikita Series

Modern Works

AB   Analecta Bollandiana

AIR   E. J. Yarnold, *The Awe-Inspiring Rites of Initiation*

CCSG   Corpus Christianorum Series Graeca

---

1. The numbering of Theodore's sixteen catechetical sermons, the last five of which are on the rites of initiation, varies among the published editions and translations. I will refer the reader to the edition of R. Tonneau because he conveniently divides each sermon into numbered sections. *BH* 1–5 in this book will correspond to *Homilies* 12–16 in that edition. Translations will be from the Mingana edition, and will be cited by page number only. Note that this edition includes a preliminary sermon on the Lord's Prayer among the catecheses on the initiation rites, thus making up six chapters. Hence, *BH* 1–5 correspond to Chapters 2-6 in the Mingana edition.

CCSL	Corpus Christianorum Series Latina
CSCO	Corpus Scriptorum Christianorum Orientalium
CSEL	Corpus Scriptorum Ecclesiasticorum Latinorum
GCS	Die griechischen christlichen Schriftsteller der ersten (drei) Jahrhunderte
GLS	Grove Liturgical Studies
HJ	Heythrop Journal
JEH	Journal of Ecclesiastical History
JTS	Journal of Theological Studies
LSJ	*A Greek-English Lexicon.* Ed. H. G. Liddell and R. Scott, rev. S. Jones, 9th ed. Oxford: Clarendon Press, 1985.
NPNF	Nicene and Post–Nicene Fathers
OCA	Orientalia Christiana Analecta
OCP	Orientalia Christiana Periodica
PGL	*A Patristic Greek Lexicon.* Ed. G. W. H. Lampe. Oxford: Clarendon Press, 1961.
PG	Patrologiae Cursus Completus: Series Graeca. Ed. J.-P. Migne. Paris: J. P. Migne, 1857–66.
PL	Patrologiae Cursus Completus: Series Latina. Ed. J.-P. Migne. Paris: J. P. Migne, 1878–90.
PO	Patrologia Orientalis. Ed. R. Graffin and F. Nau. Paris: Firmin-Didot, 1907–.
RHE	Revue d'histoire ecclésiastique
RSV	Revised Standard Version of the Bible
SC	Sources chrétiennes
SL	Studia Liturgica
SP	Studia Patristica
TS	Theological Studies
TU	Texte und Untersuchungen zur Geschichte der altchristlichen Literatur
VC	Vigiliae Christianae
WCJ	L. McCauley and A. A. Stephenson, trans., *The Works of Cyril of Jerusalem.*

Introduction

A. General Scope and Significance of the Book

Cyril of Jerusalem has long been recognized as one of the most significant influences on the development of liturgical practices in the Greek-speaking church of the fourth century. His episcopate (c. 350 to 387) largely coincided with the period when the Church revitalized Jerusalem, bringing it from a religiously vitiated Roman town to the most prominent and symbolically significant center of Christianity, the Holy City. Under the inspiration of Constantine, the city reclaimed its importance as the foremost holy place where the saving acts of Christ occurred, and it soon became a major center for pilgrimages from all over Christendom. The securing and enhancing of the Holy Places began a year after the Council of Nicaea (326). From Cyril's baptismal sermons (351) and the testimony of Egeria some thirty years later, we can see that the catechetical program and liturgical life of the local church under Cyril's guidance and inspiration developed in conjunction with the renewed interest in the Holy Places. By the 380s, a burgeoning Holy Week incorporated all the significant sites of Christ's Passion and Resurrection into its ceremonies. Through the ever growing number of pilgrims, the Holy City and its vibrant liturgical life became widely known and emulated throughout Christendom. Cyril's key role as bishop in the life, growth, and prominence of the Jerusalem church makes him one of the most important sources for understanding the Church in the fourth century.

The corpus of writings traditionally attributed to Cyril is small—one letter to the emperor Constantius, one homily *(On the Paralytic at the Pool)*, a few homiletic fragments, and a set of prebaptismal catechetical sermons. These latter sermons consist of an introductory procatechesis and eighteen Lenten catecheses preached to candidates preparing for baptism. In addition, there are five sermons on the initiation rites delivered after Easter to the newly baptized, which have also been traditionally attributed to Cyril, but whose authorship has in recent centuries been questioned. These sermons, called the *Mystagogic Catecheses,* are of special value both as a witness to the way the rites of initiation (baptism, chrismation, and Eucharist) were performed in fourth-century Jerusalem and for the rich sacramental theology they contain.[1] The principal endeavor of this study is to resolve this authorship question.

What is the significance of such a task? Since the only contender against Cyril is his successor, John II of Jerusalem (bishop 387–417), it can at least be granted that M represents the Jerusalem rites of initiation in the latter half of the fourth or the beginning of the fifth century. But given the considerable interest in recent decades in the development of the liturgical rites of this region's traditions, particularly with regard to the Eucharist and to the rites of anointing during initiation, a more precise dating and an analysis of the ritual developments represented by C and M would be of great value for any liturgical scholar interested in the history and cross-influence of these rites.[2] Of equal importance is simply knowing whether M represents the mind of Cyril or his successor. It is certainly in the interest of Cyrilline studies to know whether we can reliably regard M as a source for understanding his theology. At the same time, if M were included among the works of John of Jerusalem, this would greatly extend our knowledge of this controversial bishop. As will be shown, there is also the possibility that M represents an annual catechetical syllabus shared by both bishops. But even in this case, we would wish to know which bishop may have had the greater hand in its content. It is hoped, then, that settling this authorship question can contribute significantly to studies in the areas of Cyril's life and theology and to the history and theology of the Jerusalem liturgy.

B. The State of the Authorship Question

Ever since 1574, when Josias Simmler pointed out discrepancies in the attributions of authorship among the manuscripts of the catechetical writings (P, C, and M), which had been ascribed traditionally to Cyril, a long series of varied attempts have been made to address the question of the authorship of M. To date, however, there has been no thorough treatment of the problem. The following survey of the key points of the authorship question is intended to give the reader a sense of the broad scope of the issue, to outline the

---

1. See the bibliography for details of the sources used for these works. Hereafter, the following abbreviations will be used: P for the *Procatechesis*, C for the *Catecheses*, M for the *Mystagogic Catecheses*, Hom. for the *Homily on the Paralytic at the Pool*, and Let. for the *Letter to Constantius*.

2. See, in particular, the studies of P. Bradshaw, S. Brock, G. J. Cuming, E. Cutrone, E. Ratcliff, B. Spinks, and G. Winkler in the bibliography.

various elements involved, and to begin to assess their importance. It will also help with setting out the principles of the argument that will be utilized and the minimum requirements needed in order to arrive at a final decision.

The association of John of Jerusalem's name with M was the first problem that came to light. Simmler published a catalogue of books that included an edition of Cyril's works by John Grodecq. The edition appears in the catalogue as part of a list of Greek books that were purchased by the city of Augsburg; in this list, C and M are attributed to John of Jerusalem. Based only on this information, Simmler proposed that perhaps the works were John's but had been deliberately ascribed to another, namely, Cyril to give them greater authority.[3] The list that he referred to, however, was simply a bill of sale for the books, a hundred manuscripts purchased in 1545 by the library in Augsburg. The bill included a manuscript described as containing eighteen prebaptismal catecheses and five mystagogic catecheses and attributed the whole set to John.[4] The list was inaccurate, however, for in fact the manuscript in the collection contains P, C, and M, and only with reference to M is there mention of an author, namely, John. Not until the 1703 edition of Cyril's works by Thomas Milles was this inaccuracy rectified, but only because he had access to a more detailed catalogue, not because he examined the manuscript itself.[5] At this early stage, the attribution question was pitted against the literary tradition (references by other authors to M citing Cyril as author), which favored Cyril, and opinion was split.[6]

3. Josias Simmler, *Biblioteca instituta* (Tiguri: Apud Christophorum Froschoverum, 1574), 153.

4. This list of the sale is preserved in codex *Vindobonensis 9734*, fol. 2. The codex is reproduced by C. Graux, *Essai sur les origines de fond grec de l'Escurial*, Bibliothèque de l'école des hautes études, 46 (Paris: F. Vieweg, 1880), 413–17.

5. The manuscript in question, formerly in the Augsburg library, was moved to Munich in 1806 and is now known as *Monacensis gr. 394*; it will be considered below in detail.

6. In favor of John: Antonio Reisero, *Index manuscriptorum bibliothecae Augustanae* (Augsburg: sumtu Theophili Goebelii, 1675), 33; André Rivet, *Critici Sacri libri IV* (Geneva: in officina Iacobi Chouet, 1642), III.8, 281–82; Robert Cocus, *Censura quorumdam scriptorum* (London: impensis G. Barret, 1623), 123; F. Combefis, *Bibliotheca Patrum Concionatoria* (Paris: sumptibus Antonio Bertier, 1662), 1.10. In favor of Cyril: David Hoeschelius, *Catalogus Graecorum codicum qui sunt in bibliotheca reipublicae Augustanae Vindelicae* (Augsburg: ad insigne pinus [only], 1595), 20–22; Marcus Velserus, *Augustanae Vindelicae bibliothecae catalogus Graecorum manuscriptorum codicum et ecclesiasticorum* (Ingolstadt: excudat Adam Sartorius, 1602); reprinted as an appendix entitled *Catalogi MSS Graecorum et aliorum etiam codicum*, in A. Possevino, *Apparatus sacri ad scriptores Veteris et Novi Testamenti* II (Cologne: apud Ioannem Gymnicum, 1608), Appendix, 66. On this issue of attribution, see also: Thomas Milles, in the preface to his edition of Cyril's works, PG 33.1225; Touttée, *Dissertatio secunda*, ch. 3, PG 33.136–42; Wilhelm Karl Reischl and Joseph Rupp, eds., *S. Cyrilli: Opera quae supersunt omnia*, 2 vols. (Munich: Sumptibus Librariae Lentneriane, 1848–60; repr. Hildesheim: Georg Olms, 1967), 1:cxlv.

Later, the matter of internal evidence arose when the theology of *M* was challenged. Edmé Aubertin in a work on the Eucharist argued that the teaching of the real presence (as found in *M* 4) was unknown in these early centuries.[7] He did not find Simmler's citation of the list of Augsburg manuscripts convincing of anything certain. Arguing also from style, manuscript attestation, and literary tradition (noting significantly that none of the most ancient authors mentions *M*), he was willing to say, as André Rivet previously suggested, that *C* was Cyril's but *M* was not.[8] Periodically scholars have taken up this topic but never as the subject of a thoroughgoing study.

Consistently, the position against Cyril that deals with the liturgical theology of *M* argues that it is too advanced for Cyril's time.[9] A brief study by P. T. Camelot compared the baptismal theology of *C* (*C* 3.3, 4, 11, 12) with that of *M* (M2.4–7).[10] He noted a number of theological differences. While willing to admit that the two sets of lectures have different goals (introductory instruction in the rudiments of faith as opposed to mystagogy for the enlightened), which could account for the more developed theology of *M*, he concluded that the differences are great enough to place *M* in a time after the life of Cyril. Lastly, some scholars have addressed the possible presence of Origenisms in *M*, which would suggest the influence of John, a known Origenist.[11]

The questions concerning the manuscripts and the literary tradition were

7. *De Eucharistia sive Coenae Dominicae Sacramento libri tres contra praecipuos Adversariorum Partium Scriptores* (Davantrie: Typis Johannis Columbii, 1654).

8. *De Eucharistia*, Book II, 422.

9. Theodor Schermann, review of *Die Brotbitte des Vaterunsers*, by J. P. Bock, *Theologische Revue* 19 (1911): 575–79; Severien Salaville, "Une question de critique littéraire: Les Catéchèses Mystagogiques de S. Cyrille," *Échos d'Orient* 17 (1915): 531–37 (against Schermann); Josef Andreas Jungmann, *Die Stellung Christi im liturgischen Gebet*, Liturgiegeschichtliche Forschungen, vols. 7–8 (Münster: Aschendorff, 1925), 217; Jungmann suspends his judgment against Cyril (without, however, arguing in his favor) in the second revised German edition, Liturgiewissenschaftliche Quellen und Forschungen, vols. 19–20 (Münster: Aschendorff, 1962), XXI*; English trans., *The Place of Christ in Liturgical Prayer*, trans. A. Peeler (London: G. Chapman, 1965), 246–47; Georg Kretschmar, *Studien zür fruchristlichen Trinitätstheologie*, Beiträge zur historichen Theologie, no. 21 (Tübingen: Mohr, 1956), 165–69; idem, "Die frühe Geschichte der Jerusalemer Liturgie," *Jahrbuch für Liturgik und Hymnologie* 2 (1956): 22–46; William Telfer, *Cyril of Jerusalem and Nemesius of Emesa*, Library of Christian Classics, no. 4 (Philadelphia: Westminster, 1955), 39–40.

10. P. T. Camelot, "Note sur la théologie baptismale des Catéchèses attribuées à Saint Cyrille de Jérusalem," in *Kyriakon: Festschrift Johannes Quasten*, ed. P. Granfield and J. A. Jungmann, 2 vols, 2:724–29 (Münster: Aschendorff, 1970).

11. Kretschmar, *Studien zür fruchristlichen Trinitätstheologie*; idem, "Die frühe Geschichte der Jerusalemer Liturgie"; E. Bihain, "Une vie arménienne de S. Cyrille de Jérusalem," *Le Muséon* 76 (1963): 340 n. 73; *WCJ*, 2:147, 159 n. 24, 165 n. 15, 196 n. 19, 200 nn. 39, 41.

freshly examined by W. J. Swaans in 1942.[12] In addition, he compared M with its corresponding readings in the *Armenian Lectionary* and concluded that these traditions indicate that C and M are separate works that were united at a later date. His cautious but definite conclusion was that there were enough incongruities with common authorship to make it imprudent to place M among the works of Cyril. Hence, he decided there was no reason to deny the validity of the attribution to John of Jerusalem found in the oldest Greek manuscript of M. His article also included a substantial criticism of past arguments, and his conclusions still carry much weight.

Since Swaans's study, the issue of external witnesses has gained more importance as a result of the latest critical edition of the *Armenian Lectionary*.[13] Further, the more accurate dating of the pilgrimage of Egeria to the years 381 to 384, when Cyril was still bishop, makes her testimony newly relevant.[14] Hence, these witnesses need to be fully reconsidered.

Other questions, apparently engendered by Swaans's study, concern the precise relationship between C and M. Are they a complete set of sermons preached in the same year?[15] If not, how far apart in time are they? Were they published independently? And does M in any way depend on C for its content? One proposal is that, unlike C, which is a transcription of one year's prebaptismal sermons, M could represent something like a "diocesan script, subject to continual revision," such that it had its source with Cyril but was revised by John.[16] A. Paulin suggested that M was not allowed to be published in the mid-fourth century because of the still strict observance of the *disciplina arcani* (the practice of keeping the most sacred elements of the faith secret), and only when this practice was relaxed was it published.[17] Further, he

12. W. J. Swaans, "À propos des 'Catéchèses Mystagogiques' attribuées à S. Cyrille de Jérusalem," *Le Muséon* 55 (1942): 1–42.

13. *Le codex arménien Jérusalem 121*, ed. and trans. Athanase Renoux, PO 35.1, 36.2. The lectionary's particular relevance as an external witness will be considered in Chapter 2.

14. Paul Devos, "La date du voyage d'Égérie," *AB* 85 (1967): 165–94. See also John Wilkinson, *Egeria's Travels to the Holy Land*, 2d rev. ed. (Warminster, England: Aris and Phillips, 1981), 237–39, 330, for a full survey of this question of date.

15. For a study on the date of M, see Clemens Beukers, "'For our Emperors, Soldiers and Allies'. An Attempt at Dating the Twenty-Third Catechesis by Cyrillus of Jerusalem," *VC* 15 (1961): 177–84.

16. *St. Cyril of Jerusalem's Lectures on the Christian Sacraments. The Procatechesis and the Five Mystagogical Catecheses*, ed. F. L. Cross (London: S.P.C.K., 1951), xxxvi–xxxix; Johannes Quasten, *Patrology*, 4 vols. (Westminster, Maryland: Christian Classics, Inc., 1983–86), 3:364–66; WCJ, 2:147–48.

17. Antoine Paulin, *Saint Cyrille de Jérusalem Catéchète* (Paris: Editions du Cerf, 1959), 53.

said it seemed to be more like the extant notes of the preacher rather than a transcription by listeners. Paulin's hypothesis attempts to explain three issues: the different styles between *C* and *M*, the absence of *M* in the primitive Syriac and Armenian versions of Cyril's catecheses, and the association of both Cyril and John with *M* at a later date. All the implications of these hypotheses had yet to be fully explored.

The difference in style between *C* and *M* has been noted as far back as Aubertin in 1633 and is a fairly regular feature in any survey of the authorship question. Very few scholars, though, have attempted much more than a hypothesis for explaining the differences. Paulin had suggested *M* was a rough sketch of sermons, and A. A. Stephenson pointed out the difference of subject matter between *C* and *M*,[18] but only E. J. Yarnold attempts a proper comparison of the two texts by actually citing several examples.[19] To evaluate seriously the question of style, however, demands a much more extensive analysis than has yet been attempted.

Finally, and only recently, Yarnold has presented a case against John but only superficially and with reference to only one work of John's.[20] A fuller examination is in order.

Although Swaans's significant article settled the authorship question for some time, subsequent studies on various topics relevant to Cyril and fourth-century liturgy and theology have gradually weakened his most important arguments. The result is that among modern references to the *Mystagogic Catecheses* we find an even split of opinion concerning the question of their authorship.[21]

The current state of the question, therefore, demanded a new and com-

---

18. *WCJ*, 2:145–46.

19. E. J. Yarnold, "The Authorship of the *Mystagogic Catecheses* Attributed to Cyril of Jerusalem," *HJ* 19 (1978): 147–49.

20. Ibid., 146–47.

21. For example, in favor of Cyril: Cross, *St. Cyril's Lectures on the Christian Sacraments*, xxvi–xxxix; Karel Deddens, "Annus liturgicus? Een onderzoek naar de betekenis van Cyrillus van Jeruzalem voor de ontwikkeling van het 'kerkelijk jaar'" (Ph.D. diss., Oosterbaan & Le Cointre, 1975), 72–84; Yarnold, "The Authorship of the *Mystagogic Catecheses*"; G. Hellemo, *Adventus Domini: Eschatological Thought in 4th Century Apses and Catechesis*, Supplements to Vigiliae Christianae, 5 (Leiden: Brill, 1989), 146–48. Against Cyril: M. Richard, "Bulletin de patrologie," *Mélanges de science religieuse* 5 (1948): 281–82; Wilkinson, *Egeria's Travels*, 258; Peter Walker, *Holy City, Holy Places? Christian Attitudes to Jerusalem and the Holy Land in the Fourth Century* (Oxford: Clarendon Press, 1990), 410. Undecided: Berthold Altaner and Alfred Stuiber, *Patrologie*, 8th ed. (Freiburg: Herder, 1978), 312 (a change of mind from his 1950 edition, 269); *WCJ*, 2:147–48; Auguste Piédagnel, ed., *Cyrille de Jérusalem: Catéchèses mystagogiques*, trans. Pierre Paris, SC 126 *bis* (Paris: Éditions du Cerf, 1988), 38–40, 185–87.

plete evaluation. Past arguments in all of the areas cited above needed to be reevaluated for their own merit and then reconsidered in the light of more recent and relevant independent studies. A systematic comparison of the content of M with Cyril's Lenten catecheses in the areas of liturgical rite, spirituality, catechetics, theology, and literary style could determine the presence or absence in M of Cyrilline characteristics. This comparative study had hitherto received only partial treatment due to the extent of the task. Further, since there had not yet been a thorough comparative analysis between M and three known works of the contending author, John of Jerusalem, Cyril's successor, I included such an analysis. Lastly, concerning the question of style, besides conducting a general analysis of common terms, phraseology, and rhetorical style, I carried out a computer-based stylometric analysis (statistical analysis of literary style) of the texts to evaluate the uniformity of style between Cyril's *Catecheses* and M.

C. Principles of Argumentation and Possibilities of Outcome

It will be helpful to clarify ahead of time the parameters of the argument that will be involved in the handling of this question of the authorship of M as well as to consider the possible outcomes.

Historically, the challenges to the Cyrilline authorship of M have been characterized by two basic approaches. The first tries to give an account of the presence of John's name in certain manuscripts. The second approach, which is much less straightforward, tries to determine whether or not M is either too late for Cyril to be its author or contains material that is demonstrably non-Cyrilline. This second approach has been pursued only in order to provide an explanation for the manuscript attributions of M to John. In fact, if those manuscripts containing John's name were not known, it is doubtful whether much, if any, attention would have been paid to the differences between C and M. The first approach has received minimal attention but deserves careful reconsideration, especially in light of the fact that the studies to date have not yet substantially considered a second manuscript, the Arabic codex, that ascribes M to John. Inasmuch as C is unquestionably Cyril's, and C and M have traditionally been treated as a single work, the second approach has characteristically dealt with evidence suggesting that the two texts were published and handed on independently. This in itself is no argument against Cyrilline authorship (though some scholars were led to think it was), for it would only suggest at most that the two texts represent catechetical preaching from different years, both of which could be within the time of Cyril's episcopate. The real concern, rather, is the nature of the independence of M from C; for example, are they separated by such a time span, or do they contain such different theological or stylistic features, that it necessitates proposing two different authors?

The overall requirements for a final judgment remain as they have in the past. A decision in favor of Johannine authorship must come from showing either that M is too late for Cyril, that the manuscripts with John's name are accurate in their ascriptions, or that the content of M is convincingly not from Cyril. For a pro-Cyril decision, it would suffice to show that M need not be dated after 387 when Cyril died,[22] that the manuscript attributions to John are not indisputable, and that certain cited differences between C and M can be explained as originating from the same author.

At the same time, some other possibilities need to be mentioned. I have already noted the idea that John's name may have been associated with M, even if he did not author it, because he may have preached or even revised the text. These options need be considered seriously only if no other explanation can be put forward for why John's name appears on some of the manuscripts. The option that John merely preached M would not affect a verdict that M is the work of Cyril. As for the option that John may have revised the text, this could be shown only if there are significant non-Cyrilline features in M suggesting the presence of another hand; and in that case, unless the features were clearly non-Johannine, we could judge John to be the most likely candidate for author. Hence, a comparison of M with the other works of Cyril will also have to bear in mind the extent and nature of any non-Cyrilline features in order to come to a judgment about John's possible part in its composition.

---

22. The date for the death of Cyril had traditionally been set at 386. The most recent study by Pierre Nautin, "La date du *de viris inlustribus* de Jérôme, de la mort de Cyrille de Jérusalem et de celle de Grégoire de Nazianze," *RHE* 56 (1961): 33–35, shows that the more likely, and now commonly accepted, date is 387.

Historical Background
and Contexts

CHAPTER I

ℭℴℭ

Cyril of Jerusalem and His Church

A. Introduction

The many facets of a question of authorship can be fully understood and treated only when they are seen in their proper context. To conduct an examination of the *Mystagogic Catecheses* for signs of Cyrilline characteristics, we need to know something of Cyril himself and the life of the Jerusalem church he served. This is particularly so since the work in question is most probably separated by some thirty or so years from Cyril's other known works, which date from the earliest stage of his career.[1] Anything that can be known about the formative influences on Cyril, his upbringing, his education, his career, and the historical and cultural milieu in which he lived, will give us insight into his personality, character, and spiritual development. As well, the more we know about the Jerusalem church, its cultural milieu and theological struggles, and the development of its catechetical and liturgical life, the better we can situate Cyril in the context in which he was formed by his local church and took part in shaping its future. Besides providing a general background, a survey of these various areas will establish what developments in the local church were taking place and how Cyril was involved in them. This survey will give us a better understanding not only of the young Cyril of the *Catecheses* but also the elderly bishop of the late fourth century. The chapter will cover the life and ministry of Cyril and the revival of the Jerusalem church in the fourth century, with particular attention to its catechetical program. The survey of the catechetical program will include a brief look at Cyril's sermons with a view to determining where we are likely to find evidence for establishing the authorship of *M*.

---

1. The question of the date of *M* will be considered in Chapter 2.

B. Cyril of Jerusalem, Life and Ministry

1. Early Life

Tradition has it that Cyril was born in Jerusalem or in its environs to Christian parents in the year 313. This year was to be remembered, however, for the much more momentous event of Constantine's Edict of Milan, which gave Christians full freedom to practice their religion. Despite all the risks involved with being embraced by the secular world, this turning point gave the Church an opportunity to flourish. It was also a time of great development in the Church's administrative structure and, more pertinent to our concerns, its liturgical life.

Born when he was, and with his vocation to ministry in the Church, Cyril was poised to play a major role in its growth. But many obstacles lay ahead of him. Arianism, for example, broke out when he was but a few years old and remained a constant threat to orthodoxy.[2] While this heresy was sometimes a catalyst for major developments in trinitarian theology, it was also on occasion the cause of outright persecution. More than once Arian leaders sent Cyril and other orthodox bishops into exile. Only at the Council of Constantinople (381), a few years before Cyril's death, was this heresy finally successfully suppressed and condemned.

Nothing is directly known of Cyril's upbringing; the short biographical note from the early liturgical calendar for his feast on March 18 mentions only that he was born of pious parents of orthodox faith and was brought up during the reign of Constantine. He had at least one sister, whose son, Gelasius, he appointed as bishop of Caesarea c. 366. His comments about honoring one's parents suggest that his own upbringing was a nurturing experience in a close-knit family:

The first virtuous observance in a Christian is to honor his parents, to requite their trouble, and to provide with all his power for their comfort: for however much we

2. Arius (d. 336), while a priest in Alexandria, preached a subordinationist view of the Trinity, whereby the Son, though divine, was nonetheless created, hence, was neither equal to nor coeternal with the Father. The traditional orthodox view was that the Son was equally divine and coeternal with the Father. At the Council of Nicaea (325) the term *homoousios*, "of the same substance," was proposed to convey this belief against the Arians; this position was sometimes called consubstantialist. Later, some proposed the term *homoiousios*, "of like substance," with a view to preserving the divinity of the Son, while also preserving the distinction between the Father and Son. This intermediate view was sometimes referred to negatively as "semi-Arian," for if the Son were thought to be anything other than of the same substance with the uncreated Father, he could be construed to be in some way less than fully divine: subordinate, or even created.

may repay them, yet we can never be to them what they as parents have been to us. Let them enjoy the comfort we can give, and strengthen us with blessings.[3]

Cyril's comments in various parts of the *Catecheses* on the condition of the holy places before they were restored would suggest that he was at least raised in Jerusalem.[4] He would, then, have grown up in the fervor of Constantine's religious revitalization of the city.[5]

In *C* 12.1, 33, and 34, Cyril refers to the Order of the Solitaries and praises their practice of chastity in such a way that suggests he himself may have embraced such a life—one characterized by asceticism, works of charity, and celibacy—from an early age. He was probably ordained to the diaconate by his bishop, Macarius, who died in 335, and to the priesthood by Maximus around 342. Eight years later he was bishop of the Holy City. As a promising young deacon and presbyter in Jerusalem, he would have witnessed the many political and doctrinal vicissitudes taking place among the major churches after the Council of Nicaea as allegiances to the orthodox and Arian positions shifted back and forth. This should be kept in mind as we interpret the troubled events leading up to his consecration as bishop. Since the more substantial material we have on Cyril's life coincides with his ecclesiastical career, a close and careful scrutiny of these sources is essential for sorting out the details of his entrance into ecclesiastical life and correctly assessing Cyril's character and theological leanings.

2. Cyril's Ministry in the Jerusalem Church

a. Contradictions and Controversies: Interpreting the Sources

Five key witnesses provide us with information on Cyril's time in office, but they present a portrait full of controversy and contradiction. We need to assess each of them carefully.[6]

---

3. *C* 7.16. Unless otherwise noted, translations are my own.

4. See *C* 12.20; 13.32; 14.5, 9.

5. For a summary of attempts to reconstruct Cyril's early life, see *The Catechetical Lectures of St. Cyril,* trans. E. H. Gifford, NPNF, 2d ser., vol. 7 (Oxford: Parker, 1894; repr. Peabody, Mass.: Hendrickson, 1994), i–ii. For Cyril's probable origins in Jerusalem see Walker, *Holy City, Holy Places?* 31–34.

6. We should note the following about the historians as sources: Theodoret (393–466) wrote his history c. 449–50. He had a strong anti-heretical bent, especially against the Arians. He was well educated and experienced in controversy, but was perhaps biased toward the orthodox Fathers. Socrates (380–450) was an educated historian and lawyer. He is noted as an objective and sincere writer who is careful with his sources (evidenced by his own revised edition of his history). He covers events up to the year 439. Sozomen was born in Palestine but resided in Constantinople and was contemporary with Socrates. He wrote his history between 439 and 450.

1. Rufinus (c. 345–410):

At Jerusalem, however, Cyril received the episcopate after Maximus, there having been some confusion over his ordination, and he was wont to vacillate, sometimes in belief, more often in allegiance.[7]

The charge that Cyril vacillated in belief and allegiance stems, no doubt, from the facts that (1) he eventually took a stand against Acacius, his pro-Arian metropolitan[8] who appointed him bishop, and (2) that he later associated with those of the homoiousian party (those who proposed saying of the Son that he is of like substance with the Father, for example, Silvanus of Tarsus, Basil of Ancyra, Eustathius of Sebaste, and George of Laodicea) during his first exile (357 to 359) and at the Council of Seleucia (359).[9]

2. Jerome (c. 340–420):

Maximus, who followed Macarius as fortieth bishop of Jerusalem, died this year [352]. After him the Arians took over the Church, that is, Cyril, Eutychius, Cyril again, Irenaeus, Cyril for a third time, Hilary, and then Cyril for a fourth time. Cyril had been ordained presbyter by Maximus, but after the death of Maximus, Acacius, bishop of Caesarea, with other Arian bishops, promised the bishopric to Cyril if he renounced his ordination by Maximus and served in the Church as deacon. For this impiety he was rewarded the see. On his deathbed, Maximus appointed Heraclius his successor, but Cyril persuaded him to revert to the rank of presbyter from that of bishop.[10]

It seems, according to Jerome, that Maximus attempted to protect his diocese from Arian rule by choosing his own successor, Heraclius. Acacius would have none of that and intervened. That Cyril was the choice of an Arian, led Jerome to conclude that he was of that party. What is worse, he got the see as a reward for publicly turning his back on his bishop!

3. Sozomen (early fifth century) echoes Jerome:

The adherents of Acacius and Patrophilus, having ejected Maximus, turned over the church of Jerusalem to Cyril.[11]

He has a better style than Socrates, on whom he depends for much of his material (or on a source common to both), but is not quite as historically exacting; he includes many legends. See Quasten, *Patrology*, 3:532–38, 550–51; Altaner, *Patrologie*, 274–75.

    7. *HE* 10.24, GCS Eusebius 2.2, 989.

    8. A metropolitan is the equivalent of a modern-day archbishop. Church authority was organized according to Roman custom; a metropolitan had authority in a province over his comprovincial bishops.

    9. Theodoret, *HE* 2.22; Socrates, *HE* 2.39–40; Sozomen, *HE* 4.22–23, 25.

    10. *Chronicle* an. 352 (PL 27.683–84).

    11. *HE* 4.20. The translations of Socrates are from *Church History from A.D. 305–439*, trans. A. C. Zenos, NPNF, 2d ser., vol. 2 (Oxford: Parker, 1890; repr. Peabody, Mass.: Hendrickson, 1994).

He also, it seems, thought Cyril was pro-Arian in his early years but eventually embraced orthodoxy. For in his account of the council of 381, Sozomen groups Cyril among a hundred and fifty bishops who recognized the consubstantiality of the Trinity and adds that he "at this time had renounced the tenets of the Macedonians which he had previously held."[12]

4. Socrates (c. 380–450) gives virtually the same testimony as Sozomen:

Acacius and Patrophilus, having ejected Maximus, bishop of Jerusalem, installed Cyril in his see.[13]

Cyril of Jerusalem, who at that time recognized the doctrine of the *homoousion,* having retracted his former opinion. . . .[14]

5. Theodoret (c. 393–460) records the synodical letter from the council of 381 which says of Cyril:

We make known that the right reverend and most religious Cyril is bishop, who was some time ago canonically ordained by the bishops of the province, and has in several places fought a good fight against the Arians.[15]

It is clear from these witnesses that there were complications of some sort with Cyril's ordination and attainment of the see, as well as some questions about his doctrinal positions. At the same time, the theology of the *Catecheses* gives no reason to think Cyril was anything but orthodox in his thinking and teaching.[16] What can we make of this mixed testimony?

Five observations about these sources will make sorting out the details of Cyril's career easier. First, the most important of these witnesses is Jerome; he is closer to the events and gives more details. But, while Jerome's account of the basic facts concerning the circumstances of Cyril's ordination and consecration are probably accurate, there is reason to believe that his interpretation of the events he reports is biased against Cyril. He lived in the dio-

---

Those of Sozomen are from *Church History from A.D. 323–425,* trans. Chester D. Hartranft, NPNF, 2d ser., vol. 2 (Oxford: Parker, 1890; repr. Peabody, Mass.: Hendrickson, 1994).

12. *HE* 7.7. Macedonius (d. c. 362), as bishop of Constantinople, championed the semi-Arian position at the Council of Seleucia.

13. *HE* 2.38.

14. *HE* 5.8.

15. *HE* 5.9. The translations of Theodoret are from *Church History,* trans. Blomfield Jackson, NPNF, 2d ser., vol. 3 (Oxford: Parker, 1892; repr. Peabody, Mass.: Hendrickson, 1994).

16. See William Telfer, *Cyril of Jerusalem,* 19–24; Joseph Lebon, "La position de saint Cyrille de Jérusalem dans les luttes provoquées par l'arianisme," *RHE* 20 (1924): 181–210, 357–86; R. C. Gregg, "Cyril of Jerusalem and the Arians," in *Arianism: Historical and Theological Reassessments,* ed. R. C. Gregg, Patristic Monograph Series, no. 11 (Cambridge, Mass.: Philadelphia Patristic Foundation, 1985), 85–109.

cese of Jerusalem from 386 to 420, but on unfriendly terms with John, who succeeded Cyril. He had a heated falling out with John over questions of Origenist theology.[17] By association, he perhaps judged Cyril to be of a similar, that is, unorthodox, mind. With any such prejudice against Cyril's orthodoxy, it is understandable that an appointment by Acacius, a professed Arian, could be reason for doubt in Jerome's mind as to Cyril's views on Arianism.

Second, the notion in Socrates and Sozomen (who wrote in the middle of the fifth century) that Cyril earlier held a Macedonian view could also derive from his association with the homoiousians, for Macedonius was among this group at Seleucia.[18]

Third, a connection with Macedonius may also stem from the fact that Cyril's installation (350/51) coincided with the replacement of Paul of Constantinople (a zealous Nicene) with Macedonius, and may have been regarded as "part of the general anti-Nicene *revanche* of 351."[19] But while his preferred trinitarian terminology classifies him as a homoiousian, making him vulnerable to being labeled semi-Arian, no evidence exists, other than that he was acquainted with the individuals who preferred this terminology, for forming a judgment that Cyril aligned himself with any single group against another.

Fourth, Lebon thinks that by the time Socrates and Sozomen were writing, the various terms for any position short of strict orthodoxy, for example, semi-Arian, homoiousian, and Macedonian, were interchangeable.[20]

Fifth, without more concrete evidence, it is difficult to be certain at the time of his consecration (c. 350/51) what Cyril's doctrinal position was concerning the trinitarian status of the Son, since at this time theological positions concerning the controversial term *homoousios* were still far from refined, and the more politically astute were careful about expressing definite views. As Telfer puts it, it was a time when "doctrinal loyalties were still a matter over which many, if not most, kept their own counsel."[21]

Now that we can better interpret these sources in their proper contexts,

---

17. Jerome's stance against John is chronicled in *Against John of Jerusalem* (PL 23.355–98). For a general account see J. N. D. Kelly, *Jerome: His Life, Writings, and Controversies* (London: Duckworth, 1975), 195–209.

18. Socrates, *HE* 2.39–40; Sozomen, *HE* 4.13, 22. Epiphanius also groups Cyril in a semi-Arian splinter group at Seleucia with Basil of Ancyra, George of Laodicea, Silvanus of Tarsus, and Macedonius (*Panarion* 73.23, 27).

19. See *WCJ*, 1:22; Socrates, *HE* 2.27–28; Sozomen, *HE* 4.2.

20. Lebon, "La position de saint Cyrille," 182, 382–83.

21. *Cyril of Jerusalem*, 24.

we can look afresh at the latter half of Cyril's life, his career as bishop. First, we need to explain why his initial appointment as bishop was questioned, and second, why he would "repudiate" his ordination to the priesthood. Third, we will see that the controversies he was involved in were actually more matters of church order than doctrine. And fourth, we need to explain why he would at least appear to "vacillate" in loyalty and doctrine from anti-Arian to pro-Arian parties, while in fact he was a steady proponent of the orthodox position.

b. Difficulties from the Start: Bishop Maximus

A major contributor to the problems with Cyril's ordination and consecration was his predecessor, Bishop Maximus, who had incurred the censure of his metropolitan, Acacius. This made Cyril's entrance into his ministry potentially problematic in two ways: first, Acacius could question the validity of any exercise of Maximus's duties, such as his ordination of Cyril or the naming of a successor, and second, he would no doubt consider anyone loyal to Maximus to be opposed to himself.

To sort out what happened we need to go back to the Synod of Tyre, held in the eastern part of the Empire in 335, under the authority of the then pro-Arian emperor Constantine. The majority voice in this synod was pro-Arian, and a major issue they dealt with was accusations against the anti-Arian Athanasius, then bishop of Alexandria. The charges were ostensibly over matters of ecclesiastical administration but were no doubt driven by doctrinal concerns, with the result that Athanasius was deposed and ordered into exile.[22] Maximus was present at this synod and, probably out of unexamined loyalty to his fellow bishops and the emperor, was party to the judgment against Athanasius.[23] In 342, the Synod of Serdica was convened in the West under the protection of the new western emperor, the anti-Arian Constans. Athanasius was present (apparently anticipating vindication), much to the consternation of a group of pro-Arian eastern bishops—Acacius being among them. These eastern bishops refused to meet or begin any conference until Athanasius departed. When this was not permitted by the leaders of the synod, Acacius and his party withdrew in protest and were condemned by the remaining members of the synod.[24] Cyril's bishop, Maximus,

22. Sozomen, *HE* 2.25.
23. Ibid.
24. Athanasius, *Apologia contra Arianos (Apologia secunda)* 50.3, in *Athanasius Werke* 2.1, ed. H. G. Opitz (Berlin and Leipzig: De Gruyter, 1934–35), 131; Socrates, *HE* 2.20; Sozomen, *HE* 3.11. See also Socrates, *HE* 2.8 and Sozomen, *HE* 3.6.

was again present, but this time sat with the western anti-Arian bishops—though he also had the support of fourteen other Palestinian bishops. They all gave their support to Athanasius and voted to reinstate him in his see in Alexandria. Hence, Maximus found himself in the uncomfortable position of having condemned his own metropolitan, Acacius! He no doubt feared that some sort of retaliation was forthcoming.

This rift between Maximus and many of his fellow eastern bishops became graver in 346, when he extended hospitality to Athanasius on his return from exile to Alexandria and sent a letter to the church at Alexandria congratulating them on the return of their bishop.[25]

c. Maximus's Desperate Move, Acacius's Reaction

However Cyril may have been involved in these matters, the crisis point came when Maximus, nearing his death (348–49), became concerned about a suitable successor. Such an appointment would normally be made jointly by the bishops of the province and with the consent of the metropolitan (according to canons 4 and 6 of the Council of Nicaea[26]), in this case Acacius in Caesarea. But Maximus, fearing that these bishops with Arian leanings would appoint an Arian bishop, opted to act alone and consecrated a successor of his own choosing, Heraclius.[27]

Such an independent act by the Jerusalem church was not without precedent (indeed, according to Sozomen, Maximus himself was appointed by Macarius for the very same reason of keeping his local church free of Arian influence).[28] This show of independence reflects the long-running battle of ecclesiastical jurisdiction between Caesarea and Jerusalem. Nicaea acknowledged a special status for Jerusalem in its seventh canon: "Since there prevails a custom and ancient tradition to the effect that the bishop of Aelia[29] is to be honored, let him be granted everything consequent upon this honor, saving

25. Socrates, *HE* 2.23–24; Athanasius, *Apologia contra Arianos* 57, in *Athanasius Werke* 2.1, 136–37. Even though Constans, who ruled the West, approved the reinstatement of Athanasius at the Synod of Serdica, his brother Constantius, who ruled the East, refused to let him return immediately to Alexandria. Only Constans's threat of military force finally made his brother change his mind (Socrates *HE* 2.22).

26. Norman P. Tanner, ed., *Decrees of the Ecumenical Councils* (London: Sheed & Ward, 1990), 7–8.

27. It would seem that, as suitable as Cyril ultimately proved to be as the bishop of Jerusalem, at this time he was relatively young (about 35 years old), and Heraclius was "next in line."

28. Sozomen, *HE* 2.20.

29. The pre-Constantinian Roman name for Jerusalem.

the dignity proper to the metropolitan." The canon, however, does not specify what unique privileges Jerusalem could enjoy; hence there was room for
conflict of interpretation.[30] Maximus's appointment of Heraclius was, therefore, open to challenge as irregular, and Acacius could claim to be acting
within his rights when he declared the appointment of the new bishop void,
censured Maximus, and named Cyril as successor. This, it seems, would have
put Cyril in a position to choose either to defend Maximus's action on the basis of the so-called privileges of the Jerusalem church, or, out of respect for
overall church order, be obedient to his metropolitan. Complying with
Acacius, of course, also left him open to being suspected of Arianism.

d. Cyril's Decision

We know that Cyril indeed accepted the appointment and as a result incurred the suspicion of being an Arian. What we need to explore is why he
complied. Telfer thinks that (1) Cyril was not sympathetic with the "desper-
ate course" Maximus took in his appointing Heraclius, and (2) that he "had
come to believe that Maximus had forfeited his own bishopric in his attachment to the ruined cause of Athanasius."[31] That is, Maximus had risked censure from his metropolitan and lost. Seeing that no advantage would result
from defending Maximus's action, the practical choice, Telfer concludes,
would be for Cyril to maintain good order with his metropolitan and comply
with Acacius's decision. Seen in this way, Cyril's choice would be a bold
stance against his local church, behavior not in keeping with his long and
successful association with it.

Telfer, however, does not consider a few other aspects of the situation,
and other interpretations are possible. First of all, let us consider the case
from Acacius's point of view. Does his choice of Cyril necessarily mean that
the two of them held the same doctrinal ground? The clear non-Arian theology of the *Catecheses* and Cyril's consistent stance against Acacius in subsequent years would suggest that Acacius actually misjudged Cyril's thinking,
and by appointing him bishop, unknowingly played into the hands of the
Jerusalem church. Believing that he was appointing someone sympathetic to
his views, he actually chose a loyal member of the Jerusalem church and, as
time showed, an anti-Arian. Contrary to Jerome's suspicions, Cyril was not
necessarily placed in a compromising position; he could still be loyal to the

30. Tanner, *Decrees of the Ecumenical Councils,* 8–9. On this subject in general, see *WCJ,*
1:13–21.

31. *Cyril of Jerusalem,* 24.

needs of his local church while accepting the appointment by Acacius. Assuming his local church knew Cyril well, it is hard to think that they would have been much disappointed in the ruling from Caesarea.[32]

Second, as Stephenson notes, Acacius probably would not have acted until the death of Constans in 350, or perhaps not even until the defeat of Magnentius in 351, which left the Arian Constantius in sole power; it was only then that "a strong anti-Athanasian policy became possible."[33] This would mean that Heraclius would have been bishop for about two years, sufficient time for the local church to realize that having Cyril replace Heraclius, in compliance with Caesarea, would be of no disadvantage to them. This does not imply that Heraclius was a poor bishop, only that Cyril was considered just as promising. That Heraclius apparently stepped down and remained as presbyter under Cyril (as suggested by Jerome's account) would further indicate that the Jerusalem church found the whole situation acceptable.

Telfer's view of these events would have Cyril faced with a choice of either supporting or dissociating himself from Maximus and the Jerusalem church. But if it is true that the appointment of Cyril took place sometime after the death of Maximus, that he was misjudged by Acacius to be an Arian, that he was actually favored in the eyes of his local church, and that Heraclius cooperated with the decision, then a different conclusion emerges. Instead, no critical decision was necessary because by abiding by the wishes of the metropolitan, he was actually opting in favor of his local church.

e. Did Cyril Renounce His Ordination?

We cannot be certain of the truth of the allegation that Cyril renounced his ordination by Maximus. If it is true, it could be because he wished to comply with church order—the act need not be seen as a sign of vacillating allegiance. While we do not know the exact date of his ordination, we can surmise that it was after 342, for the following reasons. The only acceptable grounds for such a renunciation would be if the ordination was deemed invalid, and the only reason for its being invalid is if Maximus was at that time prohibited from exercising his right to ordain. Such a ban was apparently one of the results of the fateful Synod of Serdica in 342, where, because he sup-

32. This misjudgment on the part of Acacius is another indication that Cyril was a native of Jerusalem and not Caesarea. A native of Caesarea would not only be an unlikely choice for the Jerusalem bishopric, since customarily such appointments involved the choice of the local clergy and people, but he would also have been better known to the bishop of Caesarea than Cyril apparently was. See Walker, *Holy City, Holy Places?* 32.

33. *WCJ*, 1:21–22.

ported Athanasius and opposed the eastern bishops, Acacius judged Maximus to have forfeited his bishopric, and any subsequent ordinations could be ruled invalid.[34]

We can see from the above account of the events surrounding Cyril's ordination and consecration that there is nothing in the events themselves that would reveal anything certain about Cyril's doctrinal leanings, only that he complied with church order, and Jerome's grouping him with Acacius as an Arian is unfounded. It is only after Cyril commenced serving his church as its bishop and principal catechist that he exhibits much more of his character and theology.

f. Cyril, Bishop of Jerusalem

It was not long before it became clear where Cyril stood with regard to his metropolitan. In 354/55, responding to needs stemming from a famine, Cyril sold off some church property to assist the poor. According to Sozomen, Acacius ostensibly accused Cyril of acting without his approval, thus mismanaging church property, but was in fact using the incident as a pretext for having Cyril deposed for his doctrinal views.[35] From one point of view this confrontation with Acacius could suggest that Cyril suddenly changed his allegiance from Caesarea to Jerusalem and thus showed a vacillating doctrinal position. Such a view may be behind the statement of Rufinus, noted above, that Cyril "was wont to vacillate, sometimes in belief, more often in allegiance." The more sympathetic view of Cyril would see this event as another indication that Acacius had come to realize too late that he had underestimated Cyril's mind and heart both on matters of doctrine and on the ecclesiastical status of the Jerusalem church.

Cyril's bold stance in defending the ecclesiastical rights of his church against Caesarea was solidified by his refusal, according to Socrates, to answer a provincial summons to account for the alleged mismanagement of property, and in 357 Acacius deposed him.[36] Thus began the first of his three periods of exile (357 to 359). He submitted an appeal to the emperor and went to stay with Bishop Silvanus in Tarsus, whose church greatly enjoyed his teaching.[37] His appeal was included among the business of the Council of Seleucia two years later (359). A major dispute over matters of doctrine broke

---

34. See Telfer, Cyril of Jerusalem, 23–24; WCJ, 1:21. It must be remembered that rival factions would all too often mutually censure each other from one synod to the next.

35. HE 4.25; Socrates, HE 2.40.　　　　36. HE 2.40.

37. Theodoret, HE 2.22.

out and when it was clear to Acacius and his followers that they were going to lose out, they left. In their absence the remaining bishops took up Cyril's case and ruled in his favor. He was free to return to Jerusalem.[38]

But Acacius was not to be deterred and renewed his attack on Cyril. He personally took the matter up with the emperor at a synod in Constantinople and succeeded in turning him against Cyril.[39] The synod deposed Cyril "on various pretenses" and the emperor banished him from Jerusalem.[40] But this exile was short-lived (360 to 361); within a year Constantius was dead, the new emperor, Julian, canceled all sentences of banishment, and Cyril returned to Jerusalem for five years.[41] While we do not know for certain the place of his banishment, according to Theodoret he passed through Antioch on his way back to his see.[42]

In 366, Valens reestablished the ecclesiastical policies of Constantius, and Cyril was driven from his see for a third time.[43] This, the longest of his exiles, lasted eleven years, until the death of Valens in 378, whereupon Gratian reinstated Cyril, and Cyril lived out the remaining years of his life in office.[44] This last exile was no doubt the most painful because it appears that the life of his church suffered some deterioration in his absence. When Gregory of Nyssa visited the Holy City right after Cyril had returned, he was much discouraged by the lack of piety and respect for the Holy Places, which were increasingly subjected to commercialization. But recovery was rapid. Egeria's description of her visit just a few years later (to which we will return in some detail below) reveals an impressively vibrant spirituality among the pilgrims and local worshipers. Cyril's final vindication came in 381 at the Council of Constantinople, where he took a leading role among the defenders of the Nicene faith and was publicly acclaimed as both the rightful bishop of Jerusalem and a consistent opponent of Arianism.[45]

3. Conclusion: A Profile of Cyril

a. Personal Character

Even from this limited information about Cyril's life, we can draw a few conclusions about his character and how it is reflected in his theology. If the

---

38. Socrates, *HE* 2.40; Sozomen, *HE* 4.22.   39. Theodoret, *HE* 2.23.
40. Sozomen, *HE* 4.25; Socrates, *HE* 2.42.   41. Socrates, *HE* 3.1; Sozomen, *HE* 5.5.
42. *HE* 2.22.   43. Sozomen, *HE* 6.12.
44. Sozomen, *HE* 7.1; Socrates, *HE* 5.2; Theodoret, *HE* 5.2.
45. Theodoret, *HE* 5.9.

above interpretation of the events surrounding his ordination and consecration is correct, we can see that Cyril had an independent character. He showed practical and pastoral wisdom in steering his way through the crisis leading to his eventual appointment. On the one hand, he showed respect for church order in abiding by the ruling of Acacius when he censured Maximus and subsequently called into question the validity of his own ordination, yet at the same time he was able to honor the integrity and needs of his local church. Finally, when he could no longer balance outright loyalty to both his metropolitan and his local church, he took a brave stand in matters of doctrine and the traditional claims of his church for certain privileges of ecclesiastical autonomy. If we accept Sozomen's account, the issue of doctrine was more critical: the moment of truth came when his own doctrinal position, and not just that of his former bishop Maximus, was challenged by Acacius.

b. Theology

The content of the *Catecheses* shows that from early on Cyril's theological views were decidedly anti-Arian. This is so even though there is no specific mention of Arius or Arianism.[46] On the other hand, it is hard to say how close Cyril was to the hard-line conservative interpreters of the anti-Arian Council of Nicaea, sometimes referred to as the Nicene party. The following points suggest that he may have been closest to the more centrist homoiousian party. First, the term *homoousios* is notably lacking in the *Catecheses* even though there is lengthy teaching on the nature of the Son. Second, the anti-Arian language of the Nicene Creed seems not to have had any influence on the wording of the creed used in Cyril's church. Cyril's creedal statement on the Son reads: "the only-begotten Son of God, who was begotten true God of the Father before all worlds, by whom all things were made" (*C* 11.21). The Nicene Creed omitted any reference to a time when the Son was begotten (before all worlds), and includes that the Son was begotten "from the substance of the Father, God from God, light from light, true God from true God, begotten not made, consubstantial *(homoousios)* with the Father."[47] Third, Cyril attacks the extreme views of the hard-line Nicene, Marcellus of Ancyra (though without mentioning his name).[48] Lastly, his preferred trini-

---

46. See in particular Gregg, "Cyril of Jerusalem and the Arians," 88–93.

47. Tanner, *Decrees of the Ecumenical Councils*, 5.

48. The radical interpretation of *homoousios* blurred the distinction between the Father and the Son. To counter this Cyril says, "The Son is very God having the Father in himself, not changed into the Father, for the Father was not made human, but the Son" (*C* 11.17). Later he

tarian language is similar to that of his "associates" at Seleucia who proposed using "like" *(homoios)* rather than "same" *(homos)*:

C 4.7: Believe . . . in our Lord Jesus Christ, . . . like (ὅμοιον) in all things to him who begot him.

C 11.4: Son of the Father, like (ὅμοιος) in all things to his genitor.

C 11.9: Since the Father is very God, he begot the Son like (ὅμοιον) to himself, very God.

C 11.18: The Son is like (ὅμοιος) in all things to him who begot him.

But, in fact, nearly the same can be said of Athanasius's trintarian language. He also was critical of Marcellus, and as late as 355/60 (almost ten years after Cyril's writing) was comfortably using the language of "likeness in substance" with regard to the Son, for it had come gradually to take on a meaning that did not jeopardize a belief in the eternal divinity of the Son in relation to the Father.[49] This was a time of uncertainty when the doctrines of Nicaea, especially concerning the term *homoousios*, were gradually being pondered and refined.

A few final points would indicate that Cyril steered a cautious middle path through these controversial times. The fact that Acacius would appoint Cyril as bishop indicates that he was not easily identified with a hard-line Nicene party. Two statements from the *Catecheses* indicate the more careful traditionalist approach he took. At *C* 11.17 on the Son he says:

Let us never say there was a time when the Son was not; nor let us accept that the Son is the Father (υἱοπατορίαν);[50] but let us walk the king's road, and turn neither to the left hand nor to the right.

The first part of this quotation refers to the Arian position, but the position cited by the second part, while safely condemnable as Sabellian,[51] could also be construed as an extreme homoousian view, that is, a view hard-line Nicenes could be accused of holding. According to Socrates, "neither party

counters another noted heresy held by Marcellus: "If you ever hear anyone say that the kingdom of Christ shall have an end, abhor the heresy. . . . A certain one has dared to affirm that after the end of the world Christ shall reign no longer" (*C* 15.27).

49. See *Apologia contra Arianos* 1.3, 2.2, 3.1; *De decretis* 23; *De synodis* 53. See also J. N. D. Kelly, *Early Christian Doctrines,* 5th rev. ed. (San Francisco: Harper & Row, 1978), 242–45.

50. This term is also found at *C* 4.8, *C* 11.16, and *C* 15.9.

51. A third-century theologian who, in an attempt to safeguard the monotheism and the unity of the Godhead (making him a monarchian), held that the persons of the Trinity only differed as a succession of modes or operations (making him also a modalist). In particular, this position failed to acknowledge the distinct subsistence of the Son.

appeared to understand distinctly the grounds on which they calumniated one another. Those who objected to the term *homoousios* conceived that those who approved it favored the opinion of Sabellius."[52] Such seems to have been the case with Marcellus of Ancyra. A staunch defender of *homoousios* at Nicaea, his extreme anti-Arian position led him dangerously close to Sabellianism, which brought condemnation from both Arians and Orthodox alike.[53] For Cyril the safety of the king's road is to be preferred, and the signposts for the road are the Holy Scriptures:

But in learning and professing the Faith, acquire and keep only that which is now handed on to you by the Church, and which is made fast out of all the scriptures. . . . For the Faith was not composed as seemed good to men; but from all the scriptures the most important points are gathered, making up one complete teaching of the Faith. (C 5.12)

It would seem safe, then, to regard Cyril as one who put great stock in traditional teaching grounded in Scripture. During the upheaval of the Arian controversy he was party neither to the Arians nor to the staunch Nicenes, but held a secure middle path. His association with the homoiousian party at Seleucia would suggest he found no fault with their views, but it is impossible to say whether at any time he subscribed to or promoted any particular views beyond what we find in the *Catecheses*.

C. The Jerusalem Church— Fourth-Century Revival

Now that we know something of Cyril himself, we can turn to the local church that he served. We know Cyril primarily as a catechist, so we need to understand both how the church in Jerusalem prepared Cyril for this ministry and how he in turn played a role in shaping its catechetical program. We will explore how Constantine revived Jerusalem and made it into the Holy City in which he memorialized the saving events of Christ by what were to become known as the Holy Places. We will then analyze the catechetical program, both its history and organization, in order to see exactly where Cyril is to be placed in its development and administration.

---

52. Socrates, *HE* 1.23.

53. Socrates, *HE* 1.36, 2.20. See Eusebius, *Contra Marcellum* and *De ecclesiastica theologia*; Ps.-Athanasius, *Fourth Discourse against the Arians*, chapters 3–4, 8–29. On the association of the term υἱοπατορία with Marcellus, see Eusebius, *De ecclesiastica theologia* 1.1 and 2.5. See also J. N. D. Kelly, *Early Christian Creeds*, 3d rev. ed. (London: Longman, 1972), 240–43.

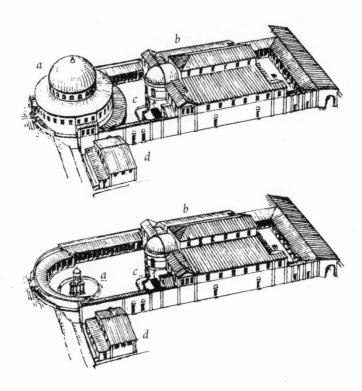

Figure 1.1 The Church of the Holy Sepulchre in the fourth century according to Conant, shown with and without the rotunda over the Anastasis; (a) Anastasis (b) Martyrium (c) Golgotha (d) Baptistry

1. *The Holy City*

As has been already mentioned, the fourth century was a time of virtual
rebirth for the church in Palestine. This, again, was due primarily to two factors, the conversion of Constantine and the natural significance of the region, especially Jerusalem, as the geographical focus of the saving events of
God in Christ. Eusebius, in his *Vita Constantini*, 3.25–39, gives a fairly reliable
account of the emperor's massive building plan, a consequence of his desire
to express his piety and fervor. With additional inspiration from his mother,
Helena, he soon thoroughly transformed the city into a major center for pilgrims. The most notable of the buildings was the basilica complex built on
the holy places of Golgotha and the Tomb; this was the venue for the
Jerusalem catecheses (Figure 1.1). As early as 333 (two years before the dedication of the basilica), the sites drew a notable pilgrim all the way from Bor-

deaux, "whose 'travelogue' remains a fascinating window into the early years of the emerging 'Holy Land.'"[54] Egeria's pilgrimage some fifty years later shows how extensive this development had become. Not only had numerous places associated with the life of Christ been singled out and commemorated, many with churches, but the city's liturgical life incorporated many of the places into its sometimes exhausting services.[55] Besides being of interest to pilgrims, the city, especially the Mount of Olives, was also particularly attractive to new monastic communities.[56] In nearby Bethlehem, Jerome founded his famous monastery.

However, although the Christian community in Jerusalem was flourishing during this time of renewal, the city as a whole did not undergo a complete Christian renewal. There was still a substantial pagan population, and the city had all the characteristics of any large urban center with a variety of people. Late in the century both Gregory of Nyssa and Jerome describe the presence of considerable evil, immorality, and idolatry.[57] It is important to keep this in mind when considering Cyril's pastoral duties. His catechesis is thorough and sound, and the liturgical life is vibrant and inspiring, giving the impression of a secure Christian lifestyle, yet the day-to-day life in the city continued to have its many dangers and temptations.

2. The Significance of the Holy Places for Cyril

Cyril's involvement with the Holy Places is one area that reveals how he exercised his role as presbyter, bishop, and catechist during this time of development. By the time he was consecrated (350/51) much of the work to recover and memorialize, by structure and rite, the sacred Christian places had already taken place, but substantial changes were still to come, and as bishop he no doubt took a leading role. Cyril's particular penchant for appreciating and making use of the Holy Places as tangible witnesses to the faith is evident in his use of them not only in liturgical celebrations but also in his catechesis.[58] He gave much thought to the impression he could make on his lis-

54. Walker, *Holy City, Holy Places?* 17. See all of Chapter 1 for an account of this period of development.

55. See in particular Egeria's account of the Holy Week services (*IE* 30–40). On the general topic of fourth-century pilgrimage see Wilkinson, *Egeria's Travels;* E. D. Hunt, *Holy Land Pilgrimage in the Later Roman Empire A.D. 312–460* (Oxford: Clarendon Press, 1982); and Kelly, *Jerome.*

56. See Hunt, *Holy Land Pilgrimage,* 167.

57. See Gregory of Nyssa, *Ep.* 17 and Jerome, *Ep.* 58.4.

58. See in particular, the studies of Antoine Paulin, *Saint Cyrille de Jérusalem Catéchète;* Walker, *Holy City, Holy Places?* ch. 1.4; and Gregory Dix, *The Shape of the Liturgy* (Westminster, London: Dacre Press, 1945; repr. San Francisco: Harper & Row, 1982), 350–53.

teners through the use of down-to-earth imagery and examples, drawing picturesque analogies even from the natural and physical sciences.[59] For Cyril, Christ and the Holy Spirit are not abstract entities to be pondered, but persons to be encountered. Their divine activity is close and personal:

Do not think that because he [Christ] is now absent physically, he is therefore also absent spiritually. He is here present in our midst listening to what is said of him, seeing your inward thoughts. (C 14.30)

In truth the Holy Spirit is great and all-powerful. Think about how many of you are sitting here now, how many souls are present. He is working appropriately for each one, and being present in our midst, beholds the disposition of each, his reasoning and conscience, and what we say and think and believe. (C 16.22)

For Cyril, the Incarnation, the physically tangible manifestation of God, was particularly meaningful. It represented a divine endorsement of the physical realm, against any notion of denying or transcending this world. It affirmed the close and personal involvement of God in the lives of fallen but redeemable humanity. Thus quite naturally, Cyril's teaching on salvation is very much wrapped up with his teaching on the Incarnation: "If the Incarnation was a fantasy, salvation is a fantasy as well" (C 4.9).[60]

The special meaning that the Incarnation and the personal encounters with Christ and the Holy Spirit had for Cyril made the Holy Places important to him, since they were the medium by which people could approach and feel close to God. Besides the numerous single references to Holy Places,[61] in three places he recites lists of *witnesses* to Christ (C 10.19–20), to his crucifixion (C 13.38–40), and to his resurrection (C 14.22–23), which include not only Holy Places, but biblical scenes and characters. Cyril suggests the role of such images as he carries on an imaginative conversation with the Old Testament prophets:

Give us a sign peculiar to the king whose coming you announce. The prophet answers and says: "See, your king shall come to you; a just saviour is he, meek, and riding on an ass, on a colt, the foal of an ass." . . . Give us a sign where the king who enters will stand. Give us a sign not far from the city, that it may not be unknown to us; give us a sign nearby and clearly visible, that being in the city we may behold the place. Again the prophet answers: "That day his feet shall rest upon the Mount of

---

59. Anatomy (C 4.22, 9.15), astronomy (C 6.3), geography (C 16.22), botany (C 9.10), and others (see especially C 9.11–16).

60. The same idea is repeated in C 12.1 and C 13.4, 37.

61. For example, Mount Tabor (C 12.16), Mount of Olives (C 4.14), Golgotha (C 5.10), the Tomb (C 14.23), the Upper Room (C 16.4), and Jerusalem (C 14.1, 17.29).

Olives, which is opposite Jerusalem to the East." Is it possible for anyone standing within the city not to behold the place?[62]

These many images and actual places provided a material medium for spiritual experiences—Cyril's listeners were fortunate that "while others can only hear, we can both see and handle" (C 13.22) these places where God in Christ was among us. Through the Holy Places, the pilgrim could somehow span the gap of time and get in touch with the original events commemorated.

This development and understanding of the Holy Places probably has much in common with pagan mystery rites, which strongly emphasized the experience of religious awe and secrecy. E. J. Yarnold has often argued that, when the emperor was engaged in his building program to commemorate the holy events, he was inspired by his own experience of the pagan rites in his upbringing. This was probably largely the cause of the Christian rites of initiation becoming understood and explained as mystery rites.[63] I will consider later how a similar attitude toward the Holy Places as awe-inspiring is evidenced in the rites of initiation as described in the mystagogy, and it will be an important feature to consider when comparing C with the disputed M. For the present I note only that the development of this attitude took place during the episcopate of Cyril.

3. The Catechumenate

In order to understand Cyril as a catechist and liturgist, we must explore the nature of the catechetical program that he inherited when he became bishop. Even though he took charge of an already existing program, it continued to develop and change; hence, we can expect to see signs of both old and new elements. Our present interest, though, is in discerning Cyril's particular influence.

The process for bringing new members into the Church, known in modern times as the catechumenate, was one of the many elements in the life of the early Church that underwent significant change in the fourth century. The name comes from "catechumen," which from earliest times was the common term used to describe those who had begun the process leading to-

---

62. C 12.10–11; translation by McCauley, WCJ, 1:233.

63. See E. J. Yarnold, The Awe-Inspiring Rites of Initiation, 2d ed. (Edinburgh: T. & T. Clark, 1994); idem, "Baptism and the Pagan Mysteries in the Fourth Century," HJ 13 (1972): 247–67; idem, "Who Planned the Churches at the Christian Holy Places in the Holy Land?" SP 18.1 (Kalamazoo: Cistercian Publications, 1985): 105–9.

ward baptism.[64] The event that probably had the most dramatic effect on the catechumenate was the change in the status of the Church as the result of the Peace of Constantine (313). The change was radical in that, from being a persecuted religion, Christianity became not just tolerated, but eventually the official religion of the state. Suddenly to be a Christian became socially and politically acceptable, even advantageous, and new members abounded. But the repercussion of this new status of the Church also had a certain detrimental effect on the catechumenate: the whole meaning of Church membership was suddenly changed, and the great numbers of new members put a strain on the existing structures. A serious reform was soon needed. By the time Cyril took over as bishop, a response to this crisis was already evident. Hence, it will be important to look briefly at (1) how the catechumenate had been developing, (2) the state into which it had deteriorated as a result of the Church's radical new status, (3) some of the steps the post-Nicene church took to meet the new needs in general, and (4) what particular changes were happening in Jerusalem.

a. The Catechumenate of the Early Fourth Century

Since New Testament times, the procedures for preparing candidates for baptism went through many stages of development. We are interested in what the catechumenate looked like by the beginning of the fourth century. The evidence suggests a well-organized program characterized by stages:[65]

1. Evangelization: how the potential candidate first encounters the Gospel message, whether by preaching or by the living witness of Christians (most pronounced in times of persecution).

2. Entrance into the catechumenate: this was in many ways the most significant step, since it required a genuine conversion and commitment to the faith. Origen likens this step to the covenant decision Joshua demands of the Hebrews at Shechem (Jos 24:14–24).[66] Suitable instruction in the faith, and, perhaps more importantly, a solid spiritual and moral formation required

---

64. The word comes from *katechumenos*, "hearers" of instruction, from the verb *katecheo*, whose first meaning is to "sound over" or "through," but also means "instruct by word of mouth." Cyril uses the term when he speaks to the latest group of candidates who are moving from the catechumenate proper to the final stage of enlightenment: "You were called a *katechoumenos*" (P 6).

65. See in general, M. Dujarier, *A History of the Catechumenate: The First Six Centuries* (New York: Sadlier, 1979). Exactly how widespread and uniform such a program was, however, is very difficult to say; see the precautionary remarks of Paul F. Bradshaw, *The Search for the Origins of Christian Worship* (London: S.P.C.K., 1992), 116–17, 172.

66. *Exhortation to Martyrdom* 17.

time, and hence, this stage of the catechumenate could last a few years. In third-century Rome, the period was normally three years, but if anyone showed signs of genuine conversion (by conduct more than by learning), he or she could be received for baptism before the end of three years.[67]

3. Final preparation for baptism: from among the large group of catechumens, those who felt ready to complete their initiation would submit their names for admission to baptism and undergo a final period of preparation. This stage also involved an examination to select only those sufficiently prepared.[68]

b. Crisis under Constantine

After the Peace of Constantine the sudden influx of new members (many hoping for the promotion of their worldly status, rather than that of their spiritual welfare) created two rather contrasting results. On the one hand, many people gained full entrance through baptism with less than adequate preparation—some even being ordained to the presbyterate at the same time. The second canon of the Council of Nicaea responded to this crisis:

Since either through necessity or through the importunate demands of certain individuals, there have been many breaches of the church's canon, with the result that men who have recently come from a pagan life to the faith after a short catechumenate have been admitted at once to the spiritual washing, and at the same time as their baptism have been promoted to the episcopate or the presbyterate, it is agreed that it would be well for nothing of the kind to occur in the future. For a catechumen needs time and further probation after baptism.[69]

On the other hand (and perhaps partially as a result of this Nicene canon), people realized that simply being a catechumen afforded sufficient privileges, since a catechumen was officially a Christian, and often postponed baptism indefinitely.[70] Thus arose the practice of an open-ended catechumenate, that is, an indefinite postponement of the final stage of applying for baptism. Parents enrolled their children as catechumens and supposedly took on the responsibility of seeing to their proper instruction. We know from the *Confessions* of Augustine that he was ritually enrolled as a catechumen as a child but subsequently did not undergo any formal program of formation in

---

67. Hippolytus, *AT* 17.
68. *AT* 20; Origen, *Contra Celsum* 3.51, 59.
69. Tanner, *Decrees of the Ecumenical Councils*, 6.
70. Ambrose, *Ex. Psalm. 118* 20.48–9 (PL 15.1499), and Augustine, *Sermon* 47.17 (PL 38.306–7) and *De catechizandis rudibus* 5.9; both denounce this problem of improper motives.

preparation for baptism, which he finally received only as a result of his personal conversion.[71] Chrysostom, Basil, Ambrose, and Gregory of Nazianzus also delayed their baptisms. Perhaps having learned from their own experience, these bishops were keenly aware of the inertia that affected the lives of many catechumens. They found it difficult to manage the gradually deteriorating catechumenate and to inspire its members to take the final step to baptism. Suddenly plunged into this situation, the fourth-century pastoral leaders lamented the inadequacies of their processes of initiation.[72]

c. Post-Nicene Renewal: The Catechumenate and the Season of Lent

One of the concrete ways the Church had begun to respond to this crisis was the development of Lent as an annual liturgical season that was to serve both as a period of renewal for the faithful and the time for formal preparation of candidates for baptism.[73] How exactly did this take place? Recent studies have suggested that before this period, neither baptism with its catechetical preparation nor a forty-day fast were always associated with Easter; the former could take place at any time, and the latter was in some places more appropriately a post-Epiphany observance corresponding to Jesus' time in the wilderness after his baptism.[74] By the end of the third century, Rome and some locales in the East were observing a three-week prepaschal season that had the baptismal catecheses as its core.[75] Chavasse and Lages carefully analyzed strata in the text tradition of the Armenian and Georgian lectionaries for evidence of changes in the length of Lent, and Lages argued that in Jerusalem, between the end of the third century and the end of the fourth,

---

71. *Confessions* 1.11.

72. See Ambrose, *Exp. in Luc.* 4.76; Chrysostom, *Hom. on John* 18.1 (PG 59.115); Basil, *De Baptismo* 1.2.13 (1545d–48b); Gregory Nazianzen, *Oration* 40.11 (on baptism).

73. The fifth canon of Nicaea seems to make a passing reference to Lent, thus indicating it was an established season by 325. But the phrase πρὸ τῆς τεσσαρακοστῆς could mean "before the fortieth of the Pasch," a day which in time came to be Ascension Day. See Thomas Talley, *The Origins of the Liturgical Year*, 2d emended ed. (Collegeville, Minn.: Liturgical Press, 1991), 63 n. 125; Severien Salaville, "La Tessarakosté au Ve canon de Nicée," *Échos d'Orient* 13 (1910): 65–72; idem, "La Tessarakosté, Ascension et Pentecôte au IVe siècle," *Échos d'Orient* 28 (1929): 257–71.

74. See Talley, *The Origins of the Liturgical Year*, 165–67; Maxwell Johnson, "From Three Weeks to Forty Days: Baptismal Preparation and the Origins of Lent," *SL* 20 (1990): 194–96.

75. See Antoine Chavasse, "La préparation de la Pâque, à Rome, avant le Ve siècle. Jeûne et organisation liturgique," in *Memorial J. Chaine*, Bibliothèque de la Faculté Catholique de Théologie de Lyon, vol. 5 (Lyons: Facultés Catholiques, 1950), 61–80; idem, "La structure du Carême et les lectures des messes quadragésimales dans la liturgie Romain," *La Maison Dieu* 31 (1952): 76–120; Mario Lages, "Étapes de l'évolution de carême à Jérusalem avant le Ve siècle. Essai d'analyse structurale," *Revue des études arméniennes*, n.s., 6 (1969): 67–102; Johnson, "From Three Weeks to Forty Days," 185–200; Talley, *The Origins of the Liturgical Year*, 168–74.

Lent grew from three to eight weeks. Its first expansion seems to have been in response to the rapid influx of new members following the Peace of Constantine. By the time of the Council of Nicaea and certainly by 330, as indicated by Athanasius in his *Festal Letters*, Lent had expanded to forty days, had taken on the symbolism of Jesus' wilderness experience, and became a proper liturgical season leading up to Easter and celebrated by all the faithful.[76] When Easter was becoming the preferred time for baptisms, the baptismal catechesis and the prepaschal fast were joined, and both were enriched. In the *Procatechesis* Cyril tells his listeners: "Your appointed time is long, you have forty days of repentance, and a great opportunity to be stripped and washed and clothed . . ." (P 4). Holy Week was added sometime after the dedication of the Holy Sepulchre Church by Constantine (335), and an additional week before Holy Week was instituted sometime before Egeria's visit (381–83), giving a total of eight weeks. The season had become an ideal opportunity not only to develop a more systematic and extensive program for the proper preparation of candidates for baptism but also for the general spiritual renewal of all the faithful (it is known from both Cyril and Egeria that the already baptized were welcome to and often present at the annual Lenten catechetical preparation for baptism).[77]

d. The Fourth-Century Jerusalem Catechumenate

What form did this renewed catechumenate take in Jerusalem? From Cyril's sermons it appears that even though he is preparing those specially selected for baptism from among the catechumens, this part of his program actually corresponds to both the second and the third stages of the program as described by Hippolytus and Origen (see above). The enrollment of candidates from among the catechumens at the beginning of Lent in the fourth century very much resembles the enrollment of converts from the stage of evangelization into the catechumenate in the previous centuries. This is evident from a comparison of descriptions of the induction process from both periods.

The third-century *Apostolic Tradition* has the following instruction for receiving converts into the catechumenate:

Those who come forward for the first time to hear the word shall first be brought to the teachers at the house before all the people come in. And let them be examined as to the reason why they have come forward to the faith. And those who bring them

76. The first letter, for the year 329, mentions a ten-day fast, but thereafter it is forty.
77. IE 46.1; C 4.3, 15.18.

shall bear witness for them whether they are able to hear. Let their life and manner of living be enquired into.[78]

The instruction follows with a list of the various lifestyles of potential catechumens and what conditions must be met if they are to be accepted; for example, prostitutes, magicians, and actors must forsake their practices. Then, when the candidates for baptism are selected (perhaps three years later), the examination is not concerned with their former way of life, but,

whether they lived piously when catechumens, whether "they honored the widows," whether they visited the sick, whether they fulfilled every good work. If those who bring them bear witness to them that they have done thus, then let them hear the Gospel.[79]

Passing this examination gained them entrance to the last stage of preparation for baptism, which, at least by the end of the third century, probably lasted for three weeks.

In contrast, the fourth-century description by Egeria of the inscription of names at the beginning of Lent for the final period of preparation, that is, the enrollment of candidates for baptism from among the catechumens, sounds more like the original reception of converts for initial instruction:

Then one by one those seeking baptism are brought up, men coming with their fathers and women with their mothers. As they come in one by one, the bishop asks their neighbors questions about them: "Is this person leading a good life? Does he respect his parents? Is he a drunkard or boaster?" He asks about all the serious human vices. And if his inquiries show him that someone has not committed any of these misdeeds, he himself puts down his name.[80]

Cyril's own comments in his introductory sermon also suggest that the candidates were much less advanced in their Christian formation compared to those in earlier times:

For we are the servants of Christ; we have welcomed each one, being doorkeepers, as it were, and have left the door unfastened. You have been permitted to come in with your souls mired in sin, and your purpose stained. Come in, you have been deemed worthy, your names have been enrolled. Do you see the august state of the assembly? Do you see the order and discipline; the reading of the scriptures, the presence of the religious, the course of the teachings? Be intimidated by the place, be edified by what appears. Depart now at an opportune time, come in tomorrow at

---

78. AT 16.1–3; translations by Dix, *The Treatise on the Apostolic Tradition*, 23.
79. AT 20.1–2; trans. Dix, ibid., 30–31.
80. IE 45.2–4; trans. Wilkinson, *Egeria's Travels*, 143–44.

your greatest opportunity [that is, when the formal instruction begins]. If you have avarice as the fashion of your soul, come in when you have put on another. Put off fornication and uncleanness and put on a brilliant garment of sobriety. . . . But if you continue with an evil purpose, the one speaking is blameless, do not expect to receive grace; for you will receive the water, but you will not receive the Spirit. (P 4)

He even addresses some who may have come in with ulterior motives; using imagery from angling, he hopes that having now been hooked, they can be converted:

Perhaps you have come in under another pretext. For a man may be wishing to court a woman, and that is why he has entered; and the same applies to women. Or often a slave wishes to please his master, or one friend another. I avail myself of the bait on the hook and admit you as one who has entered with unsound purpose, but who will be saved by a good hope. (P 5)

Dujarier regards such statements as evidence that even though the catechumenate had survived in principle, in reality it had deteriorated:

Such words cannot be found on the lips of Hippolytus or Origen a few weeks before baptism. In the fourth century the catechumenate was not what it was a hundred years earlier. The catechumens do not seem to be convinced. . . . their faith was no longer capable of transforming their lives. No special institutions supported them or placed demands on them.[81]

It seems, then, that in many respects what at one time was a three-year endeavor was now to take place in forty days. That is, in the fourth century the structure of the catechumenate, at least in Jerusalem, was such that most of the formative work for new converts took place during the season of Lent leading up to baptism at Easter. This situation helps us understand the particular challenge Cyril faced in the preparation of his candidates. It will also help in understanding the Jerusalem program, which by previous standards was longer and more substantial, as far as the final preparation for baptism was concerned. It is to that particular program in Jerusalem that we can now turn.

4. The Jerusalem Catechetical Program

This section will examine the content, organization, and manner of presentation of the Lenten catechesis (P and C) and the Easter mystagogy (M). In each of these areas we are looking for anything pertinent to include in an assessment of the question of authorship among these texts. We will consider

81. *A History of the Catechumenate*, 97.

first the content of *C* in so far as it represents the syllabus of the prebaptismal catechetical program of fourth-century Jerusalem. Then we will look at how the Lenten and Easter sermons were organized and presented as far as place, time, and style are concerned. Besides providing a basic overview of the texts, this survey will also elucidate the various factors other than the mind and style of the author(s) that would affect the correspondences, similarities, and differences among them. These factors will need to be kept in mind later when the disputed text of *M* is compared with Cyril's known work.

a. The Syllabus of the Prebaptismal Catechesis

To understand better the content of *C* as a syllabus of the prebaptismal catechesis, it will be useful to survey briefly its history up through Cyril's tenure as bishop. This will help us see better signs of Cyril's influence on its development.

It would follow that if from its origins, as noted above, the season of Lent had the baptismal preparation as its core, changes in the season would suggest corresponding changes in the catechetical program. The available evidence seems to confirm that this was indeed the case; the number of topics covered increased, and the order in which they were presented was rearranged. One of the concerns here is to establish what can be known about Cyril's particular influence on the theological and liturgical life of the Jerusalem church and thus better assess any differences between the documents written at either end of his episcopate. Hence, in this section we will look at the state of the syllabus before Cyril, the changes that occurred during his lifetime, and what influence he may have had on those changes.

For the early history of the syllabus, we can begin with another study by Mario Lages where he examines the content of the program for baptismal preparation by comparing it with three early sources: the *Armenian Ritual,* the *Armenian Lectionary,* and Cyril's *Catecheses.*[82] The *Armenian Ritual* is a collection of liturgical rites used by the church in Armenia, compiled in the ninth or tenth century but representing some practices from as early as the third or fourth century.[83] It contains a *Canon of Baptism,* that is, official in-

82. Mario Lages, "The Hierosolymitain Origin of the Catechetical Rites in the Armenian Liturgy," *Didaskalia* 1 (1971): 233–50.

83. For the *Armenian Ritual* see F. C. Conybeare, ed., and A. J. Maclean, trans., *Rituale Armenorum. Being the Administration of the Sacraments and the Breviary Rites of the Armenian Church together with the Greek Rites of Baptism and Epiphany Edited from the Oldest MSS.* (Oxford: Clarendon Press, 1905). The *Canon of Baptism* is on p. 89; the translation used is by Lages from "The Hierosolymitain Origin," 233.

structions for preparing candidates for baptism, which represents a very early practice:

CANON OF BAPTISM

[1]When one makes a Christian, first of all, it is not right to let him into the church. [2]But he shall have hands laid on him three weeks before the baptism, [3]during which he may learn from the Wardapet [instructor] both the faith and the baptism of the Church. [4]First of all the Godhead of the Holy Trinity, [5]and the creation and the coming to be of (all) creatures, [6]and next the election of just men. [7]After that, the birth of Christ and in order all the economy, [8]and the great mystery of the cross and the burial, [9]and the resurrection and the ascension unto the Father, [10]and the second coming, [11]and the resurrection of the flesh, and the rewarding of each according to his works.[84]

The *Armenian Lectionary*, the earliest manuscripts of which reflect fourth- and fifth-century practices, contains a schedule of readings from Scripture for the liturgies throughout the year, including those in Jerusalem. The part that will concern us is the list of nineteen readings assigned to the catechetical sermons.[85]

Lages shows by a comparative analysis that these three sources, the *Canon of Baptism*, the readings for the catecheses from the *Armenian Lectionary*, and the *Catecheses*, all belong to and show an expanding and developing Jerusalem tradition. The *Canon of Baptism* represents the earlier Jerusalem practice of a three-week program of baptismal preparation that predates Cyril. The other two texts reflect later stages, when the program had grown in length and content. There are some points, though, that Lages overlooks in his comparative analysis, and he underestimates what can be known of the development of the catechetical syllabus, especially if we include the text of the Creed of Jerusalem, which the candidates professed at baptism. This text also shows evidence of development in coordination with the fourth-century catechetical program.

This creed of Cyril's church has long been considered a significant component in the development of creedal formulas, especially with regard to the one formulated and adopted along with the Nicene Creed at the Council of Constantinople in 381.[86] It is often argued that since the Creed of Jerusalem

---

84. The prohibition against letting the candidate enter the church probably reflects the generic practice of keeping those not yet initiated, including catechumens, from full access to the Christian mysteries.

85. The readings for the catechetical sermons are listed at Lectionary entry no. 17.

86. See Kelly, *Early Christian Creeds*, 311–31, for a full account of the studies and arguments. The expanded Creed of Constantinople more fully addressed matters of Arianism and added statements on the Holy Spirit.

bears such a close resemblance to the one adopted at Constantinople that Cyril, who was a leading figure at that council, played a significant part in the design of the latter, perhaps even offering the very formula of his church as a basic model.[87] Kelly is hesitant about the idea of the council being so bold as to actually formulate a new creed at this time, especially when at the same time the Creed of Nicaea was reaffirmed. He proposes instead that a ready-made creed, which was born out of the experience of the baptismal cate-chetical programs of local churches, was presented and found to be an ac-ceptable expression of the "Nicene faith," even though it was not the very words of the creed of 325. This view acknowledges the fact that during the period between the two councils various creeds were still being formulated and is still open to the possibility that Cyril and his creed were a significant influence in 381.

Table 1.1 illustrates some of the changes that took place in the catechetical syllabus, as well as in the creedal formulas, during Cyril's episcopate. It com-pares four items: the early Jerusalem catechetical syllabus (represented by the *Canon of Baptism*), the lectionary readings designated for the catechetical ser-mons, a later stage of the catechetical syllabus represented by Cyril's *Catech-eses,* and the articles of the Jerusalem creed.[88]

An adequate analysis of the full implications of this comparative chart de-mands more time and space than is here available. It is only necessary at the moment to take note of what it shows concerning the development of the catechetical syllabus in Cyril's time and to consider the extent of Cyril's in-volvement in this development.

One item needs prior clarification. The lectionary has nineteen readings, yet Cyril preached only eighteen sermons in this set from the year 351. Inas-much as Cyril covers two topics, resurrection of the flesh and the Church, in one sermon (*C* 18), and cites both readings, and since he stated in a number of places that he was short of time,[89] it seems that at least for this one year, Cyril compressed the two last sermons into one. Under normal circum-stances there would have been nineteen sermons. The chart attempts to de-

87. Such is Stephenson's view, *WCJ*, 1:60–65.

88. The reconstruction of the creed of Jerusalem is problematic since the titles of sermons 6 to 18, which comprise the articles of the creed, are a later addition, and the text of the creed is nowhere cited in its entirety (probably due to the *disciplina arcani*, cf. *C* 5.12, 18.21); hence, we must cull the creed from the text of the sermons. The text of the creed in Table 1.1 follows the guidelines of Anthony A. Stephenson, "The Text of the Jerusalem Creed," *SP* 3 = TU 78 (Berlin: Akademie-Verlag, 1961), 303–13.

89. *C* 16.32; *C* 17.20, 30, 34; *C* 18.16, 22.

pict the more usual program and has thus split *C* 18 into two parts, each part corresponding to a separate reading from the lectionary.

We can now look at how the syllabus developed during the fourth century. A step-by-step examination of the subject matter of the two syllabi and the lectionary readings (shown in the first three columns of the chart) will enable us to determine where and why changes took place. What is first evident is a twofold division of material in the catechesis. Part I focuses in general on penance, baptism, and life in Christ, and Part II on the formal catechesis on the creed. Verse three of the *Canon of Baptism* says the candidate will learn about faith and baptism. This could reflect a division of parts at this early stage (early fourth century?), that is, a treatment of baptism distinct from a treatment of the content of the faith. In the syllabus from the *Catecheses* (col. 3), sermons 1–4 could constitute a distinct set of instructions on baptism: the first two sermons on purification and penance are introductory to the third sermon, focused solely on baptism, and the fourth follows with the complementary theme of the virtuous life of the newly baptized Christian.

But what about *C* 5? To answer this, let us look first at the Armenian *Canon of Baptism*. It is not clear whether "learning the faith" refers to learning about the theological virtue of faith, or, more probably, to all of Part II, the catechesis on the creed (vv. 4–11, that is, the content of the faith). Though we cannot be certain, the word for "faith" here may be a technical term corresponding to the Greek term πίστις, the word commonly used for creed.[90] The topic of *C* 5, though, is not the content of the faith, but the virtue of faith in general. At the end of this sermon (section 12), Cyril makes a reference to some sort of rite for formally handing on the creed to the candidates; this sermon on the virtue of faith seems to lead up to and prepare the candidates for this rite. It is probable, then, that this separate fifth sermon with its reading and rite was an addition to the earlier catechetical syllabus reflected in the *Canon of Baptism*.

When we look at Part II, the *Catechesis on the Creed*, we see that the topics of the syllabus in the Armenian canon are fewer and that they follow a salvation-history order. In contrast, the lectionary readings and Cyril follow the more familiar trinitarian order of the formal creeds, focusing more on theological ideas than events. Distinct articles on the persons of the Trinity and on the Church are missing from the syllabus of the *Canon of Baptism*. Though the topic "the Godhead of the Trinity" (v. 4 of the *Canon of Baptism*)

---

90. See, for example, *C* 4.2, 17; 5.12 (six times); 17.34.

Table 1.1 The Catechetical Syllabus

Part I. Introduction

The Catechetical Syllabus from the Armenian Ritual's Canon of Baptism	Armenian Lectionary Readings	The Catechetical Syllabus from Cyril's Catecheses	The Jerusalem Creed culled from Cyril's Catecheses
vv. 1–2: penitential liturgical rites (with catechesis?)	1–2: Is. 1.16–20; Ez. 18.20–23: Invitation to purification and penance	C 1–2: general theme of penance	
v. 3b: learning about Baptism	3: Rom. 6.3–14: Baptism	C 3: Baptism	(IX. and in one Baptism of repentance for the remission of sins ?)
(penitential / moral teaching?)	4: Col. 2.8–3.4: Life according to true faith in Christ, not according to false teaching	C. 4: Summary Points of Doctrine / Virtue founded on Christ and true doctrine	
v. 3a: learning about Faith (separate topic?)	5: *Heb. 11.1–31: Faith*	C 5: Faith	

Part II. Catechesis on the Creed

vv. 4–5: Godhead of the Holy Trinity / and the creation and coming to be of (all) creatures	6: Is. 45.17–26: Meditation on the works of God and on God himself	**C 6: One God (original creation topic moved to C 9)**	I. We believe in one God,
(no parallel)	7: *Eph. 3.14–4.13: Miscellaneous trinitarian themes, especially on Father*	C 7: The Father	the Father
v. 6: The election of just men	8: Jer. 32.19b–44: Greatness of God is manifest in his election of just men	**C 8: The Almighty (lection includes v. 18 on the might of God; the election of just men is a minor theme)**	Almighty,
(v. 5: Creation)	9: *Job 38.2–40.5: Creative wisdom*	C 9: Maker of Heaven and Earth …	Maker of Heaven and Earth, of all things visible and invisible (9.4).
(no parallel)	10: *I Cor. 8.5–9.23: Unique Lordship of Jesus Christ*	C 10: One Lord Jesus Christ	II. And in one Lord, Jesus Christ (7.4),
(no parallel)	11: Heb. 1.1–2.1: Jesus Christ, the only Son of God	C 11: The Only-Begotten Son of God	the only-begotten Son of God, who was begotten true God of the Father before all worlds, by whom all things were made (11.21).

v. 7: The birth of Christ and in order all the economy	12: Is. 7.10–8.10: " . . . a virgin shall conceive . . . "	C 12: Was incarnate and made man	III. [Who for us and for our salvation, came down from heaven and] was of the Virgin and the Holy Spirit made Man (4.9; 12.3; 12.13).
v. 8: And the great mystery of the cross and burial	13: Is. 53.1–54.5: The man of sorrows . . .	C 13: Was crucified and buried	IV. Who was crucified and buried, [and descended into Hell] (see 4.10–11; 13.38–39; 14.3, 11, 17, 18)
v. 9: And the resurrection and ascension to the Father	14: I Cor. 15.1–28: Resurrection, (Seating at God's right hand)	C 14: Rose from the dead, ascended, seated at God's right hand	V. Who rose on the third day,
			VI. and ascended into Heaven, and sat down on the right hand of the Father (14.24),
v. 10: And the second Coming	15: Dan 7.2–27: Vision of the Ancient of Days and the Son of Man	C 15: He shall come in glory . . . (lection begins with v. 9)	VII. and is to come in glory to judge the living and the dead; of whose kingdom there will be no end (15.2)
(no parallel)	16: I Cor 12.1–7: Charisms and the Spirit	C 16: Holy Spirit (A)	VIII. and in one Holy Spirit, the Paraclete, who spoke through the prophets (17.3).
(no parallel)	17: I Cor 12.7–27: Charisms and the Spirit / Mystical Body of Christ	C 17: Holy Spirit (B)	
(v. 3b: Baptism - covered above in Part I)	(3: Rom. 6.3–4: Baptism - covered above in Part I)	(C 3: Baptism - covered above in Part I)	IX. and in one Baptism of repentance for the remission of sins,
v. 11a, b: And the resurrection of all flesh / and the rewarding of each according to his works	18: Ez. 37.1–24: Vision of the resurrection	C 18a: Resurrection of the Flesh (chs 1–21; rewarding of the each acc. to works, ch. 4)	X. and in one Holy Catholic Church,
(no parallel)	19: I Tim. 3.14–16: The Mystery of the Church	C 18b: a) One Holy Catholic Church (chs 22–27)	XI. and in the resurrection of the flesh,
(no parallel)	(no parallel)	b) Life Everlasting (chs 28–31)	XII. and in eternal life (18.22).

implicitly includes the Father, Son, and Spirit, the lack of the separate mention of the Father and Holy Spirit, while material on the Son is included (vv. 7–10 of the *Canon of Baptism*), shows that the logic of its order is not the usual trinitarian format of the creeds. The absence of any mention of the Church need not be too surprising since, although this topic is included in some baptismal creeds, it does not seem to appear as an article in any of the creeds published by the major synods before the Council of Constantinople.[91]

When the syllabus from the *Canon of Baptism* is compared with the lectionary readings, we can spot some particular signs of growth. While each topic in the *Canon* has a corresponding reading in the lectionary, seven readings in the lectionary (nos. 7, 9, 10, 11, 16, 17, and 19) have no distinct corresponding topic in the *Canon*. However, when we compare the readings with the next two columns, we see that each of these readings corresponds to one of Cyril's topics as well as an article (or sub-point of an article) of the creed.

In the expanded program represented by the lectionary readings and the syllabus from the *Catecheses,* each person of the Trinity is the focus of separate topics. Reading 7 corresponds to a sermon on the Father. Readings 10 and 11 have been assigned to sermons on Christ, perhaps reflecting an increased interest in the person of the Son in the aftermath of Nicaea. Readings 16 and 17 with their corresponding sermons provide an extensive treatment of the person of the Holy Spirit. While reading 6 originally fits well with the combined topic of Godhead / creation, by Cyril's time the theme of creation has given way to a treatment of the one God. The syllabus deals with creation separately in *C* 9 with a new reading (no. 9) from Job. Finally, there is the addition of reading 19 with its sermon on the Church.

There are also minor modifications to the readings that seem to be the work of Cyril himself. Reading 8 fits very well with v. 6 of the Armenian canon (the election of just men), but as they stand, verses 19b–44 have little to do with Cyril's theme, the might of God. Cyril's reading, however, begins with vv. 18b–19a: "The great God and the mighty Lord, great in counsel, and mighty in works, the Lord omnipotent, of great name. . . ." This adaptation provides an ideal scriptural reference for the new topic, "God the Almighty." Another minor adjustment occurs in *C* 15. The lectionary reading is Dn 7:2–27, but Cyril has shortened it to begin with v. 9, excising introductory material and beginning immediately with the vision of the Ancient of Days.

91. See Kelly, *Early Christian Creeds*, 263–95.

Table 1.2 Final Four Articles of the Creed

Lectionary Readings	Syllabus from Catecheses	Jerusalem Creed 351	Creed of Constantinople 381
(v. 3b Baptism)	(C 3 Baptism)	———————	———————
Second Coming	Second Coming	Second Coming	Second Coming
Holy Spirit	Holy Spirit	Holy Spirit	Holy Spirit
Resurrection	Resurrection	Baptism	Church
Church	Church	Church	Baptism
———————	Eternal Life	Resurrection	Resurrection
———————	———————	Eternal Life	Eternal Life

That Cyril adapted the readings to suit these baptismal sermons, probably the first of his career as a bishop, suggests that the lectionary list of readings did not originate with him; rather, some form of the list must have been in place when he became bishop.

Lastly, when we compare the final articles of the Jerusalem Creed that the candidates recited with the two topics of *C* 18 and the lectionary readings, we see some discrepancies that suggest that changes in the syllabus and creed may have been in progress. The final four articles of the creed are baptism, the Church, the resurrection, and eternal life. The readings, however, and the topics of the *Catecheses* agree with one another in placing baptism in the third sermon and in reversing the order of the resurrection and the Church. Further, Cyril has added a section on the eternal life (*C* 18.28–31), which has no corresponding reading. There does not seem to be anything in the syllabus or readings, nor any pedagogical advantage to the instructor, that would suggest a need to add a topic or change the order of articles. It appears as if something other than the catechesis was influencing the structure of the creed, perhaps creedal formulas from other churches, while the syllabus of the catechesis and the readings were not being kept completely up to date. If we were to add the creed adopted at Constantinople in 381 to our chart, we would see yet another indication of this ongoing development, a switch between the articles on the Church and baptism.[92] This is shown in Table 1.2.

It could be that Cyril knew other creeds from other churches and was trying to bring the Jerusalem church's creed in line with what he thought was

---

92. For the text of the Constantinople Creed, see Tanner, *Decrees of the Ecumenical Councils*, 24.

becoming the more widely accepted form. That the catechetical syllabus with its scheduled readings seems to lag behind the creed Cyril has his candidates memorize is probably simply due to the conservative nature of liturgy.[93] Adding a topic or making a minor alteration in one's sermons was apparently not very disruptive, but bringing the syllabus and readings fully into line with the preferred order of the creed would involve rearranging the lectionary; apparently such a change was not deemed absolutely necessary nor worth the trouble.

All of these points suggest (as implied by the arrangement of the chart in Table 1.1) a progression of development whose earliest stage is reflected in the *Canon of Baptism,* followed by the lectionary, then by Cyril's syllabus with its readings showing some minor adjustments of the lectionary readings, and finally by the recited creed.

Our final concern in this section is how much involvement Cyril himself had in this development of the catechetical program. Since the text of *C* comes from the year 351, some twenty years after Lent had already grown to forty days, coupled no doubt with an expansion of the catechesis, Cyril probably inherited many of the changes. The development that seems to have already taken place up to the time of *C* goes hand in hand with what was noted above about the need to revamp the catechumenate in the wake of the Peace of Constantine, and there is no reason to think that the development would suddenly stop when Cyril took office, especially since in the following thirty years theological debate continued to be very active. By the end of his episcopate, Cyril had brought about some significant liturgical advances with the addition of an eighth week of Lent to make room for the elaborate Holy Week services, and we could assume that he would be just as attentive to and involved in the maintenance of the catechetical program. In fact, certain signs of stratification in the text of *C* suggest later changes in the program; these will be dealt with below when the content of *C* is treated. His numerous years in exile no doubt exposed Cyril to the practices of other churches and the views of fellow clergy, providing him with incentive and material for enriching his own church's rites.

Two external witnesses claim it was Cyril himself who drew up the lectionary in coordination with the catechetical syllabus, itself defined by the articles of the local church's creed. From the eighth century John Awjnec'i,

---

93. The literary witnesses of the *Catecheses* and the sources for the lectionary show a virtually unchanged list of readings for nearly a century (see *Armenian Lectionary* no. 17).

in his *Synodal Oration,* says that, "according to each article of faith, he assembled and ordained readings from the divine writ resembling each (article). . . ."[94] A fifteenth-century Armenian life of Cyril credits him with establishing both the list of readings and the catechesis for Lent.[95] Both Lages and Bihain are willing to give some weight to these passages, allowing Cyril credit for making necessary adaptations in the program. But again, since the Church had already for some time been enjoying the freedom to enhance its liturgy and catechumenate, they both think that the readings and syllabus existed in some form before 351.

Telfer's assessment of the Jerusalem tradition provides a balancing perspective that emphasizes Cyril's traditionalist side, lest he be thought too much of an innovator. He agrees that the foundation from which the *Catecheses* were preached was no doubt an early, pre-Nicene tradition that Cyril inherited. In subsequent years he developed the syllabus as needed. The lack of any reference by Cyril to Arius or the Nicene term *homoousios* (some twenty-five years after the council) suggests that he is guided by a well-established church tradition "impervious to contemporary theological disturbances."[96] Even though we do not know for certain how Cyril may have addressed Arianism in his sermons as the controversy unfolded during the following thirty years, if we are guided by his principles stated in 351, namely that he teaches a faith founded on Scripture and ecclesiastical tradition (cf. *C* 5.12), it is probably true that he avoided "engaging in the speculative ideas that formed the currency of the Arian controversy."[97] Telfer's concluding statement seems to be a fair assessment:

Cyril represented and conserved a venerable teaching tradition, that of the Church of Aelia-Jerusalem, which, for all its vicissitudes, had known no absolute severance since the first days of the faith. This tradition molded these lectures of Lent, 350, that

---

94. John Awjnecʻi, *Matenagrut ʻiwnkʻ*, 2d edition (Venice: I Tparani Srboyn Ghazaru, 1953), 17–19; translation by Lages, "The Hierosolymitain Origin," 236. Renoux, in his edition of the *Armenian Lectionary* (PO 36.2, 233n), cites this source as Jean d'Ojun in *Domini Johannis Ozniensis philosophi Armeniorum Catholici opera,* Armenian text with Latin translation by R. Aucher (Mkrtič Augerean) (Venice: Typis PP. Mechitaristarum, 1834), 26–27. He adds another: *Paris Arm. MS 114,* 13th c., fol. 83. This work is on the feasts of the Church, their origins, and different rites. The manuscript is described in F. Macler, *Catalogue des Manuscrits Arméniens et Georgiens* (Paris: Imprimerie Nationale, 1908), 56.

95. The text is in Armenian codex 224, folios 267–69, in the Mechitarist Library in Vienna; it is edited with a Latin translation in Bihain, "Une vie arménienne de S. Cyrille de Jérusalem," 319–48; see section III.1–2.

96. *Cyril of Jerusalem,* 61–63.

97. Ibid.

have come down to us. And though they were delivered a quarter of a century after Nicaea, yet, by the deliberate policy of Cyril, they bring to us the voice of the ante-Nicene Church.[98]

Although this account of the Jerusalem tradition emphasizes the strong orthodox foundation that was "impervious to contemporary theological disturbances," it does not rule out the possibility that Cyril was open to creative doctrinal development within the bounds of orthodoxy. The extent to which his doctrine did develop will be addressed later in the appropriate context.

As this last section has indicated, there is quite sufficient reason to think that during his episcopate Cyril was engaged in the modifying and adapting of his church's rites and catechesis according to the needs of the times. This point will be of some importance when comparing the texts of *C* and *M*, since they represent a thirty or so year difference in time.

b. The Organization and Presentation of the Lenten and Easter Catechesis

We can now turn our attention to how the prebaptismal catechesis and mystagogy were presented insofar as this has a bearing on identifying authorship. We will begin with assessing to what extent an annual program of catechesis, rather than the influence of any single author, might be the cause of common features between the texts. We will then examine in turn where the sermons were preached, the amount of time allotted to them, and what form, or style, was used to preach them. The topic of form and style will include considering how the different goals of each set of sermons might affect how their styles compare, and how catechetical and pedagogical techniques might also explain common or distinguishing characteristics. The present goal is to determine carefully in each of these areas where we are likely to find evidence to assist in establishing the authorship of *M*.

We begin with assessing the influence of the annual program. Since the *Armenian Lectionary* (which was in use long after the time of Cyril and John) cites prebaptismal and mystagogic sermons as part of the annual cycle of liturgical events, the content of *C* and *M* will reflect as much the content of the catechetical program in the Jerusalem church as they will the ideas of the individual bishop who might be preaching. For this reason, we will have to evaluate any comparisons between *C* and *M* in light of whether or not they simply represent the syllabus of an annual program or an individual author. An announcement in the Lenten catechesis that a particular topic will be

98. Ibid.

treated more fully in the Easter Week sermons, or, conversely, a reference in *M* to an earlier treatment of a topic in *C*, would show nothing more certain than that each year, as a part of the program, certain topics or explanations were reserved for the appropriate set of catecheses.[99] For example, in *C* 18.33, Cyril announces the Easter Week program, but in *M* 1.9 it could be John who refers back to the prebaptismal syllabus. What would probably be similar in the program from year to year are such basic topics as the articles of the creed and the initiation rites themselves. Hence, any example cited for its topical content would need to be assessed to see whether it principally represents more the annual program than the mind of a single author.

The task of understanding precisely how the annual program was organized year to year is difficult because this was a time of rapid change, and our evidence comes from either end of a thirty-year period, the *Catecheses* from 351 and the witness of Egeria in 381 to 383. When pertinent, I will consider what can be said in general about the organization of the catechetical syllabus in the time of *M*, but time and space do not permit a detailed treatment of this difficult, though fascinating, question.[100]

We now have to address the place, time, and style of presentation of the sermons, and we begin with the *Catecheses*. Egeria is quite explicit about the location and time allotment used by the bishop for his Lenten catecheses. She says that the bishop sits in a chair in the Martyrium with all of the candidates around him in a circle, and teaches "from six to nine in the morning *(ab hora prima usque ad horam tertiam)* all during Lent, three hours' catechesis a day" *(IE* 46.1, 4).

Before considering how this block of time was used, the designation of "three hours" needs some qualification. By the ancient reckoning of daily time 6:00 a.m., the *hora prima,* is sunrise regardless of the time of year. This would mean that "6:00 a.m." (sunrise) in December, when the days are shortest, would be about one hour nearer to noon, and in June, about an hour further away. By modern clock time, only at the equinox (March 21/22) would

99. See for example, *C* 13.19; *C* 16.26; *C* 18.33; *M* 1.9; *M* 5.1.

100. Many attempts have been made to reconcile the varied evidence in order to reconstruct the Jerusalem Lenten program, still an unconcluded task. The following are the principal ones: Fernand Cabrol, *Les Églises de Jérusalem: La discipline et la liturgie au IVe siècle* (Paris: H. Oudin, 1895), 143–59; Anthony A. Stephenson, "The Lenten Catechetical Syllabus in Fourth-Century Jerusalem," *TS* 15 (1954): 103–16; Telfer, *Cyril of Jerusalem,* 34–35; Johnson, "Reconciling Cyril and Egeria"; Talley, *The Origins of the Liturgical Year,* 168–74; John F. Baldwin, *The Urban Character of Christian Worship: The Origins, Development, and Meaning of Stational Liturgy,* OCA 228 (Rome: Pontificium Institutum Studiorum Orientalium, 1987), 90–93.

"six to nine" be a full three hours. According to Wilkinson, Egeria's main account of the Jerusalem liturgy came from the year 383; Easter was on April
9th that year, and Lent would have begun eight weeks before, on February
13. Sunrise at the beginning of Lent would be at about 6:45 a.m. on the sundi-
al, though on April 3rd, seven weeks later it was at about 5:45 a.m. Hence,
through the duration of Lent this block of time for the catechesis would
grow from about two and a quarter to just over three hours. The length of
the longest sermon, C 13, is about 6800 words, roughly a forty-five minute
talk. Keeping in mind that the text of C originates some thirty years before
Egeria's journey, so that some modifications had occurred in the program,
still some explanation is needed for the great length of time set aside for the
catecheses. How was the rest of the time spent?

From other information Egeria gives, it seems that the exorcisms, which
began "first thing in the morning, right after the morning dismissal in the
Anastasis" (46.1),[101] took up the first portion of this time. According to P 14
the exorcisms were done individually while others waited, reading and praying; hence these might have taken some considerable time. Further, time
was probably allowed for translations of the sermons. Egeria says of the
mystagogy that translations were made into Syriac for the benefit of the
non-Greek speakers (IE 47.3), and we can reasonably assume that this practice prevailed for the prebaptismal instruction as well. By doubling the time
of the longest sermon to accommodate a translation, we get one and a half
hours. This leaves an hour or so for the exorcisms.

There is some significant variation in the lengths of the individual sermons of C, which means that more time was left over on some days than on
others, but we have no reason to think that the full time was necessarily tak-
en up every day. Still, time could have been set aside for questions. Or, since
the audience also contained godparents and some of the faithful, available
time may have been used for their participation in the catechesis, say, in
group discussions. At C 15.18, Cyril addresses members of the audience who
have "begotten children by catechizing," reminding them of the importance
of their duties to preserve them in the Truth. These would be the godparents, and his comments suggest that the title was more than symbolic.

___

101. That is, 6:00 A.M., or sunrise. In 24.1–2 and 27.4, Egeria describes the morning liturgical
schedule up to the morning dismissal. She notes three points of time: Cockcrow (pullo primo),
Dawn, or first light (coeperit lucescere), and Morning, or full light (iam luce). The last morning
service begins at dawn and ends with dismissal at sunrise, or full light, immediately after
which, during Lent, the exorcisms began (46.1).

Hence, the "three hour" morning period of teaching is reasonably compatible with the text of *C*, considering that time was needed at least for exorcisms and translations, if not also for catechizing by others than Cyril.

Next, what can we note about the *Catecheses* as far as its manner or style of presentation is concerned? One notable feature, according to a scholion at the end of *C* 18, is that the text is a transcription of a single year's instruction as it was delivered by Cyril.[102] The term σχεδιασθεῖσα, "improvised," "delivered extempore," occurs in the title of each of the sermons of *C*, though this does not mean that the catechist spoke entirely off the top of his head. Accomplished orators of this era carefully prepared themselves before speaking and memorized the substance, or even the entirety, of their speech. According to the standards set by the first-century rhetorician, Quintilian, an orator was expected to deliver entirely from memory any speech written out beforehand; though, alternatively, for one who was capable, the use of brief memoranda was allowed for the extempore delivery of an unwritten speech. The reading of a prepared text was strongly discouraged. At least some command of extempore speaking was deemed necessary in case the speaker encountered an unexpected change in circumstances or inspirations of the moment.[103] We know from G. Julius Victor that the same basic standards for oratory prevailed in the fourth century.[104] Hence, we can surmise that the use of the term "improvise" is intended to indicate simply that the text is a transcription of an oration rather than a text prepared by the preacher and intended for separate publication. This means that we have recorded in *C* considerably more than just a complete syllabus of a program but Cyril's own rendering of the various topics. We should therefore be able to discern his style in the choice of images, examples, turns of phrase, vocabulary, favorite topics, or topics he thinks are more important than others. Hence,

102. The scholion reads: "Many other catecheses were delivered year to year, both before baptism and after the newly enlightened were baptized; but only these were taken down when they were spoken and written by some scholars in the year 352 of the appearance of our Lord Jesus Christ. And in these you will find partly treatments of all the necessary doctrines of the faith which ought to be known; and answers to the Greeks and to those of the circumcision, and to the heresies; and the moral precepts of Christians of all kinds, by the grace of God." The year 352 as reckoned by the Greeks is equivalent to 360 in the Christian calendar. This is no doubt an estimation by the writer. See A. Doval, "The Date of Cyril of Jerusalem's *Catechesis*," *JTS*, n.s., 48 (1997): 129–32. The scholion may have the *Procatechesis* in mind. *P* could come from another year, though no doubt exists that it is Cyril's or that it has the same oratorical style as *C*. More will be said on this below when we consider the manuscript tradition.

103. *Institutio Oratoria* X.vi–vii.

104. G. Julius Victor, *Ars Rhetorica*, ed. R. Giomini and M. S. Celentano (Leipzig: Teubner, 1980); see pp. 95–96.

some passages will be valuable for discerning the specific characteristics of the preacher, that is, the author.

These same questions of place, time, and style need to be asked about M. We can begin with where and when the bishop delivered these Easter Week sermons. Others have often cited their noticeable shortness, compared to the Lenten catechesis, as indicating a significant difference in style. But the difference is not as pronounced as it would seem at first sight, when we take into consideration the time, place, and method of delivery.

Egeria is not as explicit about the length of time for the delivery of the mystagogy during the week following baptism; she only says it begins in the morning after the dismissal from the dawn service in the Martyrium and after everyone has moved to the Anastasis.

The bishop stands leaning against the inner screen in the cave of the Anastasis, and interprets all that takes place in baptism. . . . He always speaks in Greek, and has a presbyter beside him who translates the Greek into Syriac so that everyone can understand what he says. (IE 47.1–2)[105]

She does not say for how long this lasted; all we know is that after a midday meal they went to the Eleona on the Mount of Olives for a service (IE 39.3). Hence the entire morning was available for catechesis, or at least a duration of time equal to what had been allotted for the prebaptismal instruction.

The only significant anomaly is the comparative lengths of the sermons of C (3966 word average) and those of M (1092 word average), considering that the topics of M are clearly of equal or greater import. This anomaly, though, can be deceptive. First of all, the respective lengths in words of M 1–5 are 1156, 887, 817, 765, and 1839. As they stand, M 1 and M 5 are longer than the two shortest of the Lenten sermons, C 1 (1084) and C 8 (1004); the two next shortest sermons in C are C 5 (2147) and C 7 (2300) words in length.

One factor that would affect the length of M concerns the form of the received text as compared to its original oratorical form. Hence we will consider this matter of style next and then assess what evidence a comparison with C in these areas might yield.

In answer to the problem of the difference in length as well as style between C and M, A. Paulin has suggested that M is more probably in the form of "preacher's notes" than a transcription of the delivered sermons.[106] This

---

105. Translation by Wilkinson, *Egeria's Travels*, 145–46.
106. *Saint Cyrille*, 53.

hypothesis of Paulin's was proposed primarily in light of the influence of the *disciplina arcani,* which would have prevented *M* from being recorded when it was delivered or even published in any form for some time.[107] It offers an explanation for the different style of *M* (that is, its lack of many of the oratorical features of the Lenten sermons, and its "pedestrian and threadbare" theological explanations),[108] for why the texts of *C* and *M* are often separate in ancient versions, and for how the text of *M,* if published at a later date, may have been attributed to both Cyril and John. This hypothesis warrants some further consideration.

A study by P. E. Arns lends more weight to the possibility that *M* existed as notes or a rough draft.[109] He illustrates with several examples from contemporary oratorical practice the custom of writing notes or rough drafts of works on sheets of paper. Two words in particular refer to this initial stage of writing, *scheda* and *chartula.* A *scheda* is a sort of final draft, the state of a manuscript before final transcription.[110] According to Isidore, a *scheda* is what has been emended but not yet published.[111] Jerome similarly uses *chartula* to refer to a small slip of paper, or a draft, the minutest of which his adversaries may examine for signs of heresy.[112]

These examples cited by Arns do not necessarily have to do with the preparation of sermons, but in the case of the paschal sermons of Zeno, bishop of Verona (d. c. 370), it has been argued that the text we possess is a compilation of Zeno's preparatory drafts of sermons written on loose sheets of paper.[113] A study by Alexander Olivar shows that oratorical practice varied among the Fathers: for example, Maximus of Turin carefully memorized his prepared texts, and Ambrose preferred to do the same—though he was quite capable of improvising if needed—while Jerome and Augustine are known

107. In Milan, however, Ambrose's mystagogy was transcribed (evidenced by comments of the moment, particularly at the ends of the sermons) even though he acknowledges the rule of secrecy (*DS* 1.1).

108. Stephenson, *WCJ,* 2:146.

109. P. E. Arns, *La technique du livre d'après Saint Jérôme* (Paris: E. de Boccard, 1953).

110. Ibid., 18–19.

111. "Scheda est quod adhuc emendatur et necdum in libris redactum est." Isidore also notes that the word *scheda* is derived from Greek: ἡ σχέδη, leaf, page; τὸ σχεδάριον, sketch, rough draft. Cf. *Etymologiae* 6.14.8.

112. Arns, *La technique,* 16–17; he cites Jerome's *Epistula ad Ctesiphontem* 133.12 and *Epistula ad Amandum Presbyterum* 55.4.

113. See Gordon Jeanes, *The Day Has Come! Easter and Baptism in Zeno of Verona,* Alcuin Club Collections, no. 73 (Collegeville, Minn.: Liturgical Press, 1995), 43–49. The following argument is in large measure indebted to Jeanes's research in this area.

for their ability to improvise.[114] Even the accomplished extempore speaker, though, was expected to be prepared, and the use of *memoranda* in lieu of a fully memorized text was permissible. Quintilian's observations on the use of written material are particularly interesting. First of all, writing is an important prerequisite:

As regards writing, this is never more necessary than when we frequently have to speak extempore. For it maintains the solidity of our speech and gives depth to superficial facility.

Then, on method:

It is a common practice with those who have many cases to plead to write out the most necessary portions, most especially the beginning of their speeches, to cover the remainder of that which they are able to prepare by careful premeditation, and to trust to improvisation in emergency, a practice regularly adopted by Cicero as is clear from his notebooks.

After pointing out that such notes of other speakers have been discovered, he concludes:

I admit the use of brief memoranda and notebooks *(brevem adnotationem libellosque)* which may even be held in the hand and referred to from time to time.

He strongly disapproves, though, of using a full text of a speech or even summaries of what has already been written.[115]

It seems more evident now that the Greek term σχεδιασθεῖσα does not strictly mean "improvising" in the sense Quintilian uses, delivering a speech without any preparation, such as would be needed in an emergency. It would be most unlikely that Cyril would deliver his *Catecheses* in this manner. If the term is to have any meaning, then, it would seem to be closest to the practice of premeditated speaking based on a sort of précis of the intended final delivery, allowing for adequate opportunity for improvising as needed.

In light of the above, Paulin's proposal that the text of *M* is in the form of "preacher's notes" has much more substance. The mystagogue no doubt had some form of written text for his preparation. The text of *M* is too developed to be mere *memoranda;* it seems to fit best the description of notes or a notebook that was studied closely and served as an outline for an expanded and elaborated final delivery.

114. A. Olivar, "Preparacion e Improvisacion en la Predication Patristica," in *Kyriakon: Festschrift Johannes Quasten,* 2 vols. (Münster: Aschendorff, 1970), 2:736–67.

115. *Institutio Oratoria* X.vii.28–32; ed. and trans. H. E. Butler, Loeb Classic Library, vol. 127 (London: W. Heinemann, 1922), 149–51.

There are two other reasons for thinking that *M* is a preparatory text that was elaborated when preached. One comes from internal evidence in the text of *M* itself, and the other is suggested by some observations of Egeria.

As for internal evidence, unlike *C*, *M* does not have the term "improvise" in the title. While this omission in itself does not mean that *M* is not a transcription of delivered sermons, certain features in the text nonetheless indicate that it does not represent a final oration. While *C* contains many remarks pertinent to the moment of the delivery (for example, apologies for the length of the sermon or encouragement to the listeners in their weariness: *C* 13.22, 15.33, 16.32, 17.20, 17.30, 18.17), no such asides are in *M*. Certain rhetorical features such as the invention of objections in order to introduce a further aspect (*C* 2.16, 13.19, 13.26), or the practice of *praeteritio* where the preacher nonetheless explains what he says he will pass over (*C* 17.31), or what he is too ashamed to speak of (*C* 6.33), are likewise absent in *M*.[116] In contrast to *C*, *M*'s topics are of much greater import and are given a noticeably shorter and terser treatment. This would be understandable if the text consisted of notes that served as a basis for expanded improvised sermons.

Egeria's account of how the teaching took place points out another important feature of the sermons and suggests that the style of the bishop was such that the final delivery involved an improvised elaboration of whatever was prepared. With regard to the Lenten catechesis, she draws a comparison with the usual homilies at the Eucharist:

When the bishop sits in the Church and preaches, expounding each of these points in a similar manner, ladies and sisters, the faithful utter exclamations; but when those who come to the catechesis hear what is said and expounded, God knows, their exclamations are far louder. (*IE* 46.4)[117]

We must realize that the bishop is not, strictly speaking, delivering an oration but conducting a course of instruction during which a certain amount of improvisation could be expected, depending on how receptive the audience is or whether they have questions. A presentation of the fundamentals of the Christian faith, which could last for a couple of hours, would no doubt include the handling of questions on various points and call for a certain amount of improvisation on the part of the preacher to provide adequate answers; in so doing he would be exercising more his role as teacher than preacher. The above description is of the Lenten catechesis; thus it seems

---

116. See Yarnold, "The Authorship of the *Mystagogic Catecheses*," 147.
117. Trans. Wilkinson, *Egeria's Travels*, 144–45.

reasonable to suppose that what was transcribed in *C* is considerably more than what had been prepared by the bishop and less than all that was said during each session. The same can be reasonably said for the mystagogy, namely, that *M* is a basic text of prepared points to deliver, whereas the actual preaching involved handling questions and improvising as needed (in this sense, the text would be better described as teacher's, rather than preacher's, notes).

Egeria's description of the audience response to the mystagogy is similar to what she says of the Lenten catechesis:

The bishop relates what has been done, and interprets it, and, as he does so, the applause is so loud that it can be heard outside the church. Indeed the way he expounds the mysteries and interprets them cannot fail to move his hearers. (*IE* 47.2)[118]

It is hard to imagine such a response to the existing text of *M*, but it does contain passages that suggest that, when expanded, could certainly elicit an impassioned response. Stephenson rightly detects a certain jejune and pedestrian literary style in *M* as the text stands, but he is not justified in saying that the theology is unworthy of Cyril.[119] The texture of the sermons, though threadbare, is nonetheless made up of rich theological ideas and imagery: initiation is a mystical entry into Paradise on earth (*M* 1.1); the typological figure of the Exodus is fulfilled in Christ and presently realized in baptism (*M* 1.3); the prebaptismal anointing is associated with the cross of Christ and symbolizes mystical participation in his suffering and death (*M* 2.3); the font serves as both tomb and womb (*M* 2.4); the effects of chrismation and communion bear a vivid sacramental realism (*M* 3.3; 4.3), to cite just a few. These various ideas and images are like so many unshelled kernels; a final oration based on the text of *M* could surely yield sermons as substantial as the Lenten ones and worthy of the enthusiastic response Egeria describes.

The fact that *M* is probably in the form of *schedae* does not completely rule out comparing it to *C* for similarities in preaching style. Even though the text of *M* does not reveal the extempore speaking style of the author as a preacher, nor exist in the form of a foundational text ready for delivery (rather than as simple "notes," or the mere listing of topics), it does fit together as a basic oration, and it is possible to make a useful comparison with the prebaptismal sermons.

Two factors remain to be considered that are relevant to the style and

118. Trans. ibid., 145–46.
119. *WCJ*, 2:146.

presentation of the sermons. First is the subject matter and purpose of each set, and second is the catechetical and pedagogical technique.

Some have proposed that the contrasting subject matter of the sermons suggests a difference in style and, hence, different authors. It seems, though, that the nature and purpose of these very different kinds of instructions are what dictate the noted contrasts.

C is instruction in the fundamentals of the Christian faith where theological ideas are presented and explained. *M* builds on the foundation of the prebaptismal catechesis and is more directly a commentary on the rites of initiation. Presupposing the material from the Lenten instruction, *M* would not need to explain much of the theology that lies behind the rites.[120]

But "commentary on the rites" is not really a sufficient description. *Mystagogia,* a "leading into mystery," connotes more than just explanation or abstract understanding. In the opening sermon the mystagogue points out that the experience of the initiation rites is what is significant; it is the experience that teaches:

Since I well knew that seeing is more persuasive than hearing, I awaited this opportunity of finding you more responsive to my words, so that out of your personal experience I might lead you into the brighter and more fragrant meadow of the Paradise before us. (*M* 1.1)

The rites themselves, then, are the basic content of the sermons in contrast to what could be called the Christian doctrines found in *C.* The interest of the mystagogue is now to draw attention to the rites in a more contemplative than discursive way. In the same introductory passage just cited the author notes that the newly enlightened are more receptive to the mysteries as a result of their baptism, and his choice of a word to describe what he is setting out to do is suggestive: "so let me carefully educate (παιδεύσωμεν) you in this so you may know the true significance of what happened to you on the evening of your baptism" (*M* 1.1). In *P* 4 Cyril uses the term in a similar way concerning the candidates' initial experience among the faithful: "Be intimidated by the place, be taught (παιδεύθητι) by what you see." This term "educate" has a broader sense than instruct or explain. Its basic sense is to bring up or rear a child, to educate. It suggests more than just rational understanding; it includes the broader intuitive dimension of experience, the forming of character and values.[121]

120. *WCJ,* 2:145–47; Yarnold, "The Authorship of the *Mystagogic Catecheses,*" 148.
121. Cyril uses παιδευθῶσιν at *C* 12.14 to speak of Christ more easily "instructing" people by his taking on of human nature; at 15.3, he says: "Let the converts of the Manichees be in-

In comparing *M* with the Lenten sermons, Stephenson rightly notes (even if exaggerating) that "awe and exclamations of pious wonder have taken the place of understanding."[122] In fact, exclamations are quite common in *C*,[123] but the lack in *M* of a thoroughgoing theological explanation of the topics probably reflects the difference in the subject matter and goals of the sermons, as well as the draft form of *M*. The mystagogue stays very close to the actions and images of the rites and enhances the experiential dimension by the regular use of typology and imaginative examples. The apologetic approach found in *C* (cf. *C* 4.12, 14.15–17), which seeks to strengthen the faith of the candidates against Jewish and heretical adversaries, is noticeably missing. Further, the hortatory approach, where Cyril seeks to deepen and reinforce the conviction of listeners by the sheer repetition of examples (cf. *C* 2.7–19, 10.19), is sharply minimized in *M* so as not to detract from the force of the unparalleled experience of the rites themselves.

While this understanding of the nature and purpose of *M* and its subject matter in comparison to *C* does not indicate one author rather than another, it does leave open the possibility that it was authored by Cyril and will help in evaluating *M*'s use of particular ideas, terms, and examples in comparison to *C*.

Finally, we need to consider whether the teaching techniques exhibited in the mystagogy and the Lenten instruction evidence single or dual authorship. Bearing in mind that some of these techniques are shared by many catechists of the period (for example, the use of typology is not a peculiar feature of any one author), at the same time, the particular choice of and use of a type could identify one preacher's style more than another's. The same would be the case with any stock theological ideas or explanations. Each case will need to be examined in its context in order to see if any distinguishing features can be discerned.

D. Summary and Conclusions

This chapter has attempted to provide a background of useful data concerning Cyril and his church to aid the examination of the *Mystagogic Catecheses* for characteristics of Cyrilline authorship.

---

structed (παιδευέσθωσαν) and no longer make these luminaries their gods . . ."; he exhorts not just to the gaining of information but for fuller and deeper conversion. In contrast, the normal term for teach or instruct in matters of faith is διδάσκω. It occurs about fifty times in *C* and only once in *M* (5.17) where it refers to the Lord's teaching on prayer.

122. *WCJ*, 2:147.

123. See, for example, *C* 3.15; 5.10; 6.10, 12, 18; 8.4; 13.31.

From the survey of his life, Cyril has emerged as an orthodox yet non-partisan, independent thinker. His orthodoxy, great respect for tradition and the Scriptures as the foundation for all doctrine, as well as his talent and expertise as a theologian and catechist, are evident from the theologically well-grounded and thorough *Catecheses* delivered when he was a young bishop. At the same time he showed a strong and independent character in taking a stance against his metropolitan on more than one occasion, enduring three periods of exile as a result. In the end, he overcame all doubts about his beliefs as evidenced by the authority he exercised at the Council of Constantinople.

Although as a theologian and a catechist he had a particular dedication to the Scriptures as the foundation for all teaching on the faith, he nonetheless also saw great value in his broad knowledge of secular topics as an aid in his catechesis. His devotion to the Holy Places, especially Golgotha, and a special interest in a theology of the Incarnation also marked his catechetical style, which regarded learning by experience as being as important as learning by simple instruction. This latter characteristic is perhaps best reflected in the liturgical enhancements that took place under his pastoral leadership. These included developments in the structure of the liturgy, the catechetical program and syllabus, and the lectionary. These indications of an independent and innovative mind, seen in conjunction with changes in the external rites and practices, would suggest that over the period of his career, a certain amount of development occurred in Cyril's thinking and catechesis. The likelihood of such development will have to be borne in mind when evaluating anything common or dissimilar between *C* and *M* to see whether or not it truly represents the mind of a common author.

Certain other external features that could affect how the two sets of sermons might compare with one another were also explored. Similarities in content, style, or pedagogy may result from the fact that the content of the sermons represents an established annual catechetical syllabus and not just the individual catechist. At the same time, differences may stem from a variance in form and subject matter of the texts rather than from separate authors. The ultimate goal will be to assess numerous traits of *M*, especially similarities and differences with the *Catecheses*, in light of these guidelines and carefully weigh them as evidence for or against common authorship.

ʂɔɕ

The *Mystagogic Catecheses*
Manuscript Tradition, Literary Tradition, and Date

A. Introduction

Three items remain to complete the context in which we can best study the texts of these sermons. First, we need to sort out the manuscript tradition of *M* with its complicated author attributions; second, we will assess the literary tradition of writers who make references to *C* and *M;* and third, we have to establish a workable date for *M*.

B. Manuscript Tradition and Author Attribution

1. *Introduction*

The issue of author attribution involves rendering some account of the presence or absence of one or both of Cyril's and John's names in the manuscripts.[1] The task is complicated by the fact that the texts of *C* and *M* are not always published together, and the attributions are not always to the whole set of catecheses, but to individual parts.

We can begin with charting the "family history" of the Greek manuscripts. Figure 2.1 shows how these are most probably related.[2] According to how closely they resemble each other, that is, how little variation there is between any one manuscript and another, they can be arranged much like a family tree. As the vertical scale indicates, the oldest dates from about the tenth century and the most recent from the seventeenth. Piédagnel groups them into three families represented by α = A; β = B, C, D, E; and γ = F, G,

---

1. See Appendix for details concerning the manuscripts.
2. The figure is based on that drawn up by Piédagnel, *Cyrille de Jérusalem*, 58–59. I have not included two principal manuscripts, *Coislinianus 227* and *Neapolitanus-Vin. 8*, because the authors' names have been lost through mutilation to the manuscripts.

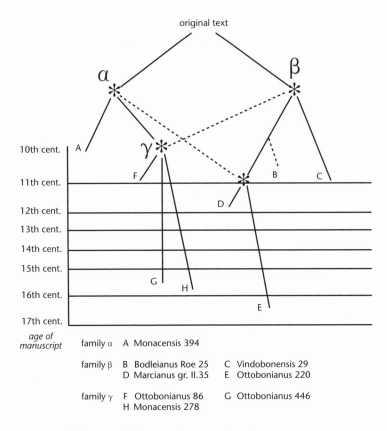

Figure 2.1 Family history of the Greek manuscripts of *M*

H. Manuscripts that are older and exhibit the least amount of variation from the majority readings are considered more reliable representatives of the original.

Piédagnel compared these three families and made the following observations. In the first case, there are passages in α that are identical to the corresponding passage in β but do not agree with the corresponding passages in γ; secondly, there are cases where α agrees with γ but differs from β; finally, there are cases where β and γ have the same reading but differ from α. Since the first two cases occur more frequently, he concluded that family α is superior. The dotted line in the figure connecting β with γ indicates the weak, but existent, relationship between these two families based on the number of readings that agree. The pair DE is, according to Piédagnel, "relatively inde-

Table 2.1 Principal Manuscripts of *M* Grouped according to Attributions

1. No author mentioned for *C*; *M* ascribed to John	*Monacensis 394*
2. *C* ascribed to Cyril; *M* ascribed to John	*Sinaïticus (Arabic) 366*
3. *C* ascribed to Cyril, *M* ascribed to Cyril and John	*(Ottobonianus 86,* mutilated in beginning) *Ottobonianus 446* *Monacensis 278*
4. *C* ascribed to Cyril, no author mentioned for *M*	*Vindobonensis Theol. gr. 29* *Bodleianus Roe 25*
5. *C* ascribed to Cyril, no author mentioned at the beginning of *M*, but Cyril mentioned in table of contents of *M*	*Marcianus gr. II.35 Ottobonianus 220*

pendent" from the others in its family and shows an occasional important agreement with family α—hence, the dotted line connecting this pair of manuscripts with α. Similarly, the single dotted line for B, *Bodleianus Roe 25*, indicates that it exhibits more than the average number of independent readings yet shows affinity with the others in its family.

Now, if we take this information and compare it to the manuscripts grouped according to the various ways the attributions appear, we find an interesting correlation. (See Table 2.1; for the sake of completeness, the Arabic manuscript is included.)

These groupings according to ascriptions correspond to Piédagnel's family groups in Figure 2.1: group 1 *(Monacensis 394)* to family α, group 3 *(Ottobonianus 86, Ottobonianus 446, Monacensis 278)* to family γ, group 4 *(Bodleianus Roe 25, Vindobonensis Theol. gr. 29)* to β, and group 5 *(Marcianus gr. II.35 and Ottobonianus 220)* to the "sub-family" of β. We will return below to evaluate the significance of this correspondence.

A few additional introductory observations should be made. The important Arabic *Sinaïticus 366* is included in the table because of the mention of authors, but it does not have a place in the family history of the Greek manuscripts. We should also note that there is no manuscript of *M* alone. Nor does any bear only Cyril's name at the beginning of *M*. However, his name does occur by itself heading the table of contents of *M* in the two manuscripts in group 5. Further, no manuscript numbers the eighteen sermons of *C* and the five of *M* consecutively 1 to 23.

The variety of ascriptions has given rise to several hypotheses that will need consideration. First of all is the possibility of copyists' errors when transcribing the author's name. Second, the two texts may not always have been together in some if not all of the strands of the manuscript tradition; therefore, the bringing together of the two works could easily have resulted in the dropping, adding, supplanting, or combining of authors' names. Third, with regard to M alone, if it originally had no author ascribed to it, it could have acquired one of either or both of Cyril's and John's names. For while any copyist would have known that these were Easter sermons preached by the local bishop, he would not necessarily know precisely who was in office the year they were preached.

First let us address the simpler question of the possibility of an error on the part of a copyist, and then we can turn to the evidence for the independence of the two texts in the tradition. We will then be in a better position to weigh all the possible permutations of the ascriptions.

2. *The Possibility of Scribal Error*

This issue pertains to the two manuscripts that bear John's name alone at the head of M. We can begin with the Munich codex, *Monacensis 394,* which has received the most attention, and then consider the Arabic codex, *Sinaïticus 366.*

a. *The Munich Codex*

The most significant feature of this manuscript is that no author is mentioned with reference to the first nineteen catecheses *(P* and *C)*, while John of Jerusalem is mentioned twice with reference to M. His name first appears in the table of contents at the beginning of the manuscript (fol. 2ᵛ), heading the list of the contents of M, and then later, just before the text of M itself in its introductory title (fol. 199ʳ). The following points would seem to indicate that the copyist of this manuscript was being faithful to his original.

A copyist's error would amount to either an inadvertent substitution of one name for another or adding the wrong author's name where one was lacking. It is barely conceivable that the two names are alike enough that one could look like the other when hastily written: Κυρίλλου / Ἰωάννου (Cyril / John). Blurring υρι could result in reading ωα, and a poor execution of λλ could look like νν. But such a mistake is highly unlikely, all the more so since John's name occurs twice. One could propose that the table of contents entered late into the tradition, and a single attribution was copied into the table, but as there is no evidence as yet that this manuscript acquired additional content at different points in its history, this proposal cannot stand.

Difficulties also arise if we consider the possibility that an author's name was added where one was lacking. Since there is only one author's name involved in this manuscript, if it were added by a copyist, then he was originally dealing with a text (or texts) with no name at all. Placing John's name where it occurs and mentioning no author for *P* and *C* would mean that he clearly knew that *M* was John's and *P* and *C* were not and that he did not know the author of *P* and *C*. But almost certainly he would only know that *P* and *C* were not John's if he knew who their true author was, and in that case, if he felt at liberty to insert John's name for *M*, he would no doubt include an author for *P* and *C*. But since there is no author mentioned for *P* and *C*, it seems much more probable that John's name was not added but copied from an original, and that in the history of this manuscript, *M*, with its attribution to John, existed apart from *P* and *C* and was at some time joined with them. Here is the first indication that the texts were not always joined.

Another peculiar feature of this manuscript is a break that occurs in the table of contents between the end of the list for *C* on folio 2ʳ to the top of folio 2ᵛ where the list for *M* begins. This could suggest that *M* with its list of sermon titles existed independently from *C* (certain other manuscripts have the table of contents for *M* listed separately).[3] Such a division, though, is not later reflected in the actual text, for *M* follows immediately after the scholion at the end of *C* 18 on the same side of the folio (199ʳ).

A certain difference in format between *C* and *M* also exists. At the end of each catechesis of *C* is an abbreviated reprise of the title and a line number. This form of a reprise in not found in *M*, suggesting again that the two sets of lectures do not share a common original redactor. With regard to *Monacensis 394*, then, it would seem that in its early tradition *M* was joined to *C* and *P* and already had John's name ascribed to it. Further, there is no reason to believe that author attributions were in any way the result of scribal errors.

b. The Arabic Codex

Only one other manuscript, the Arabic *Sinaïticus 366*, bears a sole attestation to John at the head of *M*.[4] Concerning this manuscript, Piédagnel only says that it contains all of the *Catecheses* and that it is "a copy of a model identical to that of *Monacensis gr. 394*."[5] That is, the manuscripts from which each

---

3. See Appendix, manuscripts *Ottobonianus 220* and *Marcianus gr. II.35*.
4. Assistance on this manuscript was graciously provided by Penelope Johnstone at the Oriental Institute, Oxford University.
5. Piédagnel, *Cyrille de Jérusalem*, 23 n. 2.

of these copyists produced theirs were identical. If this is true, then the Arabic codex would not need to be regarded as a significant additional witness. But, in fact, the manuscript lacks *P* and exhibits certain differences from the Munich codex, which would suggest that, at least in its entirety, it was not copied from the same immediate model.[6] Unlike the Munich manuscript, this Arabic codex has no table of contents; further, Cyril's name does occur in the title of *C* 1 with which the manuscript begins and again in the title of *C* 8. There is no scholion after *C* 18 as there is in the Munich codex; there is instead a prayerful concluding note by the scribe and a date, March 909 (fol. 217ʳ). The text of *M* begins on a new folio (218ʳ) as follows: "In the name of the Father, and of the Son, and of the Holy Spirit, the one God. Mystagogia 1, of John, Archbishop of Jerusalem." The titles for the sermons in *M* among the Greek manuscripts in general exhibit some variation, and, in this case, the Arabic titles do follow very closely those of the Munich manuscript. The title "archbishop" is notably different from the title "bishop" in the Munich codex. According to Bihain, the titles "archbishop" and "patriarch," where they occur in some of the Greek and Armenian manuscripts, are anachronistic; such titles were not instituted until the Council of Chalcedon. The more authoritative manuscript tradition (family α headed by *Monacensis 394*) uses the simple title of bishop.[7]

The fact that *C* bears the name of Cyril and *M* that of John, and that the scribe concludes the transcription of *C* with his signature, a date, and a prayerful commending of his scribal work to God and the saints (all before *M* begins on a separate folio), gives the impression that the copyist is either dealing with two separate texts that he himself is joining or copying a single edition in which the two texts were exhibited as two distinct parts. Again, there is no indication that scribal error has affected author attribution.

It is beyond the scope of this present study to conduct a comparison of these two manuscripts to determine their relationship to each other. The variations in the titles suggest that they are not as close as Piédagnel proposed. Nonetheless, these differences have to do with lists of contents and titles, which could reflect adaptations according to the style and culture of the local copyist or translator, and not, by Piédagnel's estimation, with the body of the text. Respecting his judgment that the two codices are closely related, the Arabic manuscript ought not to be regarded as an independent witness,

---

6. Piédagnel may have meant by "catecheses" the Lenten sermons without the introductory sermon; as well, to copy from a model need not mean to copy it in its entirety.

7. Bihain, "Une vie arménienne," 325 nn. 16–18.

and its attribution of *M* to John alone thus carries very limited additional weight as a second witness.

3. Manuscript Evidence for C and M as Independent Texts

a. The Evidence

The idea that *C* and *M* were once independent is of some significance, and so we will briefly consider further evidence for it and then return to the particular issue of attestation. The Syro-Palestinian fragments contain *P* and *C*, and an Armenian version contains only *C*.[8] Swaans regarded this as a strong indication that there never was an Armenian version of *M*, but subsequent to his study, citations of *M* 5 in several Armenian homilies have been discovered. It is still uncertain, though, whether an Armenian version of *M* was ever published on its own.[9] The analysis of the text of these Armenian homilies citing *M* has indicated that their style is of great antiquity (between fifth and seventh century) and that the original was most probably Syriac and not Greek.[10] Egeria noted in her diary that the sermons were translated into Syriac when they were delivered, and therefore it would not be surprising if a Syriac version was transcribed and handed on. Some other Greek manuscripts are without *P*, and the versions of *P* by itself, sometimes found among works of Basil,[11] indicate that this introductory sermon circulated on its own. Finally, there are two Greek manuscripts that lack *M*, *Holkham gr. 32* and *Patmos gr. 669*. The likely parent of the Patmos manuscript, *Marcianus gr. II.35*, has *M* in a disordered state; hence, these two manuscripts probably also belong to a tradition that originally lacked *M*.

There seems, then, to be sufficient reason from the manuscripts themselves to conclude that the texts of *P, C*, and *M* have not always been handed

---

8. See Appendix.

9. See Appendix. For the Armenian homilies, see Athanase Renoux, "Une version arménienne des Catéchèses Mystagogiques de Cyrille de Jérusalem?" *Le Muséon* 85 (1972): 147–53. G. Garitte thinks that the Armenian tradition conserved the eighteen *Catecheses* as a separate corpus because they constituted a commentary on the group of scriptural texts listed at no. 17 of the *Armenian Lectionary;* since there is no reading for *P*, it was not conserved. See G. Garitte, "Les catéchèses de Cyrille de Jérusalem en arménien: fragments d'un manuscrit du IXe siècle," *Le Muséon* 76 (1963): 95.

10. Opinion is split on this issue of a Syriac or Greek original, and a detailed philological study is still needed. See Garitte, "Les catéchèses," 108.

11. Codex *Regius 476* (ol. 1824), fols. 253–58; see Henri Omont, *Inventaire sommaire des manuscrits Grecs de la Bibliotheque Nationale*, 2 vols. (Paris: A Picard, 1888), 1.1:53–54. *Barroci gr. 191*, fols. 164–70 (*C* 9 is also on fols. 170–76); see Henry Octavius Coxe, *Catalogue of Greek Manuscripts in the Bodleian Library* (Oxford: E Typographeo Academico, 1853), col. 324.

on together, and that even from the earliest times, at least in some places, probably circulated independently. Given this evidence, two further questions present themselves: (a) why did the texts exist independently, either originally, or by being separated, and (b) why (especially if different authors are involved) were they joined?

b. Independent Redactions of P, C, and M

It is not difficult to see how P could stand on its own. The *Procatechesis,* as a prologue, was addressed to a general audience that included catechumens not enrolled for baptism. Some manuscripts (e.g., *Ottobonianus 446*) have a scholion after P that indicates that the catecheses following it are reserved only for the baptized or for baptismal candidates, implying that P was available to a wider audience.

In a similar manner, C can be seen as a separate set of catecheses for those enrolled for baptism but not yet initiated. Two of the early uses of C by other authors have to do with explaining the creed, and in one case the citations are part of the instruction of baptismal candidates.[12]

M, on the other hand, represents instruction reserved for the initiated alone. The practice of secrecy regarding these most central mysteries of the faith, the *disciplina arcani,* was very strong at this time. Right from the start, Cyril cautions against divulging any of the catechesis to strangers (P 12). The same sentiment is reflected in the scholion sometimes found after P. Hence, we can conclude that there would be nothing odd about M originally being independent from C, and, in fact, good reason to think that this was the case. It was only later that a text of M would surface for publication and be joined to C in the tradition.

c. Why the Sermons Were Joined

A reasonable explanation exists for why C and M were eventually joined. Both texts represent parts of a catechetical program in the Jerusalem church, as opposed, say, to the personal homilies of a particular bishop. The scholion at the end of C 18 mentions how such lectures were delivered every year, and most significantly, the *Armenian Lectionary,* representing a time extending long after Cyril, refers to mystagogic sermons in its rubrics. Hence, Cyril's successor, John, would have continued the practice of delivering the Easter Week mystagogy. To whatever extent, and for whatever reasons the texts

---

12. Rufinus in his *Expositio Symboli* and Niceta of Remesiana in his *Instructio ad competentes.* These will be considered in more detail below.

may have existed independently, they could easily and understandably have been joined together as an integral representation of an entire catechetical program.

d. Conclusion

For Swaans, the evidence for separate redactions was of great importance. He argued that the only reasonable explanation for the independence of the texts is that they are the works of different authors.[13] But with a closer examination, the evidence proves to be of little value. It appears from Swaans's conclusions that throughout his discussion he assumes the defenders of Cyrilline authorship believe that *C* and *M* were preached and copied in the same year.[14] While it may be true that this was the prevailing view of his time, Swaans's single-minded attention to refuting this point seems to prevent him from considering the possibility that even if *M* were not written the same year as *C* (351), it might well have been written in any other year before the death of Cyril in 387. Hence, his argument for the separate editions of the two texts only shows that *C* and *M* represent different years. This proves nothing definitive against Cyrilline authorship, for the essential element missing from his argument is evidence that *M* was composed after Cyril's death in 387. Ironically, all of the evidence he acknowledges that shows how *C* and *M* represent different redactions could also be used to defend Cyrilline authorship. Later, based on other evidence, it will be argued that *M* represents a time some thirty years later than *C* yet before Cyril's death in 387. The likelihood that *C* and *M* are different redactions helps to explain some of the differences between the two texts.

4. The Presence of Bishop John's Name in the Manuscript Tradition

We can now turn our attention to the difficult and complex problem of the presence of John's name, clearly one of the most important features of the manuscript evidence. Josias Simmler, the first one known to have questioned Cyril's authorship of *M*, proposed that perhaps John was the author and that *M* was later ascribed to Cyril to give it more authority.[15] What he is invoking here is the principle of redaction criticism that says that the more

---

13. Swaans, "À propos des 'Catéchèses Mystagogiques,'" 24–29.

14. Ibid., 41.

15. J. Simmler, *Biblioteca instituta* (Tiguri: Apud Christophorum Froschoverum, 1574), 153. The same view is proposed by Stephenson, *WCJ*, 2:145.

unusual reading has the stronger claim for being original since it is more likely to suffer alteration than itself alter a more original reading. Thus, in this instance, it would be more probable that a less prominent original ascription to John would be supplanted by a more authoritative one than vice versa (that it came to light later that only *M* was ascribed to John in the Munich manuscript actually strengthens Simmler's proposal). Cyril, who is indisputably connected with *C*, would naturally be considered as the author of *M*, which represents an integral part of a catechetical program. But this sort of argument has very limited force in showing John to be the author, for it is actually addressing the question of why Cyril's name would supplant John's on the assumption that John is the author. But to support this assumption of Johannine authorship neither Simmler nor Stephenson offers a significant reason to regard *Monacensis 394* (or in the case of Stephenson, the Arabic manuscript as well) as having enough authority to counter the rest of the tradition. Nevertheless, since no clear argument against this option exists, we must keep it in mind when weighing the evidence in the end.

If John is not the author, why would *M* be attributed to him? Since it is likely that the original of *M* existed as an unpublished set of notes, it could easily have been in a form lacking any ascription to an author. Thus, a later compiler who wished to name an author might have conjectured that John wrote it. As both Cyril and John were preachers of mystagogic sermons, this explanation could account for John's name, and in some cases both names, being assigned to *M*.[16]

Let us review the possible options for explaining the varied attributions among the manuscripts (noting that the options are not mutually exclusive):

A. If *M* had John's name alone, then either
   1. his name alone is retained, or
   2. Cyril's is added, or
   3. Cyril's name supplants John's (or John's name is dropped when *M* is joined to *C*).
B. If *M* had Cyril's name alone, then either
   1. his name alone is retained, or
   2. John's name is added, or
   3. John's name supplants Cyril's, or
   4. Cyril's name is dropped.

16. See Yarnold, "The Authorship of the *Mystagogic Catecheses*," 145.

C. If *M* had two names, then either
  1. both names are retained, or
  2. John's name was dropped, or
  3. Cyril's name was dropped, or
  4. both names were dropped.

The existing manuscripts exhibit A.1 and C.1, and effectively eliminate B.1 and C.2 since there is no evidence of *M* headed by Cyril's name alone. At the same time, if *M* ever once had Cyril's name alone, it could have been dropped as superfluous in cases where it was combined with a text of *C* that already bore Cyril's name (B.4). Such, for example, could be the history behind *Bodleianus Roe 25*, which has Cyril's name alone with *P, C,* and *M*. Inasmuch as there are several surviving witnesses to both names, C.4 can be ruled out. It is feasible that Cyril's name could be added to John's (A.2) on the strength of associating *M* with *C* and the Jerusalem catechetical tradition shared by both bishops. But inasmuch as John's name is never associated with *C*, the addition of his name, or its even supplanting Cyril's (B.2, 3), seems only possible if there were a text of *M* alone ascribed to John. This would be so also in the case of John's name being attached to *M* on the basis of a shared Jerusalem catechetical ministry; there would be little chance of its being added if the work were already ascribed to Cyril except on the strength of a separate text ascribed to John alone. As for the remaining option, C.3, it seems highly improbable that Cyril's name would be dropped once it was attached. The remaining options, then, are:

A. If *M* had John's name alone, then either
  1. his name alone is retained, or
  2. Cyril's is added (on the strength of the Jerusalem tradition), or
  3. Cyril's name supplants John's (or John's name is dropped when *M* is joined to *C*).
B. If *M* had Cyril's name alone, then either
  1. John's name is added (but only on the authority of an extant *M* with his name), or
  2. John's name supplants Cyril's (similarly, on the authority of an extant *M* with his name), or
  3. Cyril's name is dropped (as superfluous when attached to *C*).
C. *M* had two names, and both names are retained.

The significant result of this brief analysis of options is that the presence of John's name seems only to be explained by the existence of a tradition where his name alone, or jointly with Cyril's, was originally ascribed to a separate text of *M*. We need now to examine and evaluate the evidence for the breadth and authority of such a tradition. We have already seen that the Munich and Arabic manuscripts point to the existence of a tradition of John's name alone. We can now look more closely at the manuscripts with double attribution.

5. The Problem of Double Attribution

There are three significant manuscripts that bear John's name in conjunction with Cyril's: *Ottobonianus 86, Ottobonianus 446,* and *Monacensis 278*. According to the assessments of both Piédagnel and Bihain, *Ottobonianus 446* and *Monacensis 278* are close direct descendants of *Ottobonianus 86*.[17] While this interrelationship greatly limits the force of this witness of double attribution, it is still significant. In these manuscripts, the two names head only *M* and not *C,* and the titles are identical. Swaans dismissed the idea of an original double attribution (as opposed to one name being added later) because this would imply the unlikely case that the work was understood as a collaboration.[18] But a double attribution need not be interpreted this way. Whoever would have known that John delivered such sermons in Jerusalem would also probably have known that Cyril did the same. Since such sermons could have been considered more a part of the church program than the personal sermons of a single preacher (they were delivered every year), *M* could have been considered as the work of Cyril but passed on to and used by John. Hence, it is a reasonable option that *M* originally had a double attribution when it was first published.

The likelihood of an original double attribution depends, though, on its having its own separate tradition. But this probability is somewhat lessened when we consider how the manuscripts are related to one another. The three manuscripts in question probably represent only one model, *Ottobonianus 86*. In addition, by Piédagnel's reckoning of how the manuscripts are related (see Figure 2.1), *Ottobonianus 86* is most closely related to and perhaps dependent on the model of *Monacensis 394*, the sole Greek manuscript with John's name alone at the head of *M*. These relationships suggest that the most likely explanation for the double attribution is that at some point in the tradition of

---

17. Piédagnel, *Cyrille de Jérusalem,* 21–22, 58; E. Bihain, "L'Épître de Cyrille de Jérusalem à Constance sur la vision de la croix (BHG³ 413): tradition manuscrite et édition critique," *Byzantion* 43 (1973): 268–71.

18. Swaans, "À propos des 'Catéchèses Mystagogiques,'" 41.

family α, Cyril's name was added to the heading of M, which already had John's name.

6. Conclusions

We can now look at the whole of Figure 2.1 and draw some conclusions. The presence of John's name heading M occurs in one Greek manuscript in the older and more authoritative family α. Its presence most probably originates from a separate text of M originally attributed to John and then joined to C. Family β represents a parallel tradition in which two manuscripts have no author at the head of M but Cyril is the implied author by its attachment to C, and two manuscripts name Cyril in a table of contents of M. Lastly, family γ has three manuscripts with both names heading M, but, as noted above, these are most likely of a single model. The presence of John's name in this family probably reflects the tradition of family α, and the presence of Cyril's name probably originates either from association with C or from a known Jerusalem catechetical tradition or perhaps from cross influence from family β. In light of the likelihood that M originally existed as an unpublished text of notes, then the parallel traditions of families α and β would indicate that it could just as easily have picked up either name. The option that Cyril's name supplanted John's remains only the remotest of possibilities, which cannot be substantiated by the existing evidence. The net result, then, when comparing family β against α and γ is that the tradition of family β, which associates M with Cyril, is stronger. Still, the weight of the Johannine attributions cannot be completely dismissed, but a decision in favor of Johannine authorship would have to depend on evidence drawn from other sources.

C. Literary Tradition

The literary tradition, references to and the use of P, C, and M by other writers, is, of course, of special relevance to the authorship question since these writers so often acknowledge the authors of the cited texts. I will first survey the available evidence and then assess its relevance to the question of authorship.

1. The Catecheses

Five witnesses are the nearest to Cyril chronologically but make references only to the *Catecheses*. Jerome gives the earliest account of Cyril's writing catechetical lectures, but his reference does not necessarily include the mystagogy.[19] Rufinus (d. 410) uses Cyril in his *Commentary on the Apostles' Creed*.[20] Similarly, Niceta of Remesiana (d. c. 414) makes use of Cyril in his baptismal instructions.[21] Theodoret (d. 457) cites from *C* 4 concerning Christ's birth from the Virgin in his *Eranistes* (the context is a dialogue concerning the integrity of the two natures of Christ);[22] and Severus of Antioch (d. c. 538) cites Cyril seven times in his work against John the Grammarian.[23] Only the last two witnesses name Cyril as an author; the other citations are unacknowledged.

Some later witnesses to *C* are significant since some of them, in Swaans's estimation, imply no knowledge of *M*. First is Theophanes the Confessor (d. c. 818) who, when citing Cyril's catecheses, refers to them only as delivered to "those approaching baptism" not also to those who are already baptized.[24] Georgios Hamartolos (9th c.), when listing the works of Cyril, notes the eighteen catecheses without mentioning *M*. A further reference not mentioned by Swaans, but most probably the source for Georgios Hamartolos, is the monk Alexander of Cyprus (before 614) who gives the same general information with the addition of a few quotations.[25] Photius of Constantinople (d. c. 895) refers to the catecheses *ad illuminandos* as bearing a sublime theology.[26] Why, asks Swaans, does he not at the same time mention *M*, certainly as sublime as *C*? And finally, a fourteenth-century work, the *Armenian Synaxis*, refers to Cyril's catecheses *ad illuminandos*, which is a reference to *C* not *M*.[27]

19. *De viris inlustribus* 112.

20. *Expositio Symboli* 18, ed. M. Simonetti, CCSL 20 (Turnhout: Brepols, 1961), 155 (see also PL 21.357 note g, 358).

21. *Instructio ad competentes* V.3.9, 34, in *Niceta von Remesiana: Instructio ad competentes*, ed. Klaus Gamber (Regensburg: F. Pustet, 1964), 116–17, 122; see also A. E. Burn, *Niceta of Remesiana: His Life and His Works* (Cambridge: University Press, 1905), lxx–lxxiii.

22. Ed. G. Ettlinger (Oxford: Clarendon Press, 1975); see *Florilegium 2.77*.

23. *Liber contra impium Grammaticum*, ed. with Latin trans. J. Lebon, CSCO 93–94, 101–2, 111–12 (Scriptores Syri 4–6) (Louvain: Secretariat du CSCO, 1929); the citations are in Book III, 25, 38, 41.

24. *Chronographia*, ed. Carolus De Boor, 2 vols. (Leipzig: B. G. Teubner, 1883), 1:42; PG 108.141–44.

25. Georgios Hamartolos, *Chronicon*, PG 110.661B. This section of the PG edition of the *Chronicon* is not included in the following critical text: *Chronicon*, ed. Carolus de Boor, 2 vols. (Leipzig: B. G. Teubner, 1904), 2:538–39. The relevant sections of Alexander's work, *De Inventione Crucis (BGH³)* can be found in PG 87³.4068–69.

26. *Historia Manichaeorum*, PG 102.33.

27. *Synaxaire arménien de Ter Israël*, ed. and trans. G. Bayan, PO 21, 175–78. In the eastern Church, the term "synaxis" refers to any assembly of public worship or prayer inclusive of the Eucharist.

2. The Mystagogy

Not until the middle of the sixth century do we find the first of six uses of *M* citing Cyril as author, while there are no references to *M* citing John as author. Eustratius of Constantinople (d. 582) quotes *M* 5.9–10 in his work against the Psychopannychites.[28] Anastasius the Sinaïte (d. c. 700) cites both *C* 7.14 and *M* 1.8 and in each case gives the heading: "From the Catecheses of Cyril of Jerusalem."[29] In the eleventh century, Nicon cites *M* 5.9.[30] The anonymous author of the work *On the Divine Mysteries* (not earlier than the twelfth century) cites *M* 4.6, 9, and 5.15, 21–22.[31] The *Florilegium Achridense* cites virtually the same passages as the previous example.[32] Renoux also notes seven manuscripts of an Armenian florilegium that cite the same passage as Eustratius.[33]

3. Interpreting the Witnesses

Swaans has provided the most substantial interpretation of these sources to date. Hence, we will first assess his findings and then see what new conclusions we can draw. Swaans called attention to three significant features of the literary tradition of *C* and *M* that indicated for him that the two works existed independently: first, he singled out a number of the early uses of *C* by authors who did not seem to know of *M*; second, the first citation of *M* does not come until two centuries after it was written; and third, even after we find *M* under Cyril's name, there are still citations of *C* that seem to be known independently of *M*. He argued, as he did with the manuscript tradi-

---

28. *De utriusque ecclesiae occidentalis atque orientalis perpetua in dogmate de purgatorio consensione,* ed. Leone Allacci (Rome: Typis Sacrae Congreg. de Propaganda Fide, 1655), 569; see also PG 33.305C.

29. *Questions and Answers,* PG 89.336, 356; this work probably does not entirely belong to Anastasius.

30. PG 33.313C. The passage is from Nicon of the Black Mountain, *Pandectes,* cited by Touttée from the Paris codex *Regius 880,* fol. 328. However, this is not necessarily an independent witness since it is the same passage cited by Eustratius; that is, Nicon may be using Eustratius as his source.

31. Paris codex *Regius 900,* 15th c., § 7–11, fol. 112; PG 33.315–16C.

32. See V. Masic, "Les manuscrits du Musée nationale d'Ochrida," in *Zbornik na trudovi ou Recueil de Travaux du Musée National d'Ohrid* (Ohrid, Yugoslavia: Naroden muzej, 1961), 234–35. See also Piédagnel, *Cyrille de Jérusalem,* 30 n. 1, 173 n. 3, for the details of the differences between these two citations. A florilegium is a collection of quotations or passages from notable authors.

33. Renoux, "Une version arménienne," 147–53.

tion, that the independence of the texts implies more than one author.[34] We can address these points all at once as we reassess the evidence.

The fact that there are some witnesses who appear to know only of C is understandable if the texts existed independently in the manuscript tradition itself; it has already been shown that independent redactions of C and M would not in themselves constitute evidence against Cyril as the possible author of M. But inasmuch as the silence regarding M may have been due to knowledge of it as belonging to John, or perhaps a widespread and persistent ignorance of its attribution to Cyril, Swaans's assessment of the witnesses deserves evaluation.

Swaans's argument carries weight only if it shows that among the witnesses who cite from C, an additional citation from M would have been appropriate or expected. All of the witnesses before Eustratius, however, concern doctrinal matters for which, while recourse to C would be appropriate, M would have little or nothing to offer.

As for the witnesses after Eustratius (the first witness to M as Cyril's), they also show no need to cite M. Theophanes refers to the text as "catecheses which he [Cyril] expounded for the benefit of the innumerable people who had come forward for holy baptism"; if taken rigorously, this could suggest that he knew only C, that is, the lectures for those coming forward as opposed to those for the newly enlightened. However, Theophanes is commenting on the fact that Cyril was reckoned sympathetic with the Arians for omitting the word *homoousios* in his *Catecheses*. Since C was, as it were, a brief course in the fundamentals of the Christian faith, particularly on the creed, it would be this work and not the lectures on the mysteries that he would cite to bolster his contention. His use of C alone, as distinct from M, would be because of its relevance to the subject matter and, hence, would not necessarily indicate that he did not know M. At most, it would show he regarded C as a distinct set of sermons, but Cyril himself makes a clear distinction between the catecheses and the mystagogy.

As for Photius and the *Armenian Synaxis,* the value of these witnesses would depend on how rigorously we interpret the title *ad illuminandos* as referring only to C. Strictly speaking, "for those being enlightened" is the commonly used term in the title for the lectures of C, and "for those newly enlightened" is the corresponding term in M. The former title, however, could have evolved into the more generic sense in later centuries, referring to the

34. Swaans, "À propos des 'Catéchèses Mystagogiques,'" 18–23.

whole of the catechetical instruction given to the annual group of baptismal candidates.

The real value of these witnesses for substantiating Swaans's hypothesis would be in proving that the writers, while indeed knowing of *M*, did not intend to include it in their references. But there is no such evidence. Only the witnesses of Georgios Hamartolos and Alexander (actually one source) make a specific reference to the eighteen catecheses to the exclusion of *M*.

The most that these examples show is that some witnesses, even quite late ones, probably knew only of *C* and not *M*. But the existence of separate redactions has already been recognized, based on the manuscript tradition. What the witnesses have not shown is any indication that *M* was known either as John's or not as Cyril's.

In contrast, we do have the citations of *M* as Cyril's after Eustratius. Some qualification is in order, though, concerning these. The citation of the Armenian florilegium (*M* 5.9–10) is the same as that of Eustratius (though Renoux thinks they are probably independent of each other), and Nicon also cites *M* 5.9. Hence, they may be citing each other rather than independently citing *M*, and perhaps these three should be counted as only one witness. The same situation applies to the citations in the anonymous work *On the Divine Mysteries*, which are very similar to those in the *Florilegium Achridense*. Hence, granting the possibility of interdependence, these five citations may only represent two independent sources. But with the addition of the important witness of Anastasius the Sinaïte, who cites *C* and *M* as Cyril's, the total would be three—a significant number.

In the end, then, the literary tradition shows no significant evidence against Cyrilline authorship of *M*. As regards *C*, the tradition seems to indicate that for a considerable time the two texts were known independently by some authors (only Anastasius attests that *C* and *M* were known together). This evidence parallels that of the manuscript tradition and on the same grounds shows only that the two texts probably existed independently, but it does not eliminate the possibility that Cyril could have been the author of both. As for *M*, none of these witnesses dispute Cyrilline authorship, nor do any attribute it to John. Finally, in that there are, if not a total of six, at least three independent witnesses to *M* as Cyril's and no witnesses at all to *M* as John's, the weight of evidence falls clearly in favor of Cyril.

D. The Date of *M*

1. *Internal Evidence of Date*

The only direct study of the dating of *M* from internal evidence is that of C. Beukers.[35] He draws attention to the intercessory prayers in *M* 5.8:

we call upon God for the common peace of the Churches, for the stability of the world, for the Emperors, for soldiers, and for allies. . . .

He shows that only after 382 could the liturgy have intercessory prayers for more than one emperor *and* allies (the convert Visigoths, granted the status of *socii* by Theodosius in October, 382).[36] This date would place *M* a little more than thirty years after *C* (351).

This evidence concerning the date is pertinent to two important objections to Cyrilline authorship, viz., (1) that the liturgy of *M* is too advanced for the middle of the fourth century when *C* was transcribed, and (2) that there is a discrepancy between the program of Easter Week sermons described in *C* 18.33 (which alludes to at least five different topics and perhaps as many as seven sermons) and that of *M* (four topics in five sermons). Both these objections, however, have claimed nothing more precise than that *M* does not fit well with the time of *C* and that it belongs later in the century. Beukers's date, though, can satisfy the objections: the time gap of thirty years would allow for changes in the program and still allow *M* to have been written before Cyril's death in 387. The significance of this time gap will be considered again when we look more generally at the internal difference between *C* and *M*.

2. *Contemporary Sources: The* Armenian Lectionary *and the Witness of Egeria*

Two sources contemporary with *M* and pertinent to the present question are the *Armenian Lectionary* and the *Itinerarium Egeriae*.[37] Both these sources

35. Beukers, "'For our Emperors, Soldiers and Allies'. An Attempt at Dating the Twenty-Third Catechesis by Cyrillus of Jerusalem," *VC* 15 (1961): 177–84.

36. The date of the treaty with the Visigoths is recorded in the *Chronica Minora*, ed. Theodor Mommsen, Monumenta Germaniae Historica: Auctores Antiquissimi, 9 (Berlin: Weidman, 1891), 243. That the Visigoths were considered allies is well enough attested by various accounts of their settlement. See, for example, Themistius, *Oration* 16, in *Orationes*, ed. W. Dindorf (Leipzig: C. Cnobloch, 1832), 211; *Pan. Lat.* II.22, in *Panégyriques Latins*, ed. and trans. Edouard Galletier, 3 vols. (Paris: Belles Lettres, 1955), 3:89. In particular, Synesius of Cyrene, writing in 400, in *De regno* 15 (PG 66.1093), criticizes Theodosius for showing weakness in making the Visigoths allies and granting them land.

37. The *Armenian Lectionary* has been gradually reconstructed in this century. It was first

provide evidence regarding the number and arrangement of the catechetical instructions given during Lent and Easter Week in Jerusalem in the second half of the fourth century. Of particular relevance is the information about the Easter Week mystagogy. We need to determine whether, according to this evidence, C and M belong together in Cyril's catechetical ministry or whether M comes from a different tradition.

A significant part of Swaans's argument against the Cyrilline authorship of M was based on his assessment of what was known of the *Armenian Lectionary* in the 1940s when he did his study.[38] The lectionary to which he had access showed a list of readings for each of the lectures of C but for M a list of days on which the mystagogy was preached; this latter list includes only one reference to a reading. Swaans argued that the different forms of these lists indicated that they came from different traditions and times, and hence C and M themselves were from different traditions and times; from this he also concluded that they had different authors.

However, we now have in the E manuscript a much earlier version of the lectionary—dating from at least before 415—that includes a list of readings for five days of mystagogy. This list coincides with the arrangement of M. It is not certain from E alone, though, when this arrangement began; might there have been more than five mystagogic sermons in Cyril's time?

Here the witness of Egeria is of value. In particular, recent studies of her pilgrimage have dated her visit to Jerusalem 381 through 384.[39] This means that she witnessed the liturgical program of Jerusalem when Cyril was bishop. Her account coincides in almost every respect with the lectionary as well as with M. In *IE* 39.2, we read what she says about the days and places of the assemblies for the mystagogy:

---

printed in 1905 in Conybeare's *Rituale Armenorum* (507–27), which included a translation of a tenth-century manuscript, *Arm.* 44 (usually referred to as *P*) in the Bibliothèque Nationale in Paris. Conybeare filled the gaps in this manuscript with information from *cod. Arm. d.2* in the Bodleian Library, Oxford. But these manuscripts represented a tradition much later than the fourth century. Since that time two important manuscripts have come to light, *Jer. Arm.* 121 (*J*), and *Yerevan 985 (E)*, which helped complete the early lectionary. These manuscripts are included in Renoux's edition of the lectionary. Other relevant studies by Renoux include: Athanase Renoux, "Un manuscrit du vieux lectionnaire arménien de Jérusalem," *Le Muséon* 74, 75 (1961–62): 361–85 (vol. 74), 385–98 (vol. 75); idem, "Liturgie de Jérusalem et lectionnaires arméniens," *Lex Orandi* 35 (1963): 167–99; and idem, "Le Codex Érévan 985. Une adaptation arménienne du lectionnaire hiérosolymitain," in *Armeniaca: Mélanges d'Études Arméniennes* (Ile de Saint Lazare-Venice: Mechitarist Press, 1969), 45–66.

38. Namely, the *Rituale Armenorum;* see Swaans, "À propos des 'Catéchèses Mystagogiques,'" 30–34.

39. See Devos, "La date du voyage d'Égérie." See also Wilkinson, *Egeria's Travels*, 237–39, 330, for a full survey of this question.

On the first Sunday, Easter Day itself, they assemble in the Great Church, the Martyrium, and similarly on the Monday and Tuesday; and when they have had the dismissal, then they always go with singing from the Martyrium to the Anastasis. But on the Wednesday they assemble on the Eleona, on the Thursday in the Anastasis, on the Friday on Sion, on the Saturday Before the Cross, and on the eighth day, the Sunday, they assemble once more in the Great Church, the Martyrium.[40]

According to this passage, on every day except Wednesday and Friday they assemble in the Great Church or Anastasis. Another description of the program (*IE* 47.1), however, has been difficult to reconcile with the above:

Then Easter comes, and during the eight days from Easter Day to the eighth day, after the dismissal has taken place in the church and they have come with singing into the Anastasis, it does not take long to say the prayer and bless the faithful; then the bishop stands leaning against the inner screen in the cave of the Anastasis, and interprets all that takes place in Baptism.[41]

The phrase, "during the eight days" *(per illos octo dies),* makes it appear that she has in mind sermons on each of the days of the week (beginning with Monday), making seven in all. But there are several reasons for interpreting this statement more loosely. First is the close association she makes between the Anastasis and the mystagogic preaching. Cyril himself says that these lectures will take place in the "Holy Place of the Resurrection"(*C* 18.33). Further, the five days on which mystagogy occurs, according to the lectionary, are the days when the service takes place in the Martyrium, after which they could move into the Anastasis for the mystagogy (*AL* No. 52). On the other days the service took place at other stations a good distance from the locale of the Holy Sepulchre (Wednesday at Sion, associated with the upper room where the apostles were on Pentecost, and Thursday at Eleona on the Mount of Olives, associated with the Ascension) and the congregation could not conveniently retire to the Anastasis for mystagogy because of the distance. What this suggests is that the mystagogy was inseparably attached to the Anastasis, and Egeria's statement "during the eight days" should be interpreted as meaning "on those days when the assembly is in the Martyrium."[42] Just before the above passage, Egeria quotes the bishop saying: "Do not think it [the mystery of baptism] will never be explained; you will hear it all during the eight days of Easter *(per octo dies paschales)* after you have been

40. Trans. Wilkinson, *Egeria's Travels,* 139.
41. Ibid., 145.
42. See Athanase Renoux, "Les Catéchèses Mystagogiques dans l'organisation liturgique hiérosolymitaine du IVe et du Ve siècle," *Le Muséon* 78 (1965): 357.

baptized" (46.6). Similarly, this mention of eight days need not mean every one of the eight days, but rather on days that are in Easter Week. The Yerevan manuscript of the lectionary provides similar testimony. While clearly allowing for only five mystagogic sermons, it adds the rubric, "He [the bishop] teaches in this way during Easter week up to the Sunday after Easter as is indicated in the canon."[43] Finally, in M itself the mystagogue uses a similar phrase. He begins the second sermon by referring to "these daily instructions on the mysteries"; to refer to five sermons during eight days as "daily" indicates how loosely the expression should be taken.

Hence, we can conclude that Egeria, in agreement with the lectionary, most probably witnessed five mystagogic sermons in that she speaks of five assemblies in the Martyrium/Anastasis and two stational services elsewhere.

One small discrepancy needs to be accounted for that concerns the subject matter of the sermons. The lectionary readings given in the Yerevan manuscript for the mystagogic sermons fit well with M 1–4 but not with the fifth sermon. In C 18.33, when Cyril previews the subject matter for Easter week, the last topic concerns the Christian moral life, a topic that does fit with the reading for M 5 from 1 Pt 2.1 ("So put away all malice and all guile and all insincerity"). Inasmuch as sermons four and five are on the topic of the Eucharist, it seems as if the fifth sermon on morality has been preempted by the unfinished business of the fourth sermon (though the last two sentences of M 5 before the blessing seem to be an attempt at least to make due mention of the importance of moral uprightness in preserving the grace received in baptism). Even though the subject matter of M 5 was changed, the reading itself was still retained.[44] This is one of the indications of the conservative nature of the lectionary.

3. Summary

Numerous previous studies have had difficulty accepting M as Cyril's because of problems with reconciling its five-sermon structure with testimony given by Cyril in his *Catecheses*, Egeria, and the *Armenian Lectionary*. They assumed that during his time Cyril delivered his mystagogy "each day of the week," and M was thought to represent a program that had been reduced to five sermons after the time of Cyril and Egeria but had not yet been reduced to the four-sermon program that came into effect around 415 as indicated in

---

43. PO 36.2, 326–27 (*AL* No. 52).
44. See Yarnold, "The Authorship of the *Mystagogic Catecheses*," 155–56.

the later sources of the lectionary. But with a more accurate date for Egeria's pilgrimage, along with a more careful interpretation of her testimony (as well as Cyril's) regarding the mystagogy, an earlier version of the lectionary (one that mentions five mystagogic sermons), and the realization that M can be dated to late in Cyril's career, all these difficulties have disappeared. We can thus conclude that as far as dating and external witnesses are concerned M can fit easily anywhere into the last four years of Cyril's ministry. These results do not rule out the years 387 to 415, which would be during John's term, but inasmuch as the later dating of M had been a major point in favor of Johannine authorship, these new findings have greatly strengthened the case for Cyril.

E. Conclusions

This chapter has reevaluated three areas that have figured largely in previous studies of the authorship of M: manuscript attribution, literary tradition, and date. In the areas of literary tradition and date, all previous objections against Cyrilline authorship have been shown, in the light of further studies, to be no longer tenable, and no points in John's favor have emerged.

Concerning the manuscripts, there is still uncertainty. The balance of the evidence falls only just in favor of Cyril if we consider the numbers. The presence of John's name alone at the head of M on two manuscripts continues to be a weighty point, but one with its own problems. There is no extant manuscript of M alone with John's name nor is it ever cited as his in the literary tradition. It is always connected to C, which is never attributed to him, and there are three manuscripts where he shares the attribution with Cyril. All of these points give particular credibility to the theory that the text, originally unpublished, had no attribution initially but was assigned to one or both of the bishops based on what was known of the Jerusalem catechetical tradition. Hence, while the Johannine attribution still carries some weight, the case for John's authoring M cannot rely on the manuscripts alone. This matter will be reconsidered in the final conclusions of this study.

ꙮ

A Comparative Analysis of the Lenten
and Mystagogic Catecheses

CHAPTER 3

The Initiation Rites I
Preliminary Rites and the Epicleses

A. Introduction

Much attention has been given in past studies to the way *C* and *M* exhibit certain differences in content and style that could indicate different authors. At the same time, defenders of the Cyrilline authorship of *M* have pointed out particular similarities as well as offering explanations for the differences. To date, though, these studies have been only select, random, and brief. Since the authorship question at hand depends so much on the careful weighing of numerous bits of evidence, to do proper justice to this part of the overall argument a much more complete survey is in order.

We begin our comparative analysis of the two sets of catecheses with three chapters on the rites of initiation (Baptism, Chrismation, and Eucharist). The following chapters will consider, in turn, theology and spirituality, literary style, and, finally, a comparison with the known works of John of Jerusalem. If the same author wrote both the *Catecheses* and the *Mystagogia,* we could expect to find similarities in the use of certain terms, ideas, examples, catechetical techniques, interpretations, and style wherever correlative topics are addressed. Conversely, different authors could be signaled by a lack of similarity when one would be expected. Throughout, we must bear in mind that similarities could reflect the fact that the sermons are part of an annual catechetical program such that if two authors were involved, what one says in the prebaptismal catechesis the other may echo in the mystagogy. If we are dealing with two authors, any similarities between *M* and the other two texts *(P* and *C)* would be much more the result of coincidence than if they were by the same author; this would especially be so since *P* and *C* are not commentaries on the rites and are quite different in their nature from *M*. For this reason, the number of similarities will also be a significant element—the more there are, the less chance they are due to coincidence.

Differences are to be expected since this was a time of substantial liturgical and theological change. Further, they might reflect a change between the work of the young bishop at the start of his career and the older, matured, and experienced bishop some thirty years later. Hence, on the matter of differences, each case will have to be evaluated as to whether or not it can be explained by the time gap.

The intent of this comparative analysis is to select those elements of *M* that show any sort of correlation with *P* or *C*, whether they exhibit similarities or contrasts, and to evaluate the correlation for what it may show with regard to single or dual authorship. Therefore, not every rite or topic of *M* will be analyzed.

We begin with the first mystagogic sermon, which covers the prebaptismal rites, namely, the renunciation of Satan and the contract with Christ. Briefly, in the first rite the candidates enter an outer chamber of the baptistery, face toward the west, stretch forth one of their hands, and recite a formula renouncing Satan. Then in the second rite, turning to the east, they recite a formula of allegiance to Christ. The most significant topics to consider from this first sermon are the epicleses (first introduced in the mystagogy on the renunciation of Satan) and the apparent absence of a blessing of the font. First, however, we will briefly consider two other items of some interest in the opening rites.

B. Preliminary Rites before Baptism

1. *The Outstretched Hand*

In the rite of renunciation, after facing westward, each candidate is commanded to stretch forth a hand and renounce Satan (*M* 1.2; see also *M* 1.4). This ritual of extending a single hand, as it were, against Satan is not found among *M*'s contemporaries. Ambrose does not describe any particular ritual gestures, while Chrysostom and Theodore have the candidates kneel with their arms extended toward heaven in a posture of supplication.[1] This image

---

1. Chrysostom uses the verb ἀνατείνω (stretch upward) to indicate that the hands are directed heavenward to God (*Stav.* 2.18, *PK* 3.21–22). Similarly, Theodore describes the posture as one of prayer with hands or arms extended toward God (*BH* 2.2–3).

of a single hand stretched out against Satan also appears in *P* 10. Here Cyril speaks about the armor and weapons against adverse powers that the catechesis provides and the need to be ready for battle:

Abide by the catechesis . . . for you are receiving weapons against the powerful adversary, against heresies, and Jews, and Samaritans, and Gentiles. You have many enemies, take plenty of darts, for you have many targets to throw them at. . . . The armor is ready, and the sword of the Spirit is most ready. But you must also stretch (τείνω) forth your right hand with good resolve, that you may fight the Lord's fight and overcome the adverse powers.

The addition of the image of the outstretched hand seems oddly unnecessary at first; but given the context of this passage, where Cyril is in many ways giving a preview of what is to come, he appears to be hinting at the renunciation rite the candidates will soon be experiencing rather than giving only a general picturesque exhortation. The difference in the verb form is not significant. The simple verb, τείνω, "stretch," can be used in a military sense for "aim at, direct toward" or for stretching out or presenting arms, like a shield or spear.[2] Ἐκτείνω, the term used in *M,* is the more common word for stretching out one's hands to give or receive something *(LSJ)* or additionally for prayer or a blessing *(PGL)*. But it can have a more active sense such as when Jesus cures the leper in Mk 1:41. The use of ἐκτείνω over τείνω in *M,* where a rite is being described, is probably governed by the intent to portray the ritual position taken up by the hand rather than the effect of the gesture. But the sense is combative—the candidate is clearly in an adversarial stance, and the hand is directed at Satan—even though the military images are absent. The same combative sense is expressed in *M* 1.4 where the mystagogue elaborates on the words spoken by the candidate and describes a vivid picture of personal confrontation.

You are told to say, with arm outstretched towards him as though he were present, "I renounce you, Satan." I will also tell you why you stand facing West; for you need to know. Since the West is the region where darkness appears, and he being darkness has his dominion there, therefore you look with a symbolical meaning towards the West and renounce that dark and gloomy ruler. What then did each of you stand up and say? "I renounce you, Satan, you wicked and most cruel tyrant!" What you meant was, "I no longer fear your might; for Christ has dissolved it, having partaken with me of flesh and blood, that through these He might destroy death by death and save me from bondage forever. I renounce you, you crafty and most subtle serpent.

2. *LSJ,* s.v. "τείνω", A.I.4 and A.II.2. *PGL* has no entry for this word.

I renounce you, plotter as you are, who under the guise of friendship contrived all manner of disobedience and worked apostasy in our first parents. I renounce you, Satan, the artificer and abettor of all wickedness."

2. The Movement from the Vestibule into the Baptistery

The preliminary rites in M take place in a vestibule outside the baptistery proper (see Figure 3.1). There are two references to this area. In M 1.2, it is called the vestibule *(proaulion)* of the baptistery, and in M 1.11, it is referred to as the "outer room" in contrast to the "inner room," the inner sanctum or Holy of Holies (M 2.1), which the mystagogue uses as an image of the room with the font. He also uses the imagery of Paradise for the inner room. Having renounced Satan and committed themselves to Christ in the vestibule, the candidates stand in view, as it were, of Paradise (Eden), which will soon be reopened to them (M 1.9). Among his contemporaries, the author of M alone seems to have made use of a separate room for the renunciation rite.[3]

Certain passages in P and C suggest that Cyril has such a room in mind when he anticipates the initiation events. In the opening passages of P, Cyril entices his listeners by describing how close they are to the blessings of baptism. They already have the "savor of blessedness" and the "fragrance of the Holy Spirit" on them; they are already gathering "spiritual flowers for their heavenly crowns." He also says they are already at the "entrance-hall of the palace, may the King bring you in!" This image of entering into the King's chamber probably comes from Song 1:4 and shows up again in C 3.2: "For the

---

3. Only in ancient Nisibis do we know of a baptistery (dated to 359) with an adjoining room that can be dated to the time of C. See A. Khatchatrian, "Le Baptistère de Nisibis," in *Actes du Ve congrès international d'archéologie chrétienne, Aix-en-Provence, 13–19 septembre 1954*, Studi di antichità cristiana, no. 22 (Vatican City: Pontificio Istituto di archeologia cristiana, 1957), 407–21. There is still some debate on the exact location and structure of the Jerusalem baptistery; the following are the current relevant studies: K. J. Conant, "The Original Buildings at the Holy Sepulchre in Jerusalem," *Speculum* 21 (1956): 1–49; C. Coüasnon, *The Church of the Holy Sepulchre in Jerusalem* (London: Oxford University Press for the British Academy, 1974); V. C. Corbo, *Il Santo Sepolchro di Gerusalemme*, 3 vols., Studium Biblicum Franciscanum Collectio maior, no. 29 (Jerusalem: Franciscan Printing Press, 1981); Cesare Tinelli, "Il battistero del S. Sepolcro in Gerusalemme," *Studii biblici francescani: Liber Annuus* 23 (1973): 95–104; Georg Kretschmar, *Die Geschichte des Taufgottesdienstes in der alten Kirche*, ed. K. Müller and W. Blankenburg, Leiturgica: Handbuch des evangelischen Gottesdienstes, vol. 5 (=Lief. 31–35) (Kassel: J. Stauda-Verlag, 1964–66), 205–7; Malka Ben-Pechat, "L'architecture baptismale de la Terre-Sainte du IVe au VIIe siècle: étude historique, archéologique et liturgique" (Ph.D. diss., University of Paris, Nanterre, 1986). Corbo (1:132–33), with Tinelli, proposes that the original baptistery was located on the north side of the Anastasis in the courtyard of the Patriarchate, but the reassessment by Ben-Pechat (*Catalogue*, 158) shows that their evidence represents a later, probably sixth-century, development.

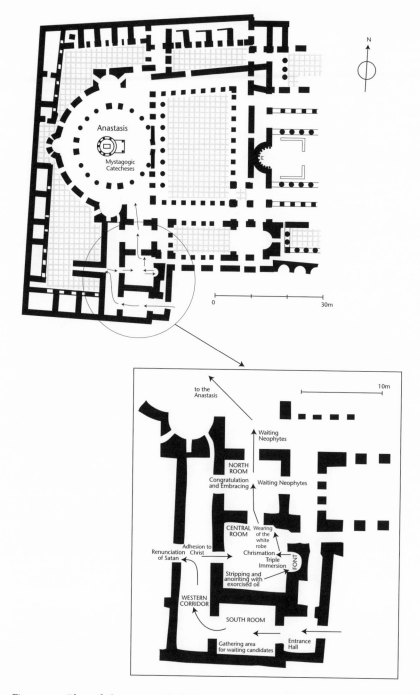

Figure 3.1 Plan of the west end of the Holy Sepulchre Church in fourth-century Jerusalem (above) based on the study of Coüasnon showing the sanctuary of the Martyrium, the Anastasis, and the baptistery. The detail of the baptistery (below) shows the itinerary of the baptismal rites.

time being, you stand outside the door, but God grant that you all might say, 'The King has brought me into his chamber.'" In *P* 15, Cyril alludes to the night of baptism, and after speaking of the purifying effect of the Lenten penance, he says of its goal:

May God at length show you that night, the darkness that shines by day, concerning which it has been said, "Darkness will not be dark to you, and the night shall be light as day." At that time may the door of Paradise be opened to each man and woman among you. Then may you enjoy the Christ-bearing fragrant waters.

There is, then, a certain correspondence of ideas here between *P/C* and *M* where a site with reference to baptism (the vestibule of the baptistery) is focused upon as a place of immediate preparation and anticipation (outer court of temple, entrance hall to palace, vantage point to Eden) before a final entrance into the baptistery (Holy of Holies, Paradise, king's chamber).

In the mystagogy about both the outstretched hand and the outer chamber, then, the parallels with corresponding ideas in *P* and *C* are noticeable yet subtle enough to suggest that they come from the mind of a single author rather than simply representing a common annual syllabus.

C. The Epicleses

In the rites of *M*, epicleses figure in the prebaptismal anointing for exorcism, the chrismation, and the Eucharist. The term is also used in several places in *C*, and a comparative analysis reveals significant correspondences. After clarifying the meaning of the term for these texts, we will examine and compare all of its occurrences in *C* and *M*. We will consider similarities and differences in the ritual use of epicleses as well as the literary style of the catechesis on them. We will then address the special problem of whether or not a rite for blessing the font was used in *C* and *M* and finish with some observations on the theology of the epicleses.

1. The Meaning of the Term

An epiclesis, in its liturgical use, is generally understood as a prayer in a rite wherein God is "called upon" (the noun *epiklesis* derives from the verb *epikaleo*) to impart the presence of the Holy Spirit for some sanctifying action, whether it is the blessing of water, the consecration of the bread and wine in the Eucharist, or even exorcism.[4] Its exact meaning in liturgical contexts is not, however, always self-evident to us from a simple literal reading of

---

4. See, for example, *C* 3.3, *M* 2.3, *M* 3.3, and *M* 5.7.

the word because it had acquired technical meanings that were not always explained. The classical meanings of the terms were still in use. For example, the verb meant (1) to "call upon" or "appeal to" someone for aid or as a witness, (2) to "call upon" or "summon" someone to appear in court, (3) to "call" someone by a name "above" (that is, in addition to) other names, as in a nickname, and (4) "call against," that is, to accuse. The noun meant "invocation," "name," "summons," or "accusation." In Christian liturgical usage, the terms took on more refined meanings.[5] The verb *epikaleo* still basically meant "call upon" in the sense of a petition to intervene or act. But also, reflecting the varied meanings of the prepositional prefix *epi* (upon), it could mean to call a divine sanctifying presence (that is, the Holy Spirit) "onto" a person or thing as in the phrase "the epiclesis of the Holy Spirit." Similarly, the substantive *epiklesis* came to mean the prayer itself said "over" a person or thing that makes the request.[6] It is the nature of established technical terms that their meaning is clear to readers and listeners of the time but not always evident to others. However, in all occurrences of these terms that will be considered, the underlying sense is a request (either as a noun or verb) of God to act in some sanctifying way.

2. The Epicleses in C and M

There are four direct and one indirect references to epicleses (translated here as invocation) in *M*:

For just as the bread and wine of the Eucharist are merely bread and wine before the invocation of the sacred and adorable Trinity, but after the invocation the bread becomes the body of Christ and the wine his blood, so the foods attached to the pomp of Satan are in themselves merely food but become impure by the invocation of the demons. (*M* 1.7)

Just as the breath of the saints and the invocation of the name of God burn like a fierce flame and drive out demons, so also the exorcised oil by the invocation of God and prayer receives such power as not only to cleanse every trace of sin with fire but also to pursue the invisible powers of evil. (*M* 2.3)

5. See F. E. Brightman, "Correspondence: Invocation in the Holy Eucharist," *Theology* 9, no. 49 (1924): 33–40, and E. G. Atchley, *On the Epiclesis of the Eucharistic Liturgy and in the Consecration of the Font* (London: Oxford University Press, 1935), 3–13.

6. See, for example, Epiphanius, *Panarion* 36.2; *AC* 7.44.3; the titles for the postcommunion and final blessing in *AC* 8.15–16, which refer to the prayers as epicleses; Basil, *De Spiritu Sancto* 66 (3.54e); Ps-Dionysius, *On the Ecclesiastical Hierarchy* 6.3.2 (PG 3.533B); Origen, *Fragmenta in Joannem* 36, in *Commentarii in Joannem*, ed. E. Preuschen, GCS Origenes 4 (Leipzig: J. C. Hinrichs, 1903), 512.12.

For just as the bread of the Eucharist after the invocation of the Holy Spirit is no longer ordinary bread but the body of Christ, so also this holy chrism with the invocation is no longer ordinary or, so to speak, common but Christ's grace. (*M* 3.3)

We entreat the merciful God to send forth the Holy Spirit upon the offerings, so that he may make the bread Christ's body and the wine Christ's blood, for everything that the Holy Spirit touches is sanctified and transformed. (*M* 5.7)

In *M* 5.19 is an indirect reference:

The offerings are holy, having received the presence of the Holy Spirit. . . .

In *C*, there are four references to epicleses used in a liturgical sense. In *C* 3.3 concerning the baptismal water, Cyril says:

For just as the offerings brought to the heathen altars, though simple in their nature, become defiled by the invocation of the idols, so contrariwise the simple water having received the invocation of the Holy Spirit and Christ and the Father acquires a power of holiness.

Then in *C* 3.12 is the following description of baptism:

For you go down into the water bearing sins; but the invocation of grace having sealed your soul, it is no longer possible for you to be swallowed up by the terrible dragon.

In *C* 4.13, Cyril speaks of the "invocation of the crucified" to drive away demons, and in *C* 6.23, the verb is used when Cyril is speaking of the Manichees invoking demons in their ceremonies:

Then having gone up on the housetop and summoned the demons of the air, whom to this day the Manicheans cause to be invoked over their abominable ceremony of the fig. . . .

Before addressing specific passages, a general overview of these varied instances will be helpful for seeing if any overall pattern emerges. (See Table 3.1; a question mark indicates an element of uncertainty.)

The examples from *M* 1.7 (a), 3.3 (c), 5.7 (d), and 5.19 (e) all refer to the eucharistic epiclesis, and so they can be considered together. *M* 5.7 (d) clearly states that God is asked to send the Spirit. The other three of this group are more elliptical and speak only of an epiclesis of the Holy Spirit and of the Trinity, but they should be understood in the same way, namely, as a request of God to send the Spirit upon the gifts that the Spirit might transform the bread and wine into the body and blood of Christ. Nothing clearly indicates that the Father is specifically the one asked.

Table 3.1 The Epicleses in *C* and *M*

Passage	Person Addressed	Object	Request	Result
a. *M* 1.7	Trinity / demons	bread & wine / food	send Spirit? / descend? transform elements	body & blood / defiled food
b. *M* 2.3	Name of God / God with prayer	person / exorcised oil	drive out demon / cleanse	cleansed soul
c. *M* 3.3	God or Holy Spirit?	bread & wine / oil	send Spirit? / descend? transform elements	body & blood / Christ's grace
d. *M* 5.7	God	bread & wine	send Holy Spirit to transform elements	body & blood
e. *M* 5.19	God?	bread & wine	send Spirit? / descend?	sanctified bread & wine
f. *C* 6.23	Demons	fig	?	?
g. *C* 4.13	Crucified	person	drive out demon	cleansed soul
h. *C* 3.3	Idols	offerings	?	defiled food
i. *C* 3.3	Trinity	water	send / descend? water receives Spirit / Word?	water with the power of holiness
j. *C* 3.12	Trinity?	person (by means of water)	sealing	baptized person / sealed soul

In *C* 3.3 (i), the Trinity is addressed, but it is not absolutely clear who acts to sanctify the water. Later (*C* 3.4), Cyril speaks of the seal of the Spirit during immersion, but Christ may also be associated with the blessing of the water. *M* 2.3 (b) and *C* 4.13 (g), which concern exorcisms, are somewhat different. Both the first epiclesis of *M* 2.3 (b) and the one in *C* 4.13 (g) suggest that the simple mention of a divine name effected the exorcism; in these cases the one being exorcised is the object involved. But the other epiclesis of *M* 2.3 (b) over the oil for exorcism involves a prayer, and it seems safe to assume that the form was similar to the other examples where God (the Trinity?) is asked to sanctify the oil by the power of the Spirit.

Finally, it is difficult to be certain about the form of the epiclesis in *C* 3.12 (j). The "invocation of grace" is most probably a reference to the baptismal formula (addressed to the Trinity), and it is the Spirit that seals (see *C* 3.4–5 where the Spirit is singled out as the person active in the font). But if this is the case, probably no specific address or request was made; rather, the formula "I baptize *N.* in the name of the Father . . ." or "*N.* is baptized in the name of the Father . . ." may have been all that was used. In *M*, the immersion rite is said to involve interrogations on a simple creed ("Do you believe in the Father? . . .) that probably sufficed for a baptismal formula. Whether this practice prevailed in 351 is not certain, but even if it did, the proclamation of the three names of the Trinity could still be regarded as an invocation. The "invocation of grace," then, can be understood as implying an address to the Trinity, and the implied request is for the Spirit to seal (C 3.3 [i] also refers to the "spiritual grace that is given with the water").

In general, while all of the examples at least imply the four basic elements of person addressed, object, request, and end product, we can discern three different patterns for the epicleses. First, with regard to simple exorcisms, the epiclesis apparently involved only naming God or, perhaps more specifically, the Crucified, and the request is to drive out demons. Second, in the more involved liturgical rites that used elements such as bread, wine, oil, and water the epiclesis involved requesting of God (the Trinity) that the Spirit sanctify the elements. In these cases, the Father does not appear ever to be specifically addressed; though with regard to the end product, either or both the Son and Spirit can be specified (for example, the body and blood of Christ, the chrism as Christ's gift of the Spirit, the Spirit present in the sanctified bread and wine, or the Spirit in the water). Lastly, the baptismal formula is noteworthy for its lack of direct address and request and the resulting action of sealing. The first two patterns are clearly shared by C and M. As for the third pattern, although M is silent about regarding the baptismal formula as an invocation, the two texts show no apparent differences in the general form of the epiclesis.

Similarities in theology among some of these examples will be considered at the end of this section. We can now consider the striking similarity M 1.7 and M 3.3 have to the passage from C 3.3 in the literary expressions used to explain the effects of the epicleses.

3. Similarities in Literary Expression

When the mystagogue comments on the epicleses in M 1.7 and M 3.3, he illustrates the power of the Spirit by contrasting the nature of the elements (bread and wine, chrism) before and after invoking the Spirit. A similar comparison is made in M 4.6 when he comments again on the bread and wine. The way this contrast is expressed in M has several striking similarities to the contrast made in C 3.3 when he is explaining the epiclesis over the font:

C 3.3: For just as the offerings brought to the heathen altars, though simple *(litos)* in their nature become defiled by the invocation of the idols, so contrariwise the simple *(litos)* water having received the invocation of the Holy Spirit, and Christ, and the Father, acquires a power of holiness.

M 1.7: For just as the bread and wine of the Eucharist are merely *(litos)* bread and wine before the invocation of the sacred and adorable Trinity, but after the invocation the bread becomes the body of Christ and the wine his blood, so the foods attached to the pomp of Satan are in themselves merely *(litos)* food but become impure by the invocation of the devils.

C 3.3: Do not regard the font as ordinary *(litos)* water; rather regard the spiritual grace that is given with the water.

M 3.3: Be sure not to regard the chrism merely *(psilos)* as ointment; for just as the bread of the Eucharist after the epiclesis of the Holy Spirit is no longer ordinary *(litos)* bread but the body of Christ, so also this holy chrism, with the invocation is no longer ordinary *(psilos)*, or so to speak, common *(koinos)*, but Christ's grace.

C 3.4: Do not regard the ordinary *(psilos)* nature of the water, but look for salvation by the power of the Holy Spirit.

M 4.6: Do not then regard the bread and wine as ordinary *(psilos)*.

The first thing to notice is the common emphasis on the real change in the ordinary elements that takes place as a result of the invocations. Second, *C* 3.3 shows a marked similarity to the way the mystagogue in *M* 1.7 and *M* 3.3 expresses his appeal to one epiclesis in order to substantiate the veracity of another. Third, in *C* 3.3 and *C* 3.4 the exhortation "do not regard" is used exactly in the same way as in *M* 4.6 and synonymously with "be sure not to regard" in *M* 3.3.

Another common feature is the use of the adjective *litos,* "mere," "ordinary," "simple," and its synonym *psilos* to refer to the elements before the invocation. According to the entries for these words in *PGL, psilos* is the more common of the two words in theological or liturgical usage for referring to something in its ordinary as opposed to its sanctified form. For example, *psilos* is used by Origen for the literal as opposed to allegorical sense of statements;[7] he also uses it in a baptismal context comparing the baptismal water to mere water before the epiclesis.[8] Athanasius uses the term to refer to the bread and wine before consecration,[9] as do Nilus of Ancyra (d. 430)[10] and Anastasius the Sinaïte (d. 700).[11] *Koinos* (common) is also used once in *M* 3.3 as a synonym for *psilos;* this term is used of the bread before the epiclesis by Irenaeus.[12] As for *litos,* the only other liturgical usage cited in *PGL* is from John of Damascus, who compares the consecrated bread to a coal in a fire; just as the coal is not mere wood but made one with the fire, so the bread of communion is not mere bread but made one with divinity.[13] In *C* and *M,* both *litos* and *psilos* are used synonymously; *litos,* the less common term in general usage, is the preferred term in *C* and is used as often as *psilos* in *M.*

An additional similarity in the first two passages compared above, *C* 3.3 and *M* 1.7, is that both draw a comparison between Christian and pagan practices. Though it is not directly quoted, 1 Cor 10:20–21 lies behind both of the passages:

What pagans sacrifice they offer to demons and not to God. I do not want you to be partners with demons. You cannot drink the cup of the Lord and the cup of demons. You cannot partake of the table of the Lord and the table of demons. (RSV)

In *M* 4.6–7, the same Pauline idea is used again to speak of the eucharistic table:

Do not regard as simple the bread and the wine, for they are the body and blood of Christ according to the declaration of the master. And the blessed David will inform you of the meaning of this mystery when he says: "You have prepared a table before me in the face of those who oppress me." What he means is this: Before your coming the demons prepared a table for men, polluted, defiled, and full of diabolical power; but after your coming, Lord, you prepared a table before me. When a man says to God: "You have prepared a table before me" what can he mean but the mystical and spiritual table which God has prepared for us in the face of, that is, opposing and confronting, evil spirits? And quite naturally, for the one table has fellowship with demons, and the other has fellowship with God.

---

7. *De Principiis* 3.1.15; 4.2.2.

8. *Fragmenta in Joannem* 36.

9. According to Eutychius Constantinopolitanus (d. 582), *Sermo de paschate et de eucharistia* 8 (PG 86.2401B).

10. Nilus of Ancyra, *Epistularum libri quattuor* 1.44, 3.39 (PG 79.405B).

11. *Hodegus* 23 (PG 89.297B).

12. *Adversus Haereses* 4.18.5.

13. *De fide orthodoxa libri quattuor* 4.13 (PG 94.1149B).

The whole of M 4 is on the topic of the reality of the change of the bread and wine into the body and blood of Christ and is essentially a commentary on the Institution Narrative.[14] The above passage, when compared with C 3.3 and M 1.7, shows the same ready association of the mystery of the transformation of the elements with the Pauline passage on Christian and pagan worship.

4. The Rite of Blessing the Font

a. The Problem

In C 3.3, when teaching about the special nature of the baptismal water, Cyril refers to an epiclesis over the water and appears to have a specific rite in mind:

Do not regard the font as ordinary water, rather regard the spiritual grace that is given with the water. . . . The simple water, having received the invocation of the Holy Spirit, and Christ, and the Father, acquires a power of holiness.

When we turn to the catechesis on the baptismal rite in M, we find a noticeable lack of any reference to a blessing of the font. If there was a distinct rite for blessing the font at the time of M, then we would certainly expect some mention of it in the mystagogy inasmuch as the mystagogue otherwise methodically comments on the other rites.

There are several possible explanations for the omission. First, there may simply have been no such rite in either of the liturgies of C or M. In this case the reference to the invocation in C 3.3 would not be to a specific ritual, and therefore it would be no surprise that M does not mention a blessing of the font. Second, a rite of blessing at the time of C may later have been dropped. This possibility, a reversion to a simpler baptismal rite, would hardly seem probable at this time of development. Lastly is the possibility that a rite of blessing existed when both C and M were preached, but it did not receive any specific mention in the mystagogy. If this were the case, we need to explain why the mystagogue passed over it.

An argument for the Cyrilline authorship of M needs to address only the last of these alternatives, for it alone represents a difference between C and M that might best be explained by the different thinking, style, or programs of two bishops. First we need to determine whether the invocation over the wa-

14. Whether or not there actually was an institution narrative in use in the time of M will be addressed later.

ter in *C* 3.3 refers to a distinct rite for blessing the font. If it does not, then the silence in *M* with regard to such a rite would not constitute a discrepancy with the content of *C*. But if it does represent a blessing rite, we then need to explain the silence about it in *M* on the assumption that, if *M* represents Cyril's liturgy and catechesis, the rite would still be performed.

b. Was There a Rite of Blessing the Font in the Time of *C*?

A distinct blessing of the font is a frequent occurrence in early initiation rites. In the West, Hippolytus mentions praying over the water *(oretur primum super aquam)* before the candidates come to it.[15] Tertullian says, "Therefore, in consequence of that ancient original privilege, all waters, when God is invoked, acquire the sacred significance of conveying sanctity."[16] Cyprian indicates that the water should first be cleansed and sanctified by the priest.[17] Zeno of Verona speaks of the baptismal water as *viva spiritu sancto* when the candidates are about to be baptized.[18] Elsewhere he says the bitter water becomes sweet through the wood of the cross,[19] though he makes no references to a specific rite of blessing the font. Ambrose in Milan uses the cross imagery in a way that strongly suggests that the blessing of the font involved a dipping of a cross into the water.[20]

In the East, the *Euchologium* of Serapion has an epiclesis of the Word upon the waters,[21] the *Apostolic Constitutions* has an epiclesis in a prayer of thanksgiving,[22] and, for Theodore, an epiclesis over the water before immersion transforms it into "the womb of sacramental birth."[23] Chrysostom, however, has no discernible rite for blessing the font. But this is probably because in his

---

15. *AT* 21.1.

16. *De baptismo* 4; trans. Edward Charles Whitaker, *Documents of the Baptismal Liturgy*, 2d ed. (London: S.P.C.K., 1970), 7.

17. *Ep.* 70.1.　　　　　　　　　　　　　18. *Tract.* 1.23.

19. *Tract.* 1.61.8.

20. *DS* 1.15–18; 2.11–14, 23; 3.14. See Yarnold, *AIR*, 107 n. 30 concerning the use of the cross in this rite.

21. *Euchologium* 7 *Prayer for the Blessing of the Water:* "King and Lord of all things, and Artificer of the world, . . . look down now from heaven and behold these waters and fill them with Holy Spirit. Let thine ineffable Word come to be in them and transform their energy and cause them to be productive [by] being filled with thy grace. . . . And as thy only-begotten Word coming down upon the waters of the Jordan rendered them holy, so now also may he descend on these and make them holy and spiritual." Text in F. E. Brightman, "The Sacramentary of Serapion of Thmuis," *JTS* 1 (1900): 263. Trans. Whitaker, *Documents of the Baptismal Liturgy*, 83.

22. *AC* 7.43.

23. *BH* 3.9.

rite of immersion, the Spirit is understood as sanctifying both water and candidate.[24]

I noted above that the reference to an invocation over the water in *C* 3.3 suggested that a blessing of the font did exist in Jerusalem. The text of *C* 3.3 does not, however, necessarily point to a distinct rite for this blessing. The invocation mentioned here could have been integrated in a rite other than one for blessing the font, namely, the immersion rite (similar to Chrysostom's), which Cyril speaks of as follows a few sections later (*C* 3.12):

> For you go down into the water bearing sins; but the invocation of grace having sealed your soul, it is no longer possible for you to be swallowed up by the terrible dragon.

Is the invocation mentioned here the same as the one over the water already mentioned in *C* 3.3? To answer this question we must first decide precisely what is meant by this "invocation of grace." Since it is specifically tied to the sealing of the candidate in the font, its most obvious referent would be the baptismal formula recited when the candidate is immersed in the water. However, to call a baptismal formula, which in its most common form does not ask or invoke God to perform any action, an invocation seems strange. Before comparing this passage with *C* 3.3, then, we must first determine whether or not it is indeed a reference to the baptismal formula.

Other sources show some precedence for calling the baptismal formula an invocation. Irenaeus says of baptism, "Being lepers in sin we are cleansed from all our transgressions by the sacred water and the invocation of the Lord."[25] In his treatise on the Holy Spirit, Basil says that when Paul omits the names of the Father and the Spirit in speaking of "baptism in Christ" (Gal 3:27, Rom 6:3), this does not mean that the invocation of the names is to be unobserved.[26] Later he adds, "In three immersions and the same number of invocations, the mystery of baptism is accomplished."[27] In the *Apostolic Constitutions*, the bishop (or presbyter) is to baptize the candidates "calling and naming over them the solemn invocation of the Father and Son and Holy Spirit."[28] In the older and simpler version of this rite from the *Didascalia*, the instruction says, "let a man pronounce over them the invocation of the di-

---

24. See *Stav.* 2.10, 25, 26.

25. *Fragment 33*, in *Libros quinque adversus haereses*, ed. W. Wigan Harvey, 2 vols. (repr. Ridgewood, N. J.: Gregg Press, 1965).

26. *De Spiritu Sancto* 28 (3.23b).   27. Ibid., 35 (3.29d).

28. *AC* 3.16.

vine names in the water."[29] Chrysostom says that his baptismal formula ("N. is baptized in the name of the Father and of the Son and of the Holy Spirit") is so worded to show that it is not the bishop who baptizes but the one whose name is invoked.[30] Dionysius describes the priest as "calling upon the threefold substance of the divine beatitude at the three immersions and emersions of him that is being perfected."[31] These examples show that even the simple baptismal formula "I baptize (or, N. is baptized) in the name of the Father, etc." could be called an epiclesis even though God is not called upon to act in a specified way. There is reason enough, therefore, to conclude that the "invocation of grace" mentioned in C 3.12 is a reference to Cyril's immersion formula, seeing that he is speaking of what happens to the candidate in the font.

We can now consider whether the earlier invocation in C 3.3 is a reference to the invocation at immersion (C 3.12) or to a separate rite of blessing the font. In C 3.3, Cyril is not outlining a sequence of rites, and so the invocation mentioned there need not be part of a separate rite. It could conceivably refer to the baptismal formula, if, as with Chrysostom, Cyril understood the formula as having a double effect where the action of the Spirit on the water and on the candidate is ritualized at the immersion. However, in C 3.3, the water specifically receives the invocation of the three names, whereas in C 3.12 the candidate is the recipient of the invocation for the purposes of sealing. Therefore it seems most probable that he is referring to two different invocations in these passages, and the earlier one represents a blessing of the font.

Another point in favor of this option is the reverse order of the divine names in the epiclesis of C 3.3. With very few exceptions (such as with Serapion) if one person of the Trinity is singled out for the sanctification of the water, it is usually the Holy Spirit.[32] This is probably why the Spirit is mentioned first in the epiclesis over the water in C 3.3. The reverse order of names

---

29. *Didascalia* 16. This text is the source for the passage from *AC* 3.16 and corresponds very closely to it; the main difference is in the specifying of the three names. The Syriac for invocation is *qrāytā*, which is the common term used elsewhere for *epiclesis*. The passage is missing from the Verona Latin fragments of this text.

30. *PK* 3.3.42.

31. *On the Ecclesiastical Hierarchy* 2.2.7 (PG 3.396D); see also Gregory of Nyssa, *Catechetical Oration* 33, 35; Isidore of Pelusium, *Epistularum libri quinque* 1.109 (PG 79.256B).

32. Irenaeus may also have the second Person in mind in *Adversus Haereses* 5.2.3: "When, therefore, the mingled cup and the prepared bread receive the Word of God (ἐπιδέχεται τὸν λόγον τοῦ Θεοῦ) and the Eucharist becomes the blood and the body of Christ. . . ."

is not unique to Cyril; it is also found in Basil's conferences on baptism.[33] But for Basil the context is not a rite involving an epiclesis. Rather, he has in mind the logical order of what is experienced by the candidates in the entire rite of initiation: first they are born from above in the Spirit (Jn 3:3); they are thus made worthy to put on Christ (Gal 3:27); and having put on Christ, they are then able to become children of God the Father (Jn 1:12).[34] It would be very surprising if Cyril were thinking of the baptismal formula (where the names are invariably in the usual order) when he gives them in the reverse order. For the present purposes it is sufficient to conclude that a rite for blessing the font existed in 351 in Jerusalem.

c. The Absence of Catechesis on the Rite of Blessing the Font in M

Since there was a rite for blessing the font c. 351, why is there no mention of it in *M*? Silence about an existing rite could result if it did not directly involve the candidates. A careful look at the movement of the candidates in the rites described by *M* yields no place where a blessing rite could occur in their sight. They begin in a vestibule of the baptistery (*M* 1.11) and then move to an inner room for the stripping and anointing (*M* 2.1). For propriety's sake, the stripping and anointing were probably in rooms where the men and women could be separated.[35] At this point they are still not at the font, for after the anointing they are "led by the hand to the sacred pool of holy baptism" (*M* 2.4). Upon arrival at the font, each person was questioned and then baptized—they perhaps had been individually led to the font out of the sight of the others. At any rate, it would be ritually awkward for a rite of blessing to take place with the candidate(s) standing naked and covered in oil ready for immersion. To accommodate the practical advantage of moving quickly from stripping to immersion to clothing again, the font could have already received a blessing before the candidates arrived. While this arrangement of the rite is conceivable, how probable is it?

Evidence from some other early rites shows that the practice of blessing the font ahead of time was normal enough. If we piece together the progres-

33. *De Baptismo* 1.2.20–23 (1560C–1565B); 1.2.27 (1572A–C), 1.3.1 (1573B).

34. A similar idea is found in his treatise *De Spiritu Sancto* 37 (3.31b). Basil is commenting on 1 Cor 12:4–6 where Paul mentions the persons of the Trinity in reverse order. He cautions against taking this as an absolute statement regarding the persons; rather, Paul is inspired by the human analogy whereby when a gift is given one first encounters the bearer of the gift (the Holy Spirit), then one thinks of the gift that is borne (the Son), and finally one thinks of the source and cause of the gift (the Father).

35. Even with the rites of exorcism the men and the women were separated (see *P* 14).

sion of Ambrose's ceremony as he outlines it in the *De sacramentis,* we find first in 1.9 that he describes the candidates approaching the font as follows: "you drew nearer, you saw the font itself, and you saw the bishop presiding over it." After some instruction relating to water and baptism, he returns to the blessing of the font (1.18). He says at that point, though, that:

when the bishop enters he first performs the exorcism on the creature that is the water and then utters invocation and prayer that the water may be sanctified.

This seems to take place before the arrival of the candidates, since in 1.9 he noted that the bishop is already presiding when they enter. This sequence of events where the candidates approach and enter the font without any intervening blessing is further suggested in 2.16 when Ambrose resumes his description of the actual progression of the rites:

You came to the font, you went down into it, you turned towards the high priest, you saw, there at the font, the levites and the priest.

In 2.20, when after some commentary he returns again to the ritual, the next act is the confession of faith followed by immersion. Once the candidates enter there is no opportunity in the sequence of rituals for a blessing over the water. Thus we can surmise, at least with Ambrose, that since the blessing of the font probably took place before their entrance, the candidates did not witness it.[36]

In the *Apostolic Tradition,* the blessing over the water takes place at "the hour when the cock crows" on the day of baptism (21.1). This is a preparatory rite before the candidates come to the water (21.2) and even before the renunciation of Satan and the prebaptismal anointing (21.6–10).

In Theodore's rite also, the candidates do not seem to witness the blessing of the water. His commentary begins in *Homily* 2 and includes the renunciation of Satan, the first anointing, and the reception of the linen stole. *Homily* 3 continues with the stripping and second anointing, immersion, reception of the white garment, and the postbaptismal anointing. Each homily consists of a brief account of each rite just as the candidates experienced it, including a description of all the ritual gestures and words they and the ministers used, and ends with a lengthy commentary. When he comes to the rite of immer-

---

36. Gordon Jeanes makes this point in slightly less detail in *The Day Has Come!* 177–78. He notes that the later Ambrosian Rite (See *Manuale Ambrosianum,* ed. Marcus Magistretti [Milan: Ulricum Hoepli, 1905], 2:205–7) even more clearly shows that the bishop precedes the others into the baptistery in order to bless the font. He also concludes that Zeno probably had the same arrangement.

sion, however, he says, "You then descend into the water that has been sanctified by the blessing of the bishop."[37] At this point the water has been sanctified already. According to Sebastian Brock, this accords with the normal structure of the rite in the Syrian tradition where the blessing of the water took place after the first anointing but before the second.[38] Theodore continues with a theological account of the blessing of the water (repeated at *BH* 3.10) but does not mention when the rite took place except to say that it was sometime beforehand:

You are not baptized only with ordinary water, but with the water of the second birth, which cannot become so except through the coming of the Holy Spirit (on it). For this it is necessary that the priest should have beforehand *(mqaddem)* made use of clear words . . . and asked God that the grace of the Holy Spirit might come on the water and impart to it the power both of conceiving that awe-inspiring child and becoming a womb to the sacramental birth.[39]

With all the attention Theodore gives elsewhere to movement, gestures, materials used, and words, it is surprising that he says nothing of this rite unless, of course, the candidates did not see it or at least were not personally involved in it.

One possible scenario for Theodore's ceremony is suggested by a description of the anointing in *BH* 3.8. The priest begins the anointing before baptism (an anointing of the whole body), but the deacons complete it.[40] While this anointing was being completed, the priest would be able to perform the blessing of the font. A possible reason for this would be to assure an uninterrupted movement from undressing to anointing to immersion. In this case, the blessing of the font would not take place precisely before the second anointing but during it.

The practice of preparing the font during the anointing is explicitly described by Dionysius. The bishop begins the prebaptismal anointing of the candidate, but the priests finish the anointing of the whole body,

---

37. *BH* 3.9, trans. *Mingana*, 54–55.

38. See Sebastian Brock, "Studies in the Early History of the Syrian Orthodox Baptismal Liturgy," *JTS*, n.s., 23 (1972): 22–23.

39. *BH* 3.9, trans. *Mingana*, 54–55.

40. "While you are receiving this anointing, the one who has been found worthy of the honour of priesthood begins and says: 'So-and-so is anointed in the name of the Father, and of the Son, and of the Holy Spirit.' And then the persons appointed for this service anoint all your body" (trans. *Mingana*, 54). This division of labor is found as early as the *Didascalia* (see ch. 16) and in many subsequent rites in the Syrian tradition; see S. Brock, "Studies in the Early History of the Syrian Orthodox Baptismal Liturgy," 40.

while he advances to the mother of filial adoption, and when he has purified the water within it by the holy invocations, . . . he orders the man to be brought forward;
and the priests conduct him near to the water and lead him by the hand to the hand
of the bishop.[41]

While the anointing is being completed, the font is blessed. Again, the only
reason for this arrangement of the rite seems to be to enhance the movement of the candidates from the anointing through the immersion. According to Brock, however, this anointing described by Dionysius technically oc-
cupies the same position as Theodore's first anointing; strictly speaking,
Dionysius does not have an anointing corresponding to Theodore's second
anointing. But Brock makes this judgment in light of the tradition as it finally became established: four anointings—one at the inscription, one on either
side of the blessing of the font, and one after baptism. Among these early
rites, the two anointings on either side of the blessing of the font show great
variety and some sharing of form and meaning.[42] Since the preimmersion
anointing for Dionysius is the same in form as Theodore's (anointing of the
whole body with the help of assistants) and as such accommodates the blessing of the font during the anointing, it is very possible that Theodore also
used this opportunity for his blessing of the font.

Although there are examples of rites where candidates do witness the
blessing of the font (for example, *Apostolic Constitutions* 7.43, the liturgy of
James of Edessa,[43] and the Armenian Rite[44]), nevertheless, the previous discussion shows that, given that a rite for blessing the font was used in
Jerusalem in the time of *C* (c. 351) and continued through the time of *M*, it
could be considered normal practice if the rite was not witnessed by the candidates. That the newly baptized were not present at the blessing could sufficiently explain the lack of any commentary on the rite. The catechesis of *M*
is already very terse compared to the contemporary catecheses of Ambrose,
Theodore, and Chrysostom and focuses on the rites as they were *experienced*
by the newly baptized—appealing to the experience of the candidates was an
expressed guiding principle of the mystagogue.

41. *On the Ecclesiastical Hierarchy* 2.2.7 (PG 3.396D).

42. See Brock, "Studies in the Early History of the Syrian Orthodox Baptismal Liturgy,"
24–40, especially 31 and 37.

43. In *Ritus Orientalium Coptorum, Synorum et Armenorum,* ed. Heinrich Denzinger, 2 vols. in
1 (Graz: Akademische Druck- u. Verlagsanstalt, 1961), 1:279–80. In contrast to the above examples, James notes that after being anointed, the candidates stand naked while the blessing of the
font takes place.

44. *Rituale Armenorum,* 94–95.

We can conclude that the silence in M regarding a rite for blessing the font, which might otherwise be construed as a significant discrepancy with the evidence of such a rite in C, does not in fact indicate that such a rite was not performed. We have every reason to believe that such a rite existed in the time of M, but since the structure of the baptismal ceremony was such that the font would need to be prepared beforehand, the candidates did not witness the blessing rite. Further, since the mystagogue keeps himself tightly bound to the essentials of what the candidates experienced, he opts to omit direct reference to the blessing of the font in his catechesis.

d. The Sanctification of the Water in C and M

Even though M does not specifically mention a blessing of the font, the mystagogue does commment on the nature of the water. Certain references to the baptismal water in M and relevant passages in C give us some idea of the theology and possible form of the blessing rite in the Jerusalem church. At the same time, a comparison of this material from C and M reveals some similarities of thought.

In M 3.1, we find a passage that seems to associate Christ with the sanctification of the water:

Christ bathed in the river Jordan, and having invested the waters with his incarnate divinity, he emerged from them and the Holy Spirit visited him.

This is only a passing comment made before a treatment of Christ's anointing by the Spirit rather than catechesis on the blessing of the font. However, since the mystagogue nonetheless mentions Christ in the Jordan, which is not pertinent to the catechesis on the chrism, he shows that the sanctification of the waters by the incarnate Son is a significant image for him.

This passage is the only place in M where any mention is made of a divine action with regard to the water. Other allusions to the water are as follows: in M 1.3, the font, "the waters of salvation," is where the demons perish just as Pharaoh did of old; in M 1.10, the font is the place where death is defeated; and in M 2.4, the water of the font is a symbol of both a tomb and a womb.

In all of these passages, the symbolic nature of the water is associated more with Christ, the one who conquers death in the tomb, than with the Spirit. For the most part, focused attention to the Spirit is reserved for the catechesis on the chrism in M 3. Additionally, the Spirit is only involved in the epicleses (and we can safely assume that the Spirit no doubt played a part in the blessing of the font no matter what precise form it took). The lack of any specific mention of the Spirit with reference to the water could be explained by the different emphases placed on the roles of the Spirit and Christ in the epicleses. The Spirit is generally understood as the agent who sanctifies, but the resulting significance of what is sanctified—namely, blessed oil, water, or chrism, for example—is understood in terms of the incarnate Son: the oil is the richness of Christ, the true olive tree (M 2.3); the water is the place where Christ defeats death (M 1.3, 10); the font is the tomb wherein one is united with Christ (M 2.4); the chrism is Christ's gift of the Spirit that instills divinity (M 3.3); and the bread and the wine are Christ's body and blood.

The mystagogue's use of the image in M 3.1 of Christ "investing the waters of the Jordan with his divinity" should not be understood as suggesting that Christ is the sanctifying agent. It is rather an example of the mystagogue's sacramental typology, the tying of a sacramental mystery to an event in Christ's life, and not a strict reference to the rite for blessing the water. The Spirit no doubt figured significantly in an epiclesis over the font, but the symbolic meaning of the water, once sanctified, is to be understood in reference to Christ and not the Spirit. This association of Christ with the water highlights the general christocentric nature of the sacramental theology of M—the initiation rites are a participation in the mysteries of Christ the incarnate Son (the Last Supper, his death, and his resurrection).

M's use of this image of Christ sanctifying the font could be, according to Quasten, an indication of a "Logos-epiclesis" theology such as is found in Serapion. However, in his estimation, this theology is more characteristic of the earlier part of the fourth century, whereas a "Spirit-epiclesis" theology was much more common after the Council of 381 greatly enhanced the theology of the Holy Spirit (as found, for example, in the *Apostolic Constitutions* and Theodore).[45] Quasten was working, however, under the assumption that M was delivered in the time of C. With the more probable date of the 380s for M, the fact that the image is still used suggests that it is particularly dear to the author of M and could be regarded as a distinguishing feature.

Significantly, we also find in C that Christ's association with water, rather than the Spirit's, is the richer and more useful catechetical idea for conveying the significance of what happens in the font. Cyril does describe the font as the place where the Spirit acts, sealing souls (C 3.3, 4, 12; C 16.24; C 17.14, 35–36), but he interprets the meaning of the font symbolically with christo-

---

45. Johannes Quasten, "The Blessing of the Baptismal Font in the Syrian Rite in the Fourth Century," *TS* 7 (1946): 308–13.

logical ideas (including in one case the sanctifying of the water). In C 3.11, the model of Jesus' baptism in the Jordan is used to show how water, once the abode of death, has been rendered powerless by Jesus' baptism, a symbol of his own death and resurrection:[46]

Jesus sanctified baptism when he himself was baptized. . . . The dragon, according to Job, was in the water, he who "received the Jordan in his maw" (Job 40:23). When, therefore, it was necessary to "crush the heads of the dragon" (Ps 74:14), descending into the water, he [Christ] bound the strong, that we might receive the "power to tread upon serpents and scorpions" (Lk 10:19). . . . Baptism draws death's sting.

Again, in C 12.15:

Christ came that he might be baptized and might sanctify baptism; he came that he might work wonders, walking upon the waters of the sea. Therefore, since before his coming in the flesh, "the sea beheld and fled; Jordan turned back" (Ps 114:3), the Lord assumed his body, that the sea might endure the sight, and Jordan receive him without fear. . . . But the devil would not have dared to approach, if he had known him. . . . His body, therefore, was made a bait to death, that the dragon, when hoping to devour it, might disgorge those also whom he had already devoured. For "death prevailed and devoured" (Is 25:8 LXX).

The theme is taken up again in C 14 on the resurrection. Sections 17–20 treat of Jonah as a type of Christ:

Jonah was cast into the belly of a great fish, but Christ of his own will descended to the abode of the invisible fish of death. He went down of his own will to make death disgorge those it had swallowed up. (C 14.17)

The association of Christ and water is also found in P 15 when Cyril wishes that his hearers might "enjoy the fragrant waters which contain Christ."

In summary, we find in these passages a strikingly common trait of linking Christ rather than the Spirit with the sanctification of the water.

5. Further Note on the Theology of the Epicleses

The above section touched on the importance in both C and M of associating Christ with the epicleses but mainly focused on the blessing of the font. We now need to examine the other three epicleses in M to see if they also share the same characteristic.

It is not surprising that in the mystagogy on the eucharistic epiclesis Christ would be of central importance in the matter of the sanctified bread

46. The following translations are by McCauley, WCJ, 1:115, 235–36; 2:43.

and wine transformed into his body and blood; hence, the christological aspect of this epiclesis should not be regarded as in any way distinctive. The two other two epicleses to consider are those over the chrism, or *myron,* and the oil of exorcism.

In the mystagogy on the epiclesis over the *myron* (M 3.3), a peculiar reference to Christ deserves special attention:

> Be sure not to regard the *myron* merely as ointment; for just as the bread of the Eucharist after the epiclesis of the Holy Spirit is no longer ordinary bread, but the body of Christ, so also this holy *myron,* after the invocation is no longer ordinary, or so to speak, common, but Christ's gracious gift and productive of the divine presence of the Holy Spirit.

Again, as in M 1.7, the author uses the eucharistic epiclesis as a model, and we can assume that "epiclesis of the Holy Spirit" really means that God is asked to impart the Spirit to sanctify the *myron.* But the parallel extends to comparing the transformed bread and wine to the *myron,* and again attention is drawn to a sacramental presence of Christ. How the difficult last clause is read, though, is important for understanding the whole paragraph. There are differing views on how one ought to understand the term *parousia* (presence) and the meaning of "Christ's gracious gift."

The genitive form of *parousia* has near unanimous manuscript attestation—the sense here is that something *of* the divine presence is brought about. However, there are two important variant readings with the dative (*Ottobonianus 446* has the dative form and *Ottobonianus 220* has a scribal correction to the dative). This form suggests an instrumental sense—it is *by* the presence or advent of the Spirit that something happens. The options for the different readings are illustrated in the following translations:

with the dative:

the *myron* is "Christ's gift of grace, and, by the advent of the Holy Ghost, is made fit to impart His Divine Nature [that is, Christ's]." (Gifford)

the *myron* is "le don du Christ, devenu par la présence de l'Esprit-Saint efficace de sa [that is, Spirit's] divinité." (Piédagnel)

the *myron* is "the gift of Christ, and by the presence of His [Christ's] Godhead, it causes in us the Holy Ghost." (R. W. Church, in F. L. Cross's edition)

with the genitive:

the *myron* "becomes the gracious gift of Christ and the Holy Spirit, producing the advent [presence?] of His deity." (Stephenson)

Stephenson argues against the first three options, which treat divinity as the object of "impart," "*devenu efficace*," "cause," (ἐνεργητικὸν γινόμενον). He says, rather, that the sacramental action brings about the advent of the divinity. Even though the renderings with the dative imply that what is meant is the producing of the divine in the anointed, that is, making the divine present (the same sense conveyed by the genitive), it still leaves the Greek awkward (divinity the object of producing) and goes against the better attested reading. Stephenson's version rightly opts for the genitive, but he does not sufficiently clarify whose divinity is being made present. The other three options try to answer this question by specifying either Christ or the Holy Spirit, but we need to ask which one best represents *M's* intention.

If we look at the previous sections (*M* 3.1–2), we can discover more of what the author understands to be happening in this rite. In *M* 3.1, he draws attention to Christ at the Jordan and makes the analogy that just as Christ was anointed by the Holy Spirit upon coming out of the water, so were the newly baptized when they emerged from the font. This typological association with Christ emphasizes that what happened to Christ happens to those who are baptized.

In *M* 3.2 he elaborates further:

Just as Christ was truly crucified, buried, and raised again, and you were deemed worthy to be crucified, buried, and raised with him in likeness, so it was with the anointing. Christ was anointed with the spiritual oil of gladness, that is, the Holy Spirit, called the oil of gladness because he is the author of spiritual joy. And you have been anointed with *myron* having become fellows and sharers of Christ.

The anointing with *myron*, symbolizing the descent of the Holy Spirit, is granted the candidate in consequence of having already become a sharer of Christ in baptism. It would be redundant to say then that the *myron* also results in a share in the divinity of Christ; ritually and typologically the anointing refers to a share in the divinity of the Spirit—chrismation is the rite for the conferring of the Spirit. Hence, the translations noted above by Piédagnel and Church rightly have the divinity of the Spirit as what is conferred with the *myron*.

Another reason to opt for the genitive form of *parousia* (of the presence) is suggested by the mystagogue's calling the *myron* (the conferring of the Spirit) Christ's gift. The most logical meaning of "Christ's gracious gift," though only apparent from the larger context of sections 1–3, is that the Spirit is the gift of Christ in the Johannine sense of the Paraclete. In other words, the anointing with the *myron* symbolizes the bestowing of Christ's promised gift of the Paraclete, and it brings about, or "produces," the divine presence of the Holy Spirit in the anointed. Thus the passage in question can be rendered: the *myron* is "Christ's gracious gift and productive of the divine presence of the Holy Spirit."

With this interpretation, the mystagogue is clearly interested in closely associating Christ with what happens in the epiclesis over the *myron* and does so in a way that fits with his general interest in tying all of the sacramental mysteries to some aspect of Christ's ministry.

Finally, let us consider the epiclesis over the oil of exorcism:

Just as the breath of the saints and the invocation of God's name burn like a fierce flame and drive out devils, so also this exorcised oil receives such power by the invocation of God and by prayer as not only to cleanse every trace of sin with fire but also to banish the invisible powers of the evil one. (*M* 2.3)

We do not know what formula was used either with the exorcism or the epiclesis over the oil. But the fact that the oil receives power shows that the invocation is understood in a way similar to the other epicleses over the bread and wine and over the *myron;* in some way the nature of the oil is changed. Although the short passage on the epiclesis itself has no immediate association with Christ, the whole of *M* 2.3 makes it clear that the blessed oil is to be understood in christological terms. The olive oil symbolizes partaking of the good olive tree, Christ; the anointed are wild shoots grafted onto the good tree (Rom 11:17–24). Its health-inducing nature symbolizes the fatness, or "richness of Christ," and purges all evil. Later, I will note how this anointing, as a "token" against evil powers (*M* 2.3), recalls the lamb's blood on the doors of the Hebrews' homes to ward off the destroyer (*M* 1.2–3) and as such probably involved a marking with the sign of the cross. The power the oil receives by virtue of the invocation is not described as the power of the Spirit but, as with the other epicleses, a power that has its meaning and source in Christ.

6. Summary and Conclusions

An examination of the basic forms of the epicleses in *C* and *M* showed no evident differences either in the epicleses for exorcisms or those for sanctifying the elements of bread, wine, and oil. More significantly, a study of specific examples revealed marked similarities in expression: (a) the explanation of one epiclesis by comparing it to another, (b) an emphasis on the real change from ordinary to sanctified elements as a result of an epiclesis, (c) the parallel use of key terms for "mere" and "do not regard," and (d) the comparison of Christian practice with pagan practice based on the Pauline text of I Cor 10:20–21. An analysis of various texts pertinent to the blessing of the water attempted to clarify the situation of this rite in Jerusalem and concluded that indeed a blessing of the water in the rites of *M* existed, but the mystagogy on this rite was passed over because the candidates either did not witness the rite or were not involved in it. A further examination of texts concerning the sanctification of the water and the epicleses over the oil of exorcism and the *myron* revealed a common preference in *C* and *M* for explaining these symbols by means of christological images rather than by reference to the Spirit. As we have have already noted, Cyril's catecheses are characterized by a strong preference for christological themes.

In that this survey of the epicleses in *C* and *M* revealed no significant differences that are not explained by differences in circumstance, the number and nature of the similarities and correspondences can be counted as a strong indication of common authorship.

CHAPTER 4

꧁ꕤ꧂

The Initiation Rites II
The Rites of Anointing and the Conferring of the Holy Spirit

A. Introduction

In the second mystagogic sermon, the author covers the rites of stripping, the prebaptismal anointing, and immersion; in the third sermon, he explains the postbaptismal anointing, or chrismation. As far as the rites are concerned, we only need to address the anointings at this time. How the mystagogy on the immersion rite compares with *C* will be addressed later, in the section on theology.

The place and significance of the two rites of anointing found in *M* need some special attention, since they exhibit notable differences from those found in *C*. The first anointing is of the whole body (including, possibly, an anointing of the forehead) with exorcised oil. It occurs before immersion and serves to symbolize both participation in Christ and protection against evil. The second anointing is administered with chrism *(myron)* to the forehead, ears, nostrils, and chest after immersion. Above all, this second anointing is the rite of reception of the Holy Spirit (*M* 3.1). In *M* 4.7, on the Eucharist, the mystagogue refers back to this second anointing in passing as a "seal" or "sign" *(sphragis);* this term is not used in the mystagogy on either of the anointing rites themselves (*M* 2 and 3).

C remains silent with regard to any anointing rite(s). This silence is understandable since instruction concerning the rites is reserved primarily for the mystagogy, but at the same time we do find references to the gift of the Holy Spirit and "sealing" in association with the immersion rite. As will be seen, Cyril also uses the term *sphragis* very frequently and broadly in *C* to describe some aspects of the activity of the Holy Spirit on the baptized other than the giving of the Spirit itself. Further, in *C* 16.26, he implies that the Holy Spirit is conferred in a rite of laying on of hands while no such rite appears in *M*. Another contrast is in the scriptural models for the rites. In *C* 3, the prevailing model for baptism is Christ at the Jordan. In *M* 3, however, the Jordan model (where Jesus is "anointed" by the Spirit) is typologically linked to the rite of chrismation, and in *M* 2, the mystagogy on baptism relies heavily on the model of Jesus' death and resurrection.

Since I have already noted that the date of *M* is most probably some thirty years or so after *C,* we can expect some changes in the rites as well as development in the thinking of a single author (especially since Jerusalem was a center of liturgical influence at this time). Therefore the ritual differences between *C* and *M* (the number and place of anointings and the laying on of hands) need not suggest different authors but rather changes resulting from liturgical development over a period of time. To assess these differences, we need to examine the changes in the Jerusalem rites exhibited in *C* and *M* in light of the ritual developments in the wider context of the Syrian tradition to see if they reflect the general trend of the time.[1] The other differences (the use and meaning of the term "seal," the scriptural models for baptism, the conferring of the Spirit) indicate more the theological and catechetical thinking of the teacher. These will be examined to see how well they correlate with the development of the rites and whether they best represent the mature thinking of a single author, namely, Cyril, or of two different ones.

It should be noted at the outset that we can speak of a "Syrian tradition" in this geographical area in only a rough way since the region has a history of racial, cultural, and linguistic differences. Gregory Dix describes the situation thus:

1. There are many studies showing that the place and significance of the anointing rites in the Syrian tradition, in contrast to the West, had gone through considerable development by the end of the fourth century: E. C. Ratcliff, "The Old Syrian Baptismal Tradition and Its Resettlement under the Influence of Jerusalem in the 4th Century," in *Liturgical Studies,* ed. A. H. Couratin and D. H. Tripp (London: S.P.C.K., 1976), 135–54; Gabriele Winkler, *Das armenische Initiationsrituale. Entwicklungsgeschichtliche und liturgievergleichende Untersuchung der Quellen des 3. bis 10. Jahrhunderts,* OCA 217 (Rome: Pontificium Institutum Studiorum Orientalium, 1982); eadem, "The Original Meaning of the Prebaptismal Anointing and Its Implications," *Worship* 52 (1978): 24–45; Sebastian Brock, *The Holy Spirit in the Syrian Baptismal Tradition,* The Syrian Churches Series, no. 9 (Bronx, N.Y.: John XXIII Center, Fordham University, 1979), especially 24–40; idem, "The Transition to a Postbaptismal Anointing in the Antiochene Rite," in *The Sacrifice of Praise,* ed. Bryan D. Spinks, Bibliotheca "Ephemerides Liturgicae," Subsidia, no. 19 (Rome: C.L.V.—Edizioni liturgiche, 1981), 215–25; idem, "Studies in the Early History of the Syrian Orthodox Baptismal Liturgy," *JTS,* n.s. 23 (1972): 16–64.

In short, Syria was an older underlying patchwork of races, languages, cultures and traditions, with a recent and different patchwork of hellenism and the surviving native cultures superimposed upon it. The underlying patchwork is *local,* but the only line of division one can draw between hellenism and the oriental traditions is purely *cultural.*[2]

While some regions in East and West Syria were completely hellenized, other areas remained strongly semitic. In the more thorough studies of the Syrian rites,[3] however, a distinction between East and West is generally made, at least in the later stages of development: the hellenizing influence had more effect near the West coast (Antioch, for example) than in the inner regions, where some early practices still survive today. It would be quite difficult, therefore, to try to isolate a single line of liturgical tradition in Syria. It is sufficient for the present purpose, however, simply to note the general trend of changes in Syrian rites in the third and fourth centuries without trying to establish direct links or influences of one local practice on another.

B. The Development of the Anointing Rite(s) in the Syrian Tradition

In this brief survey, I will outline the basic changes with regard to the anointing rites in the Syrian tradition:[4] the number of anointings, where they are placed in the whole of the initiation rite, and their symbolic meaning. After a note on terminology, we will look at the changes in the outward form of the rites and then consider the most probable influences that brought about these changes.

1. A Note on Terminology

Some clarification in terminology is in order before continuing.[5] In the earliest Syriac sources, the prebaptismal anointing invariably uses "olive oil" *(mešḥā,* Greek: *elaion)* and not *myron. Myron* is normally the term for the ointment used in the postbaptismal anointing, which was a later fourth-century

---

2. Dix, *The Shape of the Liturgy,* 174.
3. See, for example, the studies of Brock and Winkler.
4. The use of basic material and arguments for this section was guided by Winkler's *Das armenische Initiationsrituale* and "The Original Meaning of the Prebaptismal Anointing." But see also the important recent survey by Bradshaw, *The Search for the Origins of Christian Worship,* in which he cautions against seeking too strictly linear developments in liturgical practices—there may well have been a variety of parallel traditions from the earliest of times.
5. See Brock, "Studies in the Early History of the Syrian Orthodox Baptismal Liturgy," 24–40.

introduction, and when it does occur, the Syriac would use *myron*, a translit-eration of the Greek.[6]

Further, there are distinct terms for the different ritual acts. The single prebaptismal anointing of the head was regularly called "sign" or "mark" *(rušmā)*; the regular term for the anointing of the whole body was "anoint-ing" *(mšḥ)*; and the postbaptismal anointing (when it was eventually intro-duced) was normally referred to as a "seal" *(ḥatmā)*, and described some-times as an "imprinting" *(ṭbʿ)*. The Syriac translation of Theodore's rite seems to be an exception in that it shows a postbaptismal signing *(ršm)* with oil *(mešḥā)* rather than a sealing with *myron*.[7] Some confusion arises from the fact that the single Greek term *sphragis* is the word used for both "sign" and "seal," whereas the Syriac uses quite distinct terms respectively, *rušmā* and *ḥatmā*. In the translation of texts that exist in both Greek and Syriac (such as the *Acts of Thomas*, originally written in Syriac) *sphragis* is sometimes mis-takenly translated "seal" (leading one to think that the original Syriac was *ḥatmā*).[8] But in fact, the *Acts of Thomas* never uses "seal" *(ḥatmā)* for any rites of anointing, but rather "sign" or "mark" *(rušmā)*. At this early stage, *ḥatmā* normally was used only in a general sense for the whole rite of baptism.[9] The later distinction, however, between "sign" *(rušmā)* for the prebaptismal marking and "seal" *(ḥatmā)* for the postbaptismal sealing is by no means ab-solute; we can find a number of exceptions.[10]

2. Changes in the Form of the Anointing Rite(s)

a. The Early Forms

The principal sources for our knowledge of the baptismal rite in the Syri-an tradition are as follows: from the third century, the *Acts of Thomas* and the *Didascalia;* from the fourth century, the *History of John the Son of Zebedee,* the writings of Aphraates and Ephrem, *The Apostolic Constitutions,* the catecheses of Theodore of Mopsuestia, John Chrysostom, and *M;* two Armenian texts

6. A notable exception is in Chrysostom's rite (*Stav.* 2.22) where *myron* is used for the pre-baptismal anointing.

7. *BH* 3.27. The fact that the Syriac uses *mešḥā* and not *myron* (in transliteration) suggests that Theodore did not use *myron* in his rite. However, without the original Greek, we cannot be certain; it may not yet have been common practice to distinguish between the two oils when translating.

8. Compare, for example, *Acts of Thomas*, trans. A. F. J. Klijn, Novum Testamentum, vol. 5 (Leiden: Brill, 1962), 90, with Whitaker, *Documents of the Baptismal Liturgy*, 14. See also Winkler, "The Original Meaning of the Prebaptismal Anointing," 27 n. 27.

9. See, for example, the *Didascalia* chap. 3.6; 9; 10; 16.

10. See Brock, *The Holy Spirit in the Syrian Baptismal Tradition*, 107.

from the fifth century, the *Teaching of St. Gregory* (Gregory the Illuminator) and the *Agathangeli Historia;* and finally, the Armenian rite.[11] In reconstructing the history of these rites, the earliest forms of the rites are not always represented by the earliest documents, hence, we will not necessarily be referring to these documents in chronological order.

With the exceptions of *M,* the *Apostolic Constitutions,* and probably Theodore, none of the sources before the fifth century refers to a postbaptismal anointing. The earliest texts indicate a single prebaptismal anointing with olive oil, which is poured on the head. The rite recalled the anointing of priests and kings in the Old Testament and the ritualized entry into the messianic kingship of Christ; it also had associations with the coming of the Spirit. The Armenian baptismal *ordo* illustrates the theme of priest and king in the following prayer:

> Blessed art thou, O Lord our God, who hast chosen thee a people, unto priesthood and kingship, for a holy race and for a chosen people. As of old thou didst anoint priests and kings and prophets with such all-holy oil. . . .[12]

The *Teaching of St. Gregory* expresses the connections from the Old Testament to the messianic anointing of Jesus through to the present rites:

> The horn of the oil [the Old Testament anointing] was the type of the anointing of Christ. . . . Thence also Aaron was anointed to the priesthood of the Lord . . . to anoint according to the same type (no. 432). . . . The mystery was preserved in the seed of Abraham . . . until John, priest, prophet and baptist, . . . and he gave the priesthood, the anointing, the prophecy, and the kingship to our Lord Jesus Christ (no. 433), . . . and Christ gave them to the apostles, and the apostles to the children of the church (no. 469).[13]

This anointing, and not the immersion, was the principal rite of the initiation ceremony.

The close association of the Spirit with the messianic anointing has its

---

11. The text of the Armenian rite is in the *Rituale Armenorum.* The oldest manuscripts of this work that are relevant to the Armenian rite were reedited and translated into German by Winkler in *Das armenische Initiationsrituale.* Although this work represents many layers, Winkler has demonstrated that many parts of the rite are comparable to the Syrian sources of the third to the fifth centuries.

12. *Rituale Armenorum,* 93.

13. Translation from R. W. Thomson, *The Teaching of St. Gregory: An Early Armenian Catechism. Translation and Commentary,* Harvard Armenian Texts and Studies, no. 3 (Cambridge, Mass.: Harvard University Press, 1970). See also: *Acts of Thomas* 27, 132; *Didascalia* 16 (the messianic theme is also in *Apostolic Constitutions* 3.16, which is based on the *Didascalia*); Ephrem, *Hymns on Faith* 82.10, *Hymns on Virginity* 7.6.

source in the Spirit's activity in the anointing of the priests and kings of old (see Ex 40:12–13; 1 Sm 9:15; 10:1, 6, 10; 16:1–13) and the descent upon and "anointing" of Jesus at his baptism (cf. Acts 10:38, Lk 4:18). These themes are illustrated in the two following texts from the *Didascalia,* one concerning the bishop and the other an instruction on the rite itself. They indicate that the prebaptismal anointing was initiated by a laying on of hands:

[It is] the bishop through whom the Lord gave you the Holy Spirit, and through whom you have learned the word and have known God, and through whom you have been known of God, and through whom you were sealed *(ḥatmā),* and through whom you became sons of the light, and through whom the Lord in Baptism, by the laying on of the hand of the bishop, bore witness to each one of you and caused his holy voice to be heard that said, "Thou art my son: this day I have begotten thee." (ch. 9)[14]

With the laying on of the hand anoint the head only. As of old time the priests and kings of Israel were anointed, so in like manner, anoint the head of those who receive baptism, whether of men or of women. (ch. 16)[15]

Ephrem draws an association between the oil itself and the Holy Spirit:

Oil is, therefore, the friend of the Holy Spirit and Her minister.
As a disciple it accompanies Her, since by it She seals priests and anointed ones,
   for the Holy Spirit by the Anointed brands Her sheep.
In the symbol of the signet ring that in sealing wax marks its imprint,
   also the hidden mark of the Spirit is imprinted by the oil on bodies anointed in baptism and sealed in the dipping.[16]

The words "seal," "brand," "mark," and "imprint" are all from the root word *ršm,* the normal term for the prebaptismal signing with oil.

In the *Apostolic Constitutions,* the prebaptismal anointing is explicitly referred to as a "participation in the Holy Spirit" (Bk 7.22.2), and the oil is given "instead of the Holy Spirit" (Bk 3.17.1). Only in its adaptation of the *Didascalia (AC* 3.16) is there any mention of a messianic theme.

In the earliest stages, therefore, we find a single prebaptismal anointing of the head with oil and a messianic theme symbolizing the reception of the Holy Spirit. The anointing could even serve as the principal rite for initiation.

14. Translation by A. Vööbus, CSCO 402, 104.
15. Ibid., 408, 156.
16. *Hymns on Virginity* 7.6; trans. Kathleen McVey, *Ephrem the Syrian: Hymns,* Classics of Western Spirituality (New York: Paulist Press, 1989), 294.

b. Later Developments

According to Winkler, one of the first changes in the rite was in the number and motif of the prebaptismal anointings. In the third-century *Acts of Thomas* (chapters 121 and 156–58), the rite of signing with oil is extended to an anointing of the whole body that signifies healing and cleansing. Even though the original of this work is quite early, this particular anointing of the whole body is most probably a later development. Chapters 27 and 132 have only a single anointing and probably represent an earlier stratum. With the exception of chapter 157, the Greek version of this text mentions no second anointings, suggesting that in these cases the Greek represents the earlier form.[17]

In time, this full-body anointing became a widespread feature in West Syrian and Syro-Palestinian churches. The prebaptismal anointing thus became more exclusively a rite for healing and cleansing, that is, a preparatory rite, and lost its messianic and charismatic meaning. Correspondingly, the focus of initiation shifted to the immersion rite. In the *Apostolic Constitutions* (3.16–17; 7.22), the prebaptismal anointing with oil is still associated with the Holy Spirit. But with Theodore, Chrysostom, and the Jerusalem rites this association is no longer present; rather, the anointing takes on the meanings of exorcism, protection against evil, or strengthening—all as preparation for joining with Christ in his confrontation with and defeat of death.[18]

When the prebaptismal anointing was reinterpreted as a preparatory rite of cleansing and strengthening, the immersion rite also began to acquire the new symbolic meaning of a tomb, a fitting climax to the anointing rite newly interpreted as preparing the candidates for meeting death. The meaning of the original prebaptismal anointing, a sharing in Christ's messiahship and the reception of the Holy Spirit, was now out of place before immersion, and hence it was moved to the immersion rite itself or to an additional postbaptismal anointing. This resulted, for example in the case of Theodore, in three distinct rites of anointing.[19]

17. See Winkler, "The Original Meaning of the Prebaptismal Anointing," 29–31. According to Klijn, *The Acts of Thomas* was first written in Syriac, but, apparently, both copyists and translators felt no duty to be strictly faithful to the original. This explains the numerous variations between the two versions—the Greek sometimes showing the earlier form not preserved in later Syriac editions.

18. Theodore, *BH* 2.17–20; 3.8; Chrysostom, *Stav.* 2.22–24; Jerusalem, *M* 2.3.

19. Chrysostom connects the reception of the Holy Spirit and the messianic anointing with immersion, *Stav.* 2.25–26; *Hom. in epist. 2 ad Cor.,* 3.7 (PG 61.417); both themes are part of the postbaptismal anointing in Jerusalem (*M* 3). Theodore mentions the descent of the Spirit in his mystagogy on the postbaptismal anointing at *BH* 3.27 but does not address the messianic theme.

By the end of the fourth century, we find an anointing rite before immersion (sometimes in two stages) and one after. The preimmersion anointing is to prepare the candidate for passing with Christ through death and resurrection in the immersion rite. The motifs of sharing in the messianic anointing of Christ and the reception of the Spirit were moved either to the postimmersion anointing, in rites that had such an anointing (for example, *M* 3), or to the font, as with Chrysostom (*Stav.* 2.25) and Theodore (*BH* 3.25, 27). Concurrently, the symbolism of the font was changing from womb to tomb.

3. The Reasons Behind the Changes in Form

The reasons for these changes in the number and meaning of the prebaptismal anointings are complex and warrant more study than can be done here. But we can see some of the influences at work if we examine the models from which the rites were structured and derived their symbolic meaning. These are primarily scriptural, but the Jewish rite of circumcision also seems to have had an influence; we can consider them in turn.

The paradigm of the messianic anointing of kings was eventually superseded by that of the baptism of Jesus in the Jordan, and finally, motifs from the death, burial, and resurrection of Jesus were incorporated. Each paradigm served as a basis for richly symbolic rites but not always harmoniously. It will suffice for our present concern to establish a useful context for the Jerusalem rites of Cyril's time if we limit ourselves to a brief survey of the use of these models.

a. The Model of Messianic Anointing

We saw above that the prebaptismal anointing symbolized a share in the messiahship of Christ. The basis for this symbolism was the Old Testament anointing of kings and priests, which was accompanied by the descent of the Holy Spirit and the typological fulfillment of this event, namely, Christ's baptism in the Jordan. These early initiation rites, however, placed the anointing before the immersion in contrast to the order of events of Christ's baptism in the Jordan where the Spirit descends after he is baptized. In this early period of development, baptism was understood primarily as a sharing in the messianic anointing of Jesus and the reception of the Holy Spirit and tied the rite typologically only to the image of either the Old Testament anointing of kings and priests or the descent of the Spirit on Jesus. The separate image of Jesus' baptism was of secondary importance. In the *Acts of Thomas,* the focus of the initiation rite is on the anointing, with its prayers of blessing and calling down the Spirit upon the oil; for the most part the immersion is only a concluding rite (in the Greek version, two of the acts, the baptism of Gundaphorus and the baptism of the possessed women [chapters 27 and 49], make no mention at all of immersion).

The scriptural basis for this emphasis on the anointing is understandable enough. In the Synoptic accounts, the descent of the Spirit with the voice from heaven is clearly the climax of Jesus' baptism in the Jordan and the point at which the messianic associations are best exploited. In John's gospel (1:32–33) as well, the immersion is secondary; it is the descent of the Spirit that shows John the Baptist who Jesus is, and John then announces that Jesus will baptize with the Holy Spirit in contrast to John's baptizing with water. Strictly speaking, therefore, the full narrative of Jesus at the Jordan does not serve as a baptismal model, but only that part describing the descent of the Spirit.[20] Hence, the sequence of immersion after anointing suggests that the gospel accounts of Jesus at the Jordan did not on their own exert much force as a model in the early tradition, but other models may have been at work. For example, the reception of the Spirit before immersion could be part of a tradition that was based on such passages as Acts 10:44–48 (the baptism of Cornelius) where the Spirit descends before baptism.[21]

b. The Rite of Circumcision

However, evidence also exists that this early order of the rites (anointing followed by immersion) comes from the even earlier tradition of the Jewish rite of circumcision followed by baptism.[22] The East Syrian *ordo* speaks of

20. Winkler says that these early rites were modeled on Jesus' baptism and regarded as a *mimesis* of what happened at the Jordan ("The Original Meaning," 37, 42 n. 63). However, she seems to overlook the reverse order of the rites, which would conflict with any true sense of *mimesis*.

21. See Thomas Walter Manson, "Entry into Membership of the Early Church," *JTS* 48 (1947): 25–37. He sees the same order implied in Rom 5:5; Gal 3:2, 4:6, and in the account of Paul's own conversion (Acts 9:17–19). Other theories on the New Testament foundation for this order of the rites are proposed by G. G. Willis, "What Was the Earliest Syrian Baptismal Tradition?" in *Studia Evangelica* VI, ed. E. A. Livingstone, TU 112 (Berlin: Akademie-Verlag, 1973), 651–54, and Gregory Dix, "The Seal in the Second Century," *Theology* 51 (1948): 7–12.

22. Considerable material and varied opinions exist concerning the exact relationship between Jewish circumcision and the Christian rites of anointing or sealing. See, for example, G. W. H. Lampe, *The Seal of the Spirit*, 2d ed. (London: S.P.C.K., 1967), passim; Dix, "The Seal in the Second Century"; F. Gavin, *The Jewish Antecedents of the Christian Sacraments* (London: S.P.C.K., 1928); Jean Daniélou, *The Bible and the Liturgy* (Notre Dame, Indiana: University of Notre Dame Press, 1956), 7, 63; Brock, *The Holy Spirit in the Syrian Baptismal Tradition*, 38; idem, "The Transition to a Postbaptismal Anointing in the Antiochene Rite"; Manson, "Entry into Membership of the Early Church."

the baptized being "circumcised by it [the oil] with a circumcision without hands, stripping off the flesh of sins with Christ's circumcision."[23] In the fifth-century homilies of Narsai, the priest holds

> the iron of the oil on the tip of his finger; and he signs the body and the senses of the soul with its sharp edge. The son of mortals whets the oil with the words of his mouth [that is, at the epiclesis], sharpening the oil like iron to cut away iniquity.[24]

The precedent for making this correlation between circumcision and baptism is the text from Col 2:11–12:

> In him also you were circumcised with a circumcision made without hands, by putting off the body of flesh in the circumcision of Christ; and you were buried with him in baptism, in which you were also raised with him through faith in the working of God, who raised him from the dead. (RSV)

The symbolic and typological significance of circumcision with reference to baptism remained popular in the following centuries.[25] Brock thinks that the choice of the anointing of the forehead as a replacement for circumcision could very well be drawn from the practice, according to the Talmud, of anointing priests with the letter *chi* on their foreheads.[26]

c. The Model of Jesus' Baptism

Rather than supporting the early ritual form of the prebaptismal anointing, the model of Jesus' baptism in the Jordan actually contradicted it, and the resulting tension probably had some effect on the subsequent changes. Any desire to regard the initiation rites as truly a *mimesis* of the Jordan events would exert some influence on moving the immersion rite before the anointing.[27] Both Theodore's homilies (*BH* 3.22–27) and the Jerusalem mystagogy (*M* 3.1), describe a postbaptismal anointing that is explained in terms of the

---

23. Text in *Liturgia sanctorum apostolorum Addaei et Maris* (Urmiah [Rezaiyeh]: Typis Missionis Archiepiscopi Cantuariensis, 1890), 68 (trans. Brock, *The Holy Spirit in the Syrian Baptismal Tradition*, 98).

24. *Homily* 22. *The Liturgical Homilies of Narsai Translated into English with an Introduction by Dom R. H. Connolly; with an Appendix by Edmund Bishop*, Texts and Studies, no. 8.1 (Cambridge: University Press, 1909), 41–42.

25. The correlation between circumcision and baptism can be seen in the following texts: *Epistle of Barnabas* 9; Justin, *Dialogue with Trypho* 19, 24, 29, 41, 43, 114; the *Odes of Solomon* 11; Ephrem, *Hymns on the Epiphany* 3; Asterius of Amasea, *Homily on Psalm 6* (PG 40.445A); Chrysostom, *Hom. in Eph* 2:2 (PG 62.9); Ps-Chrysostom, *De occursu Christi* (PG 50.807).

26. Brock, "The Transition to a Postbaptismal Anointing," 219. He cites the Babylonian Talmud, Kerithoth 5b, Horayoth 12a.

27. Georg Kretschmar also makes this point in passing in "Recent Research on Christian Initiation," *SL* 12 (1977), 92.

descent of the Spirit on Christ after his coming up from the water. For these two authors the correspondence of the rites to the sequence of the events at the Jordan is an important element for teaching that the rites are a *mimesis* of what happened to Jesus.

In Jerusalem, the importance of the Jordan model was already showing itself in the *Catecheses*. In *C* 3.11–14, Cyril presents the events at the Jordan as a prototype for the rite of initiation. The sequence of topics (not necessarily implying separate rites of immersion and chrismation) corresponds to the sequence of events at the Jordan: conformity with Christ in his own baptism (sections 11–12) is followed by an explanation of the reception of the Holy Spirit (sections 13–14).

d. The Model of Jesus' Death and Resurrection

In addition, a second scriptural model began to emerge as influential, namely, Christ's passage through death and resurrection as treated by Paul in Romans 6. The symbolism of the font shifts from a womb to a tomb wherein one is buried and raised with Christ.[28] This model and shift of font symbolism were easily accommodated now that the prebaptismal rites were more rites of preparation leading to the climax of immersion in the font/tomb where the old sinful self dies so as to arise anew with Christ (Rom 6:1–11). Theodore's commentary shows an intermediary stage where the theme of the font as a womb where one is reborn is prominent, while at the same time immersion is likened to union with Christ in his death and resurrection (see *BH* 3.5 and 9). For *M*, on the other hand, the theme of death and resurrection with the font as tomb is prominent though a remnant of the birth symbolism remains in a brief secondary reference to the font as a womb of second birth (*M* 4.2).

e. The Immersion Rite Becomes Preeminent

Some impetus for development probably came also from reflecting on the richness of the symbolism of immersion. The candidate's passage through water not only hearkens back to the Old Testament stories (the Flood and the passage through the Red Sea) but more importantly to the New Testament passage of Christ through the tomb from death to life. By the fourth century, as shown in Chrysostom (*Stav.* 2.10–11, 25–26), Theodore (*BH* 3.11– 25), and Cyril (*C* 3.11–12 and *M* 2.4–7), the immersion rite receives considerable attention.

28. Cyril, *C* 3.12, *M* 2.4–7; Chrysostom, *Stav.* 2.10–11; Theodore, *BH* 3.1–7, 9–14; *AC* 3.17, 7.22, 43; Narsai, *Homilies* 21–22 (fifth century). See also Ratcliff, "The Old Syrian Baptismal Tradition," 142–49; Brock, *The Holy Spirit in the Syrian Baptismal Tradition*, 38, 58–59.

In Chrysostom's rite in particular, the immersion is the high point. There is no longer a prebaptismal rite for the reception of the Spirit, nor is there a postbaptismal anointing for this purpose; rebirth in Christ and the reception of the Spirit are both ritualized by immersion. He shows, from another source, that the theme of messianic anointing was also transferred to the font, "in this manner you also become a king, a priest, and a prophet in the bath."[29] The immersion rite has become equal to or even greater in importance than anointing.

For Theodore as well the immersion is central even though he does have a postbaptismal anointing. But some debate exists about whether Theodore's postbaptismal anointing is for the conferring of the Spirit or whether it even genuinely belongs to the text; he would be alone among his Antiochene contemporaries if his rite included this anointing.[30]

As to the genuineness of the text, Yarnold argues well against the radical solutions of Mitchell (the text is a later addition) and Lampe (the anointing is metaphorical) and offers the simpler solution that since this was about the time when a postbaptismal anointing for the Holy Spirit was being introduced, there is no reason against Theodore's homilies being the first to record its use. One indication that it was a newly developed rite (but still of secondary importance to the immersion rite) is that it receives a mere two paragraphs of commentary compared to a full seventeen sections on the immersion (BH 3.9–25).

As to whether the rite is for the conferring of the Holy Spirit, certain ambiguities in the text have led to different interpretations:

When Jesus came out of the water He received the grace of the Holy Spirit who descended like a dove and lighted on Him, and this is the reason why He is said to have been anointed: "The Spirit of the Lord is upon me, because of which the Lord hath anointed me." . . . It is right, therefore, that you also should receive the signing (rušmā) on your forehead. When the priest signs you he says: "So-and-so is signed in the name of the Father, and of the Son, and of the Holy Spirit," so that it may be an indication and a sign to you that it was at the naming of the Father (b-šumāhā d-Abā), Son, and Holy Spirit that the Holy Spirit descended (etā) on you also, and you were anointed and received grace; and He will be and remain with you.[31]

---

29. Hom. in epist. 2 ad Cor., 3.7 (PG 61.417).

30. Chrysostom has no postbaptismal anointing. The Apostolic Constitutions does have one in all three of its versions of baptismal ceremonies (3.16, 7.22, 7.44) but not for the conferring of the Spirit. See L. L. Mitchell, Baptismal Anointing, Alcuin Club Collections, no. 48 (London: S.P.C.K., 1966), 41; Lampe, Seal of the Spirit, 202 n. 4; Yarnold, AIR, 208 n. 65.

31. BH 3.27, trans. Mingana, 68.

Even though in his earlier mystagogy on the immersion, Theodore spoke of the graces of the Father, Son, and *Spirit* (*BH* 3.20–21, 24–25), the prevailing theme was a second birth and adoption through union with Christ. Nothing was clearly said about the gift of or abiding presence of the Spirit. This theme is taken up only in the commentary on the postbaptismal anointing just quoted. The fact that the rite closely parallels what happened to Jesus after he came up from the water would suggest that it signifies the conferring of the Spirit. But (recalling that Theodore is commenting on the rites before they take place) when he says that the signing indicates that "the Holy Spirit descended *(etā)* on you also," the past tense, *etā*, would suggest rather that the descent of the Spirit already occurred in the immersion.

f. The New Catechumenate and Hellenism

Two other factors probably had some influence on the meaning and form of the rites of anointing. We recall that after the Peace of Constantine, the catechumenate added a final stage of preparation coinciding with the season of Lent. This stage was formal and intense, preparation being the principal theme. This emphasis on preparation would have enhanced any association of preimmersion anointing with the ideas of cleansing, strengthening, and exorcism.

Further, the rise of Hellenistic influence on Christian culture following Constantine's conversion probably affected changes in the anointing rites, for there was a tendency to push the Jewish origins of Christianity into the background. Hence, the influence of the rite of circumcision gave way to a more complete modeling of baptism after Jesus' baptism in the Jordan where the messianic "anointing" of Jesus takes place after immersion (whether or not it was ritualized separately from immersion).[32]

In summary, it appears as if a desire to pattern the rites of initiation more closely after an event in the life of Christ gradually led to abandoning a structure based on the circumcision rite and adopting in its place the events at the Jordan. The preimmersion rites became preparatory since the passage through the Jordan (the font) was now the focal point. And just as Jesus was "anointed" by the Spirit afterward, so too a postimmersion anointing was introduced with a messianic anointing motif. Concurrently, the font easily took on the symbolism of the tomb in which Jesus was buried and from which he rose, and thus Jesus' passage from death to life could also serve as a model on another level.

32. See Brock, "The Transition to a Postbaptismal Anointing," 219.

C. The Jerusalem Rites

We can now examine how C and M are situated in these developments. The following areas will be considered: the anointing rites (with an excursus on the term "seal"), the conferring of the Holy Spirit through the rite of laying on of hands, and the scriptural basis for the catechesis on the rites.

1. The Anointing(s)

Unfortunately, Cyril makes no direct reference to a rite of anointing in his Lenten sermons, so it is impossible to be sure of the structure of the rite(s) around the year 351. His silence is not surprising, though, since he reserved specific catechesis on the rites for the mystagogy. In C 3, he speaks of the immersion rite but only in the context of the theology of baptism that is pertinent to the creedal article he is teaching: "We believe in one baptism for the forgiveness of sins." Hence, we cannot know for certain how many anointings were in the Jerusalem rite around 351, but on the strength of the Syrian tradition as considered above, we can assume that it included at least a preimmersion anointing.

Even with the lack of references to specific *rites* of anointing, the frequent use of the term "seal" reflects what the rites of anointing have traditionally symbolized. By closely examining Cyril's use of the term, we can arrive at some idea about how rites of anointing and the gift of the Spirit probably were performed when he delivered his *Catecheses*. Since his use of the term is varied, some background on its general meaning and use is in order.

a. The Meaning and Uses of the Term "Seal"

The substantive *sphragis* can mean either a seal or signet that makes an impression (such as in a government seal on a document) or the impression itself. More generally it can mean any distinguishing mark. The verb form can mean to enclose, authenticate, or confirm with a seal; or more generally, to make or leave a mark. In patristic usage, the basic meaning is the same, but writers widely used the term in a variety of theological senses. Among them are (1) the idea of a mark identifying one as Christian,[33] the sign of the cross,[34] or in an inward sense, a mark signifying the possession of the Holy Spirit;[35] (2) the idea of attestation or confirmation as in a profession of faith that

---

33. *Rituale Armenorum*, 389, 390, 392.
34. Eusebius, *Demonstratio evangelica* 7.14; *Sibylline Oracles* 8.244.
35. Origen, *Fragmenta ex commentariis in Eph. 1.13*, in J. A. F. Gregg, "Fragmenta ex commentariis in Eph. 1.13," *JTS* 3 (1902): 243; Basil, *De Spiritu Sancto* 64 (3.54b).

serves as an attestation of conversion and adherence to Christ[36] or the episco-pal chrismation in baptism;[37] (3) the idea of conformation, being conformed to the divine image imprinted on the soul in baptism;[38] and (4) an apotropaic sense whereby the seal serves as a protection against demonic powers.[39] For the present purposes we will briefly survey some of the uses of the term in the Syrian tradition. We will begin with the New Testament and then exam-ine key liturgical texts up through the time of Cyril's contemporaries.

Three Pauline texts lie behind the patristic use of the term. These texts are generally held to be references to Christian baptism:[40]

Eph 1:13: In him you also, who have heard the word of truth, the gospel of your sal-vation, and have believed in him, were sealed with the promised Holy Spirit, which is the guarantee of our inheritance. (RSV)

Eph 4:30: And do not grieve the Holy Spirit of God in whom you were sealed for the day of redemption. (RSV)

2 Cor 1:22: But it is God who establishes us with you in Christ, and has commis-sioned (literally "anointed") us; he has put his seal upon us and given us his Spirit in our hearts as a guarantee. (RSV)

In the first two examples, the term has the sense of authenticating or confirming one's faith, thus assuring one of God's promised blessings. But in the last one, the seal also carries the sense of an indelible mark whereby one is identified as belonging to God. In the text from 2 Cor, Yarnold sees five sacramental ideas: (1) confirmation or strengthening (establishes), (2) anoint-ing, (3) the seal or sign, (4) the giving of the Holy Spirit, and (5) the Spirit's guarantee.[41] The *sphragis,* by means of its basic sense as a visible mark (whether figuratively or physically administered in a rite), could convey any or all the meanings of (1), (2), (4), and (5). But since Paul gives no indication

36. Origen, *Hom. on Num.* 12.4; Hippolytus, *AT* 9.8 (*sphragizein* is preserved here in transliter-ation by the Sahidic version). See the following editions: *The Treatise on the Apostolic Tradition of St. Hippolytus of Rome,* ed. and trans. Gregory Dix, reedited by Henry Chadwick, 2d ed. (Lon-don: S.P.C.K., 1968), 17; *La Tradition Apostolique,* ed. and trans. Bernard Botte, SC 11 *bis* (Paris: Éditions du Cerf, 1984), 61.

37. Basil, *Adversus Eunomium* 3.5.

38. Clement of Alexandria, *Excerpta ex Theodoto* 86; Cyril of Alexandria, *Thesaurus de Trini-tate* 34, PG 75.609D.

39. Gregory Nazianzen, *Orations* 1.3.

40. See Lampe, *Seal of the Spirit,* 3–18. Much of the scholarly debate on the term "seal" has centered on whether it refers to a rite of baptism (immersion) as opposed to confirmation (anointing). It is sufficient at this point to note that Paul is referring to Christian initiation in general.

41. *AIR,* 31.

of attaching it to any rite and since *sphragis* on its own can simply mean a "marking" or "signing," the term was open to a variety of uses even outside the context of initiation rites, and we cannot expect it to be associated only with the gift of the Spirit or to be restricted to rites of anointing. In all three of these passages, the Syriac for seal is some form of *ḥatmā*.

In the early-third-century *Didascalia*, we find uses of "seal" *(ḥatmā)* that signify the baptismal rite as a whole:

He who speaks to you the Word of God, and is the cause of life unto you, and gives you the seal *(ḥatmā)* that is in Christ, love him as the apple of your eye. (Ch. 3.6)

[It is] the bishop through whom the Lord gave you the Holy Spirit, and through whom you have learned the word and have known God, and through whom you have been known of God, and through whom you were sealed *(ḥatmā)*. (Ch. 9)

As of old priests and kings were anointed in Israel, so do you likewise, with the imposition of the hand, anoint the head *(rīšā)* of those who receive baptism, whether it be of men or women; and afterwards, whether you yourself baptize, or you tell the deacons or presbyters to baptize, let a woman, a deaconess, anoint the women, as we have already said. But let a man pronounce over them the invocation of the divine names in the water. And when the woman who is being baptized has come up from the water, let the deaconess receive her, and teach and instruct her how the seal *(ḥatmā)* of baptism ought to be kept unbroken in purity and holiness. (Ch. 16)[42]

This "seal of baptism" is used in a generic sense, that is, the seal is not connected to any one part of the rite.[43]

In the late-fourth-century *Apostolic Constitutions,* a compilation of church laws and practices adapted from several sources (in particular, Books 1 to 6 are based upon the *Didascalia,* and Book 7.1–32 on the *Didache*), we find an interesting development. In *AC* 2.32.3, an ambiguous use of *sphragis* occurs that seems to echo the passage from chapter 9 of the *Didascalia* and to refer generically to two anointings: "through him [the bishop] you have been signed with the oil of gladness and the *myron* of understanding." *AC* 3.16 (based on chapter 16 of the *Didascalia*) more clearly suggests some changes in the anointing rite and the meaning of "seal." Upon emerging from the water, the instructions call for a deacon and deaconess to receive respectively the men and the women,

42. Trans. by Vööbus, CSCO 402, 34 (Syriac, 401, 37), 402, 104 (Syriac, 401, 109), 408, 156 (Syriac, 407, 173). See also *Didascalia* ch. 10, CSCO 402, 113 (Syriac, 401, 119).

43. The antiquity of this generic use of the term is attested by the second-century Acts of Paul (see *Acta Pauli. Nach dem Papyrus der Hamburger Staats- und Universitäts-Bibliothek,* ed. Carl Schmidt [Hamburg: J. J. Augustin, 1936], 32, 66, 72), and the second-century Abercios inscription (see the article "Abercius" in *Dictionnaire d'archéologie chrétienne et de liturgie,* 1:70).

so that the conferring of the seal may take place with appropriate decency. *And after that, let the bishop anoint those that have been baptized with myron.*

As we can see from a comparison to the passage cited from *Didascalia* chapter 16 above, the italicized portion has been added.

This text from the *Apostolic Constitutions* has always been puzzling because it speaks as if the "conferring of the seal" refers to a specific rite that takes place right after emerging from the water, namely, chrismation. But that possibility is problematic in light of the explanation of each of the symbols in the following chapter (*AC* 3.17): the water stands for the burial, the oil for the Holy Spirit, "the seal for the cross," and the chrism "is the confirmation of the covenant." A distinction is made here between the seal and the chrism that might suggest that two different rites are being noted. But it is not immediately clear what part of the rite the compiler has in mind when he mentions the seal, for he has already referred to the prebaptismal anointing (oil), the immersion (water), and the chrismation (chrism). The fact that the text mentions the seal in a list would indicate that it does not refer generically to the whole rite or to either or both anointings.

Part of the confusion seems to lie in a different use of *sphragis* in the two chapters. The "conferring of the seal" in *AC* 3.16 is simply a carryover from *Didascalia* chapter 16, and it is used generically for the whole rite. As for the meaning and referent for the "seal for the cross" in *AC* 3.17, two possibilities exist. The seal and the chrism could both refer to the postbaptismal anointing: the *sphragis* is the ritual gesture, a marking with a cross, and the chrism is the material used. Alternatively, the seal could refer back to the prebaptismal anointing described in *AC* 3.16. For there are, strictly speaking, two parts to this anointing of the whole body for receiving the Holy Spirit: it begins with a specific anointing of the forehead before continuing with the rest of the body. In the *Didascalia*, this anointing is of the head *(rīšā)* without specifying the forehead and recalls only the ancient anointing of priests and kings. In the corresponding text from *Apostolic Constitutions* (*AC* 3.16), it is confined to the forehead, and the instruction adds that the priestly and kingly anointing is but an ancient type now fulfilled in Christ—that is, the anointed more than just resemble the priests and kings of old, they are in fact Christians. Such an anointing, probably a marking (one of the meanings of *sphragis*) with a sign of the cross, could easily be described as a "seal for the cross."

In the *Apostolic Constitutions* 7.22 (based on the *Didache*), the postbaptismal anointing (with *myron*) is called a seal; it is not associated here with the cross but described in the Pauline sense of assurance or guarantee: a "seal of the covenants." This anointing does not represent the gift of the Spirit, which takes place in the prebaptismal anointing with oil. The sealing serves to visibly mark the newly baptized, much as circumcision did in the Jewish rites, and thus identify them as incorporated into the new covenant. The rubric adds, however, that if there is no oil or chrism, "the water is sufficient for the anointing, and for the seal, and for the confession." This is another indication that the idea of sealing is not inseparably attached to an anointing rite.

The possibility that the "seal of the cross" in *AC* 3.17 is a reference to the prebaptismal rite is strengthened by the fact that elsewhere olive oil and the olive tree are symbols of Christ and his cross. In the *Acts of Thomas*, some of the prayers over the oil make associations with the cross:

Holy oil, which was given to us for unction, and hidden mystery of the cross, which is seen through it—thou, the straightener of crooked limbs, thou, our Lord Jesus, life and health and remission of sins—let thy power come and abide on this oil, and let thy holiness dwell in it.[44]

Lord, come abide upon this oil as thou didst abide upon the tree, and they who crucified thee were not able to bear thy word.[45]

Fruit more beautiful than all other fruits, . . . power of the tree which men putting on them overcome their adversaries, . . . whose leaf is bitter, but in thy most sweet fruit thou art fair; that art rough to the sight but soft to the taste; seeming to be weak, but in the greatness of thy strength able to bear the power that beholdeth all things. . . . Let his victorious might come and be established in this oil, like as it was established in the tree [wood] that was its kin.[46]

The oil in these examples represents either healing power, strengthening, or protection against evil. All three senses find their source of meaning in the cross. In the third example, the anointing conveys the sense of sharing in Christ. This idea is used more explicitly in *M* 2.3 where the anointing symbolizes being grafted onto Christ, the true olive tree. The ideas of bitter taste,

44. Baptism of Mygdonia (Syriac version), in *Apocryphal Acts of the Apostles Edited from Syriac Manuscripts in the British Museum and Other Libraries*, ed. and trans. William Wright, 2 vols. in 1 (Amsterdam: Philo Press, 1968), 2:258; for the Greek version see vol. 2.2 of *Acta Apostolorum Apocrypha*, ed. R. A. Lipsius and M. Bonnet (Hildesheim: Georg Olms, 1959), 230 (par. 121); see also Klijn, *Acts of Thomas*, 130 (par. 121).

45. Baptism of Vizan (Syriac version), trans. Wright, *Apocryphal Acts of the Apostles*, 2:289; Greek text in Lipsius and Bonnet, *Acta Apostolorum*, 2.2:266 (par. 157); see also Klijn, *Acts of Thomas*, 148 (par. 157).

46. Baptism of Vizan (Greek version); trans. M. R. James, *The Apocryphal New Testament* (Oxford: Clarendon Press, 1924), 433.

rough sight, and weak appearance refer perhaps to the bitter and ignoble suffering of the innocent Christ shared in by the believer.

Olive oil and the olive tree are also powerful symbols for Ephrem:

> The olive tree, again, became the first-born of the trees that were buried
> in the Flood, in the likeness of its Lord Who became the
>   First-born from the house of the dead.
> Therefore the olive tree passed through the Deluge, and
>   before all else it was revived.
> It rose up and gave its leaf as a pledge for the revival of all. . . .[47]

Here the tree is a symbol of Christ himself passing from death to life with the baptismal imagery of the Flood.

In the following passage, the symbol of the tree is extended to the cross, the symbol of victory:

> It [the oil] serves as the Anointed, Reviver of all; in streams branches
>   and leaves it portrays Him. . . .
> With its branches it portrays the symbol of his victory; with its streams
>   it portrays the symbol of his mortality;
> with its leaf it portrays the symbol of resurrection, and like death the
>   Flood vomited it up.[48]

An anointing (especially of the whole body) symbolically brings one into full participation in the paschal mystery. According to Brock, early Syriac writers rarely used this interpretation of the prebaptismal anointing as a participation in Christ in a baptismal context. However, by the time of M, the oil as a symbol of participation in Christ, the true olive tree, is prominent, and the Syrian rite probably took this imagery over from Jerusalem.[49]

The prebaptismal sealing or signing on the forehead is an important feature for Cyril's contemporaries, Chrysostom and Theodore. Chrysostom gives a clear example of a preimmersion anointing that he calls a seal (sphragis) and that consists of a signing of a cross on the forehead.[50] One of the main features of this rite is to convey the sense of belonging to Christ; the seal leaves a mark of identity. This meaning would seem to be a survival

47. Hymns on Virginity 6; trans. K. McVey, Ephrem the Syrian, 288.

48. Hymns on Virginity 7; trans. McVey, Ephrem, 296. Other early examples of associating the oil with the cross include: Narsai, Homily 22; Origen, Contra Celsum 6.27.

49. Brock, The Holy Spirit in the Syrian Baptismal Tradition, 58.

50. Stav. 2.22–23. Myron is used for this anointing, and it is called a seal. The sign of the cross is implied, but in the PK series (3.27), the mark of a cross is explicitly mentioned. For Theodore (BH 2.17–19), the candidate is given the mark (rušmā) with oil (mešḥā).

of the circumcision model. Theodore gives the more elaborate account of the mark of identity with examples of sheep being branded and soldiers tattooed.[51]

For both Chrysostom and Theodore, this visible marking becomes a convenient apotropaic sign against evil. The anointing is not clearly exorcistic (a driving out of evil), but it is a protection against demons. This protective sense is probably drawn from Rv 7:2–3 (see also Ez 9:4) where the faithful are marked on the forehead before the seven angels unleash destruction upon the earth. All of these, though, hearken back to the marking of the door posts with the lamb's blood as protection from the angel of destruction in Ex 12.

Theodore also attaches the sense of confirmation or assurance to the postbaptismal signing with oil. The marking with oil is an indelible sign of a spiritual anointing that corresponds to the descent of the Spirit on Jesus after he came up from the Jordan. The durable nature of the oil attests that this spiritual anointing is guaranteed to endure.[52]

Since sealing (from its earliest use by Paul) is so closely associated with the activity of the Spirit, it is not difficult to see how over time it could ritually represent the gift of the Spirit after the immersion rite, especially since this sequence better fits the events of Christ's baptism in the Jordan and his death and resurrection. For the Jordan events in their own way prefigure the "baptism" (death and resurrection) that Jesus said he must yet undergo (Mk 10:38; Lk 12:49–50), which was followed by the outpouring of the Spirit (Jn 20:19–23; Acts 2:1–4, 14–21). In this form, found in M, the postbaptismal anointing with *myron* coincides with the gift of the Spirit and a sharing in the messianic anointing of Christ.

This short survey of the early Syrian tradition has shown the term *sphragis* used in the following ways: it can mean "seal" and refer generically to the whole rite of baptism (*ḥatmā* in Syriac); it can indicate a share in the messiahship of Christ; it can signify confirmation or assurance; it can stand for the reception of the Spirit; it can be used as a sign of the cross (perhaps traced with *myron*) or mark (*rušmā* in Syriac) of identity as belonging to

---

51. *BH* 3.17. This pastoral imagery is also in *Acts of Thomas* (see, for example, Wright, *Apocryphal Acts of the Apostles*, 2:165, 266–67; Greek text in Lipsius and Bonnet, *Acta Apostolorum*, 2.2:140 [par. 25], 238 [par. 131]; see also Klijn, *Acts of Thomas*, 76–77 [par. 25], 135 [par. 131]) and Ephrem, *Hymns on Virginity* 7; both the pastoral and military imagery is in Narsai, *Homily* 22. See also Lampe, *The Seal of the Spirit*, 5–18.

52. *BH* 3.27.

Christ; and it can serve as a protection against evil. We can now look more closely at Cyril's use of the term and see what can be concluded about the Jerusalem rites of anointing.

b. The Use of "Seal" in the Catecheses

Throughout the *Catecheses*, Cyril uses the term "seal" in a variety of ways, although he makes no specific mention of anointing rites. He uses the term twenty-eight times (of a total thirty-four) in a baptismal sense. These can be divided into four groups. In the first group, it is used in a generic sense, where the Holy Spirit seals the soul, or one is sealed in the Spirit, or even more generally, baptism itself is a seal. The remaining groups show more specified uses of the idea of a seal as a visible mark that has exorcistic or apotropaic power (second group), is a sign of attestation corresponding to circumcision (third group), or is a mark of belonging (fourth group).

The first group in which baptism is understood in a generic sense as a sealing by the Spirit has the following examples:

P 16 Great is the Baptism that lies before you, . . . a holy and indissoluble seal.

P 17 May he give you the indelible seal of the Holy Spirit.

C 1.3 Where [God] discerns a worthy motive, there he confers the seal of salvation.

C 3.3 The Holy Spirit is about to seal your souls.

C 3.4 As the water purifies the body, so the Spirit seals the soul.

C 3.4 Nor does a man who acts virtuously, but does not receive the seal by water, enter into the kingdom of heaven.

C 3.12 For you go down into the water bearing your sins, but the invocation of grace having sealed your soul, it is no longer possible for you to be swallowed up by the terrible dragon.

C 4.16 It is the Holy Spirit . . . who even now, at the time of baptism, seals your soul.

C 4.32 That receiving the seal by the Holy Spirit, we may be made heirs to eternal life.

C 16.24 To this day [the Holy Spirit] seals souls in baptism.

C 17.5 "In him you also, after believing in him, were sealed with the promised Holy Spirit" (cf. Eph 1:13).

C 17.26 The Holy Spirit not only changed Paul's blindness to sight, but imparted the seal to his soul, making him a vessel of election.

C 17.32 "But he who sealed us for this very purpose is God, who gave us the guarantee of the Spirit" (cf. 2 Cor 1:22).

C 17.35 Be mindful of the Holy Spirit . . . who is present, ready to seal your soul, and he will give you that seal.

C 17.35 "In whom you also believed and were sealed with the Holy Spirit" (cf. Eph 1:13).

C 17.37 "And do not grieve the Holy Spirit of God in whom you were sealed for the day of redemption" (Eph 4:30).

None of these references appears to restrict the sealing to any specific rite within the entire initiation ceremony even though the references to water direct attention to the immersion. Both *C* 3.4 and *C* 3.12, in particular, indicate that the outward sign of the water corresponds to the inward reality of the sealing of the soul, but since water does not of itself imprint or mark, the immersion really only functions at most as that part of the rite during which the sealing takes place. In not specifying a distinct rite of sealing, these examples indicate a generic use of the term: the initiation rites are, as a whole, a sealing by the Spirit. Cyril uses the term in the above passages without ever explaining what it means, indicating that it was a commonly used term for baptism. Without a specific qualification, it should probably be understood in this generic usage as signifying the activity of the Spirit conforming and uniting the newly baptized to Christ in a permanent and inviolable way.

The second group includes two of the passages already cited plus three others; these have to do with the efficacy of the seal as a token against evil powers:

C 1.3 [God] confers the seal of salvation, that wonderful seal, which demons tremble at and angels recognize.

C 4.14 Openly seal [the cross] upon your forehead so that the demons may behold the royal sign and flee.

C 13.36 Let the cross be the seal boldly made with our fingers on our forehead on all occasions. . . . It is a powerful safeguard . . . a grace from God, a badge of the faithful, and a terror to demons . . . Do not despise the seal as a free gift.

C 17.35 He will give you that seal at which evil spirits tremble.

C 17.36 If you are counted worthy of the grace, your soul will be enlightened, you will receive a power which you did not have, you will receive weapons terrible to the evil spirits; and if you do not cast away your arms, but keep the seal upon your soul, no evil spirit will approach you.

The two passages that concern making the sign of the cross (4.14; 13.36) do not appear to relate directly to baptism but rather to the general practice of signing oneself. Calling the sign of the cross a seal is an indication that the term is not a technical one used exclusively in the initiation rites. The other passages do concern baptism and indicate that—whatever the full significance of the baptismal seal is—it at least carries the idea of a recognizable sign. This suggests that in some form or other the spiritual sealing that takes place in baptism may have been accompanied ritually by a physical gesture like the sign of a cross, or perhaps even an anointing. It was noted above that the *Apostolic Constitutions* (3.16) associates the seal with the cross in its account of the prebaptismal anointing. For both Chrysostom and Theodore as well, the first prebaptismal anointing on the forehead leaves an identifying mark that serves as a token against evil powers.

The third group has two examples. In *C* 5.5–6, Cyril associates the baptismal seal with spiritual circumcision:

C 5.5 Being faithful in these things, [Abraham] was sealed for righteousness and received circumcision as a seal of the faith that he had while he was uncircumcised (Rom 4:11).

C 5.6 By the likeness therefore of our faith, we become the adopted sons of Abraham. And then, following upon our faith, we receive like him the spiritual seal, being circumcised by the Holy Spirit through the laver, not in the foreskin of the body, but in the heart . . . according to the Apostle: In the circumcision of Christ, being buried with him in baptism, etc. (Col 2:11–12).

Here again Cyril explains the seal in terms of the visible sign of circumcision that marks one not only as belonging to a chosen people but also as one who has made a commitment of faith. We are again left to wonder, however, whether this spiritual circumcision is actually attached to a ritual action. We can detect the possible description of a rite in *C* 5.6. By "following upon our faith," Cyril may have in mind the rite of the candidates making a profession of faith immediately before each of three immersions into the font.[53] But there is no sign of a ritual marking being performed on the candidate during immersion that would correspond to circumcision. It is worth noting here that in citing Col 2:11–12, Cyril associates the spiritual circumcision, which takes place in the font, with the death and burial of Christ; it suggests that he understands the activity of the Spirit in the sealing as forming the candidate into the perfect image of Christ in his death and resurrection.

The last group conveys the idea of the seal as a mark of belonging:

---

53. See *M* 2.4.

C 1.2 Come for the mystical seal, that you may be recognized by the Master; be numbered among the holy and spiritual flock of Christ, that you may be set apart on his right hand and inherit the life prepared for you (Mt 25:34).

C 3.3 The Holy Spirit is about to seal your souls; you are about to be enrolled in the army of the great King.

C 12.8 "I come to gather all nations and I will leave on them a sign" (Is 66:19). For from my conflict upon the cross I give to each of my soldiers a royal seal to bear upon his forehead.[54]

These passages use the idea of a recognizable mark that identifies the bearer as belonging to Christ. The first presents the image of a sheep branded by the mark of its owner, and the next two use the image of soldiers bearing a mark that shows to which army they belong. Both Chrysostom and Theodore use these two images of sheep and soldiers in describing their first prebaptismal anointing.[55] The third passage indicates that the mark is a sign of the cross, but since Cyril is not directly explaining a rite, it is not clear where and how such a marking took place.

The last mention of the seal is in *C* 18.33 (where Cyril announces the instructions on the initiation rites yet to come) and needs special attention:

After Easter's holy day of salvation . . . you will be instructed again in the reasons for everything that has been done, and receive proofs of these from the Old and New Testaments. First of the things done just before Baptism; then how you were cleansed by the Lord "in the bath of water by means of the word" (Eph 5:26); and how like priests you have become partakers of the name of Christ; and how the seal of the fellowship of the Holy Spirit has been given to you.

Each of the topics listed, namely, the partaking of the name of Christ, priestly anointing, the sealing, and fellowship with the Holy Spirit all correspond well with a chrismation rite such as we find in *M*. In striking contrast to all of the previous associations in *C* of the seal with the water, Cyril uses the term *sphragis* for a postimmersion rite, calling it a priestly and messianic anointing that grants fellowship with the Holy Spirit. A reasonable explanation offered by Stephenson suggests that *C* 18.33 is a doublet of section 32 and represents a

---

54. See Rv 7:2–3.

55. *Stav.* 2.22–23; *PK* 2.16; *BH* 2.17–19. See also F. J. Dölger, *Sphragis. Eine altchristliche Taufbezeichnung in ihren Beziehungen zur profanen und religiösen Kultur des Altertums,* Studien zur Geschichte und Kultur des Altertums, vol. 5 (3/4 Heft) (Paderborn: Ferdinand Schöningh, 1911), 32–37, with plates I, II, which illustrate how Roman soldiers were marked on their foreheads for identification. Dölger cites another example in Chrysostom, *Hom. in epist. 2 ad Cor.* 3.7 (PG 61.418).

later addition that gives an updated schedule of topics for the Easter Week catechesis at a time when the rites had developed into the form known in M.[56] Both sections announce subsequent instruction, but while section 33 announces the topics of the mystagogy that will be delivered "after Easter's holy day of salvation," section 32 seems to imply that the instruction will occur before initiation (emphasis added):

> But now that the holy day of the Passover is at hand, and you, beloved in Christ, are to be enlightened through the laver of regeneration, you will be taught again what is needed, God willing: with what devotion and order *you must come in when summoned,* for what purpose each of these holy mysteries of baptism is performed, with what reverence and order *you are to proceed* from baptism to the holy altar of God . . . so that your soul, enlightened *beforehand* by instructive discourse may come to know in each particular the greatness of the gifts God imparts to you.

These instructions are described as preparing the candidates for what they are about to do, hence they would be given before the initiation rites. Since the topics include the purpose of the mysteries and are called enlightenment, they are not just last minute practical preparations but the mystagogy proper; thus, the passage represents a time when the mystagogy was delivered before initiation rather than during Easter week, which was the case by the time of M. Except for the topic of the Eucharist, Chrysostom and Theodore delivered their mystagogy before initiation. Yarnold has also proposed that the striking textual parallels between C 18.32 and 33 suggest that the latter was intended to replace the former to take account of the new rites, but no fully revised version of C has survived.[57] Since the description of the mystagogy in C 18.33 belongs most likely to a later and revised ritual form rather than to that represented by the earlier passages, the unique use here of "seal" need not be considered an anomaly among the other uses in C. However, since it represents a more advanced stage nearer the time of M, we will have to reconsider it when examining the use of *sphragis* in M.

Before considering how sealing may have been expressed ritually, we can summarize what the term meant for Cyril. In its most fundamental sense, it signifies the permanent and inviolable nature of the Spirit's conforming the baptized to the dead and risen Christ. Founded on this basic sense the substantive meaning of seal as a distinguishing mark is also used: this new conformity with Christ is something recognizable and serves as a power against

---

56. *WCJ,* 2:180.
57. "The Authorship of the *Mystagogic Catecheses,*" 160–61.

evil; as with circumcision of old, it could also signify both a commitment of faith and a mark of belonging. With the exception of the one reference in *C* 18.33, we find no association of *sphragis* with the theme of messianic anointing. Cyril does teach about the name of Christ as meaning "anointed one" (for example, *C* 10.4, 14) or as a name imparted by the Spirit to the baptized (*P* 15, *C* 10.16) but never with reference to the term *sphragis*.

c. The Rite of Sealing in Jerusalem

To reconstruct the rite of sealing as Cyril probably knew it, we will look first at *C* and then *M*. We will then examine the differences between these two texts, which represent a thirty-year time span.

At most, only some hints exist as to whether in the time of *C* any specific rite of anointing, understood as a sealing in the Spirit rather than just signing or marking, was in use. Given the established tradition of anointing in the initiation rites both before and after *C*, we can be reasonably sure that around 351 Cyril's rites included at least one anointing. No clear evidence indicates, however, whether there was more than one, and if so, when they occurred, or whether one was clearly considered a rite of sealing.

A good reason for thinking that no specific anointing rite symbolized sealing at this early stage was that despite the references to visible markings or signs, Cyril most frequently and significantly explains the conferring of the seal as an activity of the Spirit in the context of the immersion rite. This is for Cyril the focal point of baptism, which he clearly indicates in *C* 3. While the water cleanses the body, the Spirit simultaneously seals the soul; when in the water, the candidates are to "look for salvation by the Spirit" and "receive the seal by the water" (3.4). In sections 11–12, Cyril uses the account of Jesus' own baptism to elaborate on this by showing Jesus symbolically encountering and conquering the dragon of death in the water. By virtue of participation with Jesus in the water, the baptized share in this victory.

For you go down into the water bearing sins; but the invocation of grace having sealed your soul, it is no longer possible for you to be swallowed up by the terrible dragon. . . . For if you have been "united with the likeness of the Saviour's death" (Rom 6:5), you shall also be deemed worthy of his resurrection. (*C* 3.12)

This sealing is understood as effecting a union with or a conformation to Christ through the work of the Spirit. In conclusion, then, while granting that Cyril very often uses *sphragis* generically of the whole rite of initiation, to the extent that it was possible, the immersion rite is where the idea of sealing was focused. Perhaps accompanying rites involving physical marking, for example, with oil, were seen as the external signs of what happens in the font—this was no doubt the case with Theodore—but most probably no rite other than the immersion was seen as an act of sealing.

The reason why the sealing was focused in the immersion rite in Jerusalem around 351 could be that any prebaptismal anointing for the reception of the Spirit that may have once been part of the Jerusalem tradition was no longer practiced. To regard the immersion as a sealing without involving any physical marking is similar to what we found in chapters 3 and 16 of the *Didascalia* where the whole rite is generically called the seal, or in the *Apostolic Constitutions* 7.22 where, even though it calls for a postbaptismal sealing with *myron*, the water alone could suffice for the seal in the absence of oil or *myron*. The immersion rite had become the focal point of the initiation, which was a change from the earliest Syrian tradition where the prebaptismal anointing was central; the activity of the Spirit is now centered around the font.

Two passages hint at the possibility that by the time of *C* a postbaptismal rite of anointing was in use that symbolized a sharing in the messiahship of Christ. When previewing the coming events, Cyril says, "Then may you enjoy the Christ-bearing waters in their fragrance; then may you receive the name of Christ and the power of things divine" (*P* 15). In *C* 17.28, Cyril tells the candidates that the Holy Spirit imparts the name of Christ. This reception of the name and power of Christ fits well with the effects of the chrismation as described in *M*. We might have expected this to be part of the work of the Spirit "sealing souls" in the immersion rite, but the lack of any association of the term *sphragis* with sharing in the messiahship of Christ suggests that it was ritualized separately and not understood in terms of sealing. Further, nothing indicates that the gift of the Spirit is associated with any rite other than immersion.

In summary, what this brief analysis has been able to specify regarding the Jerusalem rites around 351 corresponds with what is understood of the development of that time: the prebaptismal anointing is no longer the focus of the initiation rite; indications of a prebaptismal anointing are evident but only in the form of an apotropaic signing, which may also have signified a mark of ownership (and for which the term *sphragis* would no doubt be used); and these were probably associated with renunciation and adherence rites. The heart of the rite is the immersion, and to this is applied the idea of a sealing by the Spirit. A postbaptismal anointing symbolizing messianic anointing and strengthening may also have been in use by this time.

We can now consider whether the ritual form found in M also fits with this development, and whether it exhibits signs of continuity or discontinuity with C. By the time of M, two anointings were administered, one with olive oil before immersion and one with *myron* after immersion. The first anointing is of the whole body and not only signifies participation in Christ the cultivated olive tree (M 2.3) but also serves as a token against evil powers. This second aspect suggests that it may have involved a marking on the forehead. There is no suggestion at all of the Holy Spirit, messianic anointing, or strengthening. The postbaptismal anointing is modeled after the descent of the Holy Spirit on Jesus in the Jordan: as the Spirit descended on Jesus, so the baptized receive the Spirit with the chrismation (M 3.1). The anointing is also messianic—those anointed with *myron* are called Christs, anointed ones (*christoi*, M 3.1). The *myron* is applied to the forehead to remove the shame of Adam, to the ears to enable the hearing of mysteries, to the nose to symbolize the odor of Christ (cf. 2 Cor 2:15), and to the chest to symbolize armor against evil powers. There is nothing unusual in the form of this rite in light of the developments of the time, but how does it compare to C?

It was noted above that in contrast to C *sphragis* in M refers to the postbaptismal chrismation and not the immersion or any prebaptismal anointing. Further, the reference is made only in passing in the fourth sermon on the Eucharist and not at all in the third sermon on chrismation. This silence about chrismation in M 3 also stands in contrast to the syllabus of C 18.33, a later addition reflecting a time closer to M when the mystagogy was moved to Easter Week. In that sermon, Cyril singles out "the seal *(sphragis)* of the fellowship of the Holy Spirit" as a topic for the mystagogy on chrismation, but in M 3 not a single mention is made of the term.

One other characteristic attests to the change in the use of this term. When *sphragis* is used in M, its sense is more that of a marking or signing with oil *(rušmā* in the Syrian tradition) than the more generic Pauline sense of the seal *(ḥatmā)* of the Spirit. The mystagogue says the following at M 4.7 when citing Ps 23:5:

"You have anointed my head with oil." He has anointed your head with oil upon your forehead, by the seal which you have of God, that you may become "the engraving of the seal, the holiness of God" (Ex 28:36 LXX).

Yarnold points out that the reference from Exodus is to the engraved plate of gold bearing the words "Holy to the Lord" that Aaron should wear on his forehead.[58] This is a vivid image, but it refers only to the forehead, and *sphragis* is restricted to the sense of a sign or mark rather than a sealing in the Spirit. At the same time, though, there is something that suggests that the term *sphragis* still carried some sense of a "sealing in the Spirit" and not just a signing or marking. The mystagogue does not say that the newly baptized receive or are marked with the seal, but that they become the engraving of the seal. This odd usage connotes something more spiritual or mystical like the "sealing of souls" (*C* 3.3, 4, 12; 4.16; 16.24; 17.35) rather than just a physical marking. But on the whole, nowhere in *M* does the mystagogue properly speak of initiation as a sealing in or by the Spirit, and the contrast to what is found in *C* is still striking.

Three points, then, call for an explanation. First, why is the term *sphragis* in *M* no longer attached to the immersion rite? Second, why does it receive such little attention: completely absent in *M* 3 and only a passing remark in *M* 4 where its meaning is restricted to only a sign or mark? And third, can some account be given for the mention of *sphragis* in *C* 18.33 as if it were a distinct topic in the upcoming mystagogy, while in *M* 3 no such topic is covered?

An explanation for the shifting of the term away from the immersion may be found in the changes taking place at the time in the number and form of the rites comprising the initiation ceremonies. By the time of *M*, there is clearly a separate postbaptismal rite of chrismation, the focus of which is the conferring of the Holy Spirit, and which includes an anointing on the forehead. This rite is now modeled on the events of the Jordan where the Spirit plays a very specific and visible role. The term *sphragis* would fit more easily with chrismation since it now has a ritual expression in the form of an anointing on the forehead with *myron*. Such a shift is already evident in the doublet at *C* 18.33 as indicated above. But once the term is aptly and specifically attached to one anointing, it would be an awkward confusion of image and symbol to use it for another one, or for the entire ceremony of initiation. We could say that the rite of chrismation has drawn away the term *sphragis* from the immersion rite (thus also precluding its generic use for initiation as a whole) and at the same time has become restricted to meaning sign or mark. In *C*, the "seal of the Spirit" could be generically used of the immersion rite, since it represented both conformity to Christ in his death and res-

58. *AIR*, 86.

urrection and the reception of the Spirit. In *M*, the conferring of the Spirit is separately ritualized in the chrismation. Probably for simplicity and clarity, by the time of *M* the term would be used only for the marking with *myron* on the foreheads of the baptized. The idea of sealing would still be best associated with immersion, but an additional use of the term *sphragis* would be awkward. The teaching on the immersion is no poorer without a reference to sealing—the model of Christ's death and resurrection using the key ideas of Romans 6 and the idea of union with Christ through likeness or imitation have been sufficiently developed to provide rich and effective mystagogy.

While the above can explain the shift of the idea of the *sphragis* from the immersion to the chrismation, it does not help clarify our second concern, namely, the absence of the term *sphragis* from *M* 3 and its relegation to a passing comment in *M* 4.

Two other factors, however, can explain this omission. The first is the reading for *M* 3 from 1 Jn 2:20–28, of which the key idea is the anointing that comes from God for enlightenment; the reading makes no use of the ideas of signing or sealing. Throughout *M* 3, the mystagogue is guided by the term *chrisma*, such that to introduce the idea of the *sphragis* would be an unnecessary shift in themes. Second, the rite of chrismation in the Jerusalem church (perhaps the first to do so) was not limited to the forehead but included the ears, nose, and chest. Hence, the value in earlier rites of using the single image of the imprinting of a seal would be greatly weakened now that the anointing involves various parts of the body.

Still, where the mystagogue does speak of the anointing of the forehead, we would expect at least a passing use of the idea. Instead, he opts for the image of Adam losing his shame: the anointed countenance enables one to "behold the glory of God with unveiled face" (2 Cor 3:18). The reference is probably meant as a contrast to the mark of Cain.[59] The choice of this image is not random. The author has already introduced the typological figure of Adam along with that of a return to Paradise in *M* 1.1, 9, and 2.2—in the last passage, the candidates are said to mirror Adam naked in Paradise with no shame. When the mystagogue preaches on the topic of chrismation in *M* 3, the theme is easily picked up again, probably at the suggestion of the ending of the day's reading, "as his anointing abides in you, . . . abide in him, so that when he appears we may have confidence and not shrink from him in shame at his coming" (1 Jn 2:28 RSV).

---

59. See Yarnold, *AIR*, 81 n. 16.

The above points suggest that the idea of the *sphragis* probably never acquired any great significance for the rite of chrismation once it was no longer useful for the mystagogy on the immersion. The insignificance of the term in general is suggested by the way it is used when it does occur in *M* 4. The brief passage concerning the *sphragis* at *M* 4.7 is in itself peculiar because it has nothing to do with the topic being addressed, the Eucharist. The mention of anointing simply comes (as part of the psalm verse being cited) between two ideas that are useful eucharistic images, a table prepared by the Lord and an overflowing cup. Once he begins his exegesis on the scriptural passage, the most obvious association for the psalm reference to anointing of the head with oil is the chrismation so recently a topic in the previous sermon; even then, the association is weakened by the fact that the psalm text uses the term oil, *elaion,* and the rite uses *myron.* It is not clear whether the verse from Exodus is what suggested the term *sphragis* for the anointing on the forehead or vice versa. In the next two sections, *M* 4.8 and 9, two more scriptural citations include references to oil (Eccl 1:2, Ps 104:15) and allusions are again made to the chrismation, but no use is made of the term *sphragis;* this would suggest that *sphragis* is only mentioned in *M* 4.7 because it occurs in the citation from Exodus.

There remains for consideration the anomaly of *C* 18.33 where Cyril mentions *sphragis* as the "seal of the fellowship of the Holy Spirit" as if it were a distinct topic in the upcoming mystagogy, while in *M* 3 no such topic is covered. The other aspect of the topic, the fellowship of the Holy Spirit, is also a theme not explicitly found in *M* but mentioned a number of times in *C:*

C 1.5: Baptism bestows the fellowship of the Holy Spirit according to each man's faith.

C 14.25: The Apostles impart the fellowship of the Holy Spirit by the laying on of hands.

C 16.10: Simon Magus asked for power, not the fellowship of the Holy Spirit.

C 17.12: Christ bestowed the fellowship of the Holy Spirit on the Apostles.

C 17.25: The Apostles impart the fellowship of the Holy Spirit by the laying on of hands.

C 17.33: "the fellowship of the Holy Spirit be with you" (2 Cor 13:14).

The common phrase, "fellowship of the Holy Spirit," probably has its source in the Pauline doxologies such as the one cited in *C* 17.33. Only in *C* 1.5, though, is the gift of fellowship mentioned with direct reference to the baptized and only as a passing comment. It does not figure at all in *C* 3, the sermon on baptism. Hence, it should probably not be considered a major theme for Cyril's baptismal catechesis and mystagogy at the time of *C*. In *M*, the chrismation is clearly for the gift of the Spirit, whose divinity is instilled in the baptized (*M* 3.3), but nearly all of the numerous uses of "fellowship" concern fellowship with Christ, never the Spirit.[60] Thus, for *M* as well, the theme of fellowship with the Spirit is minimal.

In the passage from *C* 18.33, the use of *sphragis* for a postbaptismal rite and the theme of fellowship with the Holy Spirit stand, therefore, in contrast to the rest of *C* and *M*. It was noted already that *C* 18.33 probably represents a time in a stratified text tradition later than the rest of *C*, but considering the time difference of some thirty years, it may still come from a time well before *M*. In any one year topics could vary, and this passage could simply represent a time when the mystagogue chose to speak of the postbaptismal rite more strongly in terms of a sealing and fellowship with the Holy Spirit. In light of the changes in these rites during this time, we could expect a certain amount of variation as the years went by.

There is another possible explanation for the disappearance of this topic on the seal and the fellowship of the Spirit that also might reflect a time of changes. *C* 18.33 could represent a stage of development when the mystagogy was delivered on more than five days, perhaps even literally "every day" as the opening line of the section says.[61] The list of topics can be divided into a maximum of seven parts according to the use of the conjunction "and."

1. First of the things done just before baptism;
2. then how you were cleansed by the Lord . . .
3. and how like priests you have become partakers of the name of Christ;
4. and how the seal of the fellowship of the Holy Spirit has been given to you;
5. and concerning the mysteries of the altar . . .
6. and how you must approach them, and when and how to receive them;
7. and last of all, how you must conduct yourselves in word and deed.

By the time of *M*, topic seven has all but disappeared; only a token moral exhortation appears in the last paragraph of *M* 5. Topic six has also been reduced to the third- and second-to-last paragraphs in *M* 5. Topic five is split between *M* 4 and *M* 5. Topics one and two correspond fairly closely to *M* 1 and *M* 2, and topics three and four have been combined into one and covered in

60. *M* 1.4; 2.3 (three times), 2.5 (twice), 2.6, 2.7 (twice); 3.2; 4.3, 4.7 (twice); 5.22.
61. As noted above, this phrase may also mean "on each of the days a sermon is delivered."

M 3. The particular idea of the seal has been reduced to a passing comment in *M* 4, and the fellowship of the Spirit is only spoken of as Christ's gift of the Spirit through the chrism. To the extent that it was necessary to reorganize topics, perhaps topic four was one of the more expendable.

One more point concerning the chrismation needs mentioning since Stephenson cites it as a difference between *C* and *M*. He says,

> In *Myst.* 3.6 Aaron and Solomon together are the prefiguring type of the royal priest-hood which is bestowed on the candidates by the chrismation. Both Aaron and Solomon are said to have first bathed and then been anointed respectively priest and king. In the Lenten Lectures, by contrast, Solomon appears only as an example of a penitent (*C* 2.13), and "Aaron was first washed, and then became high priest" (*C* 3.5)— no anointing.[62]

The apparent contrast is easily explained. The theme of *C* 2 as a whole is re-pentance and only this aspect of the story of Solomon is pertinent. In *C* 3.5, the subject is the symbolism and typology of water. Solomon would not have been mentioned since the topic is not anointing, and further, no wash-ing is involved in the story of his anointing. The specific mention of Aaron's anointing would not be expected; it is sufficient to say he became high priest. In the mystagogy on the chrismation in *M*, however, to specify that Aaron was made high priest by anointing is appropriate.

d. Summary and Conclusions

This extensive survey of the anointing rites and the use of the term seal has attempted to clarify how the Jerusalem rites were situated in this time of development and what changes they might have undergone. The changes thus far considered, namely, the number of anointings, the shift of the idea of the seal of the Spirit away from the immersion rite, and the enhancement of the postbaptismal chrismation, in particular its symbolizing the conferring of the Spirit, all fit well with what is known of the developments in the Syri-an tradition of the time. The articulation of the postbaptismal anointing and the enhanced theme of fellowship with Christ in his Passion (which coincid-ed with the growing popularity of associating the font with the tomb and im-mersion with sharing in Christ's death and resurrection according to Rom 6)

---

62. *WCJ*, 2:179. In fact, the account of Solomon's anointing (1 Kgs 1:38–39) does not include a washing. While it is possible that the mystagogue is aware of an extra-biblical tradition, it is more probably the case (since he is not quoting the biblical accounts) that the ritual form of washing-anointing is fixed in his mind, and he inadvertently assumes that Solomon was washed before being anointed.

are two ideas that probably had their origins in Jerusalem and provide an explanation for the near disappearance of the ideas of the *sphragis* and the fellowship of the Holy Spirit. None of the contrasts between C and M with regard to the anointings need, therefore, be explained as due to the influence of an author of M other than Cyril.

2. The Conferring of the Holy Spirit and the Laying on of Hands

We noted above how in C the activity of the Spirit is predominantly associated with the rite of immersion. There appears to be no significant difference for Cyril between receiving the Spirit and receiving grace or the gifts from the Spirit. At P 4, C 3.2, and C 3.7, for example, receiving the Spirit, being received by the Spirit, and receiving the grace of the Spirit appear to have no ritual distinction; they are all associated with the font. In contrast, M speaks of the gift of the Spirit primarily in the mystagogy of the rite of chrismation. This difference is understandable, though, for it fits with the development of the rites as outlined above. The development of a distinct rite of chrismation based on the model of the Jordan would naturally convey a strong sense of the visitation of the Holy Spirit. We need to consider whether this difference involves any serious change in theology that could best be explained by proposing two different authors.

A comparison of the chrismation of M 3 and the catechesis on baptism in C 3.11–14 shows that all of the typological symbolism of the two rites in M, immersion (M 2) and chrismation (M 3), are contained, in seed, as it were, in a single rite in C. In the time of C, the conferring of the Holy Spirit took place in the immersion rite. This was still not precisely in conformity with the Gospel model of the events at the Jordan where Jesus ascends from the water before the descent of the Spirit, but it is the rite that Cyril has to explain. When he gives his catechesis, Cyril resorts to a collapsed view of the Jordan scene where the Spirit appears to descend on Jesus while he is in the water. Stephenson points out that in C 3.14 and C 17.9 Cyril speaks of the Spirit descending on Jesus while he is being baptized by John (he uses two present participles).[63] Theodore similarly presents a collapsed view of the Jordan scene in his mystagogy on the immersion rite. In his comments on the single rite of immersion with its baptismal formula, he says that the mention of the Father is to remind us of the voice from heaven (adoption), the name of the Son reminds us of the divine person in the man who was baptized, and the name of

---

63. Cf. *WCJ*, 2:178.

the Holy Spirit recalls the descent of the dove.[64] In contrast, *M* 3.1 has Jesus emerging from the Jordan first before the Spirit descends on him.

Although Cyril considers the baptism and descent as one event in the catechesis on the descent of the Spirit on Jesus (*C* 3.13–14), while these events are separated in *M*, nevertheless there is a striking parallel between both texts concerning the purpose and effects of the conferring of the Spirit:

Moreover, when you have been deemed worthy of the grace, he then gives you strength to wrestle against the adverse powers. For just as after his baptism he was tempted forty days, . . . so you likewise, though not daring before your baptism to wrestle with the adversaries, yet after you have received the grace and are henceforth confident in the armor of righteousness, must then do battle and preach the Gospel. (*C* 3.13)	After that you were anointed on the chest, so that "having put on the breastplate of righteousness, you may stand against the wiles of the devil" (Eph 6:14,11). Just as the Savior after his baptism and visitation by the Holy Spirit went out and successfully wrestled with the enemy, so you also, after your holy baptism and mystical anointing, put on the armor of the Holy Spirit, confront the power of the enemy, and reduce it. (*M* 3.4)

What in *M* is represented by a separate rite of anointing happens in *C* during the baptismal rite. In the passage from *C*, the event that serves as the occasion for receiving strength is baptism, whereas in *M*, it is the visitation by the Holy Spirit in the mystical anointing. The difference between *C* and *M* with regard to a postbaptismal rite is only a matter of relegating everything associated with the descent of the Spirit (adoption, christening, strengthening) to a rite subsequent to, but distinct from, immersion. We have already noted that the change in the rites fits in with the development of the times and does not signal a different author. On the other hand, the similarity of catechesis in the two passages does suggest that they originate from the same catechist.

Lastly, there is the matter of references in *C* to the conferring of the Spirit by the laying on of hands that is relevant here, for there is no such rite in *M*. *C* 14.25 and *C* 17.25 mention New Testament examples of laying on of hands, but the important passage is *C* 16.26 because it refers to the initiation rites:

You see the type everywhere in the Old and New Testaments. In the time of Moses, the Spirit was given by the laying on of hands, and Peter also gave the Spirit by the laying on of hands. And on you also, who are about to be baptized, the grace shall

---

64. *BH* 3.25.

soon come. But in what manner I am not telling you now, for I will not anticipate the proper season.

When Stephenson comments on this passage, he takes it as an indication that the baptized will receive the Holy Spirit through some sort of rite of laying on of hands. This not only contradicts the ritual form of *M*, but of *C* also, which in every other place associates the conferring of the Spirit with the font.[65] There is, however, one interpretation of this passage that has not been considered. When Cyril says "but in what manner," this could be taken as indicating that the conferring of the Spirit will be done in a manner different from what has been the traditional way, that is, by some other way than a distinct rite of laying on of hands. If what was said above is true, that all the events of the Jordan model are symbolized in the rite of immersion, then any laying of hands for the giving of the Spirit would have happened there. Cyril speaks of an "invocation of grace" over the candidates once they have gone down into the water (*C* 3.12); this could easily have involved a laying on of hands. Such a scene is exactly what is found in Chrysostom:

When you see the bath of water and the hand of the priest touching your head, you will not think that this is merely water, nor that only the hand of the bishop lies upon your head. For it is not a man who does what is done, but it is the grace of the Spirit which sanctifies the nature of the water and touches your head together with the hand of the priest.[66]

But by the time of *M*, the collapsed view of the Jordan has been expanded and the descent of the Spirit is ritualized in its own postimmersion rite. Now there would be no significance attached to the imposition of hands in the font; in fact, the text (*M* 2.4) suggests that the candidates submerged themselves without an accompanying minister. A vestige of the laying on of hands still exists in the chrismation, but the *myron* alone suffices to convey the idea of being anointed by the Spirit.

Hence, in neither *C* nor *M* is there any solid evidence of a rite of laying on of hands, and the passage at *C* 16.26 need not be regarded as a witness to a rite in contrast to *M*, which could otherwise indicate a non-Cyrilline source for *M*.

3. The Scriptural Model for the Jerusalem Initiation Rites

We can now consider how the differences between *C* and *M* reflect the shift in the choice of scriptural models for baptism in the Syrian tradition,

65. *WCJ*, 2:180.
66. *Stav.* 2.10.

namely, a shift from the baptism in the Jordan to the model of Christ's death
and resurrection. Again, the concern is to see whether or not the differences
represent an understandable development in the local church's rites or
whether there is any difference in theology that might suggest that M represents a different mind than Cyril's.

In C 3 (sections 6–14), the catechesis on baptism is centered on the Lord's
baptism in the Jordan for its model. In contrast, the mystagogy on the immersion rite (M 2.5–8) is entirely based on Paul's treatment of Christ's death
and resurrection in Romans 6. We have already seen that this change in
themes and models is evidenced in the Syrian tradition in general and not
just in Jerusalem. On the other hand, certain similarities between C 3 and M 2
with regard to the scriptural models are worth noting.

Even though the Jordan model is the basis for the instruction of C 3, the
reading assigned to the sermon by the lectionary (no. 17) is Rom 6:3–4, which
deals with the death and resurrection of Christ. In the middle of Cyril's catechesis on the immersion (C 3), which is otherwise based entirely on the Jordan model, he uses this text for what is really the theological climax of the
sermon:

For if you have been "united with the likeness of the Saviour's death" (Rom 6:5), you
shall also be deemed worthy of his resurrection; . . . you, by going down into the
water, and being in a manner buried in the waters, as he was in the rock, are raised
again, "walking in newness of life" (Rom 6:4). (C 3.12)

This reference to the death and resurrection and the use of the text from Romans is brief, but important, and it looks as if Cyril, almost as an aside, is introducing this new way of regarding the font as a tomb rather than a womb.

In comparison, just as in C 3.12 there is a minor introduction of the later
predominant death and resurrection model, in M 2, where the death and resurrection model is central, there are remnants of the earlier, Jordan model.
In M 2.4 concerning the immersion rite, the font primarily symbolizes the
tomb of Christ. But the mystagogue also includes a brief mention of the
more primitive idea of the font as a womb, a means of birth. The font is simultaneously a place of death and new life: "In the same moment you were
dying and being born, and that saving water was at once your grave and
your mother" (M 2.4). More significantly, in M 2.6, another sign is found of
the earlier model that looks like an attempt to propagate the newer interpretation:

No one should think, then, that baptism is merely for the remission of sins and for the grace of adoption in the way that John's baptism brought only remission of sins. We know well[67] that not merely does it cleanse sins and bestow on us the gift of the Holy Spirit—it is also the antitype of Christ's suffering.

The collapsed picture of the Jordan events is similar to what was seen in *C* 3: remission of sins (*C* 3.11), gift (descent) of the Holy Spirit (*C* 3.14), and adoption (*C* 3.14). Here we have a summary of the catechesis of *C*, to which is being added a further interpretation, a sacramental participation in the Passion of Christ. Even though the postbaptismal anointing is firmly in place with a mystagogy that associates it with the events at the Jordan (*M* 3), and the immersion rite has its own mystagogy that draws from the model of the Passion and Resurrection (*M* 2), the mystagogue in the midst of *M* 2 still feels a need to cultivate the association of baptism with the death and resurrection of Christ as if it were not a fully established association. In both sermons, we can discern a common interest in promoting the new symbolism of the font.

Another feature concerning the use of the readings for the catecheses also shows this desire to promote a new understanding of the immersion rite. The reading for *C* 3 is Rom 6:3–4, and this same reading is also designated for *M* 2 but includes the additional verses 5–14, which further elaborate the idea of sharing by imitation in the death of Christ. Even though the reading for *C* 3 ends at verse 4, Cyril, nonetheless, uses verses 5 and 6. Verse 5 is particularly important in showing how the baptized are "united with" or "planted with" the death, burial, and resurrection of Christ. This instruction is a fitting climax to what the previous sections (*C* 3.10–11) covered concerning participation in the divinity of Christ by means of his sharing in our flesh and blood (using the text from Heb 2:14). In *M* 2.7, Rom 6:5 is also a pivotal text:

In order that we might learn that all that Christ endured, for us and our salvation, he did so in truth and not in seeming, and that we all become sharers in his sufferings, Paul cries out unequivocally: "For if we have been planted with him in a death like his, so also shall we be united with him in a resurrection like his" (Rom 6:5). "Planted with" is apt, for since the true Vine was planted here, we have been planted with him by sharing in the baptism of his death.

---

67. The genitive absolute, εἰδότων ἡμῶν, is ungrammatical, and two variant readings convey a stronger sense of emphasizing a new idea and parallel the opening "no one should think" (Μηδεὶς οὖν νομιζέτω): "let him see" (ἰδέτω, omitting ἡμῶν) and "let him know" (εἰδέτω, omitting ἡμῶν).

Just as with Cyril, for M this image of being united with Christ in his death and resurrection is key to understanding what happens in the font.

That Cyril focuses on the reading from Romans to emphasize the theological significance of the immersion in the midst of describing the rite according to the more traditional model of the Jordan, and that he goes beyond the day's reading to do so, indicates that this newer interpretation is particularly meaningful for him. We can regard the similar interest on the part of the mystagogue in M, namely, to promote the new idea of sharing in the Passion of Christ in contrast to the Jordan model and to use the same Pauline image to convey this new idea, as a significant correspondence of ideas.

D. Summary and Conclusions

In this long and difficult section, I have outlined some of the changes that were taking place in the initiation rites in the Syrian tradition in order to properly assess the differences exhibited by C and M with regard to the rites of Jerusalem, since these differences could suggest more than one author. We saw that what could be deduced about the changes in the anointing rites in Jerusalem during Cyril's time fit with what can be known about the overall trends at that time. We saw further that all the other noticeable differences between C and M, namely, changes principally in the catechesis concerning the conferring of the Holy Spirit, the scriptural model used for the immersion rite, and changes in the meaning of the term *sphragis,* are correlative to the changes in the rites. No contrasts in the theology expressed in the two sets of sermons emerged that could only be explained by the thinking of two different catechists.

To ask at this point what this evidence can reveal about the question of authorship is essentially to ask whether Cyril or John was the chief inspiration in the development of the rites and the corresponding mystagogy. To propose that John instigated the changes and that M reflects his work would mean that the changes took place between 387 and 417. This is certainly enough time, but so is the period between 350/51 and 387 when Cyril was bishop. Too little is known of John to say that he was not innovative. But since from Egeria it is already known that Cyril led a church that in every other way developed an elaborate and lively liturgy by the end of his career, we could expect that he also brought about changes in the initiation rites and, as a result, the mystagogy on them. In light of the examples of similarities pointed out above, this seems the more likely case. Still the possibility exists that Cyril was responsible for the changes and John for the extant mystagogy. Hence, little can be said at this point in favor of Cyril's being the sole author of M. This past section has dealt primarily with differences between the two sets of sermons and has shown that under the circumstances they do not amount to substantial objections to the Cyrilline authorship of M. That is, important objections against Cyril have been answered; evidence *for* Cyril is considered elsewhere.

CHAPTER 5

ဗဝ်

The Initiation Rites III

The Jerusalem Anaphora

A. Introduction

The fifth mystagogic sermon has been a valuable source of information about the structure of the Eucharist in the fourth century and in particular the structure of the eucharistic prayer, or anaphora. One of the most striking features of the anaphora as presented here in the mystagogue's commentary is the absence of any reference to an institution narrative.[1] This omission suggests that either it was not in the anaphora, or if it was, there was some special reason the mystagogue passed over any commentary on it. Whether or not the narrative was present is relevant to the present study first of all because it helps to determine where the Jerusalem anaphora should be located in the history of the development of anaphoras in the fourth century and thus pertains to the dating of M. That is, the concern is whether the anaphora represents a time too late for Cyril or too early for John. Second, the presence or absence of an institution narrative and the possible reasons involved bear on the literary and catechetical style of the author of M.

---

[1]. The debate on the presence or absence of the institution narrative continues. For the various positions see F. E. Brightman and C. E. Hammond, *Liturgies Eastern and Western* (Oxford: Clarendon Press, 1896), 469; Dix, *The Shape of the Liturgy*, 197–98; WCJ, 2:194 n. 16; E. J. Cutrone, "Cyril's Mystagogical Catecheses and the Evolution of the Jerusalem Anaphora," *OCP* 44 (1978): 52–64; Kretschmar, "Die frühe Geschichte der Jerusalemer Liturgie," 22–46; idem, *Studien zur frühchristlichen Trinitätstheologie*, 165–69; Hans Lietzmann, *Mass and Lord's Supper: A Study in the History of the Liturgy*, trans. Dorothea H. G. Reeve (Leiden: Brill, 1953), 411; John Fenwick, *Fourth Century Anaphoral Construction Techniques*, GLS 45 (Bramcote Notts.: Grove Books, 1986); A. Gelston, ed. and trans., *The Eucharistic Prayer of Addai and Mari* (Oxford: Clarendon Press, 1992), 72–76; and E. J. Yarnold, "Anaphoras without Institution Narratives?" *SP* 30 (Leuven: Peeters, 1997), 395–410.

B. The Text of the Anaphora

After a brief introduction, the sermon covers an exposition of the eucharistic liturgy beginning with the lavabo and proceeding through to Communion. In the middle, the mystagogue presents the anaphora in four basic parts: the preface (M 5.4–5), the sanctus (M 5.6), the epiclesis (M 5.7), and the intercessions (M 5.8–10). If we remove the commentary, the remaining descriptive excerpts by the bishop yield the following text of the anaphora:

The preface and sanctus:

> The Priest says in a loud voice, "Lift up your hearts."
> Then you answer, "We lift them up to the Lord."
> Then the Priest says, "Let us give thanks to the Lord."
> Then you say, "It is right and just."

After this, we make mention of sky and earth and sea, sun and moon, stars and all creation, rational and irrational, visible and invisible. We recall angels, archangels, virtues, dominions, principalities, powers, thrones, and the Cherubim with many faces. . . . We recall also the Seraphim, whom Isaiah in the Holy Spirit saw standing around the throne of God. With two wings they covered the face, with two more the feet, and with two more they flew saying, "Holy, Holy, Holy is the Lord of Hosts."

The epiclesis:

> Next, having sanctified ourselves by these spiritual hymns, we beseech the merciful God to send the Holy Spirit upon the offerings that he may make the bread the body of Christ, and the wine the blood of Christ.

The intercessions:

> Next, after the completion of the spiritual sacrifice, the service without blood, we entreat God over the sacrifice of propitiation for the common peace among the churches, for the welfare of the world, for the kings, for soldiers and allies, for the sick and the afflicted, and, in a word, we all pray and offer this sacrifice for all who stand in need of help.
>
> Then we recall those who have gone to rest before us, first the patriarchs, prophets, apostles and martyrs. . . .
>
> Then on behalf also of the holy fathers and bishops who have gone to their rest before us, and in general for all who in past years have gone before us.

C. Possible Explanations

Several explanations have been offered for the omission of any discussion in M 5 of the institution narrative. First, certain portions of the anaphora may have been prayed silently out of a sense of religious awe; consequently, the portions that the congregation did not hear received no commentary. Second, there indeed may have been commentary on the institution narrative, but that portion of the text is missing from M. Third, since the mystagogy of the fourth sermon covered the topic of the Last Supper narrative and its relevance to Holy Communion, perhaps the mystagogue passes over it in the fifth sermon because he sees no need to cover it again. Finally, there is the possibility that the Jerusalem anaphora at the time of M simply lacked an institution narrative. Knowing whether or not it had an institution narrative would help in determining its date, and this in turn would show if it best belongs to the time of Cyril or of his successor, John. Therefore, we will consider these various proposals in light of some current studies in the early history of the anaphoras and of the text of M itself to decide whether or not an institution narrative was present.

D. Evidence from the History of the Anaphoras

Since Kretschmar is the only one who includes a consideration of the date of M and its author, we will look at his argument first. One of his proposals is particularly interesting because he argues that the sparse contents of the prayer, namely, its absence of a post-sanctus thanksgiving, institution narrative, and anamnesis (as well as the absence of a rite of fraction), would point to an earlier stage of liturgical development compared to its near descendant, the Liturgy of St. James (fifth century), which contains all of these elements.[2] However, this hypothesis presented a difficulty for him because he had already accepted the conclusions of Swaans that M is the work of Cyril's successor, John, which would place M very near in date to the Liturgy of St. James. He was, therefore, forced to find an explanation for why an anaphora from the late fourth or early fifth century would appear to be without these key parts found in the Liturgy of St. James. His solution was that by this time the "missing parts" had become silent prayers as a result of a heightening "sense of distance, a consequence of the anti-Arian struggles as well as the attempt to protect the holy from profanation by the masses now pressing into the Church."[3] He admits, though, that while this move to silent prayers is well attested in the latter half of the fifth century with Narsai (Homily 17), nothing verifies that this was true at the beginning of the century.

Therefore, once we set aside Kretschmar's presupposition that M is from

2. Studien zur frühchristlichen Trinitätstheologie, 165–69.
3. Ibid., 167. This is essentially the same argument put forward by Stephenson, WCJ, 2:194 n. 16.

the time of John, the evidence he cites for the simplicity of the anaphora as found in *M*, including the apparent absence of an institution narrative, actually supports dating *M* to an earlier period when Cyril was bishop rather than later. Whether such a simple form of the anaphora existed even in Cyril's time is a question Kretschmar did not thoroughly pursue, and it continues to be debated.

Most recent studies on the early anaphoras have been inclined to include *M*'s among those without an institution narrative. I will argue, however, that the evidence suggests that *M*'s anaphora did include an institution narrative.

Studies in the early history of anaphoras begin by pointing out that we are not aware of any source for these prayers in the Syrian tradition that predates *M* and gives clear evidence of the use of an institution narrative. The sources include the *Didache*, Justin (*Dialogue* 70.4, *First Apology* 66.1), *Addai and Mari*, the *Third Anaphora of St. Peter*,[4] and possibly the *Baptismal Homilies* of Theodore of Mopsuestia (if they were delivered when he was at Antioch c. 382–93). A possible exception might be the *Apostolic Constitutions*, which does have an institution narrative, but is most probably contemporary with *M*.[5] It must be emphasized, though, that the judgment that these early sources are without institution narratives is only based on the fact that they do not actually quote the words of institution. But both of the passages from Justin, especially *First Apology* 66.1, hint that an institution narrative was in use in the liturgy he knew:

For we do not receive these things as common bread or common drink; but just as our Savior, Jesus Christ, being incarnate through the Word of God, took flesh and blood for our salvation, so too we have been taught that the food that has been blessed by a word of prayer from him and that feeds our flesh and blood by transformation is both the flesh and blood of that incarnate Jesus.

Also, it is still an open question whether or not *Addai and Mari* ever had an institution narrative.[6]

4. The received text of this anaphora has an institution narrative, but it is regarded by most as a later insertion. See R. C. D. Jasper and G. J. Cuming, *Prayers of the Eucharist: Early and Reformed*, 3d rev. and enl. ed. (New York: Pueblo, 1987), 45. For the minority view, see William F. Macomber, "The Ancient Form of the *Anaphora of the Apostles*," in *East of Byzantium: Syria and Armenia in the Formative Period* (Washington, D.C.: Dumbarton Oaks, 1982), 73–88.

5. See Marcel Metzger, "La Didascalie et les Constitutions Apostoliques," in *L'Eucharistie des premiers chrétiens*, Le point théologique, no. 17 (Paris: Beauchesne, 1976), 187–93; *Les Constitutions Apostoliques*, ed. and trans. Marcel Metzger, SC 320, 329, 336 (Paris: Éditions du Cerf, 1985–87), 1:57–60. Metzger dates the work to c. 360–80.

6. See William F. Macomber, "The Oldest Known Text of the Anaphora of the Apostles Addai and Mari," *OCP* 32 (1966): 335–37; E. J. Cutrone, "The Anaphora of the Apostles: Implications

According to Cuming and Fenwick, based on its content and shape, the anaphora of *M* belongs to a time, at least in the Syrian tradition, before the inclusion of an institution narrative was common.[7] Cuming also argued that while *M*'s anaphora is usually considered an early form of *St. James*, thus belonging solely to the Syrian tradition (since both these anaphoras are centered around Jerusalem), it also has affinities with early versions of *St. Mark* from the Egyptian tradition, a unique feature of which is an epiclesis immediately after the sanctus (that is, without an intervening institution narrative).[8] Cuming says the following concerning the development of *St. Mark*:

There seems to have been a definite movement in local Egyptian rites towards developing the post-sanctus into a consecratory epiclesis, as in Coptic *St. Mark*, the Deir Balyzeh rite, and the Louvain papyrus (cf. also Cyril's *Catecheses*); whereas the Alexandrian form came under the influence of *St. Basil* and *St. James*, and deferred consecration until the second epiclesis.[9]

Further, Cuming notes that while *M* bears similarities to *St. James*, they do not share any identical text between them. He argues that this is best explained by their sharing a common (perhaps oral) tradition. He suggests that they had a common ancestor very similar to the *Strasbourg Papyrus*, a fragment of an early form of *St. Mark*, but without an institution narrative. This varied background to the Jerusalem liturgy suggests that there was considerable room for cross-influence. The following summary statement of Cuming on how these anaphoras may have developed indicates that it would not be out of place if the anaphora of *M* was without an institution narrative:

If, then, Alexandria and Jerusalem at one time used the same or a very similar liturgy, something like the *Strasbourg Papyrus* must have been in use at Jerusalem. And if the next stage in the development of the anaphora was the addition of the sanctus and an epiclesis, the beginning of the divergence between the two anaphoras is clear. At

---

of the Mar Esa'ya Text," *TS* 34 (1973): 624–42; Bryan D. Spinks, *Addai and Mari—the Anaphora of the Apostles*, GLS 24 (Bramcote Notts.: Grove Books, 1980); Jasper and Cuming, *Prayers of the Eucharist: Early and Reformed*, 39–44; Gelston, *The Eucharistic Prayer of Addai and Mari*, 72–76.

7. G. J. Cuming, "The Shape of the Anaphora," *SP* 20 (Leuven: Peeters, 1989): 333–45; idem, *The Liturgy of St. Mark: Edited from the Manuscripts with a Commentary by Geoffrey J. Cuming*, OCA 234 (Rome: Pontificium Institutum Studiorum Orientalium, 1990); idem, "Egyptian Elements in the Jerusalem Liturgy," *JTS*, n.s., 25 (1974): 117–24; Jasper and Cuming, *Prayers of the Eucharist*, 52–66, 67–73, 82–87, 88–99; Fenwick, *Fourth Century Anaphoral Construction Techniques*.

8. While the Greek text of *St. Mark* does have a consecratory second epiclesis after the institution narrative and anamnesis, this appears to be a later development under the influence of *St. James*. See Cuming, "Egyptian Elements," 119.

9. Jasper and Cuming, *Prayers of the Eucharist*, 58. In "Egyptian Elements," Cuming notes a number of other affinities (linguistic and ritual) between *M* and early Egyptian rites.

Alexandria the new sections were simply added at the end instead of or after the short doxology of *Strasbourg;* in Jerusalem they were inserted between the preface and the intercessions, thus providing the exact form described by Cyril. After them would later be added or inserted the institution narrative, anamnesis, and ultimately a second epiclesis (the first being replaced in JAS, under the influence of Egyptian Basil, by a Christological section).[10]

Cuming goes beyond the evidence when he says "something like the Strasbourg Papyrus must have been used in Jerusalem."[11] Another weak point in the hypothesis is the precise form itself of the *Strasbourg Papyrus.* Cuming's theory depends on the view that the *Strasbourg Papyrus* was complete on one leaf, but this is not certain. The text is fragmentary, and what was originally in the gaps (perhaps an institution narrative) is still debatable.[12] A final weakness is the uncertain form of *M;* it does not contain a complete text of the anaphora but only a paraphrase for the purposes of catechesis. *M*'s anaphora fits into Cuming's view of the history only if it does not have an institution narrative, which he is unable to demonstrate. While these points show that Cuming's hypothesis about the form and place of *M* has not been proved, neither has it been disproved. Therefore, as far as an argument from the history of the anaphora is concerned, we cannot be certain whether or not *M* had an institution narrative.

E. Evidence from the Anaphora of *M*

Although we have seen that it is possible that *M* may have lacked an institution narrative in light of what is known of the history of the anaphoras of the time, we must now ask how probable this might be in view of the text itself. We will consider two points. First we will examine the layout of *M* 5 itself: is there any indication of a lacuna where the institution narrative would have been if it was indeed present, or does the text present an entire and coherent anaphora? Second, we will examine *M* 4 ("On the Body and Blood of Christ"), which has the institution narrative as its central theme, for evidence indicating whether or not the institution narrative was part of the anaphora.

The four basic parts of the anaphora (preface → sanctus → epiclesis → intercessions) seem to follow immediately after each other. If *M* is a pure an-

---

10. Cuming, *The Liturgy of St. Mark,* XXXIX–XL.

11. See the review by Bryan Spinks of Cuming's edition of *St. Mark,* in *JTS,* n.s. 41 (1991), 355–58.

12. See, for example, Bryan D. Spinks, "A Complete Anaphora? A Note on Strasbourg Gr. 254," *HJ* 25 (1984): 51–55.

cestor to *St. James,* we would then expect the words of institution to occur between the sanctus and the epiclesis (preface → sanctus → institution narrative → epiclesis → intercessions). But is there any room at this point? That is, does the text of *M* show any indication of a gap that could accommodate additional material? Dix argued no. He drew attention to the use of the word εἶτα, "next," which introduces the commentary on both the epiclesis and the intercessions: preface → sanctus → next, the epiclesis → next, the intercessions (*M* 5.7–8).[13] He calls the term "one of Cyril's habitual transitions. . . . It invariably means with him what it says, *next."* Where *M* seems to omit anything, the author prefers μετὰ ταῦτα, "after this." However, the commentary on the preface (*M* 5.6) begins with "after this" even though there is no reason to think any part has been skipped between the dialogue before the anaphora (*M* 5.4–5) and the beginning of the preface. At the same time, while "after this" may not always imply that something has been passed over, the term εἶτα may still mean only "next," and Dix's point still carries some weight. Another reason for thinking that the epiclesis followed immediately after the sanctus is that the commentary begins with a reference back to the spiritual hymns just mentioned, that is, to the sanctus: "Next, having sanctified ourselves with these spiritual hymns. . . ."

What Dix did not consider, though, is the possibility that the institution narrative could have followed the epiclesis rather than preceded it (preface → sanctus → epiclesis → institution narrative → intercessions). But Cuming shows that this would be unexpected only if *M* were representative solely of the Syrian tradition, which Dix argued, but not at all surprising if it had some kinship with the early forms in the Egyptian traditions, as he himself argued.

Further, the transition from the epiclesis to the intercessions (*M* 5.8) is not as obvious as Dix suggests:

Next, after the completion of the spiritual sacrifice, the service without blood, we entreat God over the sacrifice of propitiation for the common peace of the Church.

If there was no institution narrative, the opening phrases "the completion of the spiritual sacrifice" and "the service without blood" would have to refer to the preceding epiclesis. But these phrases seem more aptly to describe an institution narrative. That this is more probably the case is suggested by the use of the term for "completion" (ἀπαρτίζω) in other sources.

Chrysostom appears to have the institution narrative in mind when he uses the term in the following passage:

13. Dix, *Shape of the Liturgy,* 196–203.

When the priest stands at the altar, his hands stretched out to heaven, calling the Holy Spirit to come and touch the gifts, there is a great stillness, a great quiet; when the Spirit gives the grace, when it comes down, when you see the sheep slain and fully prepared (ἀπηρτισμένον), do you then cause tumult?[14]

He is outlining the parts of the rite and contrasting the stillness of the people during the anaphora with their disruptive behavior during Communion. Chrysostom elsewhere uses the same term with a more direct reference to the words of institution spoken by the priest:

"This is my body," he says; these words transform the elements. And just as that which was spoken, "Increase and multiply, and replenish the earth" was said once but is for all time operative in bestowing on our nature the power of procreation, so this which was spoken once makes complete (ἀπηρτισμένην) the sacrifice at every altar in the churches from then until now and until His coming again.[15]

Irenaeus uses similar language:

For we offer to God the bread and the cup of blessing, giving him thanks because he has commanded the earth to bring forth these fruits for our nourishment. And then when we have perfected (τελέσαντες) the offering, we call upon the Holy Spirit that he may show forth this sacrifice, both the bread the body of Christ, and the cup the blood of Christ, in order that the receivers of these antitypes may obtain forgiveness of sins and eternal life.[16]

The perfecting of the offering does not clearly refer to an institution narrative, but it is distinct from the epiclesis.

The text of M 5.8, therefore, would make better sense if there was an institution narrative after the epiclesis and before the intercessions. Dix's point about the term "next" can still be valid, but in the case where the institution narrative is present, the phrase, "Next, after the completion of the spiritual sacrifice . . . we entreat God" would mean "the next thing that takes place after the spiritual sacrifice has been completed by the recitation of the institution narrative is the intercessions."

As far as the layout of the anaphora in M 5 is concerned, therefore, the following points can be made regarding the presence of an institution narrative: first, because of M's probable kinship with early Egyptian anaphoras, an institution narrative, if present, would not be out of place after a single post-sanctus epiclesis. And second, against Dix, there does seem to be room for an

---

14. *De coemeterio et cruce* 3.
15. *De proditione Judae* 1.6; trans. Dix, *The Shape of the Liturgy,* 281.
16. *Fragment 36,* in *Libros quinque adversus haereses,* ed. W. Wigan Harvey, 2:502.

institution narrative between the epiclesis and the intercessions since the mention of a "completed spiritual sacrifice," immediately preceding the intercessions, more aptly describes the institution narrative than the epiclesis.

F. Evidence from *M* 4

We can now look at the fourth sermon, which has the institution narrative as its central topic. If the anaphora contained an institution narrative, is it possible that this sermon served as the commentary on it, and for this reason no time was spent on the topic in *M* 5? Cutrone, who thinks (following Dix) that the institution narrative was not in the anaphora, regards the special attention given to it in *M* 4 as an indication that the author thought it should be present, and the catechesis was actually a key influence in its eventual inclusion.[17] He says it is characteristic of Cyril (whom he takes to be the author) to connect, as much as possible, the mystery of the sacraments to the words and deeds of Christ. But Cutrone's point about the importance of the topic to *M* would still be valid even if the institution narrative was in the anaphora. We could just as plausibly argue that the scriptural basis of the rite, namely, the account of the Last Supper, is so significant and catechetically useful as an example of a dominical act that it deserves its own sermon. That is, the importance of its place in the anaphora rather than its absence is what could warrant treating it separately. Further, since these mystagogic sermons have as their chief aim the explication of the initiation rites as they were experienced by the newly baptized, it seems unlikely that the mystagogue would devote an entire sermon to the mystery of the institution narrative if there was no corresponding rite simply to promote a new idea.

Now inasmuch as the institution narrative is essentially formulated from a scriptural text, we need to ask whether strictly speaking *M* 4 is (1) a commentary on a passage of Scripture with a liturgical theme or (2) a liturgical text currently in use—only in the latter case would it suggest the presence of an institution narrative. As it turns out, the narrative that is quoted in *M* 4.1 is not from a single scriptural text but is a conflation of 1 Cor 11:23–25 and the gospel accounts. (In the following excerpt, boldface text is from Paul and italic text is from the Synoptics):

Our **Lord Jesus Christ on the night when he was betrayed** *took bread, and when he had given thanks, he broke it and handed it to his disciples saying, "Take and eat;* **this is my body.**" *And taking the cup, and giving thanks, he said: "Take and drink; this is my blood."*

17. Cutrone, "Cyril's *Mystagogical Catecheses* and the Evolution of the Jerusalem Anaphora," 63–64.

Such a conflation is precisely what is found in the early liturgical forms.[18] In one particular study, D. Wallace-Hadrill points out the same feature concerning the sole citation of the words of institution in the works of Eusebius (*Demonstratio Evangelica* 8.1.78). Eusebius is interpreting Gen 49:12 (LXX), "His eyes shall be glad with wine," as a prophecy of the Last Supper. The wine prefigures the mystical wine that Jesus

gave to his disciples saying, "Take, drink; this is my blood, poured out on your behalf for the forgiveness of sins; **do this in memory of me.**"

Eusebius normally cites his texts with great care and accuracy; the only reasonable explanation for the conflated form is that he inadvertently quotes the liturgical form with which he would be very familiar. Wallace-Hadrill cites this as significant evidence for the presence of an institution narrative in the liturgy of Caesarea some thirty years before Cyril preached. Since at that time, Jerusalem was much more under the influence of the metropolitan see of Caesarea, the Jerusalem liturgy no doubt would have followed the same form.[19]

A further point to consider is whether sufficient time was available for mystagogy on the institution narrative in *M* 5 where we would expect to find it—too much material with too little time might explain treating it separately from *M* 5. As we noted in the previous chapter, the reading for the fifth sermon, 1 Pt 2:1, is actually suited to the topic of Christian conduct, but the material covered by the sermon is instead a necessary carryover from the previous day's unfinished topic of the Eucharist. Originally, the entire mystagogy on the Eucharist was probably assigned as the fourth topic; but owing to the importance the author places on the institution narrative, all other topics were moved to the next sermon. Even then, *M* 5 is nearly twice as long as any of the other sermons although that is primarily due to the lengthy commentary on the Our Father.

Two possible reasons exist for the extended treatment of these parts of

---

18. See especially Lietzmann, *Mass and Lord's Supper*, 20–40, where he compares a wide range of the earliest texts of the institution narrative (including the *Apostolic Constitutions*, Serapion, Basil, and Chrysostom), which are all basically conflations of Paul and Matthew with various degrees of embellishment. See also Brightman, *Liturgies Eastern and Western*, 469 n. 11; Cuming, "Egyptian Elements," 118, and *The Liturgy of St. Mark*, 123; Massey Shepherd, "Eusebius and the Liturgy of St. James," *Yearbook of Liturgical Studies*, no. 4 (Notre Dame, Indiana: Fides, 1963), 122.

19. D. S. Wallace-Hadrill, "Eusebius and the Institution Narrative in the Eastern Liturgies," *JTS*, n.s. 4 (1953): 41–42. Regarding the dating, the *Demonstratio evangelica* was written c. 315, and *M* and *C* are assumed to have been delivered together c. 350.

the Eucharist. First, both the institution narrative and the Our Father were probably recent innovations and thus warranted special attention.[20] Second, both of these topics, which far outweigh all of the others in importance to the author and therefore get the most attention, are the only parts of the Eucharistic rite that are based directly on the words and deeds of Christ. This pronounced interest in showing the christocentric dimension of all the rites, and doctrine in general, is very characteristic of Cyril.

Finally, can some account be made of the lack of any direct reference at all to the institution narrative in M 5? We could construe the passage from M 5.8 that speaks of the "completion of the spiritual sacrifice, the service without blood" as a sufficient, if oblique, mention of it. But still another reason could explain why there is not a more direct reference. Recall that the text of M is in all likelihood more in the form of "preacher's notes" than a fully prepared text or transcript of the final delivery. If this is so, the content of M includes only that for which the mystagogue needed written guidelines in his preparation. The lack of material on the institution narrative could indicate that he was adequately prepared to comment on it extempore and briefly, especially since the topic had been addressed in the previous sermon. Although it may be difficult to imagine the mystagogue not mentioning an institution narrative (if it was present in the anaphora) in his final delivery, it is not hard to see him making a brief "note" to refer to it in passing during the course of his last sermon because he had already dealt with it in the previous sermon.

G. Conclusion

While there would be nothing unusual about the absence of an institution narrative in M as far as one version of the history of the anaphoras is concerned, neither is there any historical evidence indicating the presence of one. But the internal evidence in M suggests that its anaphora did have an institution narrative and that commentary on it was confined to the fourth sermon, leaving no need for anything more than an oblique reference to it in

---

20. The *Mystagogic Catecheses* has long been considered the earliest clear witness in the East for the Our Father as a part of the Eucharist; see, for example, Dix, *The Shape of the Liturgy*, 108–9, 130–31. This judgment has been based on a mid-fourth-century date for M. Even with a later date in the 380s, it may still be the earliest witness. In the *Apostolic Constitutions*, which dates from about the same time, the Our Father is recited by the newly baptized as part of the baptismal rite after the chrismation (*AC* 3.18). However, in earlier commentaries on the Our Father, the petition for daily bread is often correlated with Communion, which suggests it had become part of the eucharistic liturgy by the early fourth century. See Josef Andreas Jungmann, *The Mass of the Roman Rite: Its Origins and Development (Missarum Sollemnia)*, trans. Francis A. Brunner, 2 vols. (New York: Benziger, 1951–55), 2:280.

the fifth sermon. However, granting the presence of an institution narrative in the anaphora of M does not conclusively place it in the time of either Cyril or John. But in addition, we must weigh the special attention given to the topics of the institution narrative and the Our Father, because they are so closely connected to the words and deeds of Christ. This special attention is characteristic of Cyril and suggests that it is his theology and style that lies behind the text.

CHAPTER 6

§☉♋

Theology and Spirituality

A. Introduction

This chapter will examine certain select themes that are commonly present in P, C, and M and that characterize the theology and spirituality of the author(s). With regard to theology, the way in which certain topics are explained can reveal underlying theological views or preferences that are distinctive to an author. Because these sermons are catechesis for beginners, they are non-speculative and orthodox; hence, we should not expect to find theological ideas or positions unique to the catechist. However, considering the wealth of material these sermons cover, we can expect considerable room for nuances of interpretation or preferences for one topic, interpretation, or example over another. Spirituality is another area where an author can exhibit an identifiable style. What particularly moves him devotionally can be reflected in his choice of topics, how he dwells on them, or how he expresses their significance.

In the area of theology, we will first look at some examples of typology and baptismal symbolism shared among the texts, then consider some texts that reveal more deeply the sacramental theology of the catechist. In the area of spirituality, we will examine two common themes, namely, the importance of the cross and the place of religious awe in the rites of initiation.

B. Comparison of Theological Themes

For the catechists of Cyril's day, the use of biblical typology was a popular method for rooting sacramental theology in Scripture. Cyril makes extensive use of this method and three particular examples have parallels in M that are worth exploring. The first two are drawn from the story of the Exodus: the passage through the Red Sea and the blood of the passover lamb. The third is Paradise, lost to the first parents but regained in baptism.

Catecheses in preparation for Christian initiation are also rich in sacramental theology. We will conclude this section with a look at two themes of sacramental theology that commonly occur in *P*, *C*, and *M*. The first is more philosophical in nature and concerns the relationship between the spiritual and the physical dimensions of the sacraments. The second has to do with the rite of renunciation; both *C* and *M* use the incarnation of Christ as well as his death and resurrection in explaining the meaning of this rite.

1. Exodus Typology: The Red Sea

In the first of his Easter Week sermons, the author of *M* begins his mystagogy on baptism with a typological interpretation of the story of the Exodus. The first thing to note is that the mystagogue presents this Old Testament text only when he is directly preaching on the first part of the renunciation rite and not on any of the subsequent rites. He does, however, indirectly allude to the two subsequent rites of anointing and immersion.

Turn now from past to present, from type to reality. Formerly Moses was sent into Egypt by God, but now, Christ is sent into the world by the Father. At that time Moses led a persecuted people out of Egypt, here Christ rescues all people from the tyranny of sin. There, the blood of the lamb was a charm against the destroyer; here, the blood of the blameless Lamb, Jesus Christ, is a sanctuary against demons. There, Pharaoh pursued the people of old up to the sea, while here, this daring and shameless demon, the author of evil, followed you up to the waters of salvation. Pharaoh was submerged in the sea, and here the devil is destroyed in the waters of salvation. (*M* 1.3)

In this vivid picture drawn by the mystagogue, the renunciation rite corresponds to the Hebrews' accepting Moses' leadership and fleeing Egypt; the lamb's blood, representing Christ's blood, symbolizes the power of the prebaptismal anointing; and the flight to the sea prefigures the flight to the font. While the Red Sea is a type prefiguring the font, it is used not so much to illustrate the water's positive effect on the candidates as its destructive effect on the evil one. The sea is not a place of passage to new life for the candidates, it is strictly a locale for deliverance from the evil one. The author makes no attempt to elaborate here or later on any ideas of the cleansing or regenerative effect of water on the baptized. Strictly speaking, therefore, he uses the Exodus typology only in the mystagogy on the preliminary rites and not with the immersion.

In contrast, the association of the Red Sea with the immersion rite is a popular theme with other catechists, no doubt following the lead of St. Paul himself who makes the association in 1 Cor 10:1–5. Commenting on this passage Chrysostom says:

Do you wish to see the symbol? I will show you the baptismal pool in which the man that we were is buried and from which the new man arises. In the Red Sea the Egyptians were drowned but the Israelites arose.[1]

The emphasis on deliverance here is similar to what we find in M, but the association is more clearly made with the rite of immersion than with the renunciation rite, and the idea of passage through the font is important. In the *Baptismal Homilies,* he describes the type more generally as a symbol of both the break from evil (renunciation) and victory over death (immersion):

You did not see the Pharaoh and his armies drowned, but you did see the drowning of the devil and his armies. The Jews passed through the sea; you have passed through the sea of death. They were delivered from the Egyptians; you are set free from the demon. (*Stav.* 3.24)[2]

Ambrose makes an even stronger association between the passage through the sea and baptism:

Consider baptism for a moment. What could be more extraordinary than this, that the Jewish people passed through the midst of the sea? And yet all the Jews who made that passage died in the desert. But he who passes through the waters of this font—that is, from earthly things to heavenly (for this is the meaning of this passage, this pasch: it is the passage of the person who is baptized; it is a passage from sin to life, from guilt to grace, from vileness to holiness)—he who passes through these waters does not die: he rises again.[3]

For Cyril, on the other hand, this theme, as with M, is also of minor importance. In the whole of the prebaptismal sermons, the only reference made to the Red Sea with a connection to baptism is in C 3.5, the sermon on the topic of baptism. Cyril is expounding on the "noblest of the four elements," water, and lists the many ways it figures in great events in sacred history. In the middle of the list, he refers to the Red Sea, but not in a way that

---

1. *Homilies on Colossians* 7.
2. Trans. P. Harkins, in *Baptismal Instructions,* Ancient Christian Writers, no. 31 (Westminster, Md.: Newman Press, 1963), 64.
3. *DS* 1.12, trans. Yarnold, *AIR,* 104. See also Tertullian, *De baptismo* 9; Didymus the Blind, *De Trinitate* 2.14; Basil, *De Spiritu Sancto* 31–33 (3.25e–28a); Zeno of Verona, *Tractatus* 2.27.

singles it out from the other events, nor does he use the idea of passage through the sea:

For Israel, freedom from Pharaoh was by means of the sea and for the world freedom from sins was "by the washing of water with the word" (Eph 5:26). (*C* 3.5)

When Cyril deals more directly with the water of baptism in this third catechesis, he chooses the Jordan River as a type for the baptismal water and combines it with the image of a dragon in the water, representing death, taken from Job 40 and Psalm 74. According to Cyril, Jesus descends into the water, binds the strong one, and renders death powerless; henceforth, all who are baptized in Christ also conquer death (*C* 3.11–12). Similarly, when the author of *M* reaches the topic of the immersion rite, he also chooses the Jordan River for his typology rather than the Red Sea. The choice of a suitable typological model seems to be more the prerogative of the catechist than one determined by a fixed annual syllabus. Hence, the fact that an otherwise rich and popular example of baptismal typology should play such a minor role in both *C* and *M* can be regarded as a common distinctive feature of the two texts.

2. Exodus Typology: The Lamb's Blood

In *M* 1.2–3, when giving a brief account of the Old Testament typology of the initiation rites, the mystagogue makes a reference to the smearing of blood on the Hebrews' doors in order to ward off the angel of death:

There, Moses was sent by God into Egypt; here, Christ is sent by his Father into the world. There, Moses was to lead an oppressed people out of Egypt; here, Christ rescues all the people of the world overwhelmed by sin. There, the blood of a lamb turned away the destroyer; here, the blood of the blameless lamb, Jesus Christ, is made a token (φυγαδευτήριον) against demons. (*M* 1.3)

In this listing of types, which intends to mirror the rites leading up to the font, the smearing of the lamb's blood on the doors corresponds to the prebaptismal anointing that serves among other things as a protection from evil powers. This is confirmed in the mystagogy on the prebaptismal anointing (*M* 2.3), where it is the exorcised oil that the author calls a φυγαδευτήριον, a "token" or "charm" that can drive away demons:

The exorcised oil, then, is a symbol of the participation in the richness of Christ; it is a token (φυγαδευτήριον) that puts to flight every trace of the enemy's power. (*M* 2.3)

The most commonplace meaning of the word is a place of refuge, like a city (this is the only meaning given in *LSJ*). Lampe gives the additional definition "that which puts to flight," citing *M* 1.3 along with two other references from Macarius of Egypt[4] and John Climacus.[5] The term as it is used in *M* 1.3 connotes more the idea of a visible sign "that puts to flight" than a location of refuge. The term is used again in *M* 2.3 suggesting that the same typological imagery of the lamb's blood is intended (though it is not explicitly stated) since no new image is introduced that suitably represents the power of a charm or token.

In *C* 13.3 (in the sermon on the crucifixion), we find a use of the lamb's blood image that is noticeably similar to the examples in *M*. Cyril is presenting reasons for glorying in the cross even though it appears as foolishness to the eyes of unbelievers. For one of his examples, he compares and contrasts the blood of the paschal lamb to the blood of Christ:

C 13.3: In the time of Moses, the lamb drove the destroyer far away, but did not the Lamb of God, who takes away the sins of the world, all the more take away our sins? The blood of an irrational sheep brought about salvation; does not the blood of the only begotten all the more save? If anyone should disbelieve the power of the Crucified, let him ask the demons. If anyone disbelieves our words, let him believe what he sees. Many have been crucified throughout the world, but of none of these have demons been frightened. But when they behold even the sign of the cross of Christ, crucified for us, they shudder.

M 1.3: There, Moses was sent by God into Egypt; here, Christ is sent by his Father into the world. There, Moses was to lead an oppressed people out of Egypt; here, Christ rescues all the people of the world overwhelmed by sin. There, the blood of a lamb turned away the destroyer; here, the blood of the blameless lamb, Jesus Christ is made a token against demons.

In the passage from *C*, Cyril may well have in mind the apotropaic nature of his prebaptismal anointing rites,[6] though he would not be inclined to go into detail because of the *disciplina arcani*. The term used here for destroyer

4. *Homily* 25.10: The divine fire, which is the power of immortality and the illumination of souls, is also a dispeller of demons.
5. *Scala paradisi* 20. John says that alertness, in contrast to somnolence, is among other things, a token against idle thoughts.
6. See also *C* 1.3 and 17.35, 36.

(the only occurrence in *C*) is the same as that used in *M* 1.3 and 2.3 (though it is probably simply drawn from the Septuagint version of Ex 12:23). In addition to the general parallel in the use of typology, we can also detect a similarity in style. In both *C* and *M*, in addition to a simple correlation of the Old Testament type with its fulfillment, the contrasting greatness of the fulfillment over the type is also commonly emphasized:

C   the lamb under Moses
     the Lamb of God;

     the blood of an irrational sheep,
     the Blood of the Only-begotten;

     the crucifixion of others avails nothing,
     the mere sign of the cross of Christ keeps demons away.

M   Moses sent into Egypt,
     Christ sent into the world;

     Moses leads an oppressed people from Egypt,
     Christ leads the whole world from sin,

     the blood of a lamb,
     the blood of the unblemished lamb, Jesus Christ.

3. Paradise

In *M* 1.1, 4, 9, and again in *M* 2.2, the mystagogue makes allusions to Paradise:

But since seeing is clearly more persuasive than hearing, I have waited until this opportunity, that finding you more open to my words from your experience, I might lead you by the hand into the brighter and more fragrant meadow of this Paradise. (*M* 1.1)

I renounce you plotter, who disguised as a friend have worked all manner of wrong and caused our first parents to turn against God. I renounce you Satan author and abettor of every evil. (*M* 1.4)

When, then, you renounce Satan, trampling underfoot your whole covenant with him, you abolish your former treaty with Hell. The Paradise of God is opened to you, which was planted in the east and from which our first parent was cast out on account of his transgression. And the symbol of this was your turning from the west to the east, the region of light. (*M* 1.9)

O wondrous occasion, for you stood naked in the view of all and were not ashamed. You truly bore the imitation of the first formed Adam, who was naked in Paradise and was not ashamed. (*M* 2.2)

While the author of *M* is not unique in associating baptism with Paradise, he does have his particular nuances. A strong sense of a return to Paradise is evident—by means of baptism Paradise is regained. This is possible because of the reversal of the curse of exile (death) resulting from original sin. The return can be made only after the breaking of every alliance with Satan, enacted in the renunciation rite. This choice of imagery opens the way for speaking of Paradise as in some way physically present. The third passage shows that the baptistery itself is a symbol of Paradise; it is opened as a result of the rite of renouncing Satan that takes place in the forecourt, in sight, as it were, of the prize. Similarly, according to the first passage, the mystagogy is a sort of guided tour of the newly regained Eden.

Several passages in *P* and *C* suggest a similar use of the image of Paradise. It is first introduced in the *Procatechesis* where Cyril likens it to baptism or even the baptistery itself. After speaking of the purifying effect of the Lenten penance, the author says of its goal:

> May God at length show you that night, the darkness that shines by day, concerning which it has been said, "Darkness will not be dark to you, and the night shall be light as day." At that time may the door of Paradise be opened to each man and woman among you. Then may you enjoy the Christ-bearing fragrant waters. (*P* 15)

The features Cyril singles out, namely, the opening up of Paradise, the triumph of light over darkness, and the pleasant fragrance, are all echoed in the passages from *M*. Once they have trampled their contract with Satan (*M* 1.9), the candidates turn from the realm of darkness in the west toward the east, the region of light, to behold Paradise opening before them; they then enter a brighter and more fragrant meadow of Paradise than the one of old (*M* 1.1).

In *P* 16, he calls baptism the "delight of Paradise," and in *C* 1.4, he tells the candidates that, having moved on from being mere catechumens, they are already being "planted in the spiritual Paradise, . . . transplanted among the spiritual olive trees, being grafted from the wild into the good olive tree."

In *C* 2.7, the theme of a return to Paradise occurs again, and Cyril may be alluding to the candidates' renunciation of Satan in the outer chamber of the baptistery in sight of their goal of regaining Paradise. He encourages his listeners to be confident in the all-forgiving God and uses Adam as an example:

> He cast him out of Paradise (for because of sin he was unworthy to live there) but he "settled him opposite Paradise" that seeing whence he had fallen, and from what and into what state he was brought down, he might afterwards be saved by repentance. (*C* 2.7)

Cyril again uses this idea of the return to Paradise in *C* 13 on the topic of the crucifixion. Here he relates the story of the good thief and contrasts his entrance into Paradise with the original expulsion of Adam:

Very speedily I passed sentence upon Adam, very speedily I pardon thee. To him it was said, "In the day wherein you eat, you will surely die"; but you today have obeyed the faith, today is your salvation. Adam by the tree fell away, you by the tree are brought into Paradise. (*C* 13.31)

Since the image of Paradise is used in the baptismal catecheses of three contemporaries, Chrysostom, Theodore, and Ambrose, we need to take into account how the Jerusalem catechesis differs.

Chrysostom uses the story of the good thief to speak of Paradise in *PK* 3.19, but he makes no reference to the Paradise of Eden. In his treatment of the stripping rite, however, the imagery of Eden is used:

After stripping you of your robe, the priest himself leads you down into the flowing waters. But why naked? He reminds you of your former nakedness, when you were in Paradise and you were not ashamed. . . . Do not, then feel shame here, for the bath is much better than the garden of Paradise. There can be no serpent here, but Christ is here initiating you into the regeneration that comes from the water and the Spirit. You cannot see here beautiful trees and fruits, but you can see spiritual favors. You cannot find here the tree of knowledge of good and evil, nor law and commandments, but you can find grace and gifts.[7]

While Chrysostom finds it helpful to make use of the imagery of the garden to convey the idea of innocence, it is a limited use. The reason is that he regards the state resulting from baptism as far surpassing that of the first parents. As pure and refreshing as the flowing waters of Paradise may have been, the baptismal bath is better; evil lurked in the garden, here Christ is present giving new life; the beautiful trees and fruits of the original Eden are superseded by spiritual favors. This idea of a state greater than Paradise is expressed elsewhere when Chrysostom preaches on sin, repentance, and the forgiveness of God: "The devil drove man from Paradise; God led him to heaven. The profit is greater than the loss" (*Stav.* 2.6–7).

With Theodore as well, we find a strong sense of heaven as an advancement over any primordial state—Eden has been superseded by baptism. By means of the adherence formula, the candidate expresses the intention "to be reborn and to die with Christ and rise with him . . . so that after having re-

---

7. *PK* 3.8, trans. Harkins, *Baptismal Instructions*, 170.

ceived another birth, instead of your first one, you may be able to participate in heaven."[8] The movement is from the Fall onwards to a heavenly home rather than a return to a previous state.

Theodore's second anointing rite involves stripping, and he makes an association with Adam in Paradise similar to *M* 2.2:

As when Adam was formerly naked and was in nothing ashamed of himself, but after having broken the commandment and become mortal, he found himself in need of an outer covering, so also you, who are ready to draw nigh unto the gift of the holy baptism so that through it you may be born afresh and become symbolically immortal, rightly remove your covering, which is a sign of mortality.[9]

The imagery extends only to the clothing representing mortality; once disrobed, the candidates are in a position to relive, as it were, Adam's experience, only this time the prospect is a rebirth into new life, not death. No real sense of restoration of Paradise is evident.

Ambrose's use of the idea of Paradise is limited to theological explanations and does not figure very strongly in presenting baptismal imagery. In *DS* 2.17, he introduces the idea when speaking of the effects of baptism. Through sin, humanity became subject to death, but the original sentence of death has become the gift of life by sharing in Christ's death and resurrection. This was "to restore the heavenly gift that had been lost through the deceit of the serpent." His idea of canceling the sentence of death conveys a sense of restoration, and theologically he is very close to Cyril. But it is the promised "heavenly gift" of eternal life that was lost and is now restored; he does not use the imagery of regaining Paradise. The sense is more of continuing from the point where the original plan was interrupted.

This comparison to these other church Fathers is not meant to suggest that Cyril and the author of *M* think that heaven is no advance on Eden. In *P* 15, when he elaborates on the new Paradise that will be opened up to the initiated, he clearly has the heavenly court in mind, drawing on imagery from the Apocalypse. Rather, it is meant to show what aspects of Paradise, as symbolized by the baptismal rites, are selected and emphasized by each of the catechists. This common choice by *C* and *M* to emphasize the idea of a return to a paradisal state as well as their similar vivid use of the image of Paradise as a place to be regained is distinctive enough to suggest common authorship.

8. *BH* 2.14, trans. Mingana, 44.
9. *BH* 3.8, trans. Mingana, 54.

4. Theology of Double Sacramental Effect

In his article on the authorship of the *Mystagogic Catecheses,* Yarnold draws attention to a common characteristic in *C* and *M* that he calls a "theology of a double sacramental effect," that is, the sacrament has an effect on both the body and the soul.[10] This view contrasts with the one that regards the physical dimensions of the sacraments purely for their sign value—what happens physically only points to or is a vehicle for the spiritual dimension.[11] Yarnold cites only two texts to illustrate this shared view of *C* and *M,* but in fact several other ones can be noted, and the topic deserves closer examination (in the following examples, the terms used for body and soul are σῶμα and ψυχή). The two passages he highlights are *C* 3.4 and *M* 4.5:

For since man is twofold, a composite of soul and body, the means of purification are twofold also: incorporeal for the incorporeal, bodily for the body. Water purifies the body; the Spirit seals the soul . . . so that when the soul has been reborn through faith, the body also may receive its share in the grace through the water. (*C* 3.4)

In the new covenant there is heavenly bread and the cup of salvation that sanctify soul and body: for just as the bread corresponds to the body, the word is apt for the soul. (*M* 4.5)

Yarnold notes that this "opens the way to an extreme sacramental realism as is expressed in *M* 4.3 (see also *M* 5.15), 'his body and blood is diffused around our members.'" In the passage from *C* 3.4, Cyril adds that without both the water and the Spirit one cannot be saved.

This theology of a double sacramental effect is reflected in certain other passages:

[Simon Magus] was baptized but he was not enlightened. He dipped his body in the water, but he did not enlighten his heart with the Spirit; his body went down and came up, but his soul was not buried with Christ, nor was it raised. (*P* 2)

"For since the children are partakers of blood and flesh, he likewise also partook of the same" (Heb 2:14) that having become partakers in his presence in the flesh we

---

10. "The Authorship of the *Mystagogic Catecheses,*" 150–51.

11. See, for example, Tertullian, *De resurrectione carnis* 8: "To such a degree is the flesh the pivot *(cardo)* of salvation, that since by it the soul becomes linked with God, it is the flesh that makes possible the soul's election by God. For example, the flesh is washed that *(ut)* the soul may be made spotless; the flesh is anointed that *(ut)* the soul may be consecrated" (trans. Ernest Evans in *Tertullian's Treatise on the Resurrection* [London: S.P.C.K., 1960], 25). See also the general comments of Stephenson on this topic pertinent to the eucharistic theology of *M* in *WCJ,* 2:186–90.

might be made partakers of his divine grace. Thus Jesus was baptized that by this we again by participation might receive both salvation and honor. (*C* 3.11)

Jesus is physician of souls and bodies, curer of spirits, curing the blind in body, and leading minds into light, healing the visibly lame, and guiding sinners' steps to repentance, saying to the palsied "Sin no more," and "Take up thy bed and walk." If, therefore, anyone is suffering in soul from sins, there is the Physician for him; . . . if anyone is encompassed also with bodily ailments, . . . to such diseases Jesus also ministers. (*C* 10.13)[12]

For Cyril, the graces of the sacraments extend not just to the soul but are a benefit to the body as well. We find a similar theological interest in *M* with regard to the rite of chrismation:

[The *myron*] is applied to your forehead and organs of sense with a symbolic meaning; while your body is anointed with visible *myron,* your soul is sanctified by the holy and life-giving [*var.* hidden] Spirit. (*M* 3.3)

For this sacrament is the spiritual preserver of the body and the salvation of the soul. (*M* 3.7)

This exalted view of the physical realm aptly fits with Cyril's strong emphasis on the Incarnation. In *M,* this view is further expressed by the repeated emphasis on the reality of Christ's physical suffering, death, and resurrection as well as the corresponding experience of salvation for the baptized through their mystical, yet real, sharing in the incarnate Christ (*M* 2.2, 3, 5, 7).

5. The Relationship between the Incarnation and the Death and Resurrection in the Theology of the Renunciation Rite

The idea of participation in Christ's passion, death, and resurrection is a significant feature in the mystagogue's theology of the prebaptismal anointing and immersion in *M* 2. But the idea is introduced earlier in *M* 1, and we find a notable parallel in *C* 3.11. Commenting on the first part of the renunciation formula, the author makes use of Heb 2:14–15 to explain the confidence and courage of the candidates:

What did each of you say while standing there? "I renounce you, Satan, you wicked and most cruel tyrant; I no longer fear your power. For Christ has destroyed it, having shared with me in blood and flesh so that by means of these sufferings he might

12. Trans. Gifford, *The Catechetical Lectures of St. Cyril,* 1, 16, 61.

destroy death by death, that I might not be subject to eternal slavery" (cf. Heb 2:14–15). (M 1.4)[13]

Since this is not the most obvious scriptural text to use to elucidate the renunciation formula, it suggests that victory over Satan (death) by means of participation in Christ is an important idea for M. In C 3.11, Cyril uses this same passage from Hebrews when he is explaining how Jesus sanctified baptism:

> Being sinless, he was baptized that he might give to them that are baptized a divine and worthy grace. "For since the children are partakers of blood and flesh, he likewise also partook of the same" (Heb 2:14) that having become partakers in his presence in the flesh we might be made partakers of his divine grace. Thus Jesus was baptized that by this we again by participation might receive both salvation and honor. . . . He went down and bound the strong one in the waters. . . . The Life encountered him, that the mouth of Death might henceforth be stopped.

P. T. Camelot cites this passage as an example of how the baptismal theology of C differs from M.[14] He says that in the whole of C 3 the emphasis on participation is based on the doctrine of the Incarnation, while in M, participation is explained with reference to sharing by imitation in the death, burial, and resurrection of Christ (based on Romans 6). Further, he says that in C, Cyril emphasizes the baptism in the Jordan much more than the death and resurrection as a baptismal model. Cyril does in fact mention this latter idea of sharing in the death and resurrection of Christ in C 13.12 (immediately following the above cited passage), but Camelot regards it as having minor importance.

There are several reasons for thinking otherwise. It has already been noted that the reading assigned by the lectionary for C 3 (the Lenten sermon on baptism) is Rom 6:3–4 and that the same reading with the additional verses 5–14 is assigned to M 2 (the mystagogic sermon on baptism). It was also pointed out that when he comes to his most significant point about being planted with Christ in his death (C 3.11), Cyril goes beyond the day's reading and uses the additional verse Rom 6:5. For this reason, the section that fol-

---

13. The actual formula for the candidate seems to have been, "I renounce you Satan, and all your works, and all your pomp, and all your worship" (M 1.4, 5, 6, 8). The mystagogue, elaborating on the first part of the formula, is putting words into the candidates' mouths.

14. P. T. Camelot, "Note sur la théologie baptismale des Catéchèses attribuées à saint Cyrille de Jérusalem," in Kyriakon: Festschrift Johannes Quasten, ed. P. Granfield and J. A. Jungmann, 2 vols. (Münster: Aschendorff, 1970), 2:724.

lows (*C* 3.12) is theologically the most important point of this sermon on baptism rather than a minor or passing comment. It is the only section that speaks of the candidates' baptism in contrast to Christ's baptism, which is otherwise the focus of the surrounding sections. This itself suggests that *C* 3.12 is not an additional and secondary theological treatment of baptism, but an explanation that is coordinated with and follows on section 11. A closer examination will bear this out and suggest why, if *C* and *M* are from the same author, the passage from Hebrews is so suitable for the mystagogy on the renunciation rite in *M* 1.4.

In *C* 3.11, when Cyril draws attention to the baptism of Christ in the Jordan, he has two ideas in mind. First, he introduces the Incarnation because it is the basis of all of Christ's redemptive activity. All that is said about participation in or imitation of Christ must begin with this doctrine. Second, Cyril wants to furnish a typological validation for water baptism. The rite of baptism has John the Baptist's ministry at the Jordan as its basic ritual model. But since John's baptisms were only for remission of sins in preparation for the coming of Christ (thus they still belonged to the old order), it is only when Christ is baptized that the rite takes on a new significance. But even then, it remains a ritual model and symbol pointing to (even in Jesus' own life) the reality of his death, burial, and resurrection. This reality, to which the symbol points, is then the focus of *C* 3.12 where Cyril fuses together the symbols of the water of the Jordan and the font with the reality of the death, burial, and resurrection of Christ:

For you go down into the water bearing sins; but the invocation of grace having sealed your soul, it is no longer possible for you to be swallowed up by the terrible dragon. Having gone down dead in sins, you come up made alive in righteousness. "For if you have been united with the Saviour in a death like his, you shall also be deemed worthy of resurrection" (Rom 6:5). For as Jesus, taking upon himself the sins of the world, died, that by putting sin to death he might rise in righteousness, so you by going down into the water, being entombed, as it were in the water, just as he was in the rock, might be raised again walking in newness of life.

This account of the relationship between sections 11 and 12 of *C* 3 shows, contrary to Camelot, that the focus of the baptismal theology of *C* 3 does indeed lie in section 12 where Cyril speaks of sharing in the death and resurrection of Christ. The themes of the Incarnation and John's baptismal ministry in section 11 are necessary for presenting the argument of section 12 but are not the central focus. The extensive material on the Jordan event in *C* 3 might give the impression that it is the more important theme for Cyril (though a good part of it is devoted to a treatment of John the Baptist), but this should not distract us from the structure of Cyril's theological explanation in *C* 3, which has its focus in section 12.

According to the text from Hebrews, Christ incarnate takes on our mortal existence, he lives and dies as one of us, yet death has no hold on him; consequently, we also share by participation in his conquering of death and freedom from its dominion. As noted above, Cyril follows the same line of argument in *C* 3.11–12.

The same reasoning is used in the explanation of the first part of the renunciation formula in *M* 1.4. As a rite preliminary to baptism, the candidates are only asked to renounce Satan; they are not yet ritually enacting his defeat. According to the mystagogy, the candidates in effect pronounce Satan's impending doom as well as the reason (Christ's sharing in their mortality through the Incarnation) for their confidence that it will indeed happen. The typological interpretation in the preceding section (*M* 1.3) also has this twofold action of renunciation and subsequent destruction in mind when it describes the devil first being repudiated (according to the type of the lamb's blood on the houses) and then, after pursuing the candidate to the waters (the Red Sea), meeting his destruction.

This twofold action of renunciation and destruction corresponds respectively to the two consequences of the incarnation and the death of Christ: wresting the world from the grip of Satan in the Incarnation and finally defeating him in the Passion. That the mystagogue is concerned here only with the first of these two actions is suggested by the choice of verbs and objects in the text. By sharing in our human nature, Christ must first break the power of the devil (*M* 1.4). When summarizing in *M* 1.9, the mystagogue again refers to the breaking of the contract with Hades with the same basic verb used to describe the effect of renouncing Satan and adhering to the incarnate Christ: "you break that ancient league with Hell." The candidates have committed themselves to Christ in their act of renunciation and adherence in order that eventually, by their sharing in Christ's death through baptism, Satan might be defeated. Just as in *C* 3.11, the Incarnation is a prerequisite condition for the ultimate defeat of Satan; it is the condition under which both Christ and those who profess faith in him confront and overthrow death. In general, a close association of the Incarnation with salvation is a favorite one for Cyril: "For, if the Incarnation was a fantasy, salvation is also a fantasy" (*C*

4.9); "For if Christ . . . did not assume human nature, then we are strangers to salvation" (*C* 12.1); "The Lord took from us our likeness, that through human nature we might be saved" (*C* 12.15).

Hence, the apparent difference Camelot describes between *C* 3 and *M* with respect to the passages cited is not clearly demonstrated and ought not to be counted against common authorship. On the contrary, we found a certain correlation of ideas that fits better with the single author option.

6. Conclusions

Each of the above examples illustrated theological thinking that is to some degree distinctively similar in both *M* and Cyril's prebaptismal catecheses. None of them demands common authorship as an explanation for the similarities, yet a common author is a more probable cause than mere coincidence. Further, even though some of these topics and interpretations are shared among catechists of Cyril's time and hence could also be part of a set annual catechetical syllabus in any community, the examples shared by *C* and *M* are distinctive enough that they are best explained as the work of a single person.

We can turn now to the area of spirituality. Two ideas that stand out in these sermons for showing something of the spirituality of the author are the cross of Christ and the awe-inspiring nature of the rites.

C. Comparison of Spirituality Themes

1. The Place of the Cross in C and M

A central theme of the second mystagogic sermon is the candidates' participation in the passion of Christ by means of what can be called "iconic imitation." The mystagogue develops this from Rom 6:5: "If we have been united with him in a death like his, we shall certainly be united with him in a resurrection like his" (RSV).[15] The ritual imitation of the image, or icon, of Christ in his paschal mystery is such that, "while there is a likeness to the image of Christ, salvation is a reality" (*M* 2.5). The mystagogue repeats in *M* 2.6 that baptism is a "share by imitation in the suffering of Christ," and that baptism is the "antitype" of the suffering of Christ, that is, baptism is a symbolic rite whose corresponding reality is the death of Christ. Then in *M* 2.7, taking the cue from the reading from Paul, he says that in these initiation rites they

15. This idea of iconic imitation is well explicated by E. J. Cutrone, "Saving Presence in the Mystagogical Catecheses of Cyril of Jerusalem" (Ph.D. diss., University of Notre Dame, 1975).

experience a "likeness of death and suffering." We can see here a focused emphasis on the idea that what happens to those being baptized is in fact what happened to Christ, even though it is now experienced in the realm of sacramental ritual. This iconic imitation, which lies at the heart of M's sacramental theology, applies to the whole passage of Christ through death, burial, and resurrection (M 2.5), but participation in Christ's suffering and death is of particular interest to M. We find this emphasis in both the description of the rites (M 2.1–4) and in the commentary that follows (M 2.5–7).

In his description of the rites, the mystagogue explains the stripping and the prebaptismal anointing with reference to the Cross:

Upon entering you took off your clothing and this symbolized your stripping off "the old nature with its practices" (Col 3:9). Stripped naked, in this too you were imitating Christ naked on the cross, who in his nakedness "threw off the cosmic powers and authorities like a garment, and publicly triumphed over them on the wood of the cross" (Col 2:15). (M 2.2)

The Greek for "throw off" is ἀπεκδυσάμενον, which, as the RSV translates it, can also mean "disarm"; but for M the more literal sense of "putting off from oneself" is more appropriate in this context of imitating Christ in the rite of stripping. (The sense of disarming the cosmic powers, though, is nonetheless expressed in the second half of the passage from Colossians by means of the idea of triumph). This entire verse from Colossians is ambiguous, and the author has freely rendered it to focus on the power of the cross. In the original, the words ἐν αὐτῷ can refer either to the cross ("on the wood of the cross") or to Christ himself ("in him," as the RSV translates it). The mystagogue has opted for the latter and clarified the ambiguity by making a specific reference to the cross:

He . . . made a public example of them, triumphing over them in him. (RSV)

[He] publicly triumphed over them on the wood of the cross. (M 2.2)

This is useful for him because it enhances the imagery he is creating of Christ not only naked but on the cross. The result of his interpretation is a more effective association of the candidates in the stripping rite with the stripping of Christ on Golgotha.

At the end of M 2.2, the candidates are said also to be imitating Adam in Paradise, naked with no shame. What might appear as three separate ideas, stripping off the "old man," Christ on the cross, and Adam in Paradise are all actually related: the candidates "throwing off" the old man is in imitation of

Christ "throwing off" the cosmic powers; and thus stripped, they exhibit solidarity with Adam, a typological figure of Christ. A universal dimension of salvation is thus added, that is, the candidates join all of humanity with Christ on the cross.

The mystagogue then develops this idea of imitation into participation in his treatment of the prebaptismal anointing. Through the image of being grafted onto the cultivated olive tree, a symbol of Christ and his cross, the candidates learn of their share in Christ, the true olive tree:

Then, having disrobed, you were anointed with exorcised oil from head to toe and became sharers in Jesus Christ who is the cultivated olive tree. For you have been cut off from the wild olive tree and grafted onto the cultivated olive tree and became sharers in the richness of the true olive tree. The exorcised oil, then, was a symbol of your sharing in Christ's richness. (M 2.3)

This association with the cross is maintained by describing the subsequent movement to the font as reminiscent of Christ being taken from the cross to the tomb (M 2.4).

The three following sections (M 2.5–7) are a commentary on the rites just described. In them, the repeated refrain of the mystagogy is that what Christ truly experienced in his death, burial, and resurrection the baptized have also experienced, but they did so through a mysterious sacramental imitation. However, of these three parts of Christ's passage, the language of imitation and participation is focused more around the suffering and death than the burial and resurrection:

[Christ] did all this gratuitously for us, so that we might share his sufferings by imitating them, and in actuality gain salvation. (M 2.5)

Baptism does not merely cleanse sin and bestow the gift of the Spirit,

it is also the sign of Christ's suffering . . . a share by imitation in the true suffering of Christ. (M 2.6)

The newly baptized are to realize that

all that Christ endured, for us and our salvation, he did so in truth and not in seeming, and that we all become sharers in his sufferings. . . . In his case all these events really occurred; but in your case there was a likeness of death and suffering, but the reality, not the likeness, of salvation. (M 2.7)

Perhaps more than anything, the emotional exclamation in M 2.5 shows how much Christ's death on the cross was for the mystagogue the most important event of all:

O what transcendent loving-kindness! Christ received nails in his innocent hands and feet, and felt pain; and on me by my sharing in the suffering without pain or sweat, he freely bestows salvation. (M 2.5)

The minimal treatment of the resurrection in M is notable. In M 2.4, on the immersion rite, the font more strongly represents the tomb where Christ was buried than a womb where rebirth takes place. The more primitive Syrian use of the image of the womb for the font is here overshadowed by a new stronger association of the initiation rites with the events of the passion of Christ. This is the case throughout M. The first reference to the "waters of salvation" is in M 1.2–3 where the author presents the Old Testament types of baptism. The font is prefigured by the Red Sea, but both are cited as the place where the enemy, Pharaoh's army (that is, Satan) perish. Nothing is said of emerging into a new life, save for a passing statement of encouragement in the closing remarks (M 1.10) where he refers to the laver as "the font of new birth." In M 2 where we would expect the fullest treatment, we find only the brief additional comment that the font serves as a womb as well as a tomb:

In the same moment you died and were born; the water of salvation was both tomb and mother for you. . . . A single moment brought about both ends, and your birth coincided with your death. (M 2.4)

In M 2.7, the author has an opportunity to expound on the candidates' participation in Christ's resurrection when commenting on Rom 6:5, but the emphasis remains on the death:

In order that we might learn that all that Christ endured, for us and our salvation, he did so in truth and not in seeming, and that we all become sharers in his sufferings, Paul cries out unequivocally, "For if we have been planted [RSV: united] with him in a death like his, so also shall we be united with him in a resurrection like his" (Rom 6:5). "Planted with" is apt, for since the true vine was planted here, we have been planted with him by sharing in the baptism of his death. (M 2.7)

The image of the planting of the "true vine" has the double reference to the cross and the burial. Sharing in the suffering and death is clearly the author's focus. As for the resurrection, he lets Paul's reference to it suffice: it is simply the natural consequence of having been united with Christ in his death and burial.

This emphasis on the cross is distinctive of M in comparison to the contemporary accounts found in Chrysostom, Theodore, Ambrose, and the *Apostolic Constitutions*. Even for Eusebius, who was so closely involved with the uncovering and enhancing of the Holy Places, the cross has a lowly place.[16] When explaining the rites in his mystagogy (*Stav.* 2 and *PK* 3), Chrysostom, for the most part only speaks, and in a balanced way, of putting off or burying the "old man" and rising anew (*Stav.* 2.11, 24–25, 29; *PK* 3.12, 28–29). Elsewhere, he makes the following remarks: a passing comment concerning the renunciation rite that the contract with Satan was destroyed by being nailed to the cross (a reference to Col 2:14) (*Stav.* 3.21); a moral exhortation that, nailed to the cross with Christ, the neophytes have also crucified their passions and desires (a reference to Gal 5:24) (*Stav.* 4.28); and exegetical comments on why in Rom 6:5 Paul refers to baptism as a likeness of Christ's death (*PK* 2.8–11).

Theodore stresses the resurrection much more than *M*, treating extensively of the font as a place of second birth or regeneration (*BH* 3.2–4, 8–9, 12–13, 21). He makes only one significant reference to death when commenting on Rom 6:5:

We know that death has been abolished a long time ago, and we draw nigh unto him and are baptized with such a faith because we desire to participate in his death, in the hope of participating also in the resurrection from the dead, in the way in which he also rose. This is the reason why, when at my baptism I plunge my head I receive the death of Christ our Lord, and desire to have his burial, and because of this I firmly believe in the resurrection of our Lord; and when I rise from the water I think I have symbolically risen a long time ago.[17]

No reference is made here to the cross, and death is synonymous with burial. Only one other reference is made to burial in *BH* 3.25:

You have now received baptism, which is a second birth; you have fulfilled by your baptism in water the rite of the burial, and you have received the sign of the resurrection by your rising out of the water.

In both of these passages the resurrection receives equal if not more emphasis.

Ambrose, on the other hand, mentions the cross with nearly as much fervor as *M:*

This is a death, then, not in the reality of bodily death, but in likeness. When you are immersed, you receive the likeness of death and burial, you receive the sacrament of his cross; because Christ hung upon the cross and his body was fastened to it by the

16. See Walker, *Holy City, Holy Places?* 252–60.
17. *BH* 3.5, trans. Mingana, 52.

nails. So you are crucified with him, you are fastened to Christ, you are fastened by the nails of our Lord Jesus Christ lest the devil pull you away.[18]

As strong as this imagery is, the attempt to relate the cross with immersion is ritually awkward in comparison to M. Ambrose elsewhere more effectively and thoroughly treats the font as a symbol of healing (DS 1.15; 2.1–9) and regeneration (DS 3.1–3), presenting in the end a balanced picture of death and resurrection.

The *Apostolic Constitutions* also has only a few minor references to the cross. In AC 3.17, when listing the symbolism of the parts of the rite, the seal (most probably a reference to the prebaptismal anointing) is said to stand for the cross; in 7.22, the water symbolizes death but with no mention of the cross; and finally, 7.43.5 speaks of the crucifixion and death in association with the font, but it is just one among all the stages of the Paschal Mystery:

Look down from heaven and sanctify this water and give it grace and power, so that the one who is baptized, according to the command of your Christ, may be crucified with him, and may die with him, and may be buried with him, and may rise with him to the adoption that is in him.

That none of M's contemporaries exhibits as great an emphasis on the cross further highlights how for M the passion and death of Christ was the most important and central aspect of the Paschal Mystery. The resurrection is clearly significant but only as the natural and glorious consequence of the saving act on the cross.

A comparison with the prebaptismal sermons reveals a very similar emphasis. We have already noted that C 3, on the topic of baptism, shows signs of the emergence of a new model for baptism: the death and resurrection of Christ in contrast to his baptism in the Jordan. The use of Rom 6:3–5 introduces the idea that resurrection with Christ follows on and is dependent on having died with Christ, in other words, on "having been united with the likeness of the Savior's death" (Rom. 6.5, C 3.12). In fact, the theme of the cross permeates the whole of the *Catecheses* to the extent that Peter Walker can say of Cyril that "the cross seems to have been the apex of his system."[19]

The theme of the cross is most evident in C 13, on the article of the creed

18. DS 2.23, trans. Yarnold, *AIR*, 119. Elsewhere Ambrose refers to types of the cross (DS 2.11–13) and speaks of the font as a tomb symbolizing death, the just sentence for sin (DS 2.16–19).

19. Walker, *Holy City, Holy Places?* 256. Such is also the view of Paulin, *Saint Cyrille de Jérusalem catéchète*, 82–84, 232.

"Was Crucified and Buried," but its presence elsewhere is what demonstrates its importance for Cyril. We find that he not only teaches the significance of the cross on a theological level but also utilizes the fact that his listeners are assembled at the holy place of the crucifixion:

Yet one should never grow weary of hearing about our crowned Lord, especially on this holy Golgotha. For others merely hear, but we see and touch. (*C* 13.22)[20]

These two aspects of physical testimony and theological teaching deserve closer consideration.

Recent archaeological studies have revealed that the symmetry of the Martyrium (the main basilica of the Holy Sepulchre Church) is offset because it was constructed with the rock of Golgotha as a reference point.[21] Cyril's references to Golgotha and the cross seem to bear out the privilege of place he gives to this site. No less than thirteen references are made to Golgotha: *C* 1.1; 4.10, 14; 5.10; 10.19; 13.4, 22, 23, 26, 28, 39; 14.6; 16.4. Some of these also include references to the wood of the cross and are noteworthy in showing how important the physical witness of the holy place was to Cyril:

He was truly crucified for our sins. And should you wish to deny this, the visible place itself, this blessed Golgotha, refutes you, where, in the name of him who was here crucified, we are gathered together. Besides, the whole world has now been filled with pieces of the wood of the cross. (*C* 4.10)

His witness is the holy wood of the cross, seen among us even to this day, and by those who have taken portions thereof, from hence filling almost the whole world. . . . This holy mount of Golgotha, conspicuous in its elevation, bears witness to him. (*C* 10.19)

He was crucified, and we do not deny it; but rather do I glory in speaking of it. For if I should now deny it, Golgotha here, close to which we are now gathered, refutes me; the wood of the cross, now distributed piecemeal from Jerusalem here over all the world, refutes me. (*C* 13.4)

He refers to Golgotha and the cross far more often than to the tomb, and when he does refer to the tomb, it is more a sign of the death and burial of Christ than of his resurrection (*C* 4.11, 13.8, 14.20, 14.22). For Cyril, the more vivid sign of the latter is the stone rolled away from the tomb (*C* 10.19, 14.22).

---

20. Translations of *C* 13.22 and the remaining selections from *C* in this section are by Mc-Cauley, *WCJ* vol. 2.

21. See C. Coüasnon, *The Church of the Holy Sepulchre in Jerusalem* (London: Oxford University Press for the British Academy, 1974), 41; and H. A. Drake, "Eusebius on the True Cross," *JEH* 36 (1985): 7.

In light of this interest in the physical witness of Golgotha and the cross, it is not surprising to find a great emphasis on the cross theologically: "The Catholic Church glories in every action of Christ, but her glory of glories is the cross" (*C* 13.1). So Cyril begins the thirteenth sermon on the crucifixion and burial, and the same sentiment is reiterated as he begins his closing remarks: "Therefore, take the cross as an indestructible foundation, and build upon it the rest of your faith" (*C* 13.38). The cross holds a central place among all the doctrines of the faith:

> If any man should say that the cross is only an illusion, turn away from him. . . . For if he [Christ] was crucified in fancy only, salvation is a fancy also, since our salvation comes from the cross. If the cross is a fancy, the Resurrection is a fancy also. . . . If the cross is a fancy, the Ascension also is a fancy; and if the Ascension is a fancy, then the second coming is likewise an illusion, and everything, finally, is unsubstantial. (*C* 13.37; see also 13.4)

The sign value of the cross is greatly stressed by Cyril. Besides being a powerful token against demons and enemies of the faith, it is a positive source of sanctity for the faithful:

> Set up the faith of the cross as a trophy against objectors. When you are to dispute with unbelievers concerning the cross of Christ, first make with your hand the sign of the cross of Christ, and the objector will be silenced. (*C* 13.22)

> Let us not be ashamed to confess the Crucified. Let the cross, as our seal, be boldly made with our fingers upon our brow, and on all occasions; over the bread we eat, over the cups we drink, in our comings and our goings; before sleep; on lying down and rising up; when we are on the way and when we are at rest. . . . It is a grace from God, a badge of the faithful, and a terror to devils. (*C* 13.36)

> Let your very presence here now persuade you of the power of the Crucified. For who brought you to this assembly? What soldiers? With what bonds were you constrained? What sentence drove you here now? No, it was the saving emblem of Jesus, the cross, that has brought you all together. (*C* 13.40)

The cross is a powerful and multifaceted symbol that leads Cyril to his most extensive use of typology and his most eloquent passages. Sections 9 through 35 of this thirteenth sermon (the longest of all the sermons) are a step by step recounting of the events of the Passion and, wherever possible, he correlates events with Old Testament types: Adam with Christ (13.2, 18); the tree in the Garden of Eden with the cross (13.2, 19); the passover lamb with the sacrificed Lamb of God (13.3); the thorns and thistles reaped by Adam with the crown of thorns (13.18); the fig leaves covering the shame of

Adam and Eve with Jesus cursing the fig tree (13.18); the Garden of Eden with the garden of the crucifixion (13.19); Adam cast out of Paradise with the good thief brought back in (13.19, 30); the bronze serpent on Moses' staff with Christ on the cross (13.20); the wood of the ark with the wood of the cross (13.20); and Moses sweetening the water with wood with the water from Christ's side on the cross (13.20). The greater part of the types, Cyril says, are passed over for lack of time (13.20). Oratorically, Cyril does not just list a number of doctrinal points as he does in other sermons (such as with the resurrection in the following sermon). Instead, the sequential unfolding of the passion narrative has the effect of impressing upon his listeners the glory of the cross through vivid imagery.

The narrative reaches a climax in sections 30–31 when Cyril recounts the scene of the two thieves crucified with Christ. Even though Christ's death itself is the topic of the following section 32, it is the scene with the good thief that most moves Cyril emotionally, for it so vividly portrays the whole purpose and effect of the cross. The manner in which he freely elaborates on the scriptural text, his ecstatic exclamations, and his taking up the role of the characters in the first and second persons show how particularly meaningful the scene is for Cyril:

After rebuking his fellow robber, he says: "'Lord, remember me'; to you I direct my speech; never mind him, for the eyes of his understanding are blinded; but remember me. I do not say: 'Remember my deeds,' for I am afraid of these. Every man is well disposed to his fellow traveler; I am traveling with you towards death; remember me, your fellow wayfarer. . . ." What power, O robber, enlightened you? Who taught you to worship that despised man crucified along with you? O Eternal Light, which illumines those lying in darkness! Therefore he justly heard the words: "Be of good cheer,"—not that your deeds should cause you to be of good cheer, but because the King is here, dispensing favors. . . . "Swiftly I passed sentence against Adam; swiftly I pardon you. . . . The tree brought ruin to Adam; it shall bring you into Paradise." . . . O mighty and ineffable grace! The faithful Abraham has not yet entered, but the robber enters! Moses and the prophets have not entered, but the lawless robber enters! (C 13.30–31)

This passage reveals two significant aspects of Cyril's soteriology that are also found in M. The first is the gratuity of salvation: forgiveness and salvation are dispensed freely (M 2.5), the robber's sins are not counted against him. This act of forgiveness, which can overcome even the most serious and numerous of sins, manifests God's loving-kindness (φιλανθρωπία). This quality of God is very dear to Cyril; it is extensively treated in C 2 (on the forgiveness of sins) where he refers to it nineteen times. In the present context, he affirms it again in section 33:

> But see the wisdom of God; he preserved the truth of his sentence and the exercise of his loving-kindness. Christ took on our sins "in his body upon the tree; that we, having died to sin," by his death "might live to justice" (1 Pt 2:24). (C 13.33)

In M 2.5, it is by the φιλανθρωπία of God that Christ gratuitously died for us and freely granted us salvation.

The second aspect is the dispensation of this favor epitomized in one who shares Christ's suffering and death as a fellow traveler. The fruition of Christ's mission, which begins with the Incarnation, is to bear sinful humanity with him through death into new life—here it is not Christ who is depicted as (the new) Adam, rather the good thief is Adam being carried along through death to Paradise. The mystagogy on baptism (M 2.5–8) goes much more deeply into the mystery of salvation by participation in Christ's passion, but the element of sharing in the fruits of Christ's passion through imitation is still fundamental.

In conclusion, both C and M are characterized by a marked interest in the cross as a highly charged symbol of the Paschal Mystery. The attachment to the physical symbol of the cross and the keen theological interest in the crucifixion as the focal point of Christ's salvific act into which the newly baptized are initiated greatly outweigh attention to the resurrection. This common feature constitutes a significant similarity in theological interest and spirituality and is best explained by common authorship.

2. Spirituality of Awe

Another feature of spirituality shared by Cyril and M that Yarnold points out is the recognition of the awe-inspiring dimension of the Christian faith.[22] In M, it is principally the sacraments of initiation that are so described, and the mystagogue uses the term φρικώδης, "awe-inspiring" or "hair-raising":[23]

> Only let me tell you this: all your words, particularly those spoken at that awful hour, are recorded in the book of God. (M 1.5)

> Then the celebrant cries, "Lift up your hearts." For truly it is right at that most awful hour to have one's heart on high with God. (M 5.4)

---

22. Yarnold, "The Authorship of the *Mystagogic Catecheses*," 149–50.

23. This terminology may very well be drawn from the mystery religions. See Yarnold, *AIR*, 55–62; idem, "Baptism and the Pagan Mysteries in the Fourth Century," *HJ* 13 (1972): 247–67.

Next we pray also . . . for all who have gone before us, believing that this will be of the greatest benefit to the souls of those on whose behalf our supplication is offered in the presence of the holy, the most dread Sacrifice. (M 5.9)[24]

Cyril uses the term φρικώδης only once in C and P (C 17.36: the baptized will receive weapons that will cause terror in evil spirits), but the word φόβος, "fear," is used in other passages to express a spirituality similar to that of M. In P 9, he describes the terror caused in evil spirits in the rites of exorcism. Using an analogy of goldsmithing, Cyril likens the breathing of the exorcist, which injects fear, to the goldsmith intensifying the fire by his breath in order to purify the gold. At two other places in P, Cyril's comments reflect more generally the awe-inspiring character of full life in the Church.

If you see the believers not ministering with care, they still are secure; they know what they have received, they possess grace. But you stand at the balance point, to be received or not. Do not copy the carefree, but cultivate fear. (P 13)

Come in; you have been deemed worthy, your names have been enrolled. Do you see the august state of this assembly? Do you see the order and discipline, the reading of the scriptures, the presence of the religious, the course of instruction? Be intimidated by the place, be edified by what you see. (P 4)

This belief in the awesome nature of the sacraments is also evidenced in the practice of the *disciplina arcani*. In two texts from P, Cyril speaks of the final period leading up to baptism as initiation into mysteries, and he may even have contemporary pagan mysteries in mind as a model:

You were once called a catechumen, which means hearing with the ears, hearing about hope but without discernment; hearing mysteries but not understanding; hearing the scriptures but not understanding their depth. But you no longer hear with ears, but you hear within, because from now on the indwelling Spirit is forming your mind into a dwelling of God. (P 6)

You were once a catechumen, and I did not explain to you then what was coming. But when through experience you have attained the highest of the teaching, then you will understand that the catechumens are unworthy of hearing them. (P 12)

Two other passages from the body of the *Catecheses* reflect this characteristic of religious awe or fear in Cyril's view of the Christian life. In C 6.35, he finishes his teaching against heresies by listing the numerous things the true Church has to offer its believers in contrast to what the heretical sects provide. Included in the long list is the "teaching of fear and trembling of him

---

24. Trans. Stephenson, *WCJ*, 2:156, 193, 197.

who sends the rain." And in *C* 16.1, concerning Christ's saying on the unforgivable sin of blaspheming the Holy Spirit, he says, "a truly fearful thing is written in the Gospel." This is a fitting comment from one who places so much importance on the Scriptures as the foundation of all doctrine (cf. *C* 5.12).

Yarnold rightly points out that some indication of development is evident here. The more general comments about the fearful aspect of the faith in *P* and *C* have "blossomed into the description, drawn apparently from the mystery religions, of the rites of initiation as awe-inspiring, hair-raising."[25] That is, by the time of *M*, φρικώδης appears to have become a preferred term to describe these rites. Further, this phenomenon is not restricted to Jerusalem.

Thus, while this language cannot be considered unique to Cyril or *M*, still, the shared interest in a spirituality of awe is supportive of the possibility of common authorship. Further, the differences in language would seem to reflect a refining of terminology that accords well with the time span between *C* and *M*.

D. Conclusion

This chapter examined *P*, *C*, and *M* with regard to content by selecting themes that are shared by the three texts and characterize the theology and spirituality of the author(s) and then assessed to what extent the similarities in the choice and use of these themes were distinctive enough to indicate single authorship. Again, no single example demanded common authorship as an explanation for the similarities, but a common author proved to be the more probable reason than the coincidence of style between two authors. We can now turn to a similar examination of literary style.

25. Yarnold, "The Authorship of the *Mystagogic Catecheses*," 150.

CHAPTER 7

ℒℐℭ

Literary Style

A. Introduction

Having examined the theology and spirituality of these texts, the next step is to search for distinctive characteristics of the author's style common to *P, C,* and *M.* Since the texts are sermons, we will look at both oratorical and literary features. We will examine such characteristics as the particular choice of words, images, turns of phrase, and allusions, as well as the selection and use of examples from Scripture, in the following topics: imagery used for Satan, the use of fragrance as a symbol, the theme of "putting off the old man" in the renunciation rite, and imagery used for the anointing rites. We will finish with a survey of miscellaneous parallel terms and expressions.

B. The Imagery for Satan

In two passages in *M,* Satan appears in the image of some sort of wild beast. First, in *M* 1.10, the reading for the day's sermon (1 Pt 5:8–14) provides the image of a lion, and the mystagogue makes a further association of death with a beast:

Having been made secure by these words, "be sober." "For our adversary the devil," in the words we have just read, "prowls around like a lion, seeking someone to devour" (1 Pt 5:8). In former times "death was strong and devoured" men (Is 25:8 LXX), but at the holy and regenerating font, "God wiped away every tear from every face." (Is 25:8; Ti 3:5; Rv 7:17; 21:4)

The passage from Isaiah is a mistranslation in the Septuagint and should read, "He [the Lord] will swallow up death forever, and the Lord God will wipe away tears from all faces" (RSV). The Septuagint version has death as the one who devours and provides the author of *M* with an image of death as a devouring beast until such time as he is defeated in the water, that is, the regenerating font of baptism. The second example occurs in *M* 1.4, where the author is elaborating on the renunciation formula. He has the candidates refer to Satan as a "cunning and most vicious serpent" who led our first parents astray in Eden.

The image of the devil as a wild beast symbolizing death is also used in *P* and *C*. Besides a serpent or lion, Cyril also uses dragon, wolf, and whale. We will consider two aspects of this imagery for the devil in the following examples: the symbol of water as the place where the devil (death) abides and where he is finally encountered and defeated, and the simple portrayal of the devil as a wild beast.

1. Imagery of the Devil in the Water

The most striking passage is found in *C* 12.15 and has a close resemblance with the passage cited from *M* 1.10. Cyril is teaching on the topic of the Incarnation, on how Christ became human "that sinful humanity might become partakers of God." Having introduced the idea of Christ sanctifying baptism by being baptized himself in the Jordan, he adds:

If the Devil had known him [Christ], he would not have dared to approach him. . . . His body, therefore, was made a bait to death, that the dragon, hoping to devour it, might disgorge those also who had already been devoured. For "death was strong and devoured. And once more, God wiped away every tear from every face" (Is 25:8 LXX). (*C* 12.15)

We should notice first the common citation of Isaiah with reference to the idea of Christ conquering death either figuratively in the waters of the Jordan *(C)* or ritualized in the font *(M)*. In *M* 1.10, the mystagogue splits the passage from Isaiah so as to associate God's wiping away tears with the cleansing property of the font. While it may appear that Cyril also splits the verse here in *C* 12.15, the words "And once more" are actually part of the LXX text; Gifford and Stephenson, however, translate them as a comment of Cyril's as if he is citing a separate text. Cyril regularly introduces additional scriptural passages with "and once more," but this is probably not the case here since he has no need to split the verse, nor would there be much purpose in singling out the second half of the verse on its own. It is nonetheless notable that the passage from Isaiah is the one cited by both texts to go with the image of the devil in the water.

Cyril first uses this image of the devil as a water beast in *C* 3.11, where he explains how Christ sanctified baptism by his own baptism in the Jordan. He then uses the image of the dragon defeated in the waters in order to show how Jesus' baptism symbolizes the ultimate defeat of death through his death and resurrection:

The dragon was in the water, according to Job, "drawing up the Jordan in his mouth" (Jb 40:23). Since, then, it was necessary to "break the heads of the dragon in pieces" (Ps 74:14), he [Christ] went down and bound the strong one in the waters, that we might receive the power to "tread upon serpents and scorpions" (Lk 10:19). It was no small beast, and terrible. "No fishing vessel was able to carry one scale of his tail" (Jb 40:26 LXX): "destruction ran before him" (Jb 41:13 LXX), ravaging everything that met him. The Life encountered him, that henceforth Death might be silenced, and we who are saved might say: "O death, where is your sting? O grave, where is your victory?" (1 Cor 15:55). The sting of death is drawn by baptism.

Finally, Cyril gives an extensive treatment of the type of Jonah in his catechesis on the resurrection, devoting four sections to it (*C* 14.17–20). He also uses the opportunity for another association of the devil (death) with a water creature, this time a whale:

The one was cast into a whale's belly; the other went down of his own accord where the invisible whale of death is. He went down of his own accord so that death might cast up those whom he had devoured. (*C* 14.17)

For the author of *M*, the specific image of the defeat of the devil in the water is not as developed as in *C* (minor associations are made in *M* 1.3, where according to exodus typology, the pursuing devil perishes in the water—Pharaoh in the sea and Satan in the font—and in *M* 1.10). But we do find an interesting parallel to Cyril's use of a passage from Matthew. Cyril begins his section on Jonah with a citation from Mt 12:40:

For as Jonah was three days and three nights in the whale's belly, so shall the Son of Man be in the heart of the earth for three days and three nights.

When the mystagogue comes to associate the descent into the font with Christ's time in the tomb (*M* 2.4), of all the possible ways to describe Christ's burial, he chooses this rendering from Matthew:

For just as our Savior spent three days and three nights in the heart of the earth, so you by your first emerging were representing his first day in the earth, and by your immersion his first night.

The author clearly has the passage from Matthew in mind, and given the context of the descent into the water of the font, he probably has in mind the association of Jonah in the belly of the whale.

2. Imagery of the Devil as a Wild Beast

Second, we find references in *P* and *C* to the devil as a dangerous beast on the prowl, based on the passage from 1 Pt 5:8–14 (the day's reading for *M* 1):

But there is a serpent (δράκων) along the way watching those who pass by. Beware lest he bite you with unbelief. He sees so many who are being saved, and is "seeking someone to devour" (1 Pt 5:8). . . . And if you find anyone saying to you, "So you are going down into the water? Does not the city now have baths?" Know that it is the dragon of the sea that is laying these plots for you. (*P* 16)

Therefore we have need of divine grace, and a sober mind and seeing eyes, lest from eating tares as wheat we suffer out of ignorance; lest, taking the wolf for a sheep we become prey; and lest, supposing the destroying devil to be a good angel, we be devoured: for as Scripture says, "he goes about as a roaring lion, seeking someone to devour." (*C* 4.1)

Again he [Christ] is called a Lion, not a devourer of men, but to indicate his kingly, steadfast, and confident nature. And he is called a Lion in opposition to the lion our enemy, who roars and devours those who have been deceived. (*C* 10.3)

For the unclean devil, when he comes upon the soul of a man, . . . comes like a bloodthirsty wolf upon sheep, ready to devour. (*C* 16.15)

We could safely say that the use of this image of a wild or devouring beast is a favorite one for Cyril. The passage from *P* in particular has a combination of a number of images: the *drakon* is the monster of the sea (devouring death), a serpent (snake) that can bite an unwary traveler (recalling Satan in the Garden), and a prowling beast (in place of the usual lion in 1 Pt 5:8).

The image of the beast in *M* is not prevalent enough to say it is a favorite of the author's; the image of Satan as a lion could simply have its source in the reading set for the day. Yet, if we consider as well the additional use of the image of the serpent (*M* 1.4), the water as the place where Satan perishes, and the probable allusion to Jonah, the parallels with *P* and *C* appear to be more than coincidental and would suggest, rather, a common author.

C. The Symbolism of Fragrance

One pair of passages from *P* and *M* show a similar use of the symbolism of fragrance or perfume. *M* 1 and *P* 1 both begin with pastoral imagery:

Already a most blessed scent is upon you who are being enlightened; already you are gathering spiritual flowers for plaiting heavenly crowns. Already the sweet odor of the Holy Spirit has breathed upon you. . . . Blossoms have appeared now on the trees, may they be for fruit in the end. (*P* 1)

But since seeing is clearly more persuasive than hearing, I have waited until this opportunity, that finding you more open to my words from your experience, I might lead you by the hand into the brighter and more fragrant meadow of this Paradise. (*M* 1.1)

The passage from *P* conveys a strong sense of anticipation. The newly enrolled are in such close proximity to their new life in Christ that the signs of the richness of life in the new Paradise are already present. In the passage from *M*, they have reached the threshold of the new Paradise and are now to be guided through it.

Stephenson has pointed out the unusual comparatives in the passage from *M*, "brighter" and "more fragrant," and sees them as a continuation and development of the pastoral imagery of *P*.[1] He does not develop this point, but it is suggestive and worth exploring. Strictly speaking, the use of the comparatives means that the mystagogue and his audience understand that in the time leading up to their baptism, the candidates have been enjoying to some degree this "bright and fragrant meadow," and such indeed is the special nature of the prebaptismal candidacy. In *P* 12, Cyril explains the *disciplina arcani* and the unique condition of being no longer a catechumen but not yet an initiated Christian. The candidates are set apart from the rest of the catechumens for this period of enlightenment; they are φωτιζόμενοι, those being enlightened, and will have mysteries revealed to them that must be guarded from catechumens. Yet before initiation, they can only stand on the threshold; only when "by experience you have reached the height of what is being taught" will the reason for secrecy be clear. It would follow that if they are receiving enlightenment on the mysteries in some measure, we could also say that they are enjoying some foretaste of the fragrance and spiritual flowers of the meadow of the new Paradise. This is the intent of Cyril's opening comments in *P* 1 (in *C* 17.20, Cyril uses this image again when he compares collecting passages from Scripture to gathering flowers from a meadow). Hence, upon reaching initiation, he can speak of brighter and more fragrant meadows than what lay only at the threshold. This setting of a pastoral scene at the beginning of each series of catecheses

---

1. *WCJ*, 2:153 n. 2. He also notes this as a point in favor of identity of authorship.

and the use of the comparatives in *M* that refer back to the introductory sermon *P* suggest the style of a single author.

Other uses of the idea of fragrance indicate that both sets of catecheses
have a common fondness for this metaphor. In his introductory sermon,
Cyril wishes that the candidates may in time enjoy the "fragrant Christ-bearing waters" of baptism (*P* 15). When speaking of Holy Scripture, he says that
the *Gospel of Thomas* misleads the simple because it has only the "odor of an
evangelical title" (*C* 4.36). In *C* 6.12, he criticizes heretics who are falsely addressed by the "most sweet name of Christ." Further in *C* 12.34, he finds fault
in the use of incense for enticing pleasure when he says, "but in everything
let your incense be the prayer of sweet odor, the practice of good works and
the sanctification of bodies." Finally, concerning the Holy Spirit, Cyril says
that "his coming is gentle, the perception of him is fragrant" (*C* 16.16). The
remaining use in *M* is in reference to the chrism (*M* 3.4). Having been anointed, the newly initiated can say with Paul, "We are the aroma of Christ to
God among those who are being saved."

D. Putting off the Old Man

In the mystagogy on the preliminary rites of renunciation and stripping,
the author uses the Pauline imagery of "putting off the old man" as a
metaphor for conversion from Satan to Christ:

For you shall no more mourn, now that you have "put off the old man" (cf. Col 3:9),
but you shall keep holiday, "clothed in a garment of salvation" (cf. Is 61:10), which is
Jesus Christ. (*M* 1.10)

As soon as you entered, you put off your tunic, and this was an image of "putting off
the old man with his deeds" (Col 3:9). . . . For since adverse powers made their lair in
your members, you may no longer wear your old garment. I do not mean this visible
one, but "the old man that is corrupt through deceitful lusts" (cf. Eph 4:22). May the
soul who has once put him off never again put him on, but say with the spouse of
Christ in the Song of Songs, "I have put off my garment, how could I put it on?"
(Song 5:3). (*M* 2.2)

The following parallels are found in *C*:

"Put off the old man that is corrupt through deceitful lusts" (Eph 4:22), by confession, so that you might "put on the new man that is renewed according to the knowledge of him that created him" (Col 3:10). . . . Be numbered among the holy and spiritual flock of Christ, to be set apart on his right hand and inherit the life prepared for
you. For they to whom the rough garment of sins still clings are found on the left
hand because they came not to the grace of God. (*C* 1.2)

As you have formerly been a viper's brood, put off, he [John the Baptist] says, the slough of your former sinful life. For every serpent creeps into a hole to cast off its old skin and, having put off the old by rubbing, grows young again in body. In like manner . . . "put off the old man with his doings" (Col 3:9), and say that saying in the Song of Songs, "I have put off my garment, how could I put it on?" (Song 5:3). (*C* 3.7)

The passages in *M* are associated with the renunciation rite and the stripping, the latter being the last gesture of renunciation before "becoming partakers of Christ" in the anointing. Both of the passages from *C* are in contexts where Cyril is talking about sin and repentance; putting off the "old man" is abandoning a life of sin. Both, as well, use the imagery of a garment. In the latter, Cyril seems to be alluding to the stripping rite, for in both *M* 2.2 and *C* 3.7, respectively, the stripping of garments and rubbing off skin are specifically symbolic of abandoning the deeds of the "old man." Both *C* and *M* commonly use Eph 4:22, Col 3:9, and Song 5:3 for their useful imagery, but what is particularly striking is the stylistically similar use of the latter passage. In both *M* 2.2 and *C* 3.7, this passage is presented by the catechist as something the candidates can say as applying to themselves.

This last feature is also found in the one other use of Song 5:3 in *C*. In *C* 15, on the topic of the final judgment, Cyril again alludes to the garment as a symbol of sinful or righteous deeds, and he invites the audience to speak in the words of Scripture. Cyril is describing the scene of the final judgment with images drawn, as in *C* 1.2, from the parable of the sheep and the goats (Mt 25:31–46):

Does not the wool show the sheep, and the hairy and rough skin the goat? Similarly with you, once you have been cleansed from your sin, your deeds will be as pure wool, and your robe unstained, and you will say always, "I have put off my garment, how could I put it on?" (Song 5:3). (*C* 15.25)

E. The Prebaptismal Anointing

Two aspects of the prebaptismal anointing (*M* 2.3) can be compared with parallels in *C*. The first is the idea of participation in Christ, using the image of grafting, and the second is the exorcistic nature of the anointing.

1. The Anointing as Participation in Christ and the Imagery of the Tree and Vine

In *M* 2.3, the mystagogue develops the idea of participation in Christ by associating the anointing with olive oil with the image of Christ as the cultivated olive tree onto which the candidates, cut from a wild olive tree, are grafted.

Then, having disrobed, you were anointed with exorcised oil from head to toe and became sharers in Jesus Christ who is the cultivated olive tree. For you have been cut off from the wild olive tree and grafted onto the cultivated olive tree and have become sharers in the richness of the true olive tree. The exorcised oil, then, was a symbol of your sharing in Christ's richness. (*M* 2.3)

He draws his imagery from Rom 11:17–24 where Paul refers to his readers (Gentile Christians) as branches of the wild olive tree grafted onto the cultivated olive tree (Jewish nation), but here it is used as an image for the newly initiated and Christ.

This idea occurs again in *M* 2.7, but this time it is the true vine to which the candidates are joined:

In order that we might learn that all that Christ endured for us and our salvation he did so in truth and not in seeming and that we all become sharers in his sufferings, Paul cries out unequivocally: "For if we have been planted (RSV: united) with him in a death like his, so also shall we be united with him in a resurrection like his" (Rom 6:5). "Planted with" (σύμφυτοι) is apt, for since the true vine was planted here, we have been planted with him by sharing in the baptism of his death. (*M* 2.7)

The word σύμφυτοι is used to develop a rich set of associations. While the word can simply mean united with another, it can also mean grown together or fully cultivated.[2] The mystagogue uses this agricultural sense to introduce the image of the true vine from Jn 15:1–8. This image, with the play on the word φύω, conveys the dual sense of being joined with Christ on the cross (thus effecting a true share in his sufferings), as well as being planted with Christ in his burial.

In *C*, similar imagery is used. In his opening sermon, Cyril gives a brief exhortation to the newly enrolled on the state of mind and heart necessary to approach baptism. He includes a brief description of the new life of the believer that includes the following:

You are henceforth transplanted among the spiritual olive trees, being grafted from the wild into the good olive tree, from sins into righteousness, from pollutions into purity. You become partakers of the holy vine. (*C* 1.4)

This passage is preceded by a listing of other things to look forward to: they will be planted in the spiritual paradise, they will receive a spiritual

2. *S.v.*, *PGL* and *LSJ*.

shield, and they will receive a new name. Cyril appears to be alluding to some of the features of the rites to come. Entrance into the baptistery is entrance into paradise (*M* 1.1); one of the features of the anointing (both pre- and postbaptismal) is its protective nature, like a shield;[3] at baptism they will receive a new name, though here it is believer, while in *M* 3 it is Christian. Further, as in *M* 2.3, he uses imagery from Rom 11:17–24, the grafting onto the cultivated olive tree. And here again it is not used in the Pauline sense of comparing Gentile Christians with Jews, but sacramentally, where the cultivated olive tree is a reference to Christ. And further, as in *M* 2.3 and 7, the grafting is immediately said to result in a share in Christ, the cultivated olive (*M* 2.3), the true vine (*M* 2.7).

The fluidity of the symbols of tree and vine in *M*, in that they evoke images of both the crucifixion and, through the idea of planting, the burial, is similarly reflected in *C* in passages where images of crucifixion and burial are ambiguously used.

Adam received the sentence: Cursed is the ground in your labors, thorns and thistles shall it bring forth to you (Gn 3:17–18). For this reason Jesus assumes the thorns, that he might cancel the sentence; for this reason also he was buried in the earth, that the earth that had been cursed might receive the blessing instead of a curse. (*C* 13.18)[4]

In Paradise was the fall, and in a garden was our salvation. From the Tree came sin, and until the Tree, sin lasted. (*C* 13.19)

The Tree of Life, therefore was planted in the earth, that the earth that had been cursed might enjoy the blessing, and that the dead might be released. (*C* 13.35)

In other places, Cyril uses the image of a garden for both the crucifixion and the burial. For both locales, he uses Song 5:1: "I have come to my garden, my sister, my bride; I gather my myrrh and my spices." In *C* 13.32 (see also *C* 14.5), it is Christ who has come into the garden to be crucified, and the myrrh refers to the mixture of wine with myrrh and vinegar given to him on the cross. But then in *C* 14.11, the garden becomes the place of burial, and the myrrh refers to the myrrh, aloes, and spices brought to the tomb by the women. He also brings in the image of the planted vine:

A garden was the place of his burial, and a vine was planted there; and he has said, "I am the vine" (Jn 15:1). He was planted therefore in the earth in order that he might root out the curse that came because of Adam. . . . And what will he that is buried in

---

3. See *M* 2.3 and especially *M* 3.4.

4. See also Ambrose, *DS* 2.16–19 for a similar use of these ideas.

the garden say? "I have gathered my myrrh with my spices"; and again, "Myrrh with aloes, with all chief spices" (Song 5:1, 4:14). Now these are the symbols of the burying. (*C* 14.11)

Here the vine is planted to cancel the curse of the earth; in *C* 13.35 (above), it was the Tree of Life that cancels the curse. The tree is clearly a symbol of the cross (*C* 13.19), and given that the garden is the place of the crucifixion as well as burial, the vine evokes an image of the cross. Yet, as both are planted in the earth, Cyril can also use the image of burial. Just like *M* 2.7, we find here that same sort of double evocation of symbol.

That both texts would use the symbols of tree and vine to represent the cross is not particularly striking. But the fact that both are used in close proximity with the idea of grafting (*M* 2.3, 7; *C* 1.4) and that both are used to simultaneously evoke the images of the cross and burial, constitutes a significant parallel best explained by common authorship.

2. The Prebaptismal Anointing as Exorcistic

One of the properties of the oil used in the prebaptismal anointing is its exorcistic power:

It is the token against every trace of the enemy's power. Just as the breath of the saints and the invocation of the name of God burn like a fierce flame and drive out demons, so also the exorcised oil by the invocation of God and prayer receives such power as not only to cleanse every trace of sin with fire but also to pursue the invisible powers of evil. (*M* 2.3)

The author cites the exorcistic rite of breathing at this point for purposes of comparison, and thus we can assume it would be something familiar to the audience; but since nothing more is said of it, it was probably only used in the Lenten preparation. Apart from this anointing, *M* has nothing more about exorcisms.

Cyril makes a reference to the power of the name of Christ in expelling demons in *C* 4:

We proclaim the Crucified and the demons now tremble. Many have been crucified at times, but of what other crucified did the invocation drive demons away? (*C* 4.13)

An example with a more striking similarity to the passage in *M* occurs in the first sermon on the Holy Spirit, *C* 16:

A man still clothed with a body wrestles with many most fierce demons; and often the demon, whom many could not master with iron bands, has been mastered by

the man's words of prayer, through the power in him of the Holy Spirit. And the
mere breathing of the exorcist becomes fire to that unseen one. (*C* 16.19)

What stands out first is the mentioning together in *M* 2.3 and *C* 16.19 of
two ways of combating demons: prayer and the rite of breathing. They also
share in common the image of the breathing of the exorcist burning like a
fire and the reference to the demons as invisible or unseen. The image of fire
deserves particular attention because another similar description occurs in *P*
9 where Cyril describes the exorcisms using the analogy of a goldsmith.

For just as when those who are experienced in the goldsmith's craft apply their
breath to the fire through delicate instruments and breathe upon the gold hidden in
the crucible, stimulating the flame that surrounds it, they find what they are seeking;
so also when the exorcists infuse fear by the Spirit of God and rekindle the soul, as it
were, in the crucible of the body, the hateful demon flees. (*P* 9)

Here again, we see the image of breathing that stirs up fire and brings about
purification.

F. Miscellaneous Parallel Terms and Expressions

In the various topics treated thus far in this chapter, I have cited and dis-
cussed select parallel terms and expressions between *M* and *P/C*. Additional
examples not necessarily tied to any particular topic are worth noting.

1. *M* 2.2 and *C* 13.36 both cite Col 2:15 concerning Christ's triumph over evil
powers by means of the cross:

Stripped naked, in this too you were imitating Christ naked on the cross, who in his
nakedness "threw off the cosmic powers and authorities like a garment, and on the
wood of the cross publicly triumphed over them." (*M* 2.2)

[The cross] is the sign of the faithful and a terror to devils, for "he triumphed over
them in it, publicly making a show of them"; for when they see the cross, they are
reminded of the crucified. (*C* 13.36)

In both passages, the scriptural verse is slightly paraphrased from the original: he made a public example of them, triumphing over them in him (RSV).
The indirect object of "triumph," ἐν αὐτῷ, can either mean "in him," namely, Christ (the preferred reading for the *RSV*) or "in it," namely, the cross.
Both passages opt for the second reading. In *M* 2.2, the mystagogue has to
substitute "the wood" for "it" to make the meaning clear; in the other passage, the antecedent is obvious so no such alteration is needed.

2. Both *M* and *C* share the sentiment that it is by the grace of God, or by God's will, that the catechesis takes place. Stylistically, this idea is commonly used when either introducing commentary or with reference to what has either just been said or to previous sermons:[5]

These subjects have been treated at large, as God's grace allowed, in the previous discourses. (*M* 1.9)

When we enter, God willing, in the succeeding discourses on the mysteries, into the Holy of Holies, we shall receive the key to the rites performed there. (*M* 1.11)

By the mercy of God you have in our former assemblies received sufficient instruction about Baptism. (*M* 5.1)

Therefore, being content for the present with these testimonies from the Old Testament, we will go on, God willing, in the next lecture to the remaining texts in the New Testament. (*C* 16.32)

In the preceding lecture, dearly beloved, we set forth for your attention as best we could some small portion of the testimonies regarding the Holy Spirit; in the present, God willing, we shall touch upon, as far as possible, those that remain from the New Testament. (*C* 17.1)

But when the holy day of Easter dawns, . . . you will, God willing, receive the further necessary instruction. (*C* 18.32)

These points will, God willing, be the burden of our talks. (*C* 18.33)

And on these points, if God grant it, we will speak more fully at the proper time. (*C* 4.8)

I have spoken of it summarily, touching the main points, but if the Lord grant, I shall discuss it more fully later. (*C* 4.17)

With God's grace you will get an explanation of the remaining articles of the faith in good time. (*C* 15.33)

Thus far let these words of mine suffice, by the grace of Christ. (*C* 11.22)

Since there is much controversy, and the strife is manifold, let us proceed to resolve each point by the grace of Christ and the prayers of those present. (*C* 12.4)

Since their denials are manifold, let us attempt to adduce, by the Lord's grace, a few testimonies concerning the Passion. (*C* 13.8)

Spiritual grace is surely needed to discourse about the Holy Spirit. (*C* 16.1)

Therefore we must rely on the grace of Jesus Christ to grant us the faculty of speaking without defect. (*C* 16.2)

---

5. The remaining translations in this section are by Stephenson, *WCJ*, vol. 2, with occasional minor alterations.

3. The example of Aaron is singled out in both texts for illustrating the sequence of washing and christening:

When Moses, conferring on his brother the divine appointment, was ordering him high priest, he anointed him after he had bathed in water, and thenceforward he was called "christ." (M 3.6)

Aaron was first washed and then became high priest. (C 3.5)

4. There is a similarity in the way both texts emphasize that Christ's anointing was of divine and not human origin:

For Christ was not anointed by men with material oil or balsam; his Father, appointing him savior of the whole world, anointed him with the Holy Spirit. (M 3.2)

He is called Christ; not as having been anointed by human hands, but anointed eternally by the Father to his high priesthood over men. (C 10.4)

He did not receive the high priesthood through bodily succession, nor was he anointed with man-made oil, but before all ages by the Father. (C 10.14)

He is the true Christ, not raised to the priesthood by advancement among men, but possessing the dignity of the priesthood eternally from the Father. (C 11.1)

5. In both texts, we find a pronounced anti-docetic emphasis that Christ is truly man and that all he did for salvation truly happened, since on this alone depends the reality of salvation. In M, this idea is extended to the reality of what happens in the initiation rites:

The strange, the extraordinary, thing is that we did not really die, nor were we really buried or really crucified and raised again, . . . yet our salvation was real. Christ's crucifixion, burial, and resurrection were real; and all these he has freely made ours that . . . we may really and truly gain salvation. (M 2.5)

Christ suffered in actual fact and not in mere seeming. . . . For Christ truly underwent a real death, his soul was separated from his body, his burial was real. . . . All these things really happened to him. But for us there was a likeness of suffering and death; but salvation for us was not a likeness, but real. (M 2.7)

As Christ was really crucified and buried and rose again, . . . so also with the chrism. Christ was anointed with the mystical oil of gladness; that is, with the Holy Spirit. (M 3.2)

These [anointings] happened to them [Aaron and Solomon] figuratively, but for you they were not figurative but real, for you were really anointed by the Holy Spirit. (M 3.6)

His incarnation took place, not in appearance or fantasy but in truth. He . . . was truly made flesh from her, and truly nourished with her milk. . . . As a man he ate truly as we do. . . . He died truly as a man, but raised him who was four days dead, as God. He truly slept in the ship as man, and walked upon the waters as God. (*C* 4.9)

He was truly crucified for our sins. (*C* 4.10)

He was truly laid as man in a rock tomb. (*C* 4.11)

Jesus who was buried rose again truly on the third day. (*C* 12.2)

For we receive God the Word made man in truth, . . . not in appearance but in reality. (*C* 12.3)

Since, therefore, the image of man was falsely worshipped as God, God became truly man, that the falsehood might be destroyed. (*C* 12.15)

Jesus truly suffered for all men. For the cross was no illusion; otherwise our redemption also is an illusion. . . . Therefore his passion was real, for he was truly crucified, and we are not ashamed of it. (*C* 13.4)

6. Both *M* and *C* make use of the metaphor, κατὰ κρήμνον, "on the edge of," or "over a precipice," for speaking of the peril of the soul or recklessly losing one's soul:[6]

Not for you, either, the folly of those who, to gratify their miserable appetite, expose themselves to wild beasts in the combats in the amphitheater. . . . Of these gladiators it is fair to say that in the service of the belly, which is their God, they cast their lives away headlong in single combats. (*M* 1.6)

Are you unwilling to learn the turnings of the road to avoid falling down the precipice through ignorance? (*C* 4.20)

To stray from the one straight way is to find oneself falling down precipices time and again. (*C* 6.13)

7. Both sets of sermons exhibit similar exclamatory remarks, mostly on the topic of God's loving-kindness in forgiving sins and granting salvation. With one exception (*C* 3.15), all of them use the genitive of cause construction:

O wondrous thing! You were naked in the sight of all and were not ashamed! (*M* 2.2)

O strange and inconceivable thing! We did not really die, we were not really buried, we did not really hang from a cross and rise again. . . . O what transcendent loving-kindness! . . . Christ felt the pain: and on me without pain or labor, . . . he freely bestows salvation. (*M* 2.5)

O the greatness of the mercy of God! To those who had revolted from Him and been reduced to the direst straits He has granted so liberal a pardon for their crimes. (*M* 5.11)

6. See Yarnold, "The Authorship of the *Mystagogic Catecheses*," 149. This metaphor is also a favorite of Chrysostom's; see *Stav.* 2.7, 15; 5.5, 17 and *Homilies on Genesis* 17 (PG 53.145a, 156d).

O the great loving-kindness of God, which is mindful even of harlots in Scripture! (*C* 2.9)

O the ineffable loving-kindness of God! They despair of salvation and yet are deemed worthy of the Holy Spirit. (*C* 3.15)

O the great loving-kindness of God! Now the just, indeed, in many years of service have pleased God; but what they succeed in gaining by many years of pleasing service, this Jesus now bestows on you in a single hour. (*C* 5.10)

O all-wise providence of God that takes wicked purpose as a basis of salvation for the faithful! (*C* 8.4)

O mighty wonder! He who formerly persecuted Him, himself preaches Christ. (*C* 10.17)

O mighty and ineffable grace! The faithful Abraham has not yet entered, but the robber enters! (*C* 13.31)

8. Another distinctive feature of rhetorical style exhibited in both texts is the exhortation to the listeners that they themselves may be able to speak certain sayings from Scripture as if they were their own words:

May the soul that has once put off that old self never again put it on, but say with the Bride of Christ in the Song of Songs, "I have put off my garment, how shall I put it on?" (Song 5:3). (*M* 2.2)

You were anointed . . . upon the nostrils, that, scenting the divine oil, you may say, "We are the incense offered by Christ to God, in the case of those who are on the way to salvation" (2 Cor 2:15). (*M* 3.4)

Clad in the armor of the Holy Spirit, stand firm against the forces of the enemy and overthrow them saying, "I can do all things in the Christ who strengthens me" (Phil 4:13). (*M* 3.4)

You must be clad in those true, spiritual garments that are white and shining. Then you will be able to say with the blessed Isaiah, "Let my soul rejoice in the Lord, for he has dressed me in the garments of salvation, and with the robe of gladness he has clothed me" (Is 61:10). (*M* 4.8)

May you all be able to say, "I, like a green olive tree in the house of God . . ." (Ps 51:10). (*C* 1.4)

Up to now you have stood outside the gate, but may all of you be able to say, "The king hath brought me into his storerooms" (Song 1:3); "Let my soul be joyful in the Lord: for he has clothed me with a garment of salvation and a robe of gladness" (Is 61:10). (*C* 3.2)

"Strip off the old man with his deeds" (Col 3:9), and say in the words of the Canticles, "I have taken off my robe, how am I then to put it on?" (Song 3:5). (*C* 3.7)

But Life came running up, that the maw of death might be stopped and that all we who were saved might say, "O death, where is your sting? O grave, where is your victory?" (1 Cor 15:55). (*C* 3.11)

Indeed, even though you be faithless or of little faith, the Lord is benevolent, and shows indulgence to you when you repent; only on your part say with all sincerity, "I do believe, Lord; help my unbelief" (Mk 9:23). (*C* 5.9)

But for your part worship One, the Almighty God, . . . saying with Job, "I will call upon the Lord Almighty, who does great things . . ." (Jb 5:8 LXX). (*C* 8.8)

[Learn how the bee] gathers the honey for your use, that you also, by ranging over the sacred scriptures, may lay hold of salvation for yourself, and sated with the scriptures, you may say, "How sweet to my palate are your promises, sweeter than honey to my mouth!" (Ps 118:103). (*C* 9.13)

So with you too, once you have been cleansed of your sins, your deeds will be as pure as wool, your robe unstained, and you will say always, "I have taken off my robe, how shall I put it on?" (Song 5:3). (*C* 15.25)

9. Finally, another feature Yarnold mentions is the common use of terms to indicate whether an example is being used in a spiritual or figurative sense as opposed to a literal or physical sense (νοητός and πνευματικός for spiritual and σῶμα, αἰσθητός, or φαινόμενος for bodily or sensible):[7]

The devil is darkness, symbolized by the West, the region of visible darkness. (Cf. *M* 1.4)

For Christ was not anointed by men with material oil or balsam, . . . [he] was anointed with the spiritual oil of gladness. (*M* 3.2)

Oil is the spiritual safeguard of the body, and salvation of the soul. (Cf. *M* 3.7)

The bodily marriage of Cana is contrasted to the Eucharist. (Cf. *M* 4.2)

Communion is at the mystical, spiritual table of the Lord as opposed to the defiled table of demons. (Cf. *M* 4.7)

Solomon prophesies about spiritual bread and wine. (Cf. *M* 4.8)

The heart is strengthened by partaking of the wine as a spiritual reality. (Cf. *M* 4.9)

We do not receive visible bread and wine, but the body and blood of Christ. (Cf. *M* 4.9)

The day's sermon sets the crown on the spiritual building of edification. (Cf. *M* 5.1)

Entrust not the judgment to your bodily palate, but to unwavering faith. For in tasting you taste not bread and wine but the antitypical body and blood of Christ. (Cf. *M* 5.20)

---

7. "The Authorship of the *Mystagogic Catecheses*," 150. For the sake of simplicity, most of these citations are paraphrased.

Already you are culling spiritual blossoms for the weaving of heavenly garlands. (*P* 1)

The armor you receive is not corruptible but spiritual. The paradise into which you are to be planted is spiritual. . . . From now on, you are grafted upon the stock of the spiritual olive. . . . Grant that all may be able to say: "I, like a green olive tree in the house of God" (Ps 51:10), an olive tree not to be perceived by the senses but spiritual and luminous. (*C* 1.4)

The candidates will be sprinkled with spiritual hyssop, and united to the spiritual bridegroom. (Cf. *C* 3.1)

The visible wood of the cross and Golgotha bear witness to Christ. (Cf. *C* 10.19 and *C* 4.10)

When then you hear of God begetting, think not of bodily function, . . . God is spirit, and His generation is spiritual. (*C* 11.7)

At the crucifixion, rocks were rent because of the spiritual Rock. (Cf. *C* 13.34)

Jonah is a type of Christ who went down where the spiritual whale of death is. (Cf. *C* 14.17)

Noah is a type of Christ and the spiritual dove is a type of the Holy Spirit; spiritual wolves and other animals represent the nations guided by the Church. (Cf. *C* 17.10)

The apostles were not drunk with bodily drunkenness, but drunk with the wine of the spiritual vine. (Cf. *C* 17.18, 19)

Peter captures souls in the spiritual net of his words. (Cf. *C* 17.21)

In certain examples of this sort, Cyril is especially careful not to be taken literally, a concern also expressed in *M*:

You may no longer wear the old garment; I do not, of course, refer to this visible garment, but to "the old man, which deluded by his lusts, is sinking towards death" (Eph 4:22). (*M* 2.2)

You must go clad in white all your days. I do not, of course, mean that your ordinary clothes must always be white, but that you must be clad in those true spiritual garments that are white and shining. (*M* 4.8)

The Lavabo is not for bodily defilement. (Cf. *M* 5.2)

[Hezekiah] turned his face to the wall, and from his bed of pain his mind soared up to heaven—for no wall is so thick as to stifle reverent prayer—"Lord," he said, "Remember me" (cf. 2 Kgs 20:2, 3). (*C* 2.15)

I do not mean the regeneration of bodies but the spiritual regeneration of the soul. (*C* 1.2)

Examples, such as those above, that illustrate similarities of style are not expected in themselves to indicate identity of author, yet their nature and number can indicate degrees of probability of common authorship. Any single case could without much difficulty be regarded as representing two different authors, though some of the similarities are quite striking. But considering the number of these examples, the balance in the end is in favor of judging them as representing a common author.

G. Summary and Conclusion

In these foregoing chapters of Part Two, we have conducted a comparative survey of the contents of M and Cyril's prebaptismal *Catecheses* in the areas of rites, theology, spirituality, and literary style. We have highlighted a number of similarities and differences between the texts and assessed them for what they revealed about common or dual authorship. In all of these areas, we have made note of the principal objections to common authorship that have been brought forward in previous studies: differences in the anointing rites, the conferring of the Holy Spirit, the scriptural model for and theology of the immersion rite, as well as the apparent late form of the eucharistic rite. All of these points have been reassessed, mainly in light of the most recent scholarship, and shown to be insubstantial as evidence against common authorship. The differences have been adequately accounted for by circumstances such as the difference in date between P/C and M (which would allow for changes in rites, catechesis, and the thought of a single author) and the different purpose and subject matter of the sermons. Some additional differences were noted with regard to the blessing of the font and the use of the idea of the "seal of baptism." For these differences as well, explanations were found that precluded the necessity of positing two different authors. Lastly, throughout this comparative study a number of similarities among the texts were cited and evaluated. As with the cases of differences, these were assessed for whether they reflected the distinctive style of an author or whether they were due to external factors that could be common to two different authors. While no single example of similarity provided conclusive proof of common authorship, the nature of some of the more striking ones and the overall number of them were deemed such that they contribute considerable weight in favor of the Cyrilline authorship of M.

CHAPTER 8

The *Mystagogic Catecheses* and the Known Works of John II of Jerusalem

A. Introduction

Most of our attention thus far has been devoted to examining evidence for or against Cyril as the author of *M*. We can now consider the evidence for and against his successor, John II, who was bishop from 387 to 417. We have already dealt with the matter of manuscript attribution to John. The present concern is with looking at what can be known of John as a theologian and preacher in order to see whether anything can speak significantly for or against the possibility of his being the author of *M*.

Our knowledge of what John wrote is at present quite limited. There are only two extant works, a sermon on the topic of the Church, which has survived in Armenian, and a short profession of faith in Syriac,[1] but there are also quotations from and references to a work referred to as his *Apology* that

---

[1]. The *Sermon on the Church* is contained in MS Yerevan 993 (fols. 525r–27v). The Armenian text of the sermon is edited with a Latin rendering by Michel Van Esbroeck in "Une homélie sur l'église attribuée à Jean de Jérusalem," *Le Muséon* 86 (1973): 283–304. Van Esbroeck published an improved French translation in "Jean II de Jérusalem et les cultes de S. Étienne, de la Sainte-Sion, et de la Croix," *AB* 102 (1984): 115–25. See also Michel Van Esbroeck and U. Zanetti, "Le manuscrit Érévan 993. Inventaire des pièces," *Revue des études arménniennes*, n.s. 12 (1977): 123–67. Excerpts from the homily will be taken from this French translation. For the profession of faith (Syriac text with German translation), see *The Profession of Faith: British Mus. Add. 12 156*, in *Ungedruckte, unbeachtete und wenig beachtete Quellen zur Geschichte des Taufsymbols und des Glaubensregels*, ed. and trans. Carl Paul Caspari, 3 vols. (Christiania: P. T. Malling, 1886), 1:185–90. The excerpts I will use are from an English translation kindly provided by Dr. Sebastian Brock. Some other works have been tentatively proposed as John's: François Joseph Leroy, "Pseudo-Chrysostomica: Jean de Jérusalem; vers une résurrection littéraire," *SP* 10 = TU 107 (Berlin: Akademie-Verlag, 1970), 131–36; Michel Van Esbroeck, "Nathaniël dans une homélie géorgienne sur les archanges," *AB* 89 (1977): 155–76.

can be culled from Jerome's pamphlet *Against John*[2] and his *Letter* 82. John's *Apology* is his defense against a challenge to his orthodoxy by Epiphanius of Salamis who, with the support of Jerome, targeted John in his campaign to eradicate all influence of the third-century theologian Origen, whom Epiphanius regarded as the "spiritual father of Arius."[3]

To date, apart from the matter of manuscript attributions, scholars have put forward only some varied and limited remarks concerning John's possible authorship of *M*, hence we need to conduct a more detailed and thorough evaluation.[4] We will restrict ourselves to two areas: first a comparison of John's Origenist thinking to *M* and then a comparison of John's extant works with *M*.

B. Was John an Origenist?

Before we answer this question, some qualification is in order concerning the term "Origenist." The Alexandrian school, mainly under the influence of Clement and Origen, had established a tradition of thought that was widespread and respected. Jerome himself referred to Origen as an "immortal genius" in his *Lives of Illustrious Men* (no. 54) and continued to defend him for his exegetical work, questioning only certain doctrinal points.[5] Epiphanius's radical anti-Origen stance seems to have been the exception. Hence, by normal standards, to be labeled an Origenist in any sort of distinctive or pejorative way would mean that one seriously entertained Origen's more characteristic and questionable views.[6]

Such was the case with John of Jerusalem, judging by the letter of Epiphanius, which cites eight specific Origenist doctrines held by John: (1)

2. PL 23.355–98. A proposed reconstruction of John's *Apology* from these two sources was made by Caspari, *Ungedruckte . . . Quellen*, 1:166–72. Pierre Nautin makes a few minor improvements in "La lettre de Théophile d'Alexandrie à l'église de Jérusalem et la réponse de Jean de Jérusalem (juin-juillet 396)," *RHE* 69 (1974): 365–94. The English excerpts are taken from W. H. Freemantle's translation of *Against John*, NPNF, 2d ser., vol. 6 (repr. Peabody, Mass.: Hendrickson, 1994), 424–47.

3. Jerome, *Letter* 51.3. *Letter* 51 is a translation of the letter of Epiphanius to John, of which the original is lost.

4. See, for example, Kretschmar, *Studien zur frühchristlichen Trinitätstheologie*, 169; idem, "Die frühe Geschichte der Jerusalemer Liturgie," 26–27; Bihain, "Une vie arménienne de S. Cyrille de Jérusalem," 340 n. 73; Yarnold, "The Authorship of the *Mystagogic Catecheses*," 146–47; Piédagnel, *Catéchèses Mystagogiques*, 18–40; Stephenson, *WCJ*, 2:143–49.

5. See *Apologia adversus libros Rufini* 3.9, where Jerome remarks how he admired Origen's scriptural learning but was ignorant of his heretical teaching.

6. On the difficulties of interpreting the labeling of individuals as Origenists see Brian Daley, "The Origenism of Leontius of Byzantium," *JTS*, n.s. 27 (1976): 333–69, especially 362–69.

the Son does not see the Father (*Letter* 51.4), (2) souls are confined to earthly bodies as in a prison (51.4), (3) the devil will be saved (51.5), (4) the skins God made for Adam and Eve were human bodies (51.5), (5) the resurrected body will not be a body of flesh (51.5), (6) the biblical account of Paradise is allegorical: for example, it is a spiritual realm in the third heaven, and the trees are angelic powers (51.5), (7) the waters above and below the firmament are angelic and demonic powers (51.5), and (8) Adam no longer bore the image of God after he sinned (51.6). Given that this testimony of Epiphanius, enhanced perhaps by Jerome's free translation, is polemical in nature, we must be careful about judging it as an accurate account of John's beliefs or as indicating that John was a staunch Origenist who held the doctrines cited.

A few points suggest, though, that Epiphanius was reasonably accurate. That he cites eight unique points, some of which are specific allegorical interpretations, shows that he knew John expressed these views in some form or other. Further, he says in his letter (51.7) that John asked for three proofs from Scripture that would refute the teaching that Adam no longer bore the image of God (Epiphanius kindly offers seven), which implies that John had, at least on one occasion, taken up the challenge to his orthodoxy. Finally, in John's eventual response, the *Apology* addressed to Theophilus, the bishop of Alexandria, he plays down the matter of doctrinal issues and tries to shift the blame to Jerome as the cause of all the trouble. He claims that Jerome began stirring up the issue of doctrine as a distraction only after he himself had been accused of misconduct regarding the forced ordination of his brother Paulinian by Epiphanius that took place within John's jurisdiction.[7] John concludes the *Apology* with a statement of personal belief, supposedly to indicate his orthodoxy, but the statement is not in the form of a direct answer to the eight points cited by Epiphanius, and Jerome rightly suspects prevarication. Hence, from his avoidance of directly answering his accusers and from the nature of the detailed accusation of Epiphanius, it is fair to conclude that John entertained these views earnestly enough to regard him as a serious Origenist.

We must now consider to what extent *M* shows any sign of Origenist thought; we can then assess the possible affinity it may have with John of Jerusalem.

---

7. See *Against John* 40.

C. Origenisms in *M*

Kretschmar cited two passages in *M* that he thought exhibited Origenist influence.[8] He notes that in *M* 5.6, on the preface of the anaphora, the Seraphim are treated separately from the rest of the heavenly angelic powers:

> After this, we make mention of sky and earth and sea, . . . angels, archangels, virtues, dominions, principalities, powers, thrones, and the Cherubim with many faces, saying with David, "O magnify ye the Lord with me" (Ps 33:4). We recall also the Seraphim, whom Isaiah in the Holy Spirit saw standing around the throne of God. With two wings they covered the face, with two more the feet, and with two more they flew saying, "Holy, Holy, Holy is the Lord of Hosts" (Is 6:2–3 LXX). For this reason we recite this doxology handed on to us from the Seraphim, that we might join in the hymns of the heavenly armies. (*M* 5.6)

Kretschmar saw in this distinction of the Seraphim, with their particular doxology, an Origenist idea from *De princ.* 4.3.14 where Origen interprets the two Seraphim in the vision of Isaiah as symbols of the Son and the Spirit, and the *trisagion* as the innertrinitarian praise of the Father. On this same passage in *M*, Stephenson notes that the Seraphim are said to hide not their own faces (plural, πρόσωπα) with two of their wings, but the face (singular, πρόσω-πον), namely, that of God, which is just how Origen interprets the passage (*De princ.* 4.3.14).[9]

There are some difficulties, though, with so strict an interpretation of this passage from *M*. The separation of the Seraphim is dictated by the use of the quotation from Isaiah in which only the Seraphim appear and who alone proclaim the *trisagion*. That *M* has singled out this passage (as well as Psalm 34) in this section simply indicates a desire to ground the catechesis at all times in Scripture. He would be very pleased if his listeners realized that it is according to Scripture that the *trisagion* is "handed on" to them from the Seraphim themselves, and that the rest of the angelic praise ("Glorify the Lord with me") has David as its exemplar. Indeed, *M* is not alone in having this form. The separation of the heavenly host occurs also in both Serapion[10] and the *Dêr Balizeh Papyrus*[11] and is, therefore, not an idea unique to *M*. Final-

---

8. Kretschmar, *Studien zur frühchristlichen Trinitätstheologie*, 169; idem, "Die frühe Geschichte der Jerusalemer Liturgie," 26–27.

9. *WCJ*, 2:196 n. 19.

10. F. E. Brightman, "The Sacramentary of Serapion of Thmuis," *JTS* 1 (1900): 105.

11. Colin H. Roberts and Bernard Capelle, *An Early Euchologion: The Dêr-Balizeh Papyrus En-*

ly, the so-called separation of the Seraphim is not as absolute as it might appear. The prevailing image in the preface is rather one of a whole heavenly host than of the separation of ranks, and even the *trisagion* is not reserved for only the two Seraphim. This is implied in the concluding sentence of *M* 5.6 where the mystagogue says that, when they recite the seraphic doxology, they are joined with the whole angelic choir. This last point further suggests that the author is not giving any special thought to the number (that is, two) of Seraphim as Origen did.

As for the use of the singular for "face," *M* is not alone in this usage either. Again, Serapion and the *Dêr Balizeh Papyrus* are similar in having the singular, as well as the shortened version of the Sanctus, without the phrase "blessed is he who comes . . . ," as we find in *M*. Both Dix and Cuming interpret these points as an indication of the presence of an Egyptian tradition of Alexandria behind *M*, that is, a tradition in which Origen had a significant influence (and one that in turn influenced Origen).[12] Hence, Origen could ultimately lie behind this usage. But since it is a idea passed on in a liturgical tradition shared by others including *M*, its mere presence in *M* does not show that the author of *M* was alone responsible for it, nor that he understood it in an Origenist sense. Further, Origen's interpretation of the "face" as the face of God is suggested by the LXX text itself, which has the singular πρόσωπον, and thus reflects more an Alexandrian tradition than a particularly Origenist view. In the end, then, there is no ground for considering any of the above points in *M* 5.6 as particularly Origenist.

Kretschmar also drew attention to *M* 4.5 where we read:

There was in the Old Testament the loaves of presence; but these, being of the Old Testament, have been fulfilled. In the New Testament there is the bread of heaven and the cup of salvation, sanctifying soul and body. For just as bread corresponds to the body, so the Word suits the soul. (*M* 4.5)[13]

He thought the last puzzling sentence only understandable in light of an idea of Clement of Alexandria where, he says, the eucharistic cup, the blood, is a symbol of the Logos:

Now the blood of the Lord is twofold: one is corporeal, redeeming us from corruption; the other is spiritual, and it is with that we are anointed. To drink the blood of

---

larged and Re-edited, Université de Louvain, Institut orientaliste, Bibliothèque du Muséon, no. 23 (Louvain: Bureaux du Muséon, 1949). The actual word for the Seraphim is missing from this manuscript due to lacunae but is easily supplied from texts in its tradition.

12. Dix, *The Shape of the Liturgy,* 196–97; Cuming, "Egyptian Elements," 117–24.

13. "Die frühe Geschichte der Jerusalemer Liturgie," 27.

Jesus is to participate in His incorruption. Yet the Spirit is the strength of the Word in the same way that blood is of the body. Similarly, wine is mixed with water and the Spirit is joined to man; . . . The union of both, that is, of the potion and the Word, is called the Eucharist. . . . Those who partake of it are sanctified in body and in soul. . . . In fact, the Spirit is closely joined to the soul depending upon Him, and the flesh to the Word, because it was for it that "the Word was made flesh."[14]

But as the end of this passage suggests, it is the Spirit that corresponds to the soul, the Logos is associated with the flesh and blood. Hence, there is no strict correspondence with M's use of the Word and the cup. The similarity extends only as far as speaking in dualistic terms of soul and body and a reference to the Word. This possible connection with Clement only indicates that M may be exhibiting some signs of an Alexandrian tradition, but this is far from saying that the idea is Origenist.

That for M the bread corresponds to the body suggests quite a different interpretation. In this fourth sermon, the mystagogue is stressing all along that his listeners believe that the bread and wine in reality become the body and blood of Christ. Yet, at the same time, it is also significant that the form (τύπος, M 4.3) of the elements as bread and wine persists, with the result that

we become Christ-bearers since his body and blood is distributed through our limbs; this is how, according to the blessed Peter, "we become partakers of the divine nature." (M 4.3)

When Jesus says we are to eat his body and drink his blood, the mystagogue continues, we are to take his words spiritually lest, like the unbelieving Jews, we think he is exhorting us to cannibalism (M 4.4). A spiritual understanding affirms our belief that the Son of God in reality shares his very nature with us. But at the same time, to stress the significance of the physical bread, the mystagogue cites the Old Testament loaves of presence kept in the Temple as types prefiguring the New Testament bread of heaven and cup of salvation (M 4.5). The important contrast he wishes to make is not that unbelieving Jews saw only the physical, and we are to see only the spiritual, or that the loaves of old were physical, but the bread of heaven is spiritual; but rather, that the bread and wine mysteriously have both a physical and a spiritual nature and that both soul and body are sanctified. The final sentence of M 4.5 recapitulates this idea. When the mystagogue says that the bread is

14. *Paedagogus* 2.2 (=2.19–20 in alternate numbering system). Trans. S. Wood, *Clement of Alexandria: Christ the Educator,* Fathers of the Church, vol. 23 (Washington, D.C.: Catholic University of America Press, 1954), 111–12. See also, *Paedagogus* 1.6 (=1.43, 47).

for the body, he is referring to the physical level and is restating the idea of M 4.3 that it is through the medium of bread and wine that Christ "is distributed through our limbs." When he says that the Word suits the soul, he is restating the idea that it is not just bread, but the Word of God himself, the divine nature of which we partake. According to this interpretation, such a strong emphasis on the physical dimension of the Eucharist seems far removed from the spiritualizing tendency of Clement and Origen.

This dualism of the physical and spiritual dimensions of the Eucharist appears again in M 5.15 on the Our Father petition for "daily bread":

This holy bread is superessential, that is, ordained for the essence of the soul. . . . It is distributed into the whole of you for the benefit of soul and body.

As we have already noted, several other passages in both C and M exhibit this same notion of dualism. It has been sufficient here only to show that the passage under question from M 4.5 does not exhibit anything distinctively Origenist.

Stephenson also points out a few places in M that appear to show a similarity to Origenist thinking. The doxology at the end of M 1 hints at a subordinationist view of the Trinity: "To God with the Son and Holy Spirit be glory, power and majesty."[15] But a similar pattern occurs in P 15, which is unquestionably Cyril's:

Lift up the eye of your understanding; reflect on the angelic choir, and God sitting, Lord of all, and the Only-Begotten Son sitting with him on his right, and the Spirit present with them.

The divinity of Christ and the Spirit do nonetheless get some affirmation in M: Jesus gives to the Jordan a touch of his divinity, and the Spirit descends on Jesus at the Jordan as "like coming to rest on like" (M 3.1). Any sign of a subordinationist view of the Trinity, though, would not support Johannine authorship; it was not one of the views challenged by Epiphanius and is certainly not reflected in the opening statement of his Apology.

Stephenson also notes that some ideas in the explanation of the Our Father in M 5.15 show some similarity to Origen's exegesis on this prayer.[16] But the ideas cited are not "Origenist" in the sense of being particularly his or tending toward heresy. At the same time, Stephenson draws attention to the non-Origenist praise of John the Baptist and the efficacy of his baptism in M

15. WCJ, 2:159 n. 24.
16. WCJ, 2:200 nn. 39, 41.

2.5.[17] In fact, his overall assessment is that a "notable paucity of Origenisms in the *Mystagogiae* prompts reservations in ascribing them to John."[18]

Finally, E. Bihain[19] also drew attention to the presence of Origenisms in *M*, citing, in addition to Kretschmar, whom we have already considered, G. Walther who made a study of the patristic exegesis of the Our Father.[20] But Walther only concluded that the author of *M* was probably familiar with Origen's *De Oratione*, exhibiting a few similar ideas. He even remarks on how much the author departs from the Origenist exegesis and shows his own independent style, which is more practical and sober.[21]

We can conclude, then, that while *M* may show some signs of a tradition with roots in Origen's thought and in the Alexandrian school, which is no cause for surprise, nothing notably exhibits any extreme Origenist view that could suggest that the author was any sort of staunch Origenist. From what we know of John of Jerusalem, this weakens the possibility that he was the author of *M*. Let us now turn to the known works of John.

D. The Works of John

1. *The* Apology *of John*

As noted above, the original text of John's *Apology* sent to Theophilus of Alexandria is lost, but much of it can be reconstructed from Jerome's letter. The *Apology* is a letter from John offering first an explanation of the circumstances of his dispute with Jerome and Epiphanius and then a personal statement of faith to illustrate his orthodoxy. The first part is a brief and straightforward statement on the events of the controversy and does not manifest any distinctive features of style; hence, nothing results from a comparison with *M*. The latter half, though, contains a statement of his beliefs, and a few points of comparison can be noted.

John opens his statement by saying, "We believe that the holy and adorable Trinity are of the same substance; that they are coeternal and of the same glory and Godhead *(Sanctam et adorandam Trinitatem eiusdem substanti-*

---

17. Ibid., 165 n. 15. Stephenson points out that *M*'s praise of John the Baptist stands in contrast to Origen, who denied regeneration to the baptism administered by John *(Comm. in Joh. 6.33)* and taught that John's baptisms were not the beginning of the new dispensation *(Comm. in Rom. 5.8 [PG 14.1039B])*.

18. Ibid., 147. See also 200 n. 41.

19. "Une vie arménienne," 340 n. 73.

20. See Georg Walther, *Untersuchungen zur Geschichte der griechischen Vaterunser-Exegese*, TU 40.3 (Leipzig: J. C. Hinrichs, 1914), 22–31.

21. Ibid., 30–31.

ae et coæternam, eiusdem gloriae et divinitatis credimus) ..." *(AJ* 8). The Greek underlying "same substance" is no doubt ὁμοούσιος.[22] This is a term that is notably absent in Cyril's *Catecheses;* he prefers to use the various forms of "like" (ὅμοιος) rather than "same" (ὅμος). In *M,* there is one place where the author could use either "same" or "like," and he chooses "like":

Christ bathed in the river Jordan, and having invested the water with his incarnate divinity, he emerged from the waters and the Holy Spirit came upon him in a substantial form, like resting upon like. (*M* 3.1)

Given that a preference for "same" over "like" would still be a matter of some importance in late-fourth-century Jerusalem, and that John clearly indicates his preference for "same" in his statement of belief in *AJ* 8, we would not expect him to choose "like" over "same" in this passage, if he were the author of *M.*

One similarity between *M* and John's *Apology* is the way John stresses that the events of Christ's passion, death, and resurrection took place in a true and not imaginary fashion:

His passion also on the cross, his death and burial, which were the saving of the world, and his resurrection in a true and not in an imaginary sense, we confess *(veritate et non putative confitemur).* .... *(AJ* 23)

There is a similar concern in *M:*

Christ's crucifixion, burial, and resurrection were real ... (*M* 2.5). In order that we may realize that Christ endured all his sufferings for us and for our salvation in reality and not in make-believe, and that we share in his pains. .... (*M* 2.7)

This interest in Christ's humanity as real and not apparent, however, simply shows a concern shared by many for the error of Docetism. For the author of *M,* it is relevant to his sacramental theology: if Christ's death and resurrection were only apparent, our participation in it is also only appearance and thus our salvation as well. John is addressing the issue of the bodily resurrection, of which he had been accused of having an Origenist view:

We all hope so to rise from the dead, as he rose again; not in any foreign or strange bodies, which are but phantom shapes assumed for the moment; but as he himself rose again in that body, which was laid in the holy sepulchre at our very doors, so we in the very bodies with which we are now clothed, and in which we are now buried, hope to rise again for the same reason and by the same command. *(AJ* 23)

---

22. See Nautin, "La lettre de Théophile d'Alexandrie à l'église de Jérusalem," 373; idem, " Ὁμοούσιος unius esse (Jérôme Ep. XCIII)," *VC* 15 (1961): 42 n. 20.

The similarity between these passages is of even less significance as regards common authorship since this anti-docetic view is also strongly emphasized in C.

2. John's Profession of Faith

This text of about nine hundred words appears to have been written in the context of the Pelagian controversy in Palestine in 415.[23] Pelagius was then residing in Jerusalem and engaged in doctrinal disputes with opponents led by Jerome. He had earned the friendship of Bishop John, and when the dispute came to a head with the arrival of Orosius (a spokesman for Augustine willing to confront Pelagius openly), a synod was held under John's direction. The monk was cleared of all charges. John also attended another synod held later in Diospolis at which Pelagius again avoided condemnation.

The *Profession of Faith* includes statements on the Trinity; the Incarnation; the passion, death, and resurrection of Christ; the Ascension; the second coming; the resurrection of the dead; and a final paragraph on the creation of humans in which John presents his view on the Pelagian issue of free will and grace. The text survives only in Syriac and is not an oratorical work, so the comparisons with M are limited to a consideration of its contents.

The opening statement on the Trinity appears not to have originally used *homoousios,* but neither is there any sign of *homoios* terminology:[24]

We believe that the Holy Trinity of Father, Son, and Holy Spirit is one Godhead or Being. We understand this (Godhead) to be the same for each of them, and we acknowledge three hypostases (*qnome*), or properties, which possess equality in dignity, in eternity, in glory, in power, and in immutability. And we anathematize whoever does not consider this (to be so).

He devotes the entire middle section to the incarnate Christ in strong antidocetic language very similar to what is in the *Apology.* He concludes this section with

And just as we acknowledge that the sufferings that (occurred) in the flesh took place in truth and not in semblance, so too with the (sufferings) in his soul, (these) we believe to have occurred in truth and not in semblance.

Those who say concerning him, that when he was beaten with lashes he felt no pain, and when he was crucified he did not suffer when the nails were fixed in him, (these people) we anathematize as heretics.

23. See John Ferguson, *Pelagius* (Cambridge: W. Heffer, 1956), ch. 6.
24. Text in Caspari, ed., *Ungedruckte . . . Quellen,* 1:185–90; trans. Brock.

Again, as noted above, any similarities to *M* are of little importance since Cyril expresses the same views in *C*.

In the last section, John offers his statement on the Pelagian issue:

We acknowledge that when he created human nature, which is composed of immaterial soul and earthly body, he created it without sin—but it was not immutable—as Adam was in Paradise before transgressing the divine commandment; . . . but having made it (endowed) with the authority of (free) will, he made it having the ability to perfect virtue through care and labor, with his help and grace; but it was not incapable of sin—this (occurring) not as a result of nature forcing it, but whenever the will was negligent.

We can discern a similar train of thought in two passages in *M*:[25]

For as Christ after his baptism and the visitation of the Holy Spirit went forth and overthrew the adversary, so must you after holy baptism and the mystical chrism, clad in the armor of the Holy Spirit, stand firm against the forces of the enemy and overthrow them saying: "I can do all things in Christ who strengthens me" (Phil 4:13). (*M* 3.4)

Temptation is like a raging torrent that defies the traveler. Some people in time of temptation manage to cross this torrent without being overwhelmed by the raging waters, their prowess as swimmers saving them from being swept away by the tide. . . . Peter entered into the temptation of the denial; but though he entered, he was not drowned, but manfully swam across and was delivered from the temptation. . . . Listen again, in another passage, to a company of triumphant saints giving thanks for their delivery from temptation, . . . "We have passed through fire and through water, and you have led us out into refreshment." (*M* 5.17)

Here the author similarly acknowledges the value of personal endeavor though with God's help. Again, it is sufficient to note that Cyril expresses the same view in *P* and *C*:

"To them that love God, all things work together for the good" (Rm 8:28). Indeed God is abundant in his goodness, yet he expects in each man a genuine resolve. (*P* 1)

Our nature admits of salvation, but the proper disposition is required. (*C* 2.5)[26]

3. John's Sermon on the Church

This homily is a panegyric on the Church delivered, according to Van Esbroeck's estimate, on September 15th (10 Tishri) 394, the feast of Yom Kippur,

---

25. Trans. Stephenson, *WCJ*, 2:172, 201.

26. See also, for example, *C* 4.18–21, 7.13, 17.37. Stephenson suggests that if this view was part of the Jerusalem tradition, it could explain why Pelagius sought Palestine as place for his exile (*WCJ*, 2:211 n. 11).

and was probably occasioned by the dedication of the Church of Holy Sion in Jerusalem.[27] It is difficult to make a strict comparison between this document and M because of the differences in subject matter (Church vs. sacraments), language (Armenian vs. Greek), and type (panegyric homily vs. catechetical instruction). Yet we can make some comparisons in their content and style.

a. Style

John's sermon is marked, first of all, by strong apophatic terminology. He begins with a lengthy introduction proclaiming how any speech on divine matters is so utterly beyond human capabilities:

Terror and fascination have taken hold of me, beloved brothers in Christ, for I must speak of God. . . . How can we comprehend celestial matters: the palace of celestial dwellings inhabited by God, incomprehensible to those found below? Neither words, nor intellect, nor our sanctuary can claim to fully measure its immensity. (2–4).

He then notes that pagan learning in these matters is of no avail for comprehending the divine (11–16). He finishes this introduction by saying that it is only by means of purification and inspiration by the Holy Spirit that any such speech is possible; the florid language is redolent of gnostic mythology:

Drenched, therefore, by the waves of the Holy Spirit, . . . let us be renewed by the mercy seat and the divine spouse. Protected from the world, let our hearts and consciences be purified, uttering redoubtable words by means of the rutilant purity of the Holy Spirit. Let us advance amidst the elements in the meadows of the divine pastures, grazing the flowers of the divine books, imitating Esdras, who by means of tears of repentance was spiritualized by a seven day fast eating the flowers of the field in the vision of the angelic host. . . . (18–20)

M also exhibits a certain apophatic character and notes the need for enlightenment but does so in a noticeably different way. The mystagogue begins the first sermon with a similar concern for how he can successfully discourse on matters of such a mysterious nature but expresses it in a considerably more sober and down-to-earth way:

For some time now . . . I have desired to discourse to you on these spiritual and celestial mysteries. But I well knew that visual testimony is more trustworthy than

27. Concerning the authenticity of the manuscript attribution and the date, see Van Esbroeck, "Une homélie sur l'église attribuée à Jean de Jérusalem," 283–84, 287; idem, "Jean II de Jérusalem et les cultes de S. Étienne, de la Sainte-Sion, et de la Croix," 107–12.

mere hearsay, and therefore I awaited this chance of finding you more amenable to my words, so that out of your personal experience I could lead you into the brighter and more fragrant meadow of Paradise on earth. The moment is especially auspicious, since you became receptive to the more heavenly mysteries when you were accounted worthy of divine and vitalizing baptism. (M 1.1)[28]

The importance of having experienced the mysteries before being able to understand discourse on them was part of the practice of the *disciplina arcani*. The candidates have been in the process of being enlightened through their course of instruction before baptism (they are referred to as φωτιζόμενοι), and only when they have been enlightened through initiation can they be catechized on the most awesome mysteries of baptism and the Eucharist.

In contrast to John, though, M shows a completely different attitude toward explaining what is needed for understanding or discoursing on the divine mysteries of initiation, a topic easily as awesome as that of the Church. For M, the issue of enlightenment is entirely pertinent to the topic on hand, that is, he is conducting catechesis on some of the most profound mysteries of the faith and how the newly initiated are now capable of possessing them, yet it is sufficient simply to refer to the experience of the initiation rites themselves for conveying this point. For John, the lengthy rhetoric on the incomprehensibility of the topics at hand and the necessary means for being purified and made worthy to discourse on them are not relevant to his topic of the Church; they are introductory comments, which suggests he has a particular interest in these gnostic ideas. Further, John speaks of the need for all, himself included as preacher, to be purified and inspired before any discourse is possible. It would seem that the subject matter of M would, above all, call for the same sentiments, but the author gives no hint of any such attitude.

John builds the rest of his panegyric on an elaborate typological scheme set in a pattern of seven divine circles (apparently drawn from 4 Esd 7:80). As he moves through each circle, a different figure of the Church is presented: (1) the heaven of heavens, (2) the heavenly Jerusalem, (3) the Garden of Eden, (4) Noah's ark, (5) Mount Moriah and Abraham, and Jacob's ladder, (6) Mt. Sinai, the tabernacle, Solomon's temple, and the temple of Ezekiel's vision, and (7) the interior tabernacle. From the description of the first circle, we can get a sense of the lofty and exaggerated imagery that is persistent throughout:

28. Trans. Yarnold, *AIR*, 70.

One can speak of the first level of the divine realm as consisting of seven circles, the fiery ether where the long haired Cherubim and Seraphim, blushing, cloak themselves under the cover of their wings; they teem and sparkle amidst the collision of rocks in the fiery light, the thrones, principalities, virtues, powers, and angels gathered by the divine light in the ignited air. (27)

John follows his descriptions of these figures with exhortations to become conformed to the kind of life exemplified or symbolized by each one. With reference to the first one, the heaven of heavens, he says:

Let us come, then, friends of Christ and citizens of heaven, let us rejoice in God's royal mansions, let us be spirit and not flesh, angels and not breathing humans, Seraphim and Cherubim reciting the *trisagion* and not blood from which the Spirit escapes after doing battle against the exterior, sun and moon or morning star with the long hair, and not terrestrial reptiles who creep in the darkness. (31)

The use of such ornate language would be encouraged by the panegyric nature of the homily, hence it is difficult to gauge how much this style might have been exhibited when he delivered his mystagogic catecheses. But inasmuch as M also makes use of typology, some comparison is possible.

Strictly speaking, John goes far beyond any sort of simple typology here and moves into the more theoretical uses of allegory. Rather than citing an event, place, or person of the Old Testament as prefiguring the Church of the New Testament, which would be more the character of typology, he focuses on what his imaginative picture of the angelic life can symbolize in a moral, or tropological, sense.

This manner of allegorizing is totally absent in M. When types are used in M, the preacher remains entirely focused on the events, letting them, at it were, speak for themselves:

Pass now from the old to the new, from the type to the reality. Then, Moses was sent from God to Egypt, in our time Christ was sent from the Father into the world. Then, Moses led an afflicted people out of Egypt; now, Christ rescues all people from the tyranny of sin. As the blood of the Lamb was a charm against the destroyer, so now the blood of Christ is a sanctuary against demons. Pharaoh of old pursued the people up to the sea; here, this daring and shameless spirit, the author of evil, followed you up to the waters of salvation. That tyrant was engulfed in the sea; this one is destroyed in the saving waters. (M 1.3)

It is necessary for you to know that this anointing is prefigured in the Old Testament. When Moses handed over to his brother the command of God, making him High Priest, after washing him in water, he anointed him and called him "Christ," anointed one, clearly because of this prefiguring anointing. Likewise, when the High Priest installed Solomon into his kingship, he anointed him after washing him in the Gihon. These things happened to them figuratively, but to you in reality, for you were truly anointed by the Holy Spirit. (*M* 3.6)

These typological expositions are remarkably sober compared to what we find in John's sermon. If John were the author of *M*, we would not expect him to exercise such restraint with these rich opportunities for typological exposition.

b. Content

As for the content of John's homily, a few points warrant a comparison with *M*. Perhaps most significant is the presence of an Origenist view on the exaltation of the soul over the body. Of the eight Origenist errors brought against John, all of them, save the first and third on the Trinity and on Satan, are related to the idea of preexisting souls falling through sin into human bodies and then regaining a spiritual existence in the resurrection. This point of view finds expression in a number of places in the homily, for example:

> Let us be spirit and not flesh, angels and not breathing humans, Seraphim and Cherubim reciting the *trisagion* and not blood from which the Spirit escapes after doing battle against the exterior, sun and moon or morning star with the long hair, and not terrestrial reptiles who creep in the darkness, praising Him always with a divine chant, without becoming flesh, food for fire and worm. (31–32)

> Come, therefore O children of Christ, who possess the talent of God, sever the roots of the flesh, the arrogance that exiled Satan, the envy that immolated Abel (45). . . . May we quit this Egypt of the flesh and insert ourselves as a branch in the cedars of God, bearing fruit in the angelic life, that we might become worthy of the Garden of Eden through meditation on the holy Mercy Seat. (55)

This last passage also accords with the sixth Origenist error cited by Epiphanius against John, the allegorical interpretation of the Garden of Eden in which the trees represented the angels of heaven.

It was shown above that in *M*, a certain theoretical distinction is made between the body and soul. But this distinction was used only for explaining the simultaneous physical and spiritual dimensions of the sacraments; there is no sign of any Origenist anthropology. In contrast, while Satan, his pomp, his works, and his worship are renounced (*M* 1.4–9), there is no hint of ascending beyond the physical into the realm of the spiritual. Somewhat similar to John, *M* uses the image of paradise regained (*M* 1.1, 9; 2.2). But life in this new Eden is characterized by a moral conversion, the renunciation of

Satan and allegiance to Christ (*M* 1.9), the putting off the "old nature, which is corrupt through deceitful lusts" (Eph 4:22) (*M* 2.2); there is no exhortation that the realm of the physical is to be transcended.

In *M* 2.2, the author uses the imagery of removing a garment (Song 5:3), symbolizing the renunciation of sin and then draws in the image of Adam in Paradise: the candidates, disrobed of their sinful nature, mirror Adam naked in Paradise with no shame. In one respect this image calls to mind the Origenist idea that Adam and Eve received physical bodies, symbolized by the clothes God made for them, only as a result of their sin,[29] and to an Origenist, this ritual disrobing might symbolize a return to this presinful spiritual existence. Yet, the image presented in *M* 2.2 is of a physical Adam naked and without shame, not a spiritual Adam who is without shame because he lacks a body. It is difficult to see John speaking in these terms with any ease.

Further, *M* expresses positive ideas regarding the physical dimension in his sacramental theology that would not seem to accord with the Origenist views attributed to John. The symbols of the rites, in particular the chrism and the eucharistic bread, are not regarded as just physical signs pointing to a spiritual reality but as symbols that are the medium for encountering Christ. It is in *M* that we first encounter one of the earliest accounts of a metabolic nature of the epiclesis: the transformed nature of the elements function on both a physical and spiritual level:

Do not regard the chrism as mere ointment. For just as the bread of the Eucharist, after the invocation of the Holy Spirit is no longer just bread but the body of Christ, so also this holy chrism after the invocation is no longer ordinary, or so to speak, common, but Christ's gracious gift and productive of the divine presence of the Holy Spirit. (*M* 3.3)

For this holy [anointing] is a spiritual safeguard of the body and salvation of the soul. (*M* 3.7)

For in the figure of bread has his body been given to you and his blood in the figure of wine, so that by partaking of Christ's body and blood, you may become of one body and blood with him. For thus we become Christ-bearers since his body and blood is distributed through our limbs; and thus it is that, according to the blessed Peter, "we become partakers of the divine nature." (*M* 4.3)

This holy bread is superessential, that is, ordained for the essence of the soul. . . . It is distributed into the whole of you for the benefit of soul and body. (*M* 5.15)

29. Epiphanius cites this idea as Origenist, but it is also found in Clement of Alexandria in *Excerpta ex Theodoto* 55.

This ready affirmation of, even sanctification of, the physical dimension is not typical of an Origenist.

Two other minor differences are worth noting. First, in his panegyric, John makes nearly three hundred scriptural allusions or citations in a sermon of about forty-five hundred words. Nearly all of them in some way are associated with the Temple or the Church, yet he makes no use of either of two texts from the prophet Isaiah (Is 2:2 and 25:6–7) that are used in *M* as a reference to the Church:

Long ago blessed Isaiah prophesied saying, "The Lord shall provide for all the nations on this mountain" (by mountain he means the Church, as elsewhere when he says, "And it shall come to pass in the last days that the mountain of the Lord will be made clear"). (*M* 3.7)

It would seem odd that, if John did preach *M*, he would use neither of these two passages from Isaiah in his panegyric, especially since he uses mountain as a typological figure in both the fifth and sixth circle (62–72).

Second, we noted above with regard to *M*'s catechesis on the preface (*M* 5.6) that he makes a point of singling out the Seraphim from the other angels as the ones who proclaim the *trisagion*. In John's homily, though, he includes the Cherubim with the Seraphim:

Let us be spirit and not flesh, angels and not breathing humans, Seraphim and Cherubim reciting the *trisagion*. (31)

There are also two points of resemblance to consider.[30] First, both texts use the language of awe. John begins his homily: "Terror and fascination has taken hold of me, beloved brothers in Christ, for I must speak of God." For *M* as well, the rites of initiation are awe-inspiring (*M* 1.5, 5.4, 9). But such language was becoming commonplace at this time, as is indicated by its frequent use by Theodore: symbols inspire fear (*BH* 2.17), initiation is an "awe-inspiring sacrament" (*BH* 3.2), and the candidates are baptized in "silence and fear" (*BH* 3.18). For Chrysostom, the rites are "awesome and ineffable mysteries" (*Stav.* 6.15) and an "awe-inspiring initiation" (*PK* 2.1; see also *PK* 1.6).

Second, both texts show an affection for the metaphor of a fragrant meadow. But in *M*, the meadow is a metaphor for Paradise newly regained, as it were, through baptism. For John it is metaphor (taken from 4 Esd 9:24) for a place of purification and enlightenment. Further, the metaphor also occurs in *P* 1 and *C* 17.20, of which there is no question of Johannine authorship.

30. On the following points see Yarnold, "The Authorship of the *Mystagogic Catecheses*," 146.

E. Summary and Conclusions

In this chapter it was first shown that John II of Jerusalem is justifiably re-garded as an Origenist. The *Mystagogic Catecheses,* on the other hand, while exhibiting some ideas characteristic of an Alexandrian tradition, revealed nothing that could be deemed peculiarly Origenist. We noted some similari-ties between M and John's writings, but we saw that they were also shared by Cyril in his *Catecheses.* Hence, no evidence in favor of John's authorship of M has emerged from a comparison of M with John's writings in the area of style and content. More significantly, a number of points, particularly in John's *Sermon on the Church,* show important differences in style and content in comparison to M. Hence, the overall balance of evidence is against the probability of John as the author of M.

CHAPTER 9

ɷ

A Stylometric Analysis of the
Mystagogic Catecheses

A. Introduction

Any thorough treatment of a question of the authorship of a literary text must seriously consider a comparative analysis of the literary style of the disputed text and texts of known authorship by means of statistics. This kind of analysis, which involves the quantification and computation of style, is called stylometry and has been practiced for well over a century. Until recent decades, though, the difficulty of adequately detecting a significant number of truly distinguishing features has greatly limited its ability to generate decisive results.[1] With advancements in computer science, it has now become much easier to collect and collate large quantities of data from texts that have been placed into what is called machine-readable form. Still, while the technology for the collection and processing of data has advanced quite considerably, the more theoretical practices of stylometry remain in a state of some uncertainty and experimentation. Given a text and the variety of measurable data that can be gathered from it (sentence length, word length, word frequencies, etc.), it is not at all certain what methods of processing the data are needed to distinguish definitively one author's style from another.

Susan Hockey believes that in this area of authorship studies is found the most use and abuse of the computer. While the use of computers has greatly enhanced the collection of data and statistical computations, the actual choices of what data are valuable, what statistical methods are most useful,

---

1. Two good introductions to the practice of stylometry are Anthony Kenny, *The Computation of Style* (Oxford: Pergamon Press, 1982); and Susan Hockey, *A Guide to Computer Applications in the Humanities* (London: Duckworth, 1980), especially ch. 6.

and, most importantly, how the results can be interpreted are still very much in an experimental stage. Only in the most favorable conditions has stylometry approached being decisive in questions of authorship.[2] Most often stylometry can only add weight to an argument that makes use of several other approaches. Such is the case in the present study; hence, it will be particularly important to set out clearly not only the details and principles of the particular method chosen but also the limits of what can be expected from this analysis of the Cyrilline texts. There is no expectation that the analysis will in itself be sufficient to decide the question of authorship; rather, it will only serve as one component of the overall study.

Because the area of stylometry is still such a wide open field with a variety of methods being tried, it was not feasible to analyze them all with an aim to determining which is the most effective. Instead, I used a method that has been recently developed in light of the most current advances in the field. This method, which is outlined below, was developed by Gerard Ledger for his analysis of the Platonic dialogues with regard to questions of authorship and chronology.[3] While following many of the basic principles of stylometry, Ledger diverged from the traditional methods in two key ways: he used only indicators of style that occur with a high frequency, and he made use of a statistical analysis method called multivariate analysis that optimizes the use of a variety of different indicators. To better understand the method being used, it will be helpful to see how it is a development of basic traditional methods.

B. Stylometry: Traditional Approaches and the Use of Multivariate Analysis

As a statistical method, stylometry must first concern itself with the distinctive features of the population being examined. The basic assumption in any statistical study is that underlying nearly any complex phenomenon of behavior, no matter how apparently random, is a discernible pattern, and the more indiscernible the pattern is to unaided observation the more useful a statistical analysis can be for discovering what that pattern is. Language is

---

2. For a good example of success see Frederick Mosteller and David Wallace, *Inference and Disputed Authorship: The Federalist* (Reading, Mass.: Addison-Wesley Pub. Co., 1964).

3. Gerard Ledger, *Re-counting Plato: A Computer Analysis of Plato's Style* (Oxford: Clarendon Press, 1989). I was fortunate to have Ledger himself supervise this stylometry project. For a review of Ledger's method and findings, see David Mealand and T. Horton, "Review of *Re-counting Plato* by G. Ledger," *Literary and Linguistic Computing* 6 (1991): 228–32.

such a phenomenon. While admitting great freedom and exhibiting immense variation, it is still by its very nature a regulated and constrained system. Individual words have conventionally limited meanings, so there are the constraints of vocabulary. Further, the arrangement of words and their various forms are not random phenomena; a complex system of grammar and syntax governs the various forms of the words and the sequence in which they occur. By its very nature, the system of language provides, as Ledger says, "an orderly matrix, a network of predictability."[4] Within this matrix, an author makes choices, and stylometry seeks to monitor these choices by means of selected measurable features that can be quantified and computed.

In traditional methods, the features of literary style that have been typically singled out as measurable fall into three groups: vocabulary (e.g., the frequency of key words), format (e.g., sentence length, word length, or word position), and syntax (e.g., the use of certain grammatical forms). An analysis usually begins by carefully selecting text samples so that they adequately represent the whole population of the author's work. It then carefully selects measurable stylistic features, counts their occurrences, and calculates statistical averages. In this manner, a stylometric profile can be constructed for an author. Throughout all of this, of course, other forces that influence style are borne in mind, such as date, genre, and subject matter. The particular challenge to stylometry in questions of authorship is to use an analytical method that can adequately discern, above all other forces, the particular influence of the author on a literary style.

It is not difficult to imagine every author having a particular style of vocabulary, format, or syntax. Nor is it difficult to identify many countable elements of style. But one particular difficulty stylometric studies have had is finding significant stylistic features in a great enough frequency to truly distinguish one author from any other. The most frequently occurring word in Greek prose, "and" (καί), only occurs at a rate of about five percent. For even the most frequent words to act as discriminators, extremely large samples need to be studied. This is the limitation of straightforward word frequency studies. A variation on this method that results in a higher percent of frequency measures the word position as well. For example, the position of the postpositive particle δέ in Greek prose sentences is thought to vary enough from author to author to distinguish one work from another.[5]

4. *Re-counting Plato*, 2.
5. See, for example, S. Michaelson and A. Q. Morton, "Identifying Aristotle," *Computer Calepraxis* 1 (1972): 13–42.

Hence, while the word in itself may only have a frequency of about one percent compared to all words, it may occur as the second word of a sentence at a rate of forty percent of all sentences in any sampling, and this percentage can vary considerably from author to author. This method, though, is limited by the reduction of elements to be counted in any sample; for in this case it is sentences and not words that are being counted. In the case at hand, the text of the *Mystagogic Catecheses* has only 5,464 words, which limits the usefulness of any of the more traditional approaches for reaching any significant results. Ideally, a method is needed that can yield measurements of stylistic features of a high frequency and at the same time make use of the greatest number of elements in the selected samples.

The methods briefly described above are characterized by the analysis of samples of text according to a single selected variable, such as the frequency of a word, length of sentence, or word position. This kind of analysis, which uses a single variable, is called univariate analysis. Even when multiple variables are used, the method remains univariate if the measurement of each variable stands on its own and is not evaluated in combination with other variables.

Lutoslawski[6] used five hundred features in his studies of Plato, and Kenny[7] used ninety-nine in his analysis of New Testament texts, yet the variables were measured individually and not in any combinational form. A univariate analysis can determine, for example, the average sentence length, average word length, and frequency percentage of "and" in a sample of Shakespeare, but it does not yield measurements of any two or more of these features in various combinations. Inasmuch as combinations of variables can be just as much an indication of stylistic characteristics as individual variables, the univariate method is greatly limited in its ability to provide data for an overall profile of style based on a large number of variables.

A more recently applied method answers these difficulties and is much more suitable for use with texts of a small size. This is the method employed by Ledger in his studies on Plato and utilizes what is known as multivariate analysis (MVA). This method not only measures the occurrences of individual variables but also calculates the occurrences of the different variables in any desired combination.

Ledger offers a helpful analogy for seeing how these two methods differ.[8]

6. W. Lutoslawski, *The Origin and Growth of Plato's Logic* (London: Longmans, 1897).

7. Anthony Kenny, *A Stylometric Study of the New Testament* (Oxford: Clarendon Press, 1986).

8. *Re-counting Plato*, 26–28.

Let us say that we were faced with the task of categorizing the trees of a genus into species when the trees exhibit no immediately discernible distinctive characteristics. We must resort to collecting less discernible features, such as weight of seed, volume of seed, heartwood density, density of bark, hardness of bark, weight of leaf, number of leaf stomata per unit area, and so forth. Each tree would then have its own group of measurements that could be compared with the measurements of the other trees. The advantage of multivariate analysis is that the trees are not compared by characteristics taken individually but in combination. Hence, for example, while four of the trees may be indistinguishable by seed weight or seed volume alone, when considered by seed weight and seed volume taken together, a division of the four trees into subgroups might become discernible. In such an analysis, it is not important that the measurements being used are in themselves incompatible quantities (say, grams and cm^3) for they all equally act as indicators (to varying degrees) of the single entity being sought, namely, generic affinity. Theoretically, the same holds for literary phenomena. Two samples of text may be indistinguishable by particular words taken singly, such as "and," "the," or words ending in "-ing." But they may be quite distinct when all of these words are measured in various combinations. The key to success in such an analysis is the selection of characteristics (variables) that genuinely act as indicators of generic affinity or species differentiation, or more specifically in the present task, stylistic affinity or differentiation.

The selection of measurable literary features is one of the steps in stylometric analyses that varies considerably from study to study, and it is here that we see one of the unique features of Ledger's method. He gives the following criteria for the choosing of variables (measurable features of the text):

1. They must be easily recognizable and hence easily counted by the computer without any preliminary enhancement of the machine-readable texts.

2. They must score at a sufficiently high rate to be free of the uncertainties associated with low-level distributions and also to enable us to use small samples.

3. There must be a fair chance that these variables be linked to stylistic features and not be just measurements of random and haphazard events.[9]

The first condition is of practical value for this present project given its scope and time limitations. The second is important given the size of the text of the *Mystagogic Catecheses*. The third is of greatest importance theoretically and so some explanation is in order.

9. *Re-counting Plato*, 4.

Since Greek is a highly inflected language (the words change their form according to how they function in a sentence), an author's stylistic patterns could be reflected in patterns of the occurrence of key letters that serve to mark words as different grammatical forms, parts of speech, or even choice of vocabulary. Hence, Ledger opted to analyze the words of his texts according to their orthography, that is, the variables chosen were the letters of the alphabet, and words were counted according to their alphabetical content (this will be explained in detail below).

One way for organizing the data was to predefine grammatical categories according to orthography, allocate the words into their appropriate category, and then count the words that fall into each group (for example, one such category would be the genitive singular masculine of nouns of the second declension, for they all share the common ending - ου). I did not opt for this approach because, apart from its mechanical complexity, it would also have run the risk of obscuring stylistic features by using a too narrowly defined set of grammatical features and thus introduce an undesirable level of subjectivity on the part of the analyst.[10] Ledger discovered (through trial runs on texts of known authorship) that a high degree of success could result from doing a blanket count of all words simply according to their alphabetical content. He followed the principle that the collection of too much information would be balanced out by the likelihood that the more subtle stylistic features would have a better chance of being detected. This latter approach was adopted for the present study.

C. The Stylometric Analysis of *M*

1. *The Texts*

The basic task of this analysis was to make a comparison of style among known works of Cyril, the text of *Mystagogic Catecheses,* and a selection of other texts both earlier and contemporary with Cyril. The texts that were analyzed are the following:[11]

10. See *Re-counting Plato,* 6. Hockey also makes a similar observation in *A Guide to Computer Applications,* 130.

11. The texts for Chrysostom and Basil were generously made available in machine-readable format through the cooperation of Theodore Brunner, director of *Thesaurus Linguae Graecae (TLG),* University of California at Irvine, and Susan Hockey, former director of the *Centre for Humanities Computing* at the Oxford University Computing Service. Unfortunately, the texts for Cyril were not in available form from *TLG,* and thus I had to manually load them into the computer. The other texts were obtained from the Oxford University Computing Centre's Text Archive.

Cyril of Jerusalem
known works[12]
Procatechesis (2,554 words)
Prebaptismal Catecheses 1–18 (72,709 words)

disputed work[13]
Mystagogic Catecheses (5,464 words)

Diodorus of Tarsus[14]
Commentarii in Psalmos I–L (selected) (8,095 words)

Ignatius of Antioch[15]
Collected Letters (7,697 words)

Gregory of Nyssa[16]
*De tridui inter mortem et resurrectionem domini nostri
Iesu Christi spatio* (6,155 words)

Pseudo-Chrysostom[17]
In adorationem venerandae crucis (3,828 words)

John Chrysostom[18]
Catecheses ad illuminandos 1–8 (26,080 words)
Catecheses ad illuminandos 1–2 (8,622 words)

Basil of Caesarea[19]
De baptismo (22,040 words)
De Spiritu Sancto (26,524 words)

12. The text for the *Procatechesis* was taken from *St. Cyril of Jerusalem's Lectures on the Christian Sacraments*, ed. F. L. Cross. The text of the *Catecheses* was taken from the edition of Reischl and Rupp.

13. Text from the Sources Chrétiennes edition edited by A. Piédagnel.

14. Text edited by Jean-Marie Olivier, CCSG 6 (Turnhout: Brepols, 1980); deposited into the Oxford Text Archive by Wolfram Kinzig, University of Heidelberg.

15. Text edited by Kirsopp Lake, *The Apostolic Fathers*, vol. 1 (London: W. Heinemann, 1913), 166–277.

16. Text edited by E. Gebhardt, in *Gregorii Nysseni Opera*, vol. 9 (Leiden: Brill, 1967), 273–306; deposited into the Oxford Text Archive by Hubertus Drobner, University of Paderborn.

17. Text from PG 62.747–54; deposited into the Oxford Text Archive by Wolfram Kinzig, University of Heidelberg.

18. The first set of eight sermons is taken from the Sources Chrétiennes edition by Wenger, *Huit catéchèses baptismales*. The second set comprises the two sermons edited by B. de Montfaucon in PG 49.221–40. A. Piédagnel has argued that each of the last two sermons actually belongs to two different series; see John Chrysostom, *Trois catéchèses baptismales*, ed. Auguste Piédagnel, SC 366 (Paris: Éditions du Cerf, 1990), 20–32.

19. The first of these texts was taken from PG 31.1513–1628. The second text is taken from the Sources Chrétiennes edition by Benoît Pruche, *Sur le Saint-Esprit*.

These texts were selected to provide a varied context for comparison. The *Letters* of Ignatius are included because of their early date. The others are selected because they are relatively contemporary with Cyril or deal with similar topics.

2. *Parameters of the Study*

In the best of circumstances, a disputed work can be compared with the works of two or more contending authors, and, when placed side by side, fairly significant results can arise. But the lack of surviving texts of John of Jerusalem in Greek places a severe limitation on the present study. We can only hope to determine, as far as stylometry is concerned, how similar or different M is to the works of Cyril and his contemporaries. Again, it was not anticipated that this study would result in any decisive evidence concerning the authorship of M, but it might add significant weight one way or the other. In the end, the task will be to evaluate how much weight to give the results.

Since ten texts are being analyzed, theoretically a large number of permutations are possible for comparing how stylistically similar or dissimilar M is to each of the others. However, lacking a text of John's means that only two mutually excluding outcomes will need to be considered. If M proves to be more similar to any one or more of the works other than C, then this could be regarded as weight against Cyrilline authorship. On the other hand, if M is closer to C than to all of the other works, this would give some weight toward Cyrilline authorship. No result can be interpreted as direct evidence for or against Johannine authorship. Just how a text of John's would measure up to any of the others will always be unknown; such a text could very well show itself to be as unlike M as C is or just as similar. But since John is the only contending author, weight in favor of Cyril would make John less likely to be the author, and vice versa, a result that suggests non-Cyrilline authorship would increase the likelihood that M is John's.

It will also be important to evaluate the results in light of another relevant point regarding the date of M. It has already been shown that the date of M is some thirty or so years later than that of C. If it is from the hand of Cyril, can one expect a discernible difference of style? A significant part of Ledger's work was on the chronology of Plato's *Dialogues,* and he successfully showed that an author's style is likely to change discernibly over his writing lifetime.[20]

---

20. *Re-counting Plato,* 82–91, and ch. 9.

S. Michaelson and A. Q. Morton[21] note that in general, studies have revealed that after a minimum of about thirty years a change in an author's overall style can be detected. Hence, we must be prepared to grant some degree of dissimilarity to *C* since it was written thirty years earlier than *M*. Exactly what degree of dissimilarity is to be granted will be adjudged when the statistical results are examined.

It has also been proposed that unlike *C*, *M* is in the form of "preacher's notes" rather than a transcription of delivered sermons. Even if they are notes, they nonetheless take more the form of an oratorical précis than a simple list or outline of topics. Its difference from a delivered version would be more one of length than style.

3. The Analysis

The texts were divided into sequential one-thousand-word samples, and each sample was analyzed for the alphabetic content of the words. At the advice of Ledger, twenty-eight variables were chosen. There are twenty-four total letters, but as six of them (β, ζ, ξ, φ, χ, ψ) occur at a low frequency, they were grouped together as one variable. This yielded nineteen variables from the Greek alphabet tested for their occurrence anywhere in each word. The last nine variables were select letters that were tested for their presence as word endings (since these vary according to how the words are used grammatically): α, ε, η, ι, ν, ο, ς, υ, ω.

The texts were organized into the groups of samples shown in Table 9.1. A computer concordance program produced the first stage of data:[22] for each thousand-word sample the program generated twenty-eight word counts, each representing the number of words containing each of the twenty-eight variables (for example, in the first thousand-word sample of *P,* 441 words contained an *alpha,* 162 words contained a *beta,* etc.) For the sake of simplicity, no effort was made to distinguish words that contained a variable more than once. So, for example, the word ἀλλά would be counted once for containing an alpha (α), once for a lambda (λ), and once for ending in an alpha (α). At the same time, the frequency with which this word would be contracted, losing its final alpha, would be reflected in its not being counted as containing an ultimate alpha.

---

21. Michaelson and Morton, "Identifying Aristotle," 23.

22. I used the *Oxford Concordance Program, Version 2,* which is the 1987 updated edition of the original 1981 program. Both versions were written by Jeremy Martin at the Oxford University Computing Service.

Table 9.1 Authors and Texts Sampled in the Stylometric Analysis

Author	Text	No. of samples	Label
Cyril	Catecheses (P and C)	72	P01–02; CAT0101–1806
?	Mystagogic Catecheses	5	MC01–05
Gregory of Nyssa	De tridui spatio	6	GREG01–06
Ignatius	Letters	7	IGNAT01–07
Diodorus	Commentarii	8	DIOD01–08
Ps-Chrysostom	In adorationem	4	PCHRYS01–04
Chrysostom	Catecheses 1–2	8	CHRYSA01–08
Chrysostom	Catecheses 1–8	25	CHRYSB01–25
Basil	De baptismo	21	BASILA01–21
Basil	De spiritu sancto	26	BASILB01–26

The word counts were then organized into what is called a "data set" for use with a statistical analysis program called SAS *(Statistical Analysis Systems).*[23] The twenty-eight numbers for each thousand-word sample could be regarded as forming a numerical profile. It should be noted that while the scores for each variable differ from sample to sample (a natural result of the complexity of style), there is at the same time a similarity among the values for the same variable from one sample to the next. For example, for each sample there are roughly 450 words per thousand that contain an alpha and 100 that contain a gamma. It was anticipated that beyond this visually discernible correlation of individual values among all the samples, there were also family resemblances among the samples when grouped by author that would correspond to the style of that author. These resemblances would only be seen by means of the statistical analyses.

The various SAS methods of analysis are called "procedures," and the ones that were used in the present study are the cluster procedure, the discriminant procedure, and the canonical discriminant procedure.[24] All of the procedures treated the numerical values of each sample as if they were spatial coordinates defining each sample's location relative to the others. More accurately, they are "hyperspatial" entities with twenty-eight dimensions rather than three-dimensional objects in space; but mathematically they can be treated in the same way as three dimensional objects. In a variety of ways,

23. SAS Institute Inc., *SAS User's Guide: Statistics, Version 5 Edition* (Cory, N.C.: SAS Institute Inc., 1985).
24. Cf. *SAS User's Guide: Statistics,* ch. 13 (canonical discriminant procedure), ch. 15 (cluster procedure), and ch. 16 (discriminant procedure).

these procedures produce data on the "distances" between samples (or groups of samples). In the case at hand, since the variables are chosen for their relevance to writing style, these distance measurements are regarded as the indicators of the similarity or dissimilarity of style. Two samples with roughly the same values for each of the twenty-eight variables (that is, being very similar in the alphabetic content of their words) would end up being evaluated as "spatially" very close to one another.

A cluster analysis gives a simple visual indication of whether the samples from a single author can at least roughly be grouped together or "clustered" according to their nearness, that is, similarity, to one another. The other two procedures (discriminant and canonical discriminant) are more refined and powerful processes that can indicate an actual numerical distance between each sample (or group of samples). I will briefly summarize the results of these three, gradually more refined, procedures.

The cluster procedure begins its process by calculating the total value for the entire data set.[25] It then systematically goes through each of the samples again in order to calculate which two samples if joined together (or "clustered") and counted as one, would result in the least amount of change in the value of the entire set, when this value is recalculated. These two samples are considered the closest since when clustered together they have the least effect on the overall variance among the samples. The process is then repeated though this time the new cluster is treated as one sample just like all the other samples until all the samples and clusters have been combined into one. If the chosen variables were to be effective in representing an author's style, we would expect the samples from any one author to be clustered together, at least in a general way. We could anticipate, though, that there would be a few "outliers," chance atypical samples that would skew the results away from what would be produced by the more typical samples.

In the initial cluster procedure, the first two clusters formed (at levels 181 and 180) are CAT401 with BASILB25, and IGNAT02 with IGNAT03. MC03, on the other hand, is the last individual sample to be joined to a cluster; it holds its own until there are twenty-three clusters.

This first run produced quite a bit of fragmentation. At the level of ten

---

25. This is determined by first finding the grand mean for all the samples then finding the difference of each sample from the grand mean. Those differences are then squared (to eliminate negative values) and finally added together to give the total sum of squares. This figure could be said to represent the amount of variance in the entire data set; the greater this value the greater the amount of variance.

clusters (which in ideal circumstances would show one cluster for each of the ten texts), one could see fairly well how they had fallen out. Samples of Chrysostom and Basil were mixed in among the samples of Cyril. On the other hand, P-Chrysostom was completely intact, and five of the seven samples of Ignatius formed a separate group. All six samples of Gregory were clustered together though the cluster also contained samples from four other texts. Five of the eight samples of Diodorus were in a cluster though its cluster also was shared by others. Basil B outnumbered Cyril by only one in its group. Chrys A and M were the two texts without a cluster of their own. Seven of the eight samples of Chrys A were in Cyril–1 and Cyril–2. Three of the five samples of M ended up in Cyril–2, the cluster that contained the greatest number of samples from Cyril; one other was in Cyril–1 (the next largest cluster of Cyril samples); and the last one, MC02, was grouped with Chrys B.

The first way to refine the analysis is to identify and remove the outliers. The discriminant procedure, used to identify samples that are atypical of their respective group, singled out eight such samples: CAT605, CAT1705, CHRYSB03, CHRYSB06, CHRYSB09, CHRYSB10, CHRYSB18, and BASILB26. The second way is to give some weight to the samples as groups (that is, for example, instead of having each of the samples of Diodorus stand on its own against all of the others, the program can include a value for the sample's membership in its own group, that is, the rest of the samples of Diodorus). This is done by what is called canonical discriminant analysis. This procedure also more clearly indicates the distance between any two texts. In the same way as the previous cluster analyses, the procedure considers the samples of each author independently of one another, but this time an additional set of values (canonical variables) is included in the calculations, which adds some bias to keeping the respective groups intact. In this way, some weight from the texts as a whole corpus, and not just as individual parts, is introduced into the discriminating process.

With only outliers removed, the clusters were much more homogeneous, but samples from both Chrys A and M were still drawn into other clusters. Adding canonical variables, however resulted in one cluster for each text at level ten. After this procedure only CAT604, CHRYSA02, CHRYSB13, and BASILA04 were misclassified. The samples of Cyril were all joined (at level 10) before Chrys A was joined to Chrys B (at level 9), but these latter texts were still joined before M was joined to Cyril (at level 7), as were Gregory with Basil B (at level 8). Ignatius was joined to Basil A at level 6 and then this cluster was joined to Basil B at level 5, and so on. The only misclassified sample of Cyril is grouped with M. The results of these cluster procedures were displayed in what are called tree diagrams, in which labels for the samples are arranged into their appropriate clusters. Immediate visual observation of the tree diagram at this point showed that M held itself intact as an independent text and had its closest affinity with C.

Tree diagrams give a convenient visual representation of where each text stands spatially to the others. The clusters are based on the calculation of "distances" between samples or groups, but exactly what these distances are is not clearly represented in the diagrams. The canonical discriminant procedure does, however, include these distances (called squared, or Euclidean distances) in its output, and it will be useful to see not only that M is close to Cyril but how close.

Table 9.2 gives the distances between the groups for all the samples less the eight outliers. If we look at the column under M, we can see that compared to all the other texts M has the lowest value (closest distance) with reference to Cyril. The tree diagrams also suggested that of the other texts the two that overall are the closest to each other are Chrys A and Chrys B followed by Gregory and Basil B. The utility of the table of distances is in its showing that, in fact, Basil A and Basil B are the next closest texts after Chrys A and Chrys B. The table verifies this showing a value of 14.47 for Chrys A and Chrys B and 16.37 for the two texts of Basil compared to 26.22 for Gregory and Basil B. That the cluster analysis procedure joined Gregory and Ignatius to Basil B and Basil A respectively before it joined Basil A to Basil B would be for two reasons. First, Gregory and Ignatius are themselves closer to the texts of Basil than they are to any other texts. Second, the procedure misclassified two samples with Basil B (CHRYSB13 joined at level 54, and BASILA04 joined at level 92); with these two extra samples included, the cluster procedure calculated the Basil B group as closer to Gregory than to Basil A.

The table of distances reveals a similar phenomenon for M. While the column for M shows that it is closest to Cyril, the reverse is not the case since Cyril is closer to both Chrys A and Basil B than it is to M. This was reflected in the earlier cluster analysis tree diagrams where nearly all of the samples misclassified into Cyril came from Chrys A and Basil B. The chart shows seven pairs of texts with distances less than the 28.09 for M and Cyril. More accurately, then, we can say of M only that it is closer to Cyril than it is to any

Table 9.2 Squared Distance to Group—All Samples Less 8 Outliers

From group	Cyril	M	Gregory	Ignatius	Diodorus
Cyril	0	**28.09725**	41.62159	48.36714	42.04798
M	**28.09725**	0	59.25506	47.84677	67.93818
Gregory	41.62159	59.25506	0	68.98059	90.66085
Ignatius	48.36714	47.84677	68.98059	0	84.68624
Diodorus	42.04798	67.93818	90.66085	84.68624	0
P-Chrys	109.32794	106.47101	129.94136	134.45207	172.36333
Chrys A	**19.05261**	43.09468	47.92081	69.17730	41.52402
Chrys B	34.59909	48.57465	51.64917	77.54407	63.54105
Basil A	33.99144	38.02773	34.60024	34.32685	76.34061
Basil B	**20.35063**	38.44123	**26.21893**	45.19181	47.54012

From group	P-Chrys	Chrys A	Chrys B	Basil A	Basil B
Cyril	109.32794	**19.05261**	34.59909	33.99144	**20.35063**
M	106.47101	43.09468	48.57465	38.02773	38.44123
Gregory	129.94136	47.92081	51.64917	34.60024	**26.21893**
Ignatius	134.45207	69.17730	77.54407	34.32685	45.19181
Diodorus	172.36333	41.52402	63.54105	76.34061	47.54012
P-Chrys	0	107.58218	121.16698	122.81814	122.78859
Chrys A	107.58218	0	**14.47096**	47.88513	**22.67039**
Chrys B	121.16698	**14.47096**	0	48.19092	**23.00187**
Basil A	122.81814	47.88513	48.19092	0	**16.36914**
Basil B	122.78859	**22.67039**	**23.00187**	**16.36914**	0

of the other texts. One other text, P-Chrysostom, is also closer to Cyril than it is to any of the others, but its distance is nearly twice the distance of M from Cyril and considerably more distant from Cyril than any other of the texts.

There was some concern throughout this analysis whether the large size of the Cyrilline corpus exerted any undue influence on the results. In order to check this, two final canonical discriminant analyses were run. The first split Cyril into three groups, and the second used a selected number of samples from Cyril. The results showed no significant difference from the analysis using the entire corpus of Cyril.

D. Summary of Results and Conclusions

The cluster analyses showed that the twenty-eight variables were sufficient to yield a discernible distinction among the works of the selected authors, especially when outliers were removed. There is no reason to believe that a modification of the choice of variables could not yield better results, but a greater degree of refinement was not deemed necessary for the present project. The cluster analyses showed that samples from Chrysostom, Basil, and M were the ones most commonly dispersed among the seventy-two samples of Cyril. When just the outliers were removed, Chrys A and M were the two texts not clearly defined at the level of ten clusters. Both of these texts had the majority of their samples contained in three separate clusters of Cyril, indicating a closeness of style to Cyril. It was not clear at this point whether M or Chrys A was closer to Cyril. When the canonical discriminant analysis was used, some weight was given to the texts as groups. This resulted in more homogenous clusters. This procedure also produced numerical distances between each group. The tree diagram of this analysis visually indicated that M was very close to Cyril; but the actual distance measurements among the groups confirmed that M is closer to Cyril than it is to any other text, even though Chrys A and Basil B are closer to Cyril than M is.

How can these results be interpreted with regard to M? Since this stylometric analysis is not in itself sufficient to decide the authorship question, particularly because no text of John of Jerusalem could be represented, its value is mainly in showing how its results, namely, (1) that M is closer to C than it is to any other of the texts, and (2) that M was classified so clearly among the samples of Cyril in the first cluster procedures, fit with both the traditional claim of the Cyrilline authorship of M and the evidence that the text of M is from some thirty years after C. The results also show M as a text in its own right, rather than an integral part of C, yet still very close to C. This result corresponds with the later date of M. Both of these points can be regarded as significant weight in favor of Cyrilline authorship. Only if M were the closest of all the texts to C, yet still discernible, could more weight be given to the claim that Cyril authored M (even more than if M were homogenous with C, for that would not go well with the later date of M). Finally, no result of this analysis counts against Cyrilline authorship. In fairness, though, it must be reiterated that while none of these results can be interpreted as evidence against Johannine authorship, since no text of John's was available to the analysis, the overall conclusion is that the stylometric analysis of M adds significant weight to the claim that Cyril is the author of M.

ಅಂ

Summary and Conclusions

When dealing with a question of disputed authorship of any ancient text, it is virtually impossible to establish with absolute certainty the identity of the author because of the antiquity and sparsity of evidence. We must inevitably settle for the most probable result after carefully weighing the available testimony, and the present case is no exception. In this study, I have individually addressed different aspects of the question of the authorship of the *Mystagogic Catecheses*. Each aspect has its own degree of relevance and weight in the overall question. The task remains of drawing together the results of the separate investigations and arriving at a final judgment.

Let us first review the key elements of the question, their importance, and the minimum requirements for a suitable outcome. The study was divided into three general areas, the first and most important of which was the issue of author attributions in the manuscript tradition of *M*. The presence of John of Jerusalem's name on some manuscripts is what initially sparked the controversy of authorship, and it has been the central point in all subsequent studies.

The second area concerned external evidence. Of particular interest was the date of *M* and the witness of both the pilgrim Egeria and the *Armenian Lectionary*. Earlier attempts to locate the sermons in the episcopate of Cyril or John and reconcile them with evidence from Egeria's visit to Jerusalem and the lectionary had only limited success. A more certain date for Egeria's visit to Jerusalem and new information on the lectionary, however, enabled us to construct a much more complete and accurate historical setting for *M*. A review of *M*'s literary tradition was also included.

The third and most extensive area comprised the internal comparison of the text of *M* with other texts of Cyril and John. The majority of past studies paid most attention to the differences between the texts with a view to giv- ing some credence to the manuscript attributions to John and argued for his authorship. Concurrently, defenders of Cyrilline authorship highlighted the similarities between the texts. Further, while many recognized that how M compared with the known works of John was significant, a thorough com- parative analysis of this sort had yet to be done.

The following parameters of argument were laid down as a guide for reaching an acceptable result. A decision in favor of Johannine authorship would only come from showing either that the manuscripts with John's name were accurate in their ascriptions (except, of course, if the best expla- nation for John's name in the manuscript tradition is that he delivered ser- mons inherited from his predecessor), that M is too late for Cyril, or that the content of M is convincingly not from Cyril. For a pro-Cyril decision, it would first be necessary to show that the manuscript attributions to John are not indisputable, that M need not be dated after 387 when Cyril died, and that certain cited differences between C and M can be adequately explained as originating from the same author. This much, however, would only reestab- lish Cyril as an equal contender against his challenger. A final decision in fa- vor of Cyril would have to depend on additional positive indications that the sermons are his.

We can now summarize the results. First, the study of the manuscript tra- dition provided meaningful results, even if not decisive. Among the Greek manuscripts, the presence of John's name occurs in a narrow line of the tradi- tion (families α and γ): at one time by itself in the heading of M and then sometimes in the company of Cyril's name. But at the same time, there is the parallel tradition (family β) wherein Cyril's name alone is present, and the overall balance of evidence from all of the ascriptions in the Greek manu- scripts (as far as quantity was concerned) fell in favor of Cyril. The presence of John's name, however, was not deemed to be a simple matter of a scribal error, and some other explanation was demanded. The option of Cyril's name supplanting John's remained only a remote possibility for which there was no evidence. The more probable explanation for the presence of John's name, especially in light of its conjunction with Cyril's, is that it was ascribed to an unpublished text that originally bore no name but was otherwise recog- nized as belonging to the Jerusalem catechetical tradition. As for the Arabic codex that bears John's name at the head of M, if one respects Piédagnel's judgment that it is related to the Greek *Monacensis 394*, it does not significant- ly alter the overall balance of evidence or the likely explanation of the ascriptions. The net result is that on manuscript evidence alone, the attributions of *M* to John are not sufficient for an indisputable claim that the sermons are his.

In the second area of external evidence, the reevaluation of what can be known about the date of *M* and the contemporary witnesses of Egeria and the *Armenian Lectionary* showed that there are no longer any obstacles to situating *M* in the latter years of Cyril's episcopate. No evidence precluded a date after Cyril, but all previous objections to Cyrilline authorship based on a late dating of *M* (in particular the late stage of liturgical developments) and discrepancies with Egeria and the lectionary were answered; that is, important evidence against Cyril was removed.

The results of a survey of the literary tradition also favored Cyril. The objections brought against Cyrilline authorship of *M* in this area have all been arguments from silence: on the one hand is the lack of references to *M* before the sixth century, and on the other the absence of any early witnesses to *C* who also knew of *M*. These earlier studies argued that if *M* was originally attributed to Cyril, we would expect it both to have earlier witnesses and to be grouped with *C* from the beginning.

However, the argument from silence was shown to count just as heavily against John, for there is not a single witness to *M* under his name. The most this tradition could offer in favor of John would be to corroborate a situation where *M* was originally attributed to John and in time John's name was supplanted by Cyril's. But as was shown, we have no evidence for such a situation. Further, a suitable explanation was found for the lack of references to *M*, especially by early witnesses to *C*, in concluding that *M* initially existed independently from *C* based on its later date, unique form (preacher's notes), and subject matter (sermons on the mysteries). When we added the fact that there are at least three independent witnesses that name Cyril as the author of *M*, the overall balance of evidence from the literary tradition fell strongly in favor of Cyrilline authorship.

It was also shown that this assessment of the external evidence is compatible with the interpretation of the manuscript tradition. Since *M* was originally independent of *C* and not formally published with author attribution, it is easy to see how both bishops could be equally attractive contenders as authors of *M*.

The third and most extensive part of the study was taken up with the comparison of *M* with the contents of Cyril's Lenten sermons. A systematic survey of the contents of *M* in the areas of ritual, theology, spirituality, and literary style revealed points exhibiting both differences and similarities with

C. Among these were points cited by scholars in previous studies who argued both for and against Cyrilline authorship. These were reevaluated in the light of the most recent research, and additional points hitherto not addressed were also studied.

The examination of differences between *M* and Cyril's Lenten sermons sought to assess to what extent they could be explained by the external factors of time and development or whether there was a need to explain them as originating from a different author. Here again the task was difficult because we were not dealing with certainties but adding up and weighing probabilities.

We noted that some differences between *P/C* and *M* should be expected because of the different subject matter and goal of the catecheses; even those who argued against Cyril as the author of *M* readily acknowledged this. But we saw that other factors were pertinent to explaining these differences, the most important of which was the later date of *M*. During the thirty or so years between the two sets of sermons, considerable changes and developments could take place in theology, in the structure of liturgical rites, and in the form and content of the catechetical program.

A survey of Cyril's life and career also helped show that this was a time of growth and that as bishop he would have been the leading figure in any developments. We saw him to be an orthodox thinker, a gifted pastoral leader, and a catechist. He was at heart a traditionalist but by no means conservative; he was a well educated, innovative, and creative catechist and liturgist. In his three periods of exile, he would have been involved in the life and rites of neighboring churches, and mutual influence on liturgical practice and theology no doubt took place. Hence, we could reasonably expect some degree of change in his views and interests over a span of thirty years. Unfortunately, as we do not have any undisputed text representative of Cyril's late thinking or preaching, appeals to Cyril's personal development were made only tentatively.

The most important result from examining differences was that a reasonable explanation was found for each discrepancy between the texts raised by previous studies as evidence against common authorship. For the most part, these new findings were possible because of recent studies. We saw that some of the more significant contrasts, such as the form of the anointing rites and the accompanying catechesis, were due mainly to changes in the rites, and thus there was no need to appeal solely to a change in the thinking of the catechist.

In the same comparative analysis, similarities were also assessed; this was an area that hitherto had only received cursory attention. We needed to decide how probable it was that the similarities were the result of a single author rather than of external factors such as a set syllabus in an annual program passed on from Cyril to John. Hence, attention was not directed so much to the general topics of the mystagogy as to specific examples of content and style. Overall, a striking number of similarities was unveiled, some more compelling than others, and substantial weight was added in this area to the case of Cyrilline authorship.

The comparison of *M* with the known works of John of Jerusalem was the best opportunity to uncover evidence in favor of Johannine authorship. However, no such evidence of any significance materialized. *M* was shown to lack any genuine Origenist tendencies, which could have signaled the hand of John, and what similarities were discovered were also represented in *P* and *C*, which are unquestionably Cyril's. More importantly, certain contrasts with John's works spoke against his being the author of *M*. The lack of a Greek catechetical work of John's limited the scope of this comparative analysis, but the results were nonetheless significant.

Finally, the stylometric analysis of *M* produced limited, yet significant, results. It could not furnish direct evidence against John since no Greek text of John's was available; yet to the extent that the method successfully indicated similarity and dissimilarity of style, the case for Cyril received further support since *M* turned out to be closer to *P* and *C* than to any other text in the analysis.

In the end, the only surviving significant evidence of the Johannine authorship of *M* is that of the manuscript tradition, which was shown to be in itself insufficient for ascribing *M* to him. No significant objections to Cyrilline authorship remain unanswered, and many points of comparison in the areas of theology, spirituality, and literary style reveal notable similarities between *M* and Cyril's *Catecheses;* that is, the content and style of *M* is decidedly Cyrilline rather than Johannine. In light of all the evidence, the most that can be concluded from the manuscript attribution to John is that it represents his close association with the Jerusalem catechetical tradition. Hence, we may conclude that the *Mystagogic Catecheses* ought rightfully to be included among the works of Cyril of Jerusalem.

Appendix
Principal Relevant Manuscripts

A. Munich—National Library[1]

Monacensis 394, 10th cent., 261 parchment fols.

This manuscript contains all of the catecheses, which are followed by a collection of epistles attributed to St. Ignatius. The titles and headings are in red, and the text is in clear small uncials. The text on fol. 1 begins with a general statement of contents: one *Procatechesis,* eighteen *Lenten Catecheses* for those being enlightened, and five *Mystagogic Catecheses.* A list follows of the titles of the eighteen catecheses (*P* is not mentioned in this list), which extends to the first half of fol. 2^r. There is no mention of an author, and the rest of this side of the folio is blank. The text resumes on fol. 2^v with the words, *Five Mystagogic Catecheses of John, Bishop of Jerusalem,* and a list of the titles of these five sermons. The text itself of the catecheses then begins, starting with *P,* again with no mention of an author (fols. 3–198). Each catechesis through *C* 18 is followed by an abbreviated reprise of its title and a line number. For example, after *C* 18 are the words: *Catechesis 18 on the Resurrection of the Dead, the Catholic Church, and Life Everlasting, line 763.* Following *C* 18 is an editorial note (fols. 198–99) describing how and when they were taken down and a general comment concerning their content:

Many other catecheses were delivered year to year, both before baptism and after the newly enlightened were baptized; but only these were taken down when they were spoken and written by some scholars in the year 352 of the appearance of our Lord Jesus Christ. And in these you will find in part, treatments of all the necessary doctrines of the faith which ought to be known; and answers to the Greeks and to those of the circumcision, and to the heresies, and the moral precepts of Christians of all kinds, by the grace of God.

The text of M 1 follows immediately (fol. 199) with the words: Mystagogia 1 of John of Jerusalem and a reading from the first catholic letter of Peter from "Be sober, be watchful, your adversary the devil . . ." to "To him be the dominion for ever and ever. Amen." The second sermon begins without mentioning the author: Mystagogic catechesis 2 concerning baptism, etc. Each of the other ser-

---

1. Information on these manuscripts can be found in J. C. L. Aretin, ed., *Catalogus codicum manuscriptorum Bibliothecae Bavaricae,* 4 vols. (Munich: J. E. Seidel, 1810): *Monac. 394,* 4:221–26; *Monac. 278,* 3:165–66.

mons begins in the same manner as the second, and unlike C, no reprise follows each sermon. This manuscript was in Augsburg prior to 1806. The lack of an author's name for C and John's name for M was noted by Milles and Touttée, but their information came only from the Augsburg catalogue, which printed the table of contents and the editorial note after C 18; they did not collate the manuscript itself. Reischl and Rupp valued the manuscript as much older than the Roe and Casaubon manuscripts and thus made special use of it for emending their text.

Monacensis 278, 16th cent., 473 paper fols.

This manuscript was written by Andreas Darmarius; titles and headings are in red. The manuscript lacks *P*, and the text of *C* is found on fols. 1–433. The entire text has the short heading: *Catecheses of Cyril to those being enlightened. C* 1 has the following heading: *The first catechetical sermon of Saint Cyril, Archbishop of Jerusalem, to those who are to be enlightened, delivered extempore in Jerusalem, as an introduction to those coming forward for baptism; with a reading from Isaiah: "Wash yourselves; make yourselves clean, etc."* The text of *M* is on fols. 433–68 and begins with the following title: *The first mystagogic catechesis to the newly baptized, with a reading from the first catholic epistle of Peter from "Be sober, be watchful, etc." to the end of the epistle, of the same author Cyril and of Bishop John.* Fols. 468–73 contain the *Letter to Constantius.* Reischl and Rupp note that the readings of this manuscript are very often consonant with Roe and Casaubon, and it was of only secondary use for them.[2]

B. Mount Sinai—Library of the Monastery of St. Catherine[3]

Sinaïticus 366 [*ol.* 309], dated 909, 237 parchment fols.

This manuscript is in Arabic and contains *C* and *M*. Fol. 1 begins immediately with *C* 1. At the heading of each sermon is a characteristic Arabic doxology: *In the name of the Father, and of the Son, and of the Holy Spirit, the one God*, and continues with a title very nearly identical with those of the Greek manuscripts but with a few variations. *C* 1 and *C* 8 have Cyril's name in the heading: *C* 1: *A sermon from the words of Cyril, Patriarch of Jerusalem, which he delivered extempore as an introduction to those coming forward to be baptized.* There is no editorial note after *C* 18. Instead there is a prayerful commendation by the scribe on the completion of the copying; he also notes the place and date: the Church of the Resurrection, March 909. The following heads the first mystagogic catechesis (fol. 218): *In the name of the Father, and of the Son, and of the Holy Spirit, the one God. Mystagogia 1, of John, Archbishop of Jerusalem, and a section from the first epistle of Peter the holy apostle.*

2. *S. Cyrilli*, 1:cxlvi.

3. See M. Kamil, ed., *Catalogue of All Manuscripts in the Monastery of St. Catherine on Mt. Sinai* (Wiesbaden: Harrassowitz, 1970), 29. Translations provided by Penelope Johnstone of the Oriental Institute, Oxford.

C. Vienna—National Library[4]

Vindobonensis Theol. gr. 29 [al. 55, Piédagnel, Reischl and Rupp], 11th cent., 249 parchment fols.

This manuscript contains C (fols. 155–245) and M (fols. 245–49); P is missing. The first catechesis is preceded by the title: *The first catechetical sermon of Cyril, Bishop of Jerusalem, to those who are to be baptized in Jerusalem; delivered extempore as an introduction to those coming forward for baptism; with a reading from Isaiah.* There is no other mention of an author. The first mystagogic catechesis is preceded by the title: *The first mystagogic catechesis to the newly baptized, with a reading from the first catholic epistle of Peter.* M 5 is incomplete. Its provenance is Constantinople, as noted in the manuscript by someone named Augerius Busbeckius. The manuscript also contains works of Eusebius of Pamphilia (fols. 1–61), John Philopon (fols. 61–146), and Philo (fols. 146–54). In Volume I of Reischl and Rupp (cxlvii), a manuscript of this exact description is called codex *Viennensis* 55 (al. 46); the editors note that they had not yet collated it but hoped to do so for Volume II of their work. In the *Prolegomenon* of Volume II, the same description of the manuscript is given again, but its name is changed to codex *Vindobonensis 55*.

Vindobonensis Mechitarist 273 (ol. 42)[5]

This Armenian version is thought to have been rendered in the fifth century. It contains only C and probably c omes from a Syriac and not a Greek original. It appeared for the first time in Constantinople in 1727. A second edition, based on codex *Vindobonensis Mechitarist 273* and dated to 1277, appeared in Vienna in 1832. Some ninth-century fragments have since been discovered and published.[6]

4. See H. Hunger and O. Kresten, eds., *Katalog der griechischen Handschriften der österreichischen Nationalbibliothek* (Wien: Verlag Notring der wissenschaftlichen Verbände Österreichs, 1976), 3/1:48–49. There is a fuller description in the older catalogue: Daniel de Nessel, ed., *Catalogus Codicum Manuscriptorum Graecorum . . . Bibliothecae Caesareae Vindobonensis* (Vienna: Norimbergae, typis Leopoldi Voigt, & Joachimi Balthasaris Endteri, 1690), Part I, 46–48.

5. The manuscript is described in H. V. Dashian, ed., *Catalog der armenischen Handschriften in der Mechitharistenbibliothek zu Wien* (Vienna: Mechitharisten-Buchdruckerei, 1895), 692–94.

6. See G. Garitte, "Les catéchèses de Cyrille de Jérusalem en arménien: fragments d'un manuscrit du IXe siècle," *Le Muséon* 76 (1963): 95–108, and S. Kolandjian, "New Fragments from a Manuscript of the 9th Century by Cyril of Jerusalem," *Yerevan: Banber Matenadarani* 5 (1960): 201–38.

D. England—Bodleian Library[7]

Bodleianus Roe 25 (al. 271 Reischl and Rupp),
11th cent., 223 parchment fols.

This manuscript was first collated by Thomas Milles. P and C are contained in fols. 1–200 and M in fols. 201–15. It also has the *Letter to Constantius* and the *Homily on the Paralytic* on fols. 215–23. Reischl and Rupp erroneously note that this manuscript has 294 folios and only a fragment of the *Homily on the Paralytic* on fol. 217.[8] Cyril's name occurs at the beginning of the set of catecheses on fol. 1 with these words: *The catechetical sermons of Saint Cyril, Archbishop of Jerusalem.* The text of M is entitled: *The first mystagogic catechesis to the newly baptized, with a reading from the first catholic epistle of Peter.* There is no other occurrence of an author's name.

Holkham gr. 32 (ol. Morenzenos 13, Guistiani 19),
15th cent., ii + 441 paper fols.

This manuscript contains C (fols. 3–272), followed by the Letter to Constantius (fols. 273–77) but lacks P and M. C begins with the following heading: *The first catechetical sermon of Saint Cyril, Archbishop of Jerusalem, to those who are to be enlightened, delivered extempore in Jerusalem, as an introduction to those coming forward for baptism; with a reading from Isaiah: "Wash yourselves; make yourselves clean, etc."* Bihain reckons this manuscript to be a copy of Patmos gr. 669.[9]

E. Paris—Bibliothèque Nationale[10]

Coislinianus 227 (ol. 101), 11th cent., 230 parchment fols.[11]

This manuscript was originally preserved in the monastery of the Enclystra in Cyprus. It was collated by Touttée. M is found on fols. 218–30. M 1 is preceded by the following title: *The first mystagogic catechesis to the newly baptized, with a reading from the epistle of Peter.* M 5 is missing, except for its title: *The fifth mystagogic catechesis; from the epistle of Peter, "Therefore, having laid aside all malice, etc."* It also contains C (fols. 1–218) but lacks P. The beginning of C 1, the end of C 17, and the beginning of C 18 are missing (Reischl and Rupp say that the lacunae in C are

---

7. See H. O. Coxe, ed., *Catalogue of Greek Manuscripts in the Bodleian Library*, vol. I (Oxford: E typographeo Academico, 1853).

8. *S. Cyrilli*, 1:cxlviii.

9. E. Bihain, "L'Épître de Cyrille de Jérusalem à Constance sur la vision de la croix (BHG3 413): tradition manuscrite et édition critique," *Byzantion* 43 (1973): 268–69. See also R. Barbour, *The Bodleian Library Record*, VI.5 (1960): 591–613.

10. H. Omont, ed., *Inventaire sommaire des manuscrits grecs de la Bibliothèque Nationale*, 2 vols. (Paris: A. Picard, 1888). (This catalogue is now referred to as Part I since the publication of subsequent parts). Part II is edited by R. Devreesse, *Catalogue des manuscrits grecs de la Bibliothèque Nationale II, fons Coislin* (Paris: Imprimerie nationale, 1945).

11. R. Devreesse, *Catalogue des manuscrits grecs*, 207.

the beginning and middle parts of *C* 1). There is no mention of an author in the codex.

F. Rome—Vatican Library [12]

Ottobonianus 86, 10th or 11th cent., 232 parchment fols.

This manuscript is missing some folios in the beginning; fol. 1 begins at the middle of *P* 3, and *C* begins on fol. 7 at the end of *C* 2.2. A note in the margin of fol. 1 reads: *The catecheses of Cyril*. The text of *M* is on fols. 190–206 preceded by the title: *The first mystagogic catechesis to the newly baptized, with a reading from the first catholic epistle of Peter from "Be sober, be watchful, etc." to the end of the epistle, of the same author Cyril and of Bishop John*. It also contains the *Letter to Constantius* on fols. 206–9. Reischl and Rupp call this *Ottobonianus I*.

Ottobonianus 220, 16th or 17th cent., viii + 173 paper fols.

This manuscript contains the full set of catecheses, though with some lacunae, and the *Letter to Constantius*. On the flyleaf (fol. a), Cyril's name is given in a note which announces that the codex contains *P* and *C*; the text of *P* begins (fol. b) with: *The procatechesis, or prologue to the catecheses, of Saint Cyril, Archbishop of Jerusalem*, and continues through fol. h. A short editorial note follows cautioning against lending the following catecheses to anyone but the baptized and candidates for baptism. There follows a table of contents of *C* and then the eighteen sermons. The first sermon has the heading: *The first catechetical sermon of Saint Cyril, Archbishop of Jerusalem, to those who are to be enlightened, delivered extempore in Jerusalem, as an introduction to those coming forward for baptism; with a reading from Isaiah: "Wash yourselves, etc."* *M* is contained in fols. 158–69 and is preceded by the following note: *These mystagogic catecheses are to be read only after all the preceding catecheses; the first mystagogic catechesis to the newly baptized, with a reading from the catholic epistle of Peter from "Be sober, be watchful, etc., to the end of the epistle."* The editorial note found after *C* 18 in *Monacensis 394* is found here at the end of M 5, on fol. 170; however, it is incomplete (see *Marcianus II.35*). Following the editorial note is the *Letter to Constantius*, which ends on fol. 172. On the last folio (173) is a table of contents for *M* with the following heading: *Table of contents of the mystagogic catecheses of Cyril, Archbishop of Jerusalem, for the newly baptized: five mystagogic catecheses*.

Ottobonianus 446, 15th cent., 273 paper fols.

The text of *P* and *C* is on fols. 1–189. Preceding *P* on the first folio is the following title: *The procatechesis, or prologue to the catecheses, of Saint Cyril, Archbishop of Jerusalem*. *P* is followed by a short editorial note cautioning against lending the

---

12. For the following three manuscripts see E. Féron and F. Battaglini, eds., *Catalogue des Codices graeci Ottoboniani*, (Rome: ex typographeo Vaticano, 1893), 53 *(Ott. 86)*, 128–29 *(Ott. 220)*, 249–50 *(Ott. 446)*.

following catecheses to anyone but the baptized and candidates for baptism. On fol. 8 is a table of contents for *C* with the following heading: *Eighteen catecheses of Cyril, Archbishop of Jerusalem, for those being enlightened; delivered extempore, and not polished, during one Lent to Syrians through an interpreter.* The text of *C* begins on fol. 9 with this heading: *The first catechetical sermon of Saint Cyril, Archbishop of Jerusalem, to those who are to be enlightened, delivered extempore in Jerusalem, as an introduction to those coming forward for baptism; with a reading from Isaiah: "Wash yourselves, etc."* The complete text of *M* is on fols. 189–204 preceded by the title: *The first mystagogic catechesis to the newly baptized, with a reading from the epistle of Peter, . . . of the same Cyril and of Bishop John.* The *Letter to Constantius* is found on fols. 204–8.

G. Venice—Library of San Marco[13]

Marcianus gr. II.35 [ol. Nanianus 56], 11–12th cent., 189 parchment fols.

The first three and the last two folios of this manuscript are paper and from the 16th century; they appear simply to be replacement copies of the deteriorating original beginning and ending folios. Fol. 1 has the following title: *The catecheses of Saint Cyril, Archbishop of Jerusalem.* The *verso* side begins with Sophronius's Greek version of Jerome's entry for Cyril in his *De viris inlustribus* with the heading: *The life of Cyril of Jerusalem according to Sophronius.*[14] This is followed by a list of the contents of *M*. *P* begins on fol. 2 and is followed on fol. 8 by the short editorial note cautioning against lending the following catecheses to anyone but the baptized and candidates for baptism (see above, *Ottobonianus 220, 446*). An index of *C* is on fols. 8–9, headed by the following: *Eighteen catecheses of Cyril, Archbishop of Jerusalem, for those being enlightened; delivered extempore, and not polished, during one Lent to Syrians through an interpreter.* On fols. 175–89 is *M*, but *M* 1 and 2 have been displaced to the very end of the manuscript. *M* 3–5 are followed by the editorial note found after *C* 18 in *Monacensis 394*, which recounts how the sermons were taken down (fols. 181–82); it is, however, incomplete (see *Ottobonianus 220*). Next is the *Letter to Constantius* followed finally by *M* 1–2.

H. Naples—Naples National Library[15]

Neapolitanus-Vindobonensis gr. 8, 11th cent., 170 parchment fols.

The first part of this manuscript contains the Epistles of Paul. There is no text of *P*; fols. 87–166 contain *C* and begin with the opening words of *C* 1.1; there is no

---

13. See *Bibliothecae Divi Marci Venetiarum Codices Graeci Manuscripti*, 3 vols. plus 2 vols. titled *Thesaurus Antiquus* (Rome: Istituto poligrafico dello Stato, 1967), 1:123–24.

14. Text edited by Oscar Von Gebhardt, *Der sogenannte Sophronius*, TU 14.1b (Leipzig: J. C. Hinrichs, 1896), 56. Jerome's text is in the same volume, 14.1a, no. 112.

15. See *Catalogus Codicum Graecorum Bibliothecae Nationalis Neapolitanae I* (Rome: Istituto poligrafico dello Stato, 1962), 23. The following work gives a fuller description: A. F. Kollar, ed., *Ad Petri Lambecii Commentariorum de Augusta Bibliotheca Caes. Vindobonensi libros VIII. supplemen-*

heading or ascription. *C* 11, 18, and part of 12 are missing; the end of *C* 10 is mutilated. The text of *M* (fols. 167–70) has been mutilated. The text begins with the final few words of *M* 1.1 and continues through to the first sentence of *M* 3.4.

I. Patmos[16]

Patmos gr. 669, 14th–15th cent., 100 paper fols.

The beginning of this manuscript is mutilated, but it probably lacks *P.* It contains *C* 1–18 and the *Letter to Constantius*. According to Bihain, it derives from the oldest part of *Marcianus gr. II.35* (fols. 10–175).[17]

J. Other

Codex A

A codex of *P* and *C* was found by Dionysius Kleopas in the library of the archbishop of Cyprus. This was used for a Greek edition of the *Catecheses* published in Jerusalem in 1867–68 (see Bibliography).

Syro-Palestinian fragments

Fragments of a Syro-Palestinian version have been collected, which contain only *P* and *C* 3–18. Judging from its literary style, the version is from between the fifth to seventh century.[18]

---

torum liber primus posthumus (Vienna: Typis et sumptibus Joan. Thomae Nob. de Trattnern, 1790), cols. 77–90.

16. See J. Sakellion, Πατμιακὴ βιβλιοθήκη (Athens: St. John's Monastery, 1890), 263; Bihain, "L'Épître de Cyrille de Jérusalem," 298.

17. Ibid., 268–69.

18. See J. N. P. Land, *Anecdota syriaca* (Leiden: Brill, 1874), 4:171. Land presents sixty-three fragments but without identifying them. These were identified as Cyril's with the addition of sixteen more by H. Duesing in *Christliche palästinisch-aramäische Texte und Fragmente nebst einer Abhandlung über den Wert der palästinischen Septuaginta* (Göttingen: Vandenhoeck & Ruprecht, 1906), 41–62.

Bibliography

Sources

Principal Editions and Translations of Cyril's Works

Sancti Patris nostri Cyrilli Archiepiscopi Hierosolymorum mystagogicae catecheses quinque, ad eas qui sunt recens illuminati. Quae nunc primum et Graece et Latine simul eduntur, ut qui dubitet de Latinis, ad Graecas possit recurrere, qui Graecas non satis intelligat, Latinas legat. Ed. John Grodecq. Vienna: The King's College, Society of Jesus, 1560.

Sancti Cyrilli Hierosolymorum Archiepiscopi Catecheses ex bibliotheca Henricii Memmii libellorum supplicum in Regia Magistri. Ed. William Morel. Paris: G. Morel, 1564.

Sancti Cyrilli Hierosolymorum Catecheses ad Illuminandos et Mystagogiae. Ed. John Grodecq. Antwerp: Christophorus Plantinus, 1564 (Latin text).

Sancti patris nostri Cyrilli Hierosolymorum Archiepiscopi Catecheses ex variis bibliothecis, praecipue Vaticana, Graece omnes nunc primum in lucem editae, cum Latina interpretatione Ioannis Grodecii, plerisque in locis aucta et emendata. Ed. Jean Prévot. Paris: apud Carolum Morellum, 1608.

S. Patris nostri Cyrilli Hierosolymorum Archiepiscopi opera quae supersunt, omnia; Quorum quaedam nunc primum ex Codd. MSS. edidit, reliqua cum Codd. MSS. contulit, plurimis in locis emendavit, notisque illustravit. Ed. Thomas Milles. Oxford: e Theatro Sheldoniano, 1703.

S. Cyrilli archiepiscopi Hierosolymitani Opera quae extant omnia, et ejus nomine circumferuntur. Ed. Antonii-Augustini Touttée. Paris: J. Vincent, 1720.

S. Cyrilli: Opera quae supersunt omnia. Ed. Wilhelm Karl Reischl and Joseph Rupp. 2 vols. Munich: Sumptibus Librariae Lentnerianae, 1848–60. Repr. Hildesheim: Georg Olms, 1967.

S. Cyrilli Archiepiscopi Hierosolymitani opera quae extant omnia. Ed. D. Kleopas and Photius Alexandrides. 2 vols. Jerusalem: P. Taphou, 1867–68.

The Five Lectures of St. Cyril on the Mysteries and Other Sacramental Treatises. Ed. H. de Romestin. Oxford: Parker, 1887.

The Catechetical Lectures of St. Cyril. Trans. E. H. Gifford. NPNF, 2d ser., vol. 7. Oxford: Parker, 1894. Repr. Peabody, Mass.: Hendrickson, 1994.

Catéchèses Mystagogiques de saint Cyrille en grec-latin. In *Monumenta eucharistica et liturgica vetustissima,* ed. Johannes Quasten. Florilegium Patristicum, vol. 7b, 69–111. Bonn: P. Hanstein, 1935.

St. Cyril of Jerusalem's Lectures on the Christian Sacraments. The Procatechesis and the Five Mystagogical Catecheses. Ed. F. L. Cross. Trans. R. W. Church. London: S.P.C.K., 1951.

Cyrille de Jérusalem. Ed. and trans. Maurice Véricel. Paris: Editions ouvrières, 1957.

Letter to Emperor Constantius. In *Le Grand Lectionnaire de l'Église de Jérusalem (V–VIIIe siècle)*, ed. and trans. Michel Tarchnischvili. CSCO 188–89. Scriptores Iberici 9–10, 144–40 (117–21). Louvain: Secretariat du CSCO, 1959–60.

Kolandjian, S. "New Fragments from a Manuscript of the 9th Century by Cyril of Jerusalem." *Yerevan: Banber Matenadarani* 5 (1960): 201–38.

Catéchèses baptismales et mystagogiques. Trans. Jean Bouvet. Namur: Editions du Soleil Levant, 1962.

Garitte, G. "Les catéchèses de Cyrille de Jérusalem en arménien: fragments d'un manuscrit du IXe siècle." *Le Muséon* 76 (1963): 95–108.

The Works of Cyril of Jerusalem. Trans. Leo P. McCauley and Anthony A. Stephenson. The Fathers of the Church, vols. 61, 64. Washington, D.C.: Catholic University of America Press, 1969–70.

Renoux, Athanase. "Une version arménienne des Catéchèses Mystagogiques de Cyrille de Jérusalem?" *Le Muséon* 85 (1972): 147–53.

Letter to Emperor Constantius. Ed. E. Bihain. "L'Épître de Cyrille de Jérusalem à Constance sur la vision de la croix (BHG³ 413): tradition manuscrite et édition critique." *Byzantion* 43 (1973): 264–96.

Cyrille de Jérusalem: Catéchèses mystagogiques. Ed. Auguste Piédagnel. Trans. Pierre Paris. SC 126 *bis.* Paris: Éditions du Cerf, 1988.

Editions and Translations of Works by John of Jerusalem

Apology. In *Ungedruckte, unbeachtete und wenig beachtete Quellen zur Geschichte des Taufsymbols und des Glaubensregels*, ed. Carl Paul Caspari. 3 vols., 1:185–90. Christiania: P. T. Malling, 1886 (Latin text assembled from Jerome's *Contra Ioannem*).

Profession of Faith. In *Ungedruckte, unbeachtete und wenig beachtete Quellen zur Geschichte des Taufsymbols und des Glaubensregels*, ed. and trans. Carl Paul Caspari. 3 vols., 1:185–90. Christiania: P. T. Malling, 1886 (Syriac text with German translation).

Sermon on the Church. Ed. Michel Van Esbroeck. "Une homélie sur l'église attribuée à Jean de Jérusalem." *Le Muséon* 86 (1973): 283–304.

———. In Michel Van Esbroeck, "Jean II de Jérusalem et les cultes de S. Étienne, de la Sainte-Sion, et de la Croix." *AB* 102 (1984): 99–134.

Editions and Translations of Other Patristic Authors

Acts of Paul. Acta Pauli. Nach dem Papyrus der Hamburger Staats- und Universitäts-Bibliothek. Ed. Carl Schmidt. Hamburg: J. J. Augustin, 1936.

Acts of Thomas. Acta Apostolorum Apocrypha, ed. R. A. Lipsius and M. Bonnet, vol. 2.2. Hildesheim: Georg Olms, 1959 (Greek text).

———. Trans. A. F. J. Klijn. Novum Testamentum, vol. 5. Leiden: Brill, 1962.

———. In *Apocryphal Acts of the Apostles Edited from Syriac Manuscripts in the British Museum and Other Libraries*, ed. and trans. William Wright. 2 vols. in 1, 2:146–298. Amsterdam: Philo Press, 1968 (Syriac text).

Addai and Mari. *The Eucharistic Prayer of Addai and Mari.* Ed. and trans. A. Gelston. Oxford: Clarendon Press, 1992.

Agathangelos. *La version grecque ancienne du livre arménien d'Agathange.* Ed. Guy Lafontaine. Publications de l'Institut orientaliste de Louvain, no. 7. Louvain-la-Neuve: Université catholique de Louvain, 1973.

Ambrose. *Des Sacrements, des Mystères, Explication du Symbole*. Ed. and trans. Bernard Botte. SC 25 *bis*. Paris: Éditions du Cerf, 1961.

————. *Expositio Evangelii secundum Lucam*. Ed. and trans. G. Tissot. SC 45, 52 *bis*. Paris: Éditions du Cerf, 1971, 1976.

————. *Expositio Psalmi 118*. PL 15.1261–1604.

Anastasius the Sinaïte. *Questiones et Responsiones*. PG 89.311–824.

Aphraates. *Aphraate le Sage Persan: Les Exposés*. Ed. and trans. M.-J. Pierre. SC 349, 359. Paris: Éditions du Cerf, 1989.

Apostolic Constitutions. Les Constitutions Apostoliques. Ed. and trans. Marcel Metzger. SC 320, 329, 336. Paris: Éditions du Cerf, 1985–87.

Armenian Lectionary. Ed. Athanase Renoux. "Un manuscrit du vieux lectionnaire arménien de Jérusalem." *Le Muséon* 74 (1961): 361–85; 75 (1962): 385–98.

————. *Le codex arménien Jérusalem 121*. Ed. and trans. Athanase Renoux. PO 35.1, 36.2. Turnhout: Brepols, 1969, 1971.

Armenian Rite. Rituale Armenorum. Being the Administration of the Sacraments and the Breviary Rites of the Armenian Church together with the Greek Rites of Baptism and Epiphany Edited from the Oldest MSS. Ed. F. C. Conybeare. Trans. A. J. Maclean. Oxford: Clarendon Press, 1905.

Athanasius. *The Festal Letters of Athanasius: Discovered in an Ancient Syriac Version and Edited by William Cureton*. London: Society for the Publication of Oriental Texts, 1848.

————. *Athanasius Werke*. Vol. 2.1: *Die Apologien* (1935), vol. 3: *Urkunden zur Geschichte des arianischen Streites 318–328* (1934). Ed. H. G. Opitz. Berlin and Leipzig: De Gruyter, 1934–35.

Ps-Athanasius of Alexandria. *Fourth Discourse Against the Arians*. PG 26.468–526.

————. *Athanasiana: Five Homilies, Expositio Fidei, Sermo maior*. Ed. Henric Nordberg. Societas Scientiarum Fennica, Commentationes humanarum litterarum, 30.2. Helsinki: n.p., 1962.

Augustine. *De catechizandis rudibus*. In *Aurelii Augustini Opera*. Ed. J. B. Baur. CCSL 46, 121–78. Turnhout: Brepols, 1969.

————. *Confessions*. Ed. L. Verheijen. CCSL 27. Turnhout: Brepols, 1981.

————. *Sermones*. PL 38–39.

Barnabas. *Epistle of Barnabas*. In *The Apostolic Fathers*, vol. 1, trans. Kirsopp Lake, 337–409. London: William Heinemann, 1930.

Basil of Caesarea. *Contre Eunome (Adversus Eunomium)*. Ed. and trans. Bernard Sesboüé, with Georges-Matthieu Durand and Louis de Doutreleau. SC 299, 305. Paris: Éditions du Cerf, 1982–83.

————. *Sur le Baptême (De baptismo)*. Ed. U. Neri, trans. Jeanne Ducatillon. SC 357. Paris: Éditions du Cerf, 1989.

————. *Sur le Saint-Esprit (De Spiritu Sancto)*. Ed. and trans. Benoît Pruche. SC 17 *bis*. Paris: Éditions du Cerf, 1968.

Clement of Alexandria. *Extraits de Théodote*. Ed. François Sagnard. SC 23. 2d ed. Paris: Éditions du Cerf, 1970.

————. *Paedagogus*. Ed. and trans. Marguerite Harl. SC 70, 108, 158. Paris: Éditions du Cerf, 1960–70.

Cyprian. *Epistulae*. Ed. W. Hartel. CSEL 3.2. Vienna: Geroldi, 1871.

Cyril of Alexandria. *Thesaurus de Trinitate*. PG 75.9–656.

Didascalia Apostolorum. *Didascalia et Constitutiones Apostolorum*. Ed. F. X. Funk. Paderborn: Ferdinand Schöningh, 1905 (Latin and Greek text).

———. *Didascalia Apostolorum: The Syriac Version Translated and Accompanied by the Verona Latin Fragments*. Ed. and trans. R. Hugh Connolly. Oxford: Clarendon Press, 1929.

———. *Didascaliae Apostolorum Canonum Ecclesiaticorum Traditionis Apostolicae Versiones Latinae*. Ed. Erik Tidner. TU 75. Berlin: Akademie-Verlag, 1963.

———. *The Didascalia Apostolorum in Syriac*. Ed. and trans. Arthur Vööbus. CSCO 401–2, 407–8. Scriptores Syri 175–76, 179–80. Louvain: Secretariat du CSCO, 1979 (Syriac text with English translation).

———. Ed. J. V. Bartlet. "Fragments of the Didascalia Apostolorum in Greek." *JTS* 18 (1917): 301–9.

Didymus the Blind. *De Trinitate*. PG 39.269–992.

Diodorus of Tarsus. *Commentarii in Psalmos I–L*. Ed. Jean-Marie Olivier. CCSG 6. Turnhout: Brepols, 1980.

Ps-Dionysius. *On the Ecclesiastical Hierarchy*. PG 3.369–584.

East Syrian Ordo. In *Liturgia sanctorum apostolorum Adaei et Maris*. Urmia (Rezaiyeh): Typis Missionis Archiepiscopi Cantuariensis, 1890.

Egeria. *Egeria's Travels to the Holy Land*. Trans. John Wilkinson. 2d rev. ed. Warminster, England: Aris and Phillips, 1981.

———. *Itinerarium Egeriae*. In *Itineraria et alia geographica*, ed. E. Franceschini and R. Weber. CSEL 175, 29–103. Turnhout: Brepols, 1965.

Ephrem the Syrian. *Ephrem the Syrian: Hymns*. Trans. Kathleen McVey. Classics of Western Spirituality. New York: Paulist Press, 1989.

———. *Hymnen de nativitate (Epiphania)*. Ed. and trans. E. Beck. CSCO 186–87. Scriptores Syri 82–83. Louvain: Secretariat du CSCO, 1959.

———. *Hymnen de virginitate*. Ed. and trans. E. Beck. CSCO 223–24. Scriptores Syri 94–95. Louvain: Secretariat du CSCO, 1962.

Epiphanius of Salamis. *Panarion (Adversus haereses)*. Ed. Karl Holl. GCS Epiphanius 1–3. Leipzig: J. C. Hinrichs, 1915, 1922, 1933.

Eusebius of Caesarea. *Contra Marcellum*. Ed. E. Klostermann, in *Gegen Marcell, Über die kirchliche Theologie, die Fragmente Marcells*. 2d rev. ed. Günther Christian Hansen. GCS Eusebius 4, 1–58. Berlin: Akademie-Verlag, 1972.

———. *De ecclesiastica theologia*. Ibid., 61–182.

———. *Demonstratio evangelica*. Ed. Ivar A. Heikel. GCS Eusebius 6. Leipzig: J. C. Hinrichs, 1913.

———. *De Vita Constantini*. Ed. Ivar A. Heikel. GCS Eusebius 1, 1–148. Leipzig: J. C. Hinrichs, 1902.

Eustratius of Constantinople. *De utriusque ecclesiae occidentalis atque orientalis perpetua in dogmate de purgatorio consensione*. Ed. Leone Allacci. Rome: Typis Sacrae Congregationis de Propaganda Fide, 1655.

Georgian Lectionary. *Le grand lectionnaire de l'Église de Jérusalem (V–VIIIe siècle)*. Ed. and trans. Michel Tarchnischvili. CSCO 188–89, 204–5. Scriptores Iberici 9–10, 13–14. Louvain: Secretariat du CSCO, 1959–60.

Georgios Hamartolos. *Chronicon*. PG 110.

———. *Georgii Monachi Chronicon*. Ed. Carolus de Boor (1904 ed. corr. by Peter Wirth). Stuttgart: Teubner, 1978.

Gregory Nazianzen. *Orations*. Ed. and trans. Jean Bernardi et al. SC 247, 309, 405, 270, 284, 250, 318, 358, 384. Paris: Éditions du Cerf, 1978–95.

Gregory of Nyssa. *The Catechetical Oration of Gregory of Nyssa*. Ed. J. H. Srawley. Cambridge: Cambridge University Press, 1956.

———. *De tridui inter mortem et resurrectionem domini nostri Iesu Christi spatio*. In *Gregorii Nysseni Opera*, vol. 9, ed. E. Gebhardt, 273–306. Leiden: Brill, 1967.

———. *Epistulae*. In *Gregorii Nysseni Opera*, vol. 8.2, ed. G. Pasquali. 2d ed. Leiden: Brill, 1959.

Gregory the Illuminator. *The Teaching of St. Gregory: An Early Armenian Catechism. Translation and Commentary*. Trans. R. W. Thomson. Harvard Armenian Texts and Studies, no. 3. Cambridge, Mass.: Harvard University Press, 1970.

Hippolytus. *La Tradition Apostolique*. Ed. and trans. Bernard Botte. SC 11 *bis*. Paris: Éditions du Cerf, 1984.

———. *The Treatise on the Apostolic Tradition of St. Hippolytus of Rome*. Ed. and trans. Gregory Dix, reedited by Henry Chadwick. 2d ed. London: S.P.C.K., 1968.

History of John the Son of Zebedee. In *Apocryphal Acts of the Apostles Edited from Syriac Manuscripts in the British Museum and Other Libraries*, ed. and trans. William Wright. 2 vols. in 1, 2:2–60. Amsterdam: Philo Press, 1968.

Ignatius of Antioch. *Letters*. In *The Apostolic Fathers*, vol. 1, trans. Kirsopp Lake, 166–277. London: W. Heinemann, 1913.

Irenaeus. *Contre les Hérésies*. Ed. and trans. Adelin Rousseau et al. SC 100, 152–53, 210–11, 263–64, 293–94. Paris: Éditions du Cerf, 1965–82.

———. *Libros quinque adversus haereses*. Ed. W. Wigan Harvey. 2 vols. Repr. Ridgewood, N. J.: Gregg Press, 1965.

Isidore of Pelusium. *Epistularum libri quinque*. PG 78.178–1646.

Itinerarium Burdigalense. In *Itineraria et alia geographica*, ed. P. Geyer and O. Cuntz. CCSL 175, 1–26. Turnhout: Brepols, 1965.

Jerome. Against John of Jerusalem. PL 23.355–98.

———. *Apologie contre Rufin*. Ed. and trans. P. Lardet. SC 303. Paris: Éditions du Cerf, 1983.

———. *Letters*. Ed. Isidor Hilberg. CSEL 54–56. Vienna: F. Tempsky, 1910–18.

———. *Liber de viris inlustribus*. Ed. E. C. Richardson. Leipzig: J. C. Hinrichs, 1896.

John Chrysostom. *Baptismal Homilies* (Montfaucon Series 1–2). PG 49.221–40.

———. *Baptismal Instructions*. Trans. Paul W. Harkins. Ancient Christian Writers, no. 31. Westminster, Md.: Newman Press, 1963.

———. *De coemeterio et cruce*. PG 49.393–418.

———. *De proditione Judae*. PG 49.373–92; 50.715–20.

———. *Homilies on Colossians*. PG 62.299–392.

———. *Homilies on Genesis*. PG 53–54.

———. *Homilies on John*. PG 59.

———. *Huit catéchèses baptismales* (Stavronikita Series, 1–8). Ed. and trans. Antoine Wenger. SC 50. Paris: Éditions du Cerf, 1957.

———. *Trois catéchèses baptismales*. Ed. Auguste Piédagnel. Trans. Pierre Paris. SC 366. Paris: Éditions du Cerf, 1990.

Ps-Chrysostom. *In adorationem venerandae crucis.* PG 62.747–54.

John Climacus. *Scala paradisi.* PG 88.585–1248.

Justin. *Apologies.* Ed. and trans. André Wartelle. Paris: Etudes augustiniennes, 1987.

———. *Dialogue avec Tryphon. Texte grec, traduction française.* Ed. and trans. Georges Archambault. Paris: A. Picard, 1909.

Liturgy of St. Mark. *The Liturgy of St. Mark: Edited from the Manuscripts with a Commentary by Geoffrey J. Cuming.* OCA 234. Rome: Pontificium Institutum Studiorum Orientalium, 1990.

Macarius of Egypt. *Homiliae spirituales.* PG 34.449–822.

Manuale Ambrosianum. Ed. Marcus Magistretti. Vols. 2–3 of *Monumenta veteris liturgiae Ambrosianae.* Milan: Ulricum Hoepli, 1897–1905.

Narsai. *The Liturgical Homilies of Narsai Translated into English with an Introduction by Dom R. H. Connolly; with an Appendix by Edmund Bishop.* Texts and Studies, no. 8.1. Cambridge: University Press, 1909.

Niceta of Remesiana. *Niceta of Remesiana: His Life and His Works.* Ed. A. E. Burn. Cambridge: University Press, 1905.

———. *Niceta von Remesiana: Instructio ad competentes.* Ed. Klaus Gamber. Regensburg: F. Pustet, 1964.

Odes of Solomon. Edited and translated by J. H. Charlesworth. Oxford: Clarendon Press, 1973.

Origen. *Commentarii in Johannem.* Ed. E. Preuschen. GCS Origenes 4. Leipzig: J. C. Hinrichs, 1903.

———. *Commentarii in Romanos.* PG 14.

———. *Commentaire sur S. Jean.* Ed. and trans. Cécile Blanc. SC 120, 157, 222, 290, 385. Paris: Éditions du Cerf, 1966–92.

———. *Contra Celsum.* Ed. and trans. M. Borret. SC 132, 136, 147, 150. Paris: Éditions du Cerf, 1967–69.

———. *De principiis.* Ed. Paul Koetschau. GCS Origenes 5. Leipzig: J. C. Hinrichs, 1913.

———. *Exhortation to Martyrdom.* Ed. Paul Koetschau. GCS Origenes 1. Leipzig: J. C. Hinrichs, 1899.

———. *Homilies on Numbers.* Ed. W. A. Baehrens. GCS Origenes 7. Leipzig: J. C. Hinrichs, 1921.

Photius of Constantinople. *Historia Manichaeorum.* PG 102.15–264.

Quintilian. *Institutio Oratoria.* Ed. and trans. H. E. Butler. Loeb Classic Library, vols. 124–27. London: W. Heinemann, 1921–22.

Rufinus of Aquileia. *Historia Ecclesiastica.* Ed. T. Mommsen. GCS Eusebius 2.2, 957–1040. Leipzig: J. C. Hinrichs, 1908.

———. *Expositio Symboli.* Ed. M. Simonetti. CCSL 20. Turnhout: Brepols, 1961.

Serapion of Thmuis. *The Sacramentary of Sarapion of Thmuis: A Text for Students, with Introduction, Translation, and Commentary.* Ed. and trans. R. Barrett-Lennard. Alcuin/GROW Liturgical Study, no. 25. Bramcote, Notts.: Grove Books, 1993.

———. F. E. Brightman. "The Sacramentary of Serapion of Thmuis." *JTS* 1 (1900): 88–113, 247–77.

Severus of Antioch. *Liber contra impium Grammaticum.* Ed. Joseph Lebon. CSCO 93–94, 101–2, 111–12. Scriptores Syri 4–6. Louvain: Secretariat du CSCO, 1929.

Sibylline Oracles. Oracula Sibyllina. Ed. J. Geffcken. GCS 8. Leipzig: J. C. Hinrichs, 1902.

Socrates. *Church History from A.D. 305–439.* Trans. A. C. Zenos. NPNF, 2d ser., vol. 2. Oxford: Parker, 1890. Repr. Peabody, Mass.: Hendrickson, 1994.

———. *Sokrates Kirchengeschichte.* Ed. Günther Christian Hansen and Manja Sirinjan. GCS Sokrates. Berlin: Akademie-Verlag, 1995.

Sozomen. *Church History from A.D. 323–425.* Trans. Chester D. Hartranft. NPNF, 2d ser., vol. 2. Oxford: Parker, 1890. Repr. Peabody, Mass.: Hendrickson, 1994.

———. *Historia Ecclesiastica.* Ed. J. Bidez and G. C. Hansen. GCS Sozomen. Berlin: Akademie-Verlag, 1960.

Tertullian. *Tertullian's Homily on Baptism (De baptismo).* Ed. and trans. Ernest Evans. London: S.P.C.K., 1964.

———. *Treatise on the Resurrection (De resurrectione carnis liber).* Ed. and trans. Ernest Evans. London: S.P.C.K., 1960.

Theodore of Mopsuestia. *Commentary of Theodore of Mopsuestia on the Lord's Prayer and on the Sacraments of Baptism and the Eucharist.* Ed. and trans. Alphonse Mingana. Woodbrooke Studies, no. 6. Cambridge: W. Heffer, 1932–33.

———. *Les Homélies Catéchétiques de Théodore de Mopsueste. Reproduction phototypique du MS. Mingana Syr. 561.* Ed. and trans. Raymond Tonneau with Robert Devreesse. Studi e Testi 145. Vatican City: Biblioteca apostolica Vaticana, 1949.

Theodoret of Cyrus. *Church History.* Trans. Blomfield Jackson. NPNF, 2d ser., vol. 3. Oxford: Parker, 1892. Repr. Peabody, Mass.: Hendrickson, 1994.

———. *Historia Ecclesiastica.* Ed. Leon Parmentier. 2d rev. ed. F. Scheidweiler. GCS Theodoret. Berlin: Akademie-Verlag, 1954.

Theophanes. *Chronographia.* Ed. Carolus De Boor. 2 vols. Leipzig: B. G. Teubner, 1883.

Zeno of Verona. *Zenonis Veronensis Tractatus.* Ed. B. Löftsedt. CCSL 22. Turnhout: Brepols, 1971.

Literature

Altaner, Berthold, and Alfred Stuiber. *Patrologie.* 8th ed. Freiburg: Herder, 1978.

Armstrong, G. T. "The Cross in the Old Testament according to Athanasius, Cyril of Jerusalem, and the Cappadocian Fathers." In *Theologia crucis, signum crucis: Festschrift für Erich Dinkler,* ed. Carl Andresen and Günter Klein, 19–37. Tübingen: Mohr, 1979.

Arns, P. E. *La technique du livre d'après Saint Jérôme.* Paris: E. de Boccard, 1953.

Atchley, E. G. *On the Epiclesis of the Eucharistic Liturgy and in the Consecration of the Font.* London: Oxford University Press, 1935.

Bagatti, Bellarmino. "I battisteri della Palestina." In *Actes du Ve congrès international d'archéologie chrétienne, Aix-en-Provence, 13–19 septembre 1954,* 213–27. Studi di antichità cristiana, no. 22. Vatican City: Pontificio Istituto di archeologia cristiana, 1957.

Bailey, R., and L. Dolezel. *Statistics and Style.* New York: American Elsvier, 1969.

Baldovin, John F. "A Lenten Sunday Lectionary in Fourth-Century Jerusalem?" In *Time and Community,* ed. J. Neil Alexander, 115–22. Washington, D.C.: Pastoral Press, 1990.

———. *Liturgy in Ancient Jerusalem.* GLS 57. Bramcote, Notts.: Grove Books, 1989.

———. *The Urban Character of Christian Worship: The Origins, Development, and Mean-*

ing of Stational Liturgy. OCA 228. Rome: Pontificium Institutum Studiorum Orientalium, 1987.

Bardy, Gustave. "Cyrille de Jérusalem." *Dictionnaire de spiritualité ascétique et mystique* 2.2, 2683–87. Paris: G. Beauchesne, 1953.

Baumstark, Anton. *Comparative Liturgy.* London: Mowbray, 1958.

Ben-Pechat, Malka. "L'architecture baptismale de la Terre-Sainte du IVe au VIIe siècle: étude historique, archéologique et liturgique." Ph.D. diss., University of Paris, Nanterre, 1986.

Bernard, J. H. "The Descent into Hades and Christian Baptism." *The Expositor* 11 (1916): 241–74.

Beukers, Clemens. "'For our Emperors, Soldiers and Allies'. An Attempt at Dating the Twenty-third Catechesis by Cyrillus of Jerusalem." *VC* 15 (1961): 177–84.

Bihain, E. "Le *Contre Eunome* de Théodore de Mopsueste, source d'un passage de Sozomène et d'un passage de Théodoret concernant Cyrille de Jérusalem." *Le Muséon* 75 (1962): 331–35.

——. "La Source d'un texte de Socrate (H. E. II.38.2) relativ à Cyrille de Jérusalem." *Byzantion* 32 (1962): 81–91.

——. "La tradition manuscrite grecque des oeuvres de S. Cyrille de Jérusalem." Ph.D. diss., University of Louvain, 1966.

——. "Une vie arménienne de S. Cyrille de Jérusalem." *Le Muséon* 76 (1963): 319–48.

Boismard, M. E. "I Renounce Satan, His Pomps, and His Works." In *Baptism in the New Testament: A Symposium,* ed. Augustin George et al., trans. David Askew, 107–12. Baltimore: Helicon, 1964.

Botte, Bernard. "Le Baptême dans l'église syriénne." *Orient Syrien* 1 (1956): 137–55.

Bottini, G. C., L. DiSegni, and E. Alliata, eds. *Christian Archaeology in the Holy Land, New Discoveries: Essays in Honour of Virgilio C. Corbo, OFM.* Studium Biblicum Franciscanum Collectio maior, no. 36. Jerusalem: Franciscan Printing Press, 1990.

Bradshaw, Paul F. *The Search for the Origins of Christian Worship.* London: S.P.C.K., 1992.

Brightman, F. E. "Correspondence: Invocation in the Holy Eucharist." *Theology* 9, no. 49 (1924): 33–40.

Brightman, F. E., and C. E. Hammond. *Liturgies Eastern and Western.* Oxford: Clarendon Press, 1896.

Brock, Sebastian. *The Harp of the Spirit: Eighteen Poems of St. Ephrem.* 2d enl. ed. Studies Supplementary to Sobornost, no. 4. London: Fellowship of St. Alban and St. Sergius, 1983.

——. *The Harp of the Spirit: Twelve Poems of St. Ephrem. Introduction and Translation.* Studies Supplementary to Sobornost, no. 4. London: Fellowship of St. Alban and St. Sergius, 1975.

——. *The Holy Spirit in the Syrian Baptismal Tradition.* The Syrian Churches Series, no. 9. Bronx, N.Y.: John XXIII Center, Fordham University, 1979.

——, trans. *The Liturgical Portions of the Didascalia.* GLS 29. Bramcote Notts.: Grove Books, 1982.

——. "Some Early Syriac Baptismal Commentaries." *OCP* 46 (1980): 20–61.

——. "Studies in the Early History of the Syrian Orthodox Baptismal Liturgy." *JTS,* n.s. 23 (1972): 16-64.

————. "The Syrian Baptismal Ordines (with Special Reference to the Anointings)." *SL* 12 (1977): 177–83.

————. "The Transition to a Postbaptismal Anointing in the Antiochene Rite." In *The Sacrifice of Praise*, ed. Bryan D. Spinks, 215–25. Bibliotheca "Ephemerides liturgicae." Subsidia, no. 19. Rome: C.L.V.—Edizioni liturgiche, 1981.

Burreson, Kent. "The Anaphora of the Mystagogical Catecheses of Cyril of Jerusalem." In *Essays on Early Eastern Eucharistic Prayers*, ed. Paul F. Bradshaw, 131–151. Collegeville, Minn.: Liturgical Press, 1997.

Cabié, R. *La Pentecôte: L'évolution de la cinquantaine pascale au cours des cinq premiers siècles*. Tournai: Desclee, 1964.

Cabrol, Fernand. *Les Églises de Jérusalem: La discipline et la liturgie au IVe siècle*. Paris: H. Oudin, 1895.

Camelot, P. T. "Note sur la théologie baptismale des Catéchèses attribuées à saint Cyrille de Jérusalem." In *Kyriakon: Festschrift Johannes Quasten*, ed. P. Granfield and J. A. Jungmann. 2 vols, 2:724–29. Münster: Aschendorff, 1970.

Capelle, Bernard. "L'authorité de la liturgie chez les Pères." *Recherches de théologie ancienne et médiévale* 21 (1954): 5–22.

Carrington, P. *The Primitive Christian Catechism*. Cambridge: Cambridge University Press, 1940.

Casel, Odo. "Neuere Beiträge zur Epiklesenfrage." *Jahrbuch für Liturgiewissenschaft* 4 (1924): 169–78.

Chavasse, Antoine. "La préparation de la Pâque, à Rome, avant le Ve siècle. Jeûne et organisation liturgique." In *Memorial J. Chaine*. Bibliothèque de la Faculté Catholique de Théologie de Lyon, vol. 5, 61–80. Lyons: Facultés Catholiques, 1950.

————. "La structure du Carême et les lectures des messes quadragesimales dans la liturgie Romain." *La Maison Dieu* 31 (1952): 76–120.

Conant, K. J. "The Original Buildings at the Holy Sepulchre in Jerusalem." *Speculum* 21 (1956): 1–49.

Corbo, V. C. *Il Santo Sepolchro di Gerusalemme*. 3 vols. Studium Biblicum Franciscanum Collectio maior, no. 29. Jerusalem: Franciscan Printing Press, 1981.

Coüasnon, C. *The Church of the Holy Sepulchre in Jerusalem*. London: Oxford University Press for the British Academy, 1974.

Cross, F. L. *I Peter, A Paschal Liturgy*. London: Mowbray, 1954.

Cullmann, O. *Baptism in the New Testament*. Trans. J. K. S. Reid. Studies in Biblical Theology, no. 1. London: SCM, 1950.

Cuming, G. J. "Egyptian Elements in the Jerusalem Liturgy." *JTS*, n.s. 25 (1974): 117–24.

————. "The Shape of the Anaphora." *SP* 20, 333–45. Leuven: Peeters, 1989.

Cummings, Owen. "Cyril of Jerusalem as a Postliberal Theologian." *Worship* 67 (1993): 155–64.

Cutrone, E. J. "The Anaphora of the Apostles: Implications of the Mar Esa'ya Text." *TS* 34 (1973): 624–42.

————. "Cyril's Mystagogical Catecheses and the Evolution of the Jerusalem Anaphora." *OCP* 44 (1978): 52–64.

————. "The Liturgical Setting of the Institution Narrative in the Early Syrian Tradition." In *Time and Community*, ed. J. Neil Alexander, 105–14. Washington, D.C.: Pastoral Press, 1990.

————. "Saving Presence in the Mystagogical Catecheses of Cyril of Jerusalem." Ph.D. diss., University of Notre Dame, 1975.

Daley, Brian. "The Origenism of Leontius of Byzantium." *JTS*, n.s. 27 (1976): 333–69.

Daniélou, Jean. *The Bible and the Liturgy.* Notre Dame, Indiana: University of Notre Dame Press, 1956.

————. *From Shadows to Reality: Studies in Biblical Typology of the Fathers.* Trans. Wulstan Hibberd. London: Burns & Oates, 1960.

————. *Sacramentum futuri: études sur les origines de la typologie biblique.* Paris: Beauchesne, 1960.

————. "Traversée de la Mer Rouge et baptême aux premiers siècles." *Recherches de science religieuse* 33 (1946): 402–30.

Davies, J. G. *The Architectural Setting of Baptism.* London: Barrie and Rockliff, 1962.

Deddens, Karel. "Annus liturgicus? Een onderzoek naar de betekenis van Cyrillus van Jeruzalem voor de ontwikkeling van het 'kerkelijk jaar'." Ph.D. diss., Oosterbaan & Le Cointre, 1975.

————. "Cyrille de Jérusalem et l'année liturgique." *Questiones liturgicae* 56 (1975): 41–46.

Denzinger, Heinrich, ed. *Ritus Orientalium, Coptorum, Syrorum et Armenorum.* 2 vols. in 1. Graz: Akademische Druck- u. Verlagsanstalt, 1961.

Devos, Paul. "La date du voyage d'Égérie." *AB* 85 (1967): 165–94.

Dix, Gregory. *Confirmation or the Laying on of Hands.* Theology Occasional Papers, no. 5. London: S.P.C.K., 1936.

————. "The Seal in the Second Century." *Theology* 51 (1948): 7–12.

————. *The Shape of the Liturgy.* Westminster, London: Dacre Press, 1945. Repr. San Francisco: Harper & Row, 1982.

Dölger, Franz Josef. *Der Exorzismus im altchristlichen Taufritual.* Studien zur Geschichte und Kultur des Altertums, vol. 3 (1/2 Heft). Paderborn: Ferdinand Schöningh, 1909.

————. *Sphragis. Eine altchristliche Taufbezeichnung in ihren Beziehungen zur profanen und religiösen Kultur des Altertums.* Studien zur Geschichte und Kultur des Altertums, vol. 5 (3/4 Heft). Paderborn: Ferdinand Schöningh, 1911.

Doval, Alexis. "Cyril of Jerusalem's Theology of Salvation." *SP* 37, 452–61. Leuven: Peeters, 2001.

————. "The Date of Cyril of Jerusalem's *Catecheses*." *JTS*, n.s. 48 (1997): 129–32.

————. "The Fourth Century Jerusalem Catechesis and the Development of the Creed." *SP* 30, 296–305. Leuven: Peeters, 1997.

————. "The Location and Structure of the Baptistery in the Mystagogic Catecheses of Cyril of Jerusalem." *SP* 26, 1–13. Leuven: Peeters, 1993.

Drake, H. A. "Eusebius on the True Cross." *JEH* 36 (1985): 1–22.

Drijvers, Jan Willem. "Promoting Jerusalem: Cyril and the True Cross." In *Portraits of Spiritual Authority: Religious Power in Early Christianity, Byzantium, and the Christian Orient.* Religions in the Graeco-Roman World, vol. 137, 79–95. Leiden: Brill, 1999.

Dujarier, M. *A History of the Catechumenate: The First Six Centuries.* New York: Sadlier, 1979.

Fenwick, John. *Fourth Century Anaphoral Construction Techniques.* GLS 45. Bramcote Notts.: Grove Books, 1986.

Ferguson, John. *Pelagius.* Cambridge: W. Heffer, 1956.

Finn, Thomas M. *Early Christian Baptism and the Catechumenate: West and East Syria.* Message of the Fathers of the Church, vol. 5. Collegeville, Minn.: Liturgical Press, 1992.

———. *From Death to Rebirth: Ritual and Conversion in Antiquity.* New York: Paulist Press, 1997.

———. *The Liturgy of Baptism in the Baptismal Instructions of St. John Chrysostom.* The Catholic University of America Studies in Christian Antiquity, no. 15. Washington, D.C.: Catholic University of America Press, 1967.

Fruytier, Joseph. "Cyrillus' auterschap van de myst. catechesen toch nog te redden?" *Studia Catholica* 26 (1951): 282–88.

Gavin, F. *The Jewish Antecedents of the Christian Sacraments.* London: S.P.C.K., 1928.

Giordano, N. "Lo Spirito fragranza di Cristo nelle catechesi di Cirillo di Gerusalemme." *Nicolaus* 8 (1980): 323–27.

Grace, Madeleine. "The Catechumenate within the Patristic Heritage." *Diakonia* 30, no. 2–3 (1997): 77–87.

Green, H. B. "The Significance of the Prebaptismal Seal in St. John Chrysostom." *SP* 6 = TU 81, 84–90. Berlin: Akademie-Verlag, 1962.

Gregg, R. C. "Cyril of Jerusalem and the Arians." In *Arianism: Historical and Theological Reassessments,* ed. R. C. Gregg, 85–109. Patristic Monograph Series, no. 11. Cambridge, Mass.: Philadelphia Patristic Foundation, 1985.

Gribomont, J. "Le succès littéraire des Pères grecs." *Sacris Erudiri* 22.1 (1974–75): 23–49.

Goppelt, L. *Typos: The Typological Interpretation of the Old Testament in the New.* Trans. Donald H. Madvig. Grand Rapids: W. B. Eerdmans, 1982.

Guillet, J. "Les exégèses d'Alexandrie et d'Antioch. Conflit ou malentendu?" *Recherches de science religieuse* 34 (1947): 257–302.

Hamman, Adelbert. *L'Initiation chrétienne. Cyrille de Jérusalem: Catéchèses mystagogiques; Ambroise de Milan: Traité des mystères; Jean Chrysostome: Sermon aux néophytes.* 2d ed. Lettres chrétiennes, no. 7. Paris: B. Grasset, 1980.

Hanson, R. P. C. *The Search for the Christian Doctrine of God.* Edinburgh: T & T Clark, 1988.

Hellemo, G. *Adventus Domini: Eschatological Thought in 4th Century Apses and Catechesis.* Supplements to Vigilae Christianae, no. 5. Leiden: Brill, 1989.

Hess, Hamilton. "Soteriological Motifs in the Catechetical Lectures of St. Cyril of Jerusalem." *SP* 32, 314–19. Leuven: Peeters, 1997.

Hockey, Susan. *A Guide to Computer Applications in the Humanities.* London: Duckworth, 1980.

Hunt, E. D. *Holy Land Pilgrimage in the Later Roman Empire A.D. 312–460.* Oxford: Clarendon Press, 1982.

Irshai, O. "Cyril of Jerusalem: The Apparition of the Cross and the Jews." In *Contra Iudaeos: Ancient and Medieval Polemics between Christians and Jews,* ed. Ora Limor and Gedaliahu A. G. Stroumsa, 85–104. Tübingen: J.C.B. Mohr, 1996.

Jackson, Pamela. "Cyril of Jerusalem's Treatment of Scriptural Texts Concerning the Holy Spirit." *Traditio* 46 (1991): 1–31.

———. "Cyril of Jerusalem's Use of Scripture in Catechesis." *TS* 52 (1991): 431–51.

James, M. R. *The Apocryphal New Testament.* Oxford: Clarendon Press, 1924.

Janeras, Sebastià. "À propos de la catéchèse XIVe de Cyrille de Jérusalem." *Ecclesia Orans* 3 (1986): 307–18.

Jasper, R. C. D., and G. J. Cuming. *Prayers of the Eucharist: Early and Reformed.* 3d rev. and enl. ed. New York: Pueblo, 1987.

Jeanes, Gordon. *The Day Has Come! Easter and Baptism in Zeno of Verona.* Alcuin Club Collections, no. 73. Collegeville, Minn.: Liturgical Press, 1995.

Jenkinson, W. R. "The Image and Likeness of God in Man in the Eighteen Lectures on the Credo of Cyril of Jerusalem." *Ephemerides Theologicae Lovanienses* 40 (1964): 48–72.

Johnson, Maxwell. "From Three Weeks to Forty Days: Baptismal Preparation and the Origins of Lent." *SL* 20 (1990): 185–200.

———. "Reconciling Cyril and Egeria on the Catechetical Process in Fourth-Century Jerusalem." In *Essays in Early Eastern Initiation,* ed. Paul F. Bradshaw, 18–30. GLS 56. Bramcote, Notts.: Grove Books, 1988.

Jones, C., G. Wainwright, and E. J. Yarnold. *The Study of Liturgy.* London: S.P.C.K., 1978.

Jungmann, Josef Andreas. *Die Stellung Christi im liturgischen Gebet.* Liturgiegeschichtliche Forschungen, vols. 7–8. Münster: Aschendorff, 1925.

———. *Die Stellung Christi im liturgischen Gebet.* 2d rev. ed. Liturgiewissenschaftliche Quellen und Forschungen, vols. 19–20. Münster: Aschendorff, 1962.

———. *The Mass of the Roman Rite: Its Origins and Development (Missarum Sollemnia).* Trans. Francis A. Brunner. 2 vols. New York: Benziger, 1951–55.

———. *The Place of Christ in Liturgical Prayer.* Trans. A. Peeler. London: G. Chapman, 1965.

Käsemann, E. "A Primitive Christian Baptismal Liturgy." In *Essays on New Testament Themes.* Studies in Biblical Theology, no. 41. Trans. W. J. Montague, 149–68. Naperville, Ill.: Allenson, 1964.

Kattenbusch, F. *Das apostolische Symbol.* Leipzig: J. C. Hinrichs, 1934.

Kelly, H. A. *The Devil at Baptism: Ritual, Theology, and Drama.* Ithaca: Cornell University Press, 1985.

Kelly, J. N. D. *Early Christian Creeds.* 3d rev. ed. London: Longman, 1972.

———. *Early Christian Doctrines.* 5th rev. ed. San Francisco: Harper & Row, 1978.

———. *Jerome: His Life, Writings, and Controversies.* London: Duckworth, 1975.

Kenny, Anthony. *The Computation of Style.* Oxford: Pergamon Press, 1982.

———. *A Stylometric Study of the New Testament.* Oxford: Clarendon Press, 1986.

Khatchatrian, A. "Le Baptistère de Nisibis." In *Actes du Ve congrès international d'archéologie chrétienne, Aix-en-Provence, 13–19 septembre 1954,* 407–21. Studi di antichità cristiana, no. 22. Vatican City: Pontificio Istituto di archeologia cristiana, 1957.

Kolandjian, S. "New Fragments from a Manuscript of the 9th Century by Cyril of Jerusalem." *Yerevan: Banber Matenadarani* 5 (1960): 201–38.

Krautheimer, R. "Constantine's Church Foundations." In *Akten des VII. internationalen Kongresses für christliche Archäologie, Trier, 5–11 September 1965,* 237–57. Studi di antichità cristiana, no. 27. Vatican City: Pontificio Istituto di archeologia cristiana, 1969.

Kretschmar, Georg. "Festkalender und Memorialstätten Jerusalems in altkirchlicher Zeit." In *Jerusalemer Heiligtumstraditionen in altkirchlicher und frühislamischer Zeit,* ed. G. Kretschmar and H. Busse, 29–111. Abhandlungen des deutschen Palästinavereins, no. 8. Wiesbaden: Otto Harrassowitz, 1988.

————. "Die frühe Geschichte der Jerusalemer Liturgie." *Jahrbuch für Liturgik und Hymnologie* 2 (1956): 22–46.

————. *Die Geschichte des Taufgottesdienstes in der alten Kirche.* Ed. K. Müller and W. Blankenburg. Leiturgica: Handbuch des evangelischen Gottesdienstes, vol. 5 (=Lief. 31–35). Kassel: J. Stauda-Verlag, 1964–66.

————. "Recent Research on Christian Initiation." *SL* 12 (1977): 87–106.

————. *Studien zur frühchristlichen Trinitätstheologie.* Beiträge zur historichen Theologie, no. 21. Tübingen: Mohr, 1956.

Lages, Mario. "Étapes de l'évolution de carême à Jérusalem avant le Ve siècle. Essai d'analyse structurale." *Revue des études arméniennes*, n.s. 6 (1969): 67–102.

————. "The Hierosolymitain Origin of the Catechetical Rites in the Armenian Liturgy." *Didaskalia* 1 (1971): 233–50.

Lampe, G. W. H. *The Seal of the Spirit.* 2d ed. London: S.P.C.K., 1967.

Lash, J. A. "L'onction post-baptismale de la 14e homélie de Théodore de Mopsueste: une interpolation syriaque?" In *XXIX Congrès International des Orientalistes: Resumés*, 43–44. Paris: The Congress, 1973.

Lebon, Joseph. "La position de saint Cyrille de Jérusalem dans les luttes provoquées par l'arianisme." *RHE* 20 (1924): 181–210, 357–86.

Ledger, Gerard. *Re-counting Plato: A Computer Analysis of Plato's Style.* Oxford: Clarendon Press, 1989.

Ledwich, William. "Baptism, Sacrament of the Cross: Looking behind St. Ambrose." In *The Sacrifice of Praise*, ed. Bryan D. Spinks, 199–211. Bibliotheca "Ephemerides liturgicae." Subsidia, no. 19. Rome: C.L.V.—Edizioni liturgiche, 1981.

Leroy, François Joseph. "Pseudo-Chrysostomica: Jean de Jérusalem; vers une résurrection littéraire." *SP* 10 = TU 107, 131–36. Berlin: Akademie-Verlag, 1970.

Lietzmann, Hans. *Mass and Lord's Supper: A Study in the History of the Liturgy.* Trans. Dorothea H. G. Reeve. Leiden: Brill, 1953.

Ligier, Louis. "The Origins of the Eucharistic Prayer: From the Last Supper to the Eucharist." *SL* 9 (1973): 161–85.

Logan, Alastair. "Post-baptismal Chrismation in Syria: The Evidence of Ignatius, the *Didache*, and the *Apostolic Constitutions*." *JTS*, n.s., 49 (1998): 92–109.

Lundberg, Per. *La Typologie baptismale dans l'ancienne église.* Acta Seminarii Neotestamentici Upsaliensis, no. 10. Uppsala: A.-B. Lundequistska, 1942.

Lutoslawski, W. *The Origin and Growth of Plato's Logic.* London: Longmans, 1897.

Macomber, William F. "The Ancient Form of the *Anaphora of the Apostles.*" In *East of Byzantium: Syria and Armenia in the Formative Period*, 73–88. Washington, D.C.: Dumbarton Oaks, 1982.

————. "The Oldest Known Text of the Anaphora of the Apostles Addai and Mari." *OCP* 32 (1966): 335–37.

Manson, Thomas Walter. "Entry into Membership of the Early Church." *JTS* 48 (1947): 25–37.

Martimort, Aimé Georges. *The Church at Prayer.* 3 vols. Collegeville, Minn.: Liturgical Press, 1988.

Mazza, Enrico. *Mystagogy: A Theology of Liturgy in the Patristic Age.* New York: Pueblo, 1989.

————. *The Origins of the Eucharistic Prayer.* Trans. R. Lane. Collegeville, Minn.: Liturgical Press, 1995.

McDonald, William Patrick. "Paideia and Gnosis: Foundations of the Catechumenate in Five Church Fathers." Ph.D. diss., Vanderbilt University, Nashville, 1998.

McDonnell, Kilian. *The Baptism of Jesus in the Jordan: The Trinitarian and Cosmic Order of Salvation.* Collegeville, Minn.: Liturgical Press, 1996.

Mealand, David, and T. Horton. Review of *Re-counting Plato* by G. Ledger. *Literary and Linguistic Computing* 6 (1991): 228–32.

Metzger, Marcel. "La Didascalie et les Constitutions Apostoliques." In *L'Eucharistie des premiers chrétiens,* 187–93. Le point théologique, no. 17. Paris: Beauchesne, 1976.

Meyers, Ruth. "The Structure of the Syrian Baptismal Rite." In *Essays in Early Eastern Initiation,* ed. Paul F. Bradshaw, 31–43. GLS 56. Bramcote, Notts.: Grove Books, 1988.

Michaelson, S., and A. Q. Morton. "Identifying Aristotle." *Computer Calepraxis* 1 (1972): 13–42.

Mitchell, L. L. *Baptismal Anointing.* Alcuin Club Collections, no. 48. London: S.P.C.K., 1966.

———. "The Development of Catechesis in the Third and Fourth Centuries: From Hippolytus to Augustine." In *A Faithful Church: Issues in the History of Catechesis,* ed. John H. Westerhoff and O. C. Edwards, 49–78. Wilton, Conn.: Morehouse-Barlow Co., 1981.

Mollat, Donatien. "Baptismal Symbolism in St. Paul." In *Baptism in the New Testament: A Symposium,* ed. Augustin George et al., trans. D. Askew, 63–83. Baltimore: Helicon, 1964.

Moroziuk, R. "Some Thoughts on the Meaning of *katholike* in the Eighteenth Catechetical Lecture of Cyril of Jerusalem." *SP* 18.1, 169–78. Kalamazoo, Mich.: Cistercian Publications, 1985.

Morton, Andrew Queen. "The Authorship of the Pauline Corpus." In *The New Testament in Historical and Contemporary Perspective: Essays in Memory of G. H. C. MacGregor,* ed. Hugh Anderson and William Barclay. Oxford: Blackwell, 1963.

Mosteller, Frederick, and David Wallace. *Inference and Disputed Authorship: The Federalist.* Reading, Mass.: Addison-Wesley Pub. Co., 1964.

Mullen, Roderic L. *The New Testament Text of Cyril of Jerusalem.* Atlanta, Ga.: Scholars Press, 1997.

Nautin, Pierre. "La date du *de viris inlustribus* de Jérôme, de la mort de Cyrille de Jérusalem et de celle de Grégoire de Nazianze." *RHE* 56 (1961): 33–35.

———. "La lettre de Théophile d'Alexandrie à l'église de Jérusalem et la réponse de Jean de Jérusalem (juin–juillet 396)." *RHE* 69 (1974): 365–94.

———. "Ὁμοούσιος unius esse (Jérôme Ep. XCIII)." *VC* 15 (1961): 40–45.

Olivar, A. "Preparación e Improvisación en la Predicación Patrística." In *Kyriakon: Festschrift Johannes Quasten.* 2 vols, 2:736–67. Münster: Aschendorff, 1970.

Pasquato, O. "Spirituality and Prayer in the Baptismal Catecheses of St. Cyril of Jerusalem." In *Prayer and Spirituality in the Early Church,* ed. Raymond Canning et al., 39–60. Queensland: Centre for Early Christian Studies, 1998.

Paulin, Antoine. *Saint Cyrille de Jérusalem Catéchète.* Paris: Éditions du Cerf, 1959.

Piédagnel, Auguste. "À propos des Catéchèses Mystagogiques de Cyrille de Jérusalem." *RSR* 55 (1967): 565.

Posner, Rebecca. "The Use and Abuse of Stylistic Statistics." *Archivum Linguisticum* 15 (1963): 111–39.

Quasten, Johannes. "The Blessing of the Baptismal Font in the Syrian Rite in the Fourth Century." *TS* 7 (1946): 308–13.

———. *Patrology*. 4 vols. Westminster, Maryland: Christian Classics, Inc., 1983–86.

Ratcliff, E. C. "The Old Syrian Baptismal Tradition and Its Resettlement under the Influence of Jerusalem in the 4th Century." In *Liturgical Studies*, ed. A. H. Couratin and D. H. Tripp, 135–54. London: S.P.C.K., 1976.

Renoux, Athanase. "Les Catéchèses Mystagogiques dans l'organisation liturgique hiérosolymitaine du IVe et du Ve siècle." *Le Muséon* 78 (1965): 355–59.

———. "Le Codex Érévan 985. Une adaptation arménienne du lectionnaire hiérosolymitain." In *Armeniaca: Mélanges d'Études Arméniennes*. Île de Saint Lazare–Venice: Mechitarist Press, 1969.

———. "Hierosolymitana." *Archiv für Liturgie-Wissenschaft* 23 (1981): 1–29, 149–75.

———. "La lecture biblique dans la liturgie de Jérusalem." In *Le monde grec ancien et la Bible*. Bible de tous les temps, no. 1. Paris: Beauchesne, 1980.

———. "Liturgie de Jérusalem et lectionnaires arméniens." *Lex Orandi* 35 (1963): 167–99.

Richard, M. "Bulletin de patrologie." *Mélanges de science religieuse* 5 (1948): 273–308.

Riley, Hugh. *Christian Initiation: A Comparative Study of the Interpretation of the Baptismal Liturgy in the Mystagogical Writings of Cyril of Jerusalem, John Chrysostom, Theodore of Mopsuestia, and Ambrose of Milan*. The Catholic University of America Studies in Christian Antiquity, no. 17. Washington, D.C.: Catholic University of America Press, 1974.

Roberts, Colin H., and Bernard Capelle. *An Early Euchologion: The Dêr-Balizeh Papyrus Enlarged and Re-edited*. Université de Louvain. Institut orientaliste. Bibliothèque du Muséon, no. 23. Louvain: Bureaux du Muséon, 1949.

Roberts, Colin H., and T. C. Skeat. *The Birth of the Codex*. London: Oxford University Press for the British Academy, 1987.

Salaville, Severien. "La Tessarakosté, Ascension et Pentecôte au IVe siècle." *Échos d'Orient* 28 (1929): 257–71.

———. "La Tessarakosté au Ve canon de Nicée." *Échos d'Orient* 13 (1910): 65–72.

———. "Une question de critique littéraire: Les Catéchèses Mystagogiques de S. Cyrille." *Échos d'Orient* 17 (1915): 531–37.

SAS Institute Inc. *SAS User's Guide: Statistics, Version 5 Edition*. Cary, North Carolina: SAS Institute Inc., 1985.

Schermann, Theodor. Review of *Die Brotbitte des Vaterunsers*, by J. P. Bock. *Theologische Revue* 19 (1911): 575–79.

Shepherd, Massey. "Eusebius and the Liturgy of St. James." In *Yearbook of Liturgical Studies*, no. 4, 109–23. Notre Dame, Indiana: Fides, 1963.

Simmler, Josias. *Biblioteca instituta*. Tiguri: Apud Christophorum Froschoverum, 1574.

Slusser, Michael. "Reading Silently in Antiquity." *Journal of Biblical Literature* 111 (1992): 499.

Spinks, Bryan D. *Addai and Mari—the Anaphora of the Apostles*. GLS 24. Bramcote Notts.: Grove Books, 1980.

———. "A Complete Anaphora? A Note on Strasbourg Gr. 254." *HJ* 25 (1984): 51–55.

———. "The Jerusalem Liturgy of the Catecheses Mystagogicae: Syrian or Egyptian?" *SP* 18.2, 391–95. Leuven: Peeters, 1989.

———. Review of *The Liturgy of St. Mark*, by G. J. Cuming. *JTS*, n.s. 41 (1991): 355–58.

Stauffer, S. Anita. *On Baptismal Fonts: Ancient and Modern*. GLS 29-30. Bramcote, Notts.: Grove Books, 1994.

Stephenson, Anthony A. "Cyril of Jerusalem's Trinitarian Theology." *SP* 11 = TU 108, 234–41. Berlin: Akademie-Verlag, 1972.

———. "The Lenten Catechetical Syllabus in Fourth-Century Jerusalem." *TS* 15 (1954): 103–16.

———. "St. Cyril of Jerusalem and the Alexandrian Christian Gnosis." *SP* 1 = TU 63, 147–56. Berlin: Akademie-Verlag, 1957.

———. "The Text of the Jerusalem Creed." *SP* 3 = TU 78, 303–13. Berlin: Akademie-Verlag, 1961.

Swaans, W. J. "À propos des 'Catéchèses Mystagogiques' attribuées à S. Cyrille de Jérusalem." *Le Muséon* 55 (1942): 1–42.

Talley, Thomas. *The Origins of the Liturgical Year*. 2d emended ed. Collegeville, Minn.: Liturgical Press, 1991.

Tanner, Norman P., ed. *Decrees of the Ecumenical Councils*. London: Sheed & Ward, 1990.

Tarby, Andre. *La prière eucharistique de l'église de Jérusalem*. Théologie Historique, no. 17. Paris: Beauchesne, 1972.

Telfer, William, ed. *Cyril of Jerusalem and Nemesius of Emesa*. Library of Christian Classics, no. 4. Philadelphia: Westminster, 1955.

Thompson, T. *The Offices of Baptism and Confirmation*. Cambridge: Cambridge University Press, 1914.

Tinelli, Cesare. "Il battistero del S. Sepolcro in Gerusalemme." *Studii biblici francescani: Liber Annuus* 23 (1973): 95–104.

Torchia, N. Joseph. "The Significance of Chrismation in the Mystagogical Lectures of Cyril of Jerusalem." *Diakonia* 32, no. 2 (1999): 128–44.

Tyrer, John Walton. "The Meaning of ἐπίκλησις." *JTS* 25 (1923–24): 139–50.

Van Esbroeck, Michel. "Nathaniël dans une homélie géorgienne sur les archanges." *AB* 89 (1977): 155–76.

Van Esbroeck, Michel, and U. Zanetti. "Le manuscrit Érévan 993. Inventaire des pièces." *Revue des études arméniennes*, n.s. 12 (1977): 123–67.

Victor, G. Julius. *Ars Rhetorica*. Ed. R. Giomini and M. S. Celentano. Leipzig: Teubner, 1980.

Walker, Peter. "Eusebius, Cyril, and the Holy Places." *SP* 20, 306–14. Leuven: Peeters, 1989.

———. "Gospel Sites and 'Holy Places': The Contrasting Attitudes of Eusebius and Cyril." *Tyndale-Bulletin* 41 (1990): 89–108.

———. *Holy City, Holy Places? Christian Attitudes to Jerusalem and the Holy Land in the Fourth Century*. Oxford: Clarendon Press, 1990.

Wallace-Hadrill, D. S. *Christian Antioch: A Study of Early Christian Thought in the East*. Cambridge: Cambridge University Press, 1983.

———. "Eusebius and the Institution Narrative in the Eastern Liturgies." *JTS*, n.s. 4 (1953): 41–42.

Walther, Georg. *Untersuchungen zur Geschichte der griechischen Vaterunser-Exegese*. TU 40.3. Leipzig: J. C. Hinrichs, 1914.

Whitaker, Edward Charles. *Documents of the Baptismal Liturgy*. 2d ed. London: S.P.C.K., 1970.

Wilkinson, John. *Egeria's Travels to the Holy Land*. 2d rev. ed. Warminster, England: Aris and Phillips, 1981.

———. "Jewish Influences on the Early Christian Rite of Jerusalem." *Le Muséon* 92 (1979): 347–59.

Willis, G. G. "What Was the Earliest Syrian Baptismal Tradition?" In *Studia Evangelica* 6 = TU 112, 651–54. Ed. E. A. Livingstone. Berlin: Akademie-Verlag, 1973.

Winkler, Gabriele. *Das armenische Initiationsrituale. Entwicklungsgeschichtliche und liturgievergleichende Untersuchung der Quellen des 3. bis 10. Jahrhunderts*. OCA 217. Rome: Pontificium Institutum Studiorum Orientalium, 1982.

———. "The History of the Syrian Prebaptismal Anointing in the Light of the Earliest Armenian Sources." In *Symposium Syriaca 1976*, 317–24. OCA 205. Rome: Pontificium Institutum Studiorum Orientalium, 1978.

———. "The Original Meaning of the Prebaptismal Anointing and Its Implications." *Worship* 52 (1978): 24–45.

Wolfson, H. A. "Philosophical Implications of the Theology of Cyril of Jerusalem." *Dumbarton Oaks Papers* 11 (1957): 1–19.

Yarnold, E. J. "Anaphoras without Institution Narratives?" *SP* 30, 395–410. Leuven: Peeters, 1997.

———. "The Authorship of the *Mystagogic Catecheses* Attributed to Cyril of Jerusalem." *HJ* 19 (1978): 143–61.

———. *The Awe-Inspiring Rites of Initiation*. 2d ed. Edinburgh: T. & T. Clark, 1994.

———. "Baptism and the Pagan Mysteries in the Fourth Century." *HJ* 13 (1972): 247–67.

———. *Cyril of Jerusalem*. London and New York: Routledge, 2000.

———. "Did St. Ambrose Know the Mystagogical Catecheses of St. Cyril of Jerusalem?" *SP* 12 = TU 115, 184–89. Berlin: Akademie-Verlag, 1975.

———. "Who Planned the Churches at the Christian Holy Places in the Holy Land?" *SP* 18.1, 105–9. Kalamazoo: Cistercian Publications, 1985.

Young, F. *From Nicaea to Chalcedon*. Philadelphia: Fortress, 1983.

Ysebaert, Joseph. *Greek Baptismal Terminology: Its Origins and Early Development*. Nijmegen: Dekker & Van de Vegt, 1962.

Index of Citations from Cyril's Works

Index of Ancient Persons and Works

Index of Modern Authors

Subject Index

Cyril of Jerusalem, Mystagogue: The Authorship of the Mystagogic Catecheses was designed and composed in Dante MT by Kachergis Book Design, Pittsboro, North Carolina; and printed on 60-pound Writers Offset Natural and bound by Thomson-Shore of Dexter, Michigan.